STRATEGIC FINANCIAL MANAGEMENT

(STRATEGIC INVESTMENT AND DECISION MAKING)

Dr. G.V. Satya Sekhar

MBA., Ph.D.,

Asst. Professor,
Gitam Institute of Management,
Gitam University,
Visakhapatanam – 530 045.

FIRST EDITION: 2013

MUMBAI • NEW DELHI • NAGPUR • BENGALURU • HYDERABAD • CHENNAI • PUNE • LUCKNOW • AHMEDABAD • ERNAKULAM • BHUBANESWAR • INDORE • KOLKATA • GUWAHATI

First Edition : 2013

Published by : Mrs. Meena Pandey for **Himalaya Publishing House Pvt. Ltd.**, "Ramdoot", Dr. Bhalerao Marg, Girgaon, **Mumbai - 400 004.** Phone: 022-23860170/23863863, Fax: 022-23877178 **E-mail: himpub@vsnl.com; Website: www.himpub.com**

Branch Offices :

New Delhi : "Pooja Apartments", 4-B, Murari Lal Street, Ansari Road, Darya Ganj, New Delhi - 110 002. Phone: 011-23270392, 23278631; Fax: 011-23256286

Nagpur : Kundanlal Chandak Industrial Estate, Ghat Road, Nagpur - 440 018. Phone: 0712-2738731, 3296733; Telefax: 0712-2721215

Bengaluru : No. 16/1 (Old 12/1), 1st Floor, Next to Hotel Highlands, Madhava Nagar, Race Course Road, Bengaluru - 560 001. Phone: 080-32919385; Telefax: 080-22286611

Hyderabad : No. 3-4-184, Lingampally, Besides Raghavendra Swamy Matham, Kachiguda, Hyderabad - 500 027. Phone: 040-27560041, 27550139; Mobile: 09390905282

Chennai : No. 8/2, Madley 2nd Street, Ground Floor, T. Nagar, Chennai - 600 017. Phone: 044-28144004/28144005; Mobile: 09345345051

Pune : First Floor, "Laksha" Apartment, No. 527, Mehunpura, Shaniwarpeth (Near Prabhat Theatre), Pune - 411 030. Phone: 020-24496323/24496333; Mobile: 09370579333

Lucknow : House No 731, Shekhupura Colony, Near B.D. Convent School, Aliganj, Lucknow - 226 022. Mobile: 09307501549

Ahmedabad : 114, "SHAIL", 1st Floor, Opp. Madhu Sudan House, C.G. Road, Navrang Pura, Ahmedabad - 380 009. Phone: 079-26560126; Mobile: 09377088847

Ernakulam : 39/176 (New No: 60/251) 1st Floor, Karikkamuri Road, Ernakulam, Kochi - 682011, Phone: 0484-2378012, 2378016; Mobile: 09344199799

Bhubaneswar : 5 Station Square, Bhubaneswar - 751 001 (Odisha). Phone: 0674-2532129, Mobile: 09338746007

Indore : Kesardeep Avenue Extension, 73, Narayan Bagh, Flat No. 302, IIIrd Floor, Near Humpty Dumpty School, Indore - 452 007 (M.P.). Mobile: 09301386468

Kolkata : 108/4, Beliaghata Main Road, Near ID Hospital, Opp. SBI Bank, Kolkata - 700 010, Phone: 033-32449649, Mobile: 09883055590, 07439040301

Guwahati : House No. 15, Behind Pragjyotish College, Near Sharma Printing Press, P.O. Bharalumukh, Guwahati - 781009, (Assam). Mobile: 09883055590, 09883055536

DTP by : HPH Editorial Office, Bhandup **(Asmita Pankar)**

Printed at : M/s. Aditya Offset Process (I) Pvt. Ltd., Hyderabad, On behalf of HPH.

PREFACE

Strategic Financial Management (SFM) involves various aspects of Financial Planning. Financial Planning depends on two aspects, i.e., (i) Liquidity Planning and (ii) Profit Planning. SFM is closely associated with business policy and strategic management.

Strategic management may be defined as a systematic approach of positioning the business in relation to its environment to ensure continued success and offer security from surprises. While no approach can guarantee continuous success and total security, an integrated approach to strategy formulation, involving all levels of management, can go some way in this direction. SFM focuses on designing financial plans according to corporate business environment.

This book is intended to focus on advanced topics in the area of 'Strategic Financial Management', which analyses the techniques of optimisation, corporate restructuring and turnaround management. The scope of finance managers at top-level management is increasing day by day. Global financial crisis otherwise known as global meltdown is creating new challenges to Chief Executive Officers and Chief Finance Officers. Hence, there is a dire need for implementing strategies for survival of the organisation. It is the responsibility of CFO to design capital structure of the organisation, i.e., equity and debt. Besides debt instruments such as the Euro-Dollar and bond markets, the equity capital market is another important source of financing. Evidence indicates that the final decade of the twentieth century will go down in history as the period in which much of the world discovered the stock market as a major source of funds for their global expansion. Companies will increasingly turn to the stock market to raise money. In this context, this book focuses on how ownership in publicly owned corporations is traded throughout the world. The stock market consists of the primary market and the secondary market. The primary market is a market in which the sale of new common stock by corporations to initial investors occurs. This book also focuses on international financing strategies, transnational pricing and global corporate governance practices.

— G.V. SATYA SEKHAR

PREFACE

Strategic Financial Management (SFM) involves various aspects of Financial Planning. Financial Planning depends on two aspects, i.e., (i) Liquidity Planning and (ii) Profit Planning. SFM is closely associated with business policy and strategic management.

Strategic management may be defined as a systematic approach to positioning the business in relation to its environment to ensure continued success and to keep it free from surprises. While no approach can guarantee both the success and freedom from surprises, [illegible] formulation involving all levels of management [illegible] direction. SFM focuses on designing financial policies [illegible] to support the business environment.

This book is designed to focus on the various topics in the area of Strategic Financial Management, which analyses the techniques of optimisation, corporate restructuring and long-term fund management. The scope of finance managers at top level management is increasing day by day. Global financial crisis otherwise known as [illegible] is creating [illegible] to Chief Executive Officers and Chief Finance Officers. Hence, there is a dire need for implementing strategies for survival of the organisation. It is therefore essential for CFO to design capital structure of the organisation, i.e., equity and debt. For debt, instruments such as the various Debt and Bond markets; the equity capital market is another important source of financing. Evidence indicates that the final decade of the twentieth century will go down in history as the period in which most of the world discovered the stock market as a major source of funds for their global expansion. Companies will increasingly turn to the stock market to raise money. In this context, this book focuses on how ownership of publicly owned companies are traded throughout the world. The stock market consists of the primary market and the secondary market. The primary market is [illegible] [illegible] are initially [illegible] to [illegible] investors. This book also focuses on international financing strategies, financial engineering and global corporate governance practices.

— C. V. SATYA SEKHAR

SYLLABUS

MPRBA - FM 404: STRATEGIC FINANCIAL MANAGEMENT

The objective of this course is to enable the students to understand the financing strategies in valuation and mergers in corporate entities

Unit I: Strategy Formulation - Financial Strategy for Capital Structure - Strategy for Shareholders Value Maximization - Market to Book Value - Economic Value Added.

Unit II: Corporate Valuation - Adjusted Book Value Approach - Stock and debt Approach - Direct Comparison Approach - Discounted Cash Flow Approach - Analysis of Historical Performance - Calculating Firm Value and Interpretation - Case Studies **(NP)**

Unit III: Merger and Acquisition Strategy - Corporate Restructuring - Types of Business Combinations - Motives and Benefits of Mergers and Acquisitions - Legal Framework - Strategies in Mergers and Acquisitions - Financial Synergies - Human Capital Synergies - Impact of Mergers and Acquisitions on Stakeholders - Causes for Failure of Mergers and Acquisitions **(NP)**

Unit IV: Financial Implication of Mergers and Acquisitions - Significance of Share Exchange Ratio - Significance of P/E Ratio and EPS Analysis - Illustrations **(NP)**

Unit V: Takeovers - Introduction - Kinds of Takeovers - Motives behind Takeovers - Defensive Strategies - Sell Offs - Spin Offs - Golden Parachutes - Crown Jewels - Green Mails - Poison Pills - White Knights - Financial Implications - SEBI Guidelines for Takeovers - Leveraged Buyouts **(NP)**

Caselet (Not Exceeding 200 Words)

CONTENTS

DETAILED CONTENTS

CHAPTER

1

The Conceptual Approach

CHAPTER OUTLINE

- Opening Caselet
- Structure of Strategic Financial Management Introduction
- Scope of Strategic Financial Management
- Defintions
- The Strategic Management Process
- Modernisation of Strategies
- Dimensions of Strategic Management
- Board of Directors
- Functional Aspects of Strategic Management
- Financial Strategies
- Financial Planning
- Functions of SFM
- Factors to be Considered while Estimating Financial Requirements
- SFM Relation with Other Subjects
- Profit Maximisation vs. Wealth Maximisation
- Important Issues in Profit Maximisation
- Strategic Financial Planning
- Closing Caselet
- Questions
- Keywords
- Summary
- Review Questions
- References

OPENING CASELET

A STRATEGIC MOVE

IL&FS STEPS IN AS A PROMOTER IN MAYTAS INFRA

Infrastructure Leasing and Financial Services Ltd., (IL&FS) will be the new promoter of the Hyderabad-based Maytas Infras Ltd., following the recent orders passed by the Company Law Board (CLB), which has also allowed IL&FS to nominate its managing director Hari Sankarna, joint managing director Arun K Saha, president and CEO Karunakaran Ramchand, and chairman Ravi Parthasarathy, on the board of the severely impaired entity.

As part of taking control of the Maytas management, IL&FS will increase its holding in Maytas from the existing 14.5 per cent. To start with, it has obtained approval to foreclose its rights on 22.6 per cent pledged shares. This will take its overall holding to 37.1 per cent. It may be recalled that the promoters of Maytas had raised ₹ 180 crore from IL&FS by pledging their shares. IL&FS also made an open offer to acquire 20 per cent stake of Maytas equity at a price of ₹ 112.80 per share. On completion of this open offer, IL&FS total shareholding in Maytas will rise to 57.1 per cent.

Analysts have also termed the deal a win-win situation for both parties. "Not only Maytas benefit in the entire process, but for IL&FS too, this is the best option available since it has to recover its money parked in the company as debt and equity, states KB Chokey's Deven Choksey, who feels, that it will take some time before Maytas can be turned around."

Ref: *Business India*, Sept., 20, 2009.

STRUCTURE OF STRATEGIC FINANCIAL MANAGEMENT INTRODUCTION

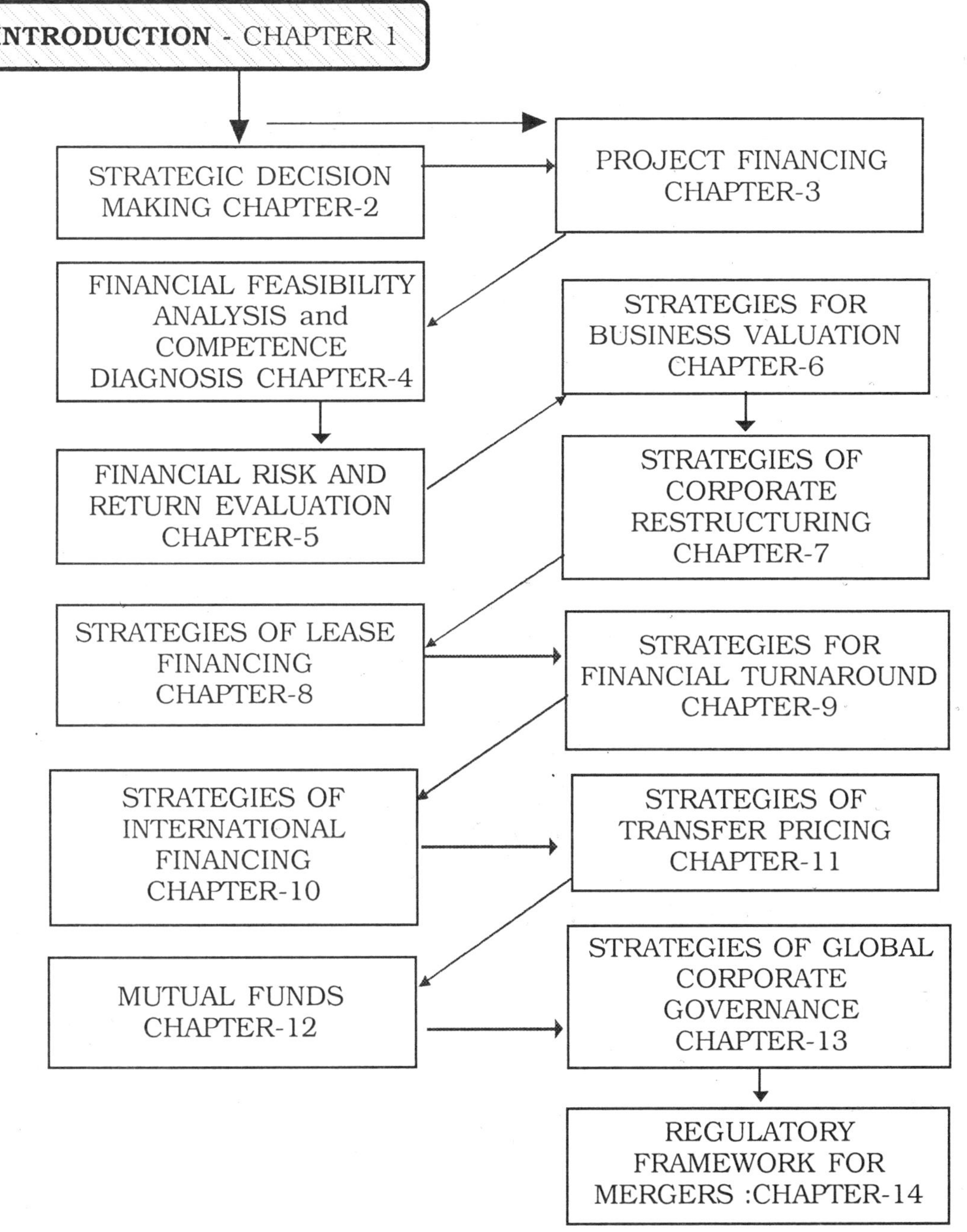

Fig. 1.1: Structure of the Book

Strategic Financial Management involves various strategies for finance and business sustainability. Finance and financial management encompass numerous business and governmental activities. In the most basic sense, the term *finance* can be used to describe the activities of a firm attempting to raise capital through the sale of stocks, bonds, or other financial instruments like commercial paper, certificate of deposits, Global Depository Receipts, etc. Financial management, in the broadest sense, can be defined as business activities undertaken with the goal of maximising shareholder wealth, utilising the principles of the time value of money, leverage, diversification, and an investment's expected rate of return versus its risk. Within the discipline of finance, there are two basic components. First, there are financial instruments. These instruments *viz.*, stocks and bonds, are recorded evidence of obligations on which exchanges of resources are founded. Effective investment management of these financial instruments is a vital part of any organisation's financing activities. Second, there are financial markets, which are the mechanisms used to trade the financial instruments of institutions, which facilitate the transfer of resources among those buying and selling the financial instruments.

Strategic Financial Management in the corporate entities is characterised, in many different cases, by the need to confront a somewhat different set of problems and opportunities. One immediate problem is issue of stocks or bonds to the public in order to raise funds. The managing director of the corporate entity must rely primarily on trade credit, bank financing, lease financing and equity to finance the business. On the other hand, many financial problems have to be faced by the larger corporations. For example, the analysis required for a long-term investment decision such as the purchase of heavy machinery or the evaluation of lease-buy alternatives, is essentially the same regardless of the size of the firm. Once the decision is made, the financing alternatives available to the firm may be radically different, but the decision process will be generally similar. Another area of particular concern for the business owner lies in the effective management of working capital. Lack of control in this crucial area is a primary cause of business failure in both small and large firms. The business manager must continually be alert to changes in working capital accounts, the cause of these changes and the implications of these changes for the financial health of the company.

SCOPE OF STRATEGIC FINANCIAL MANAGEMENT

The subject Strategic Financial Management (SFM) covers the various functions depicted in the diagram. Thus, SFM deals with strategies relating to equity fund raising, global expansion, acquisition, merger, business development plan and foreign exchange management etc. Thus, the role of financial strategist of any corporate entity depends on the scope of the strategies adopted by him. The responsibilities and functions to be carried out by him are also discussed in this chapter.

REVIEW OF LITERATURE

Alexander W. Butler *et.al*[1]., paper presents empirical evidence on the importance of market timing relative to an investment-based explanation of corporate financing decisions. Market timing and investment-based theories both predict under performance following an increase in net financing, but only market timing theories predict that the composition of firms' financing (equity compared to debt) should also forecast returns. In regressions of future excess returns on both the amount and composition of net financing, we find that the level of net financing is important in explaining subsequent under performance, but the composition is not. The results are consistent with changes in investment policy affecting expected returns and inconsistent with successful market timing.

Gustave Grullon, Geroge Kanatas and Piyush Kumar [2] study reveals that how a firm's financial structure affects the intensity with which it competes in the product market. Using a sample of firms that raise significant amounts of capital, they studied the extent of their non-price competition, as measured by their advertising expenditures, following this event. It was found that after controlling other factors, firms whose financial leverage has decreased as a result of the new funding increase, their advertising competition significantly was more than firms whose leverage has increased. They have undertaken both an instrumental variables approach.

An empirical study of capital structure and a 'reverse causality' test to address the issue of the endogeneity of the capital structure and advertising decisions and show that it is indeed capital structure changes that influence the degree of advertising competition. It was also observed that the reaction of the sample firms' industry rivals is influenced as well by their capital structures. Specifically, the study revealed that a rival firm responds more (less) aggressively — relative to it's peers — in the increase of it's own advertising, if it is less (more) levered than the sample firm in it's industry that has initiated the more intense advertising competition. Overall, the study results support the view that financial leverage appears to have a 'dampening' effect on the intensity with which a firm chooses to compete in the product market.

Craig M. Lewis, Richard J. Rogalski and James K. Sewad[3] examines the relationship between convertible debt issue announcements, announcement period share price reactions, and the profitability of the issuing firm's growth opportunities. They find that investor reactions are positively related to the profitability of the issuing firm's investment opportunities. However, the relationship does not appear to be particularly robust across several model specifications. Share price reactions are less negative (more positive) the higher the issuer's investment opportunities relative to that of the median industry performer. Thus, investors seem to react to convertible debt offerings more on the basis

---

1. Alexander W. Butler, Hess Cornaggia, Gustavo Grulon, James P. Weston, 'Corporate Financing Decisions and Managerial Market Timing, http://ssrn.com/abstract=1370403.
2. Gustave Grullon, Geroge Kanatas and Piyush Kumar, Financing Decisions and Advertising: An Empirical Study of Capital Structure and Product Market Competition, http://ssrn.com.
3. Craig M. Lewis, Richard J. Rogalski and James K. Sewad, 'Industry Conditions, Growth Opportunities and Market Reactions to Convertible Debt Financing Decisions', http://ssrn.com/abstract=1618.

of relative performance within the issuer's industry, rather than absolute measures of issuer or industry performance.

STRATEGIC MANAGEMENT

The word strategy came from the Greek word 'strategos', which means a general. At that time, strategy literally meant the art and science of directing military forces. Today strategy is used in business to describe how an organisation is going to achieve its objectives. Strategic management may be defined as a systematic approach to positioning the business in relation to its environment to ensure continued success and offer security from surprises. While no approach can guarantee continuous success and total security, an integrated approach to strategy formulation, involving all levels of management, can go some way in this direction. In simple words strategy can be defined as 'Strategy is ideas and actions to conceive and secure the future'. Strategic management is that set of managerial decisions and actions that determines the long-run performance of a corporation. It includes environmental observation, strategic planning, formulation, implementation, evaluation and control. Strategic mission consists of a long-term vision of what an organisation seeks to do and what kind of organisation it intends to become. Development of organisation completely rests on the efficiency of the decision makers. They have to base decision on present policies for achievement of future goals. Strategic management always concentrates on the anticipated aim. Future is always uncertain. Hence, strategic decisions are always incomplete and sometimes they have been based on false information. It may lead to further problems. Strategic manager should always aim at achieving pre-determined goal of the organisation.

DEFINITIONS

- **Ansoff (1965)[4]:** 'Strategy is a rule for making decisions'. Ansoff also distinguishes between policy and strategy. A policy is a general decision that is always made in the same way whenever the same circumstances arise.

- **Alfred D. Chandler, *et.al.*, (1999)[5]:** 'Strategy can be defined as the determination of the basic long-term goals and objectives of an enterprise, and the adoption of courses of action and the allocation of resources necessary for carrying out these goals. Business strategy is becoming increasingly pluralist, drawing on the insights of different disciplines and business practice in different parts of the world.'

- **Kenichi Ohame (1983)[6]:** 'The way in which corporate endeavours to differentiate itself positively from its competitors, using its relative strengths to better satisfy customer needs'.

- **Kenneth Andrews (1965):** A pattern of objectives, purpose, goals and major policies and plans for achieving these goals stated in such a way so as to define what business the company is in and is to be and the kind of company it is to be. This refers to business

4. Ansof, H. Igor, *Corporate Strategy*, New York, McGraw-Hill, 1965.
5. Alfred Dupont Chandler, Peter Hagström, Örjan Sölvell, *The Dynamic Firm: The Role of Technology, Strategy, Organization and Regions*, Oxford University Press, 1999
6. Kenichi Ohame, *"The Mind of The Strategist"*, McGraw-Hill, 1983.

definition which is a way of stating the current and desired future position of the company and the objectives, purpose, goals of major policies and plans remained to take the company from where it is, to where it wants to be.

◇ **Henry Mintzberg (1987):** Strategies are always the outcome of rational planning. They can emerge from what an organisation does it without any formal plan. In his view strategy means a pattern in a stream of decisions and actions. Intended strategies refer to the plans that managers develop. Emergent strategies are the actions that actually take place over a period of time.

◇ **Micheal E. Porter (1996):** A plan or course of action or a set of decisions/rules forming a pattern or creating a common thread. A pattern or common thread related to the organisation's activities which are classified from its policies, objectives and goals.

William F. Glueck (1972)[7]: 'Strategic Management is a stream of decisions and actions which leads to the development of an effective strategy or strategies, which help to achieve corporate objectives'. Strategy is defined as 'a unified comprehensive and integrated plan designed to assure that the basic objective of the enterprise are achieved'.

1. Corporate Strategy

Corporate strategy is concerned with broad issues, such as which types of business the company should be in. It explains overall direction in terms of its general attitude toward growth and the management of its various businesses and product lines. Strategies have an important role to play here. For example, the decision to enter or exit from a business requires sound strategic analysis. Similarly, the decision as to the appropriate business structure and policy form part of strategic development at the corporate level. Corporate strategies may fit within main categories of stability, growth and retrenchment. Thus, diversification, expansion also depends upon the strategy adopted by the company.

Corporate strategy is the way in which corporate endeavours to differentiate itself positively from its competitors, using its relative strengths to better satisfy customer needs. Corporate strategy applies to large companies, which are divided into a number of discrete and fairly autonomous units. Holding companies are the best example of corporate strategy, in which a number of companies are, grouped together, usually for financial reasons such as the efficient allocation of capital and investment. Corporate strategy is strategy of an organisation, or the sub-unit of a larger organisation is a conceptualization expressed or implied by the organisation's leader, of (1) the long-term objectives or purposes of the organisation, (2) the broad constraints and policies either self-imposed by the leader or accepted by him from his superiors that currently restrict the scope of organisation activities, and (3) the current set of plans and near-term goals that have been adopted in their expectations of contributing to the achievement of organisation objectives.

Corporate strategic manager should always aim at achieving pre-determined goals of the organisation. Further organisations have to work with brevity and variety. Thoughts should become actions. Actions will lead to results. Result-oriented action is the need of hour. Professor Kenneth Andrews defines corporate strategy as 'the pattern of major

7. William F. Glueck, *Business Policy: Strategy Formation and Management Action*, McGraw-Hill, 1972.

objectives, purposes or goals and essential policies and plans for achieving those goals stated in such a way to define what business the company is in or is to be in and the kind of company it is or is to be'.

Corporate strategy has two main aspects:

(a) Formulation of Strategy.

(b) Strategy Implementation.

(a) Formulation of Strategy: Strategy formulation is nothing but 'the process of deciding on objectives, on the changes in objectives, on the resources used to attain these objectives, and on the policies that are to govern the acquisition, used and disposition of resources'. Formulation of strategy involves decision making by corporate management that —

(i) Objectives, goals and aim of organisation can be determined.

(ii) Preparation of long and short-term plans to achieve aim and goals.

(b) Strategy Implementation: The decisions of organisation which are based on formulated strategies should be implemented in proper manner. These decisions primarily comprise administrative polices regarding resources, structure and performance measurement. The essence of strategy implementation may be said to lie in the choice of organisational structure, organisational processes and pattern of leadership appropriate for accomplishing the chosen strategy.

2. Business or Competitive Strategy

Business policy deals with how strategic business units compete in different markets. This usually occurs at the business unit level or product level. Strategies are formulated which influence the allocation of resources to these units. This allocation may be based on the attractiveness of the markets in which Strategic Business Units (SBUs) operate and the firm's competitive strengths. Business strategies may fit within the overall categories of competitive or cooperative strategies.

3. Operational Strategy or Functional Strategies

Operational Strategy explains about functional levels contributing to corporate and business strategies. This type of strategies requires various functional decision making like, Finance, Marketing, Human Resource Management, Marketing, etc. Experts decision may be required at different functional areas. For example, the finance function may formulate strategies to achieve the new dividend policy identified at the corporate strategy level. Similarly, a foreign currency exposure strategy may be developed to reduce the risk of loss through currency movements.

THE STRATEGIC MANAGEMENT PROCESS

'Strategic Management process' can be defined as 'a combination of managerial decisions and actions that determines the long run performance of a corporation. It includes environmental observation, strategic planning, formulation, implementation, evaluation and control.

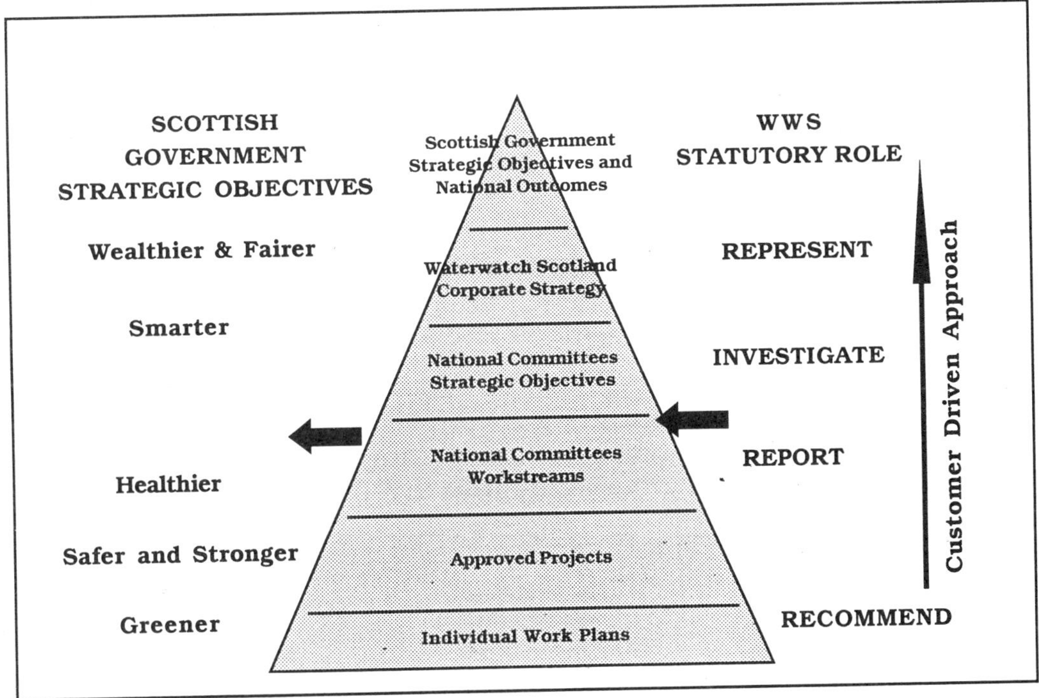

Fig. 1.2: Model Corporate Strategy of Waterwatch Scotland

Source: *http://www.waterwatchscotland.org/wp-content/uploads/2009/01/corporate-strategy.png*

CRUCIAL CONSIDERATIONS

1. **Demand Forecasting:** No business man cannot expect demand forecasting for products unless he is having strategic planning for the organisational development. Second World War created more demand for some products. Hence, long-range planning is necessary to meet the demand.

2. **Competition:** Business entities should always fight for survival. When there are new entrants in the market there will be more competition. Hence, strategic planning is necessary to face competition and to become successful business man.

3. **Technology:** Changes in technology also necessitates strategic planning. Technological advancements are useful for the development of business. More opportunities will be available to business.

4. **Scarcity:** Scarcity of the resources always forms as the basis for strategic management. When products are scarce and there will be increase in demand for the products.

MAJOR STEPS

FIRST STAGE: (DEFINITIONS)

1. **Preparation of Mission:** 'Mission' is the purpose for which organisation is established. Mission includes both a statement of organisational philosophy and purpose. An organisational philosophy establishes the values, beliefs, and guidelines for the manner in which the organisation is going to conduct its business. The first step of strategy formulation depends on well defined mission statement or organisational purpose. The mission may be described as the scope of the operation in terms of nature of business.

2. **Setting of Objectives:** Objectives are defined as ends which the organisation seeks to achieve by its existence and operation. Objectives may be internal or external objectives. Internal objectives are those which define how much is expected to be achieved with the resources that the organisation commands.

3. **Fixation of Goals:** Goals are specific, and time-based points of measurement. Generally, goals are determined by the owner or entrepreneur of the business organisation. In the case of large-scale companies, CEO (Chief Executive Officer) will determine the goals for its firm. Thus, goal of the owner will be the goal of the firm.

4. **Policies:** A policy is a definition of common purposes or organisation components. The process of strategic planning sometimes encompasses the formulation of important policies. Policies help to ensure that all units of an organisation operate under the same ground rules. They also facilitate coordination and communication between various organisational units. Policies of competitors also influence an organisation's policies.

5. **Analysis of Environment:** Business environment is always an influencing factor for decision making. There may be external or internal factors that influence business. Buyers, suppliers, government and competitors are likely to react in accordance with changes in environment. Thus business also should act in the same passion.

SECOND STAGE (FORMULATION)

6. **Formulation of Strategies:** Strategies can be formulated after clear diagnosing of the environment. Each strategy with suitable sub-strategies and alternative

strategies should be available to top management. Thus, top management always mentor the administration with strategies which can be adopted from time to time.

7. **Implementation of Strategies:** This is an important stage in strategic management process. Well designed strategies may be failed in implementation. Hence, adoptability of strategies and implementation process should be clearly mentioned while formulating strategy. It is the strategist responsibility to take care of implementing strategies in accordance with the requirements of organisation.

THIRD STAGE (EVALUATION)

8. **SWOT Analysis:** Strengths, Weaknesses, Opportunities and Threats simply termed as SWOT. Every organisation should go through SWOT analysis. It is an important tool of evaluating organisational capabilities.

9. **Evaluation:** This can be stated as last stage of strategic management process. The strategist should evaluate each strategy after implementing them. The strategy should evaluate whether there is profit maximisation or cost minimisation or achievement of long or short-term goal what ever it may be.

MODERNISATION OF STRATEGIES

Modernisation means coping with the changing environment and technology. It involves updating and upgrading technology of the organisation and training the staff. Modernisation is not only confined to physical advancement but also to the psychological development. Every organisation should concentrate on the modernisation and implementation of modern strategies for the competitor analysis. To achieve benefits of modernisation like optimisation of cost, efficiency in productivity and achieving sustainable development, modern strategies are necessary.

Modernisation of strategies may be defined as a systematic approach to preparing modern-oriented plans for the development of business in relation to its environment to ensure continued success and offer security from contingencies. An integrated approach to strategy formulation, involving all levels of management, can go some way in this direction. In simple words strategy can be defined as 'Strategy is ideas and actions to conceive and secure the future'. Modern strategic mission consists of a long-term vision of what an organisation seeks to do and what kind of organisation it intends to become. Development of organisation completely rests on the efficiency of the decision makers. They have to take decisions based on present policies for achievement of future goals.

William F. Glueck

'Strategic planning is a stream of decisions and actions which leads to the development of an effective strategy or strategies, which help to achieve corporate objectives'. Strategy is defined as 'a unified comprehensive and integrated plan designed to assure that the basic objective of the enterprise is achieved'.

REASONS FOR MODERNISATION

Modernisation is necessary for the achievement of organisation goals and objectives. Modernisation is becoming compulsory because existing technology has become outdated. The following are the important reasons for the modernisation and modernisation of strategies:

1. Modernisation is required for updating of existing technology in the organisation.
2. Modernisation is used as a tool to compete new entrants.
3. It is necessary for improvement of efficiency of organisation.
4. Modern technology and modern strategies are used for improvement of productivity.
5. It is useful to achieve optimization of cost.
6. Modernisation is required for profitability.
7. It helps in sustainable and overall development of the organisation.

POLICY

The term policy is derived from the Greek word '*politeia*' relating to policy, that is citizen and Latin word 'politis' meaning polished, that is to say, clear. According to New Webster Dictionary, policy means the art or manner of governing a nation, the line of conduct which rulers of a nation adopt on a particular question specially with regard to foreign countries, the principle on which any measure or course of action is based. While these descriptions of policy relate to any field, policy in the organisational context is defined as 'management's expressed or implied intent to govern action in the achievement of company's aims'? This definition, however, is at high level of abstraction and requires deeper analysis. It suggests that it governs actions of people in the organisation but does not say how the action is governed. Therefore, an operational definition of policy may be as follows: A policy is the statement or general understanding which provides guidelines in decision making to members of an organisation in respect to any course of action. On the basic of this definition, following features of policy can be identified:

1. A policy provides guidelines to the members of the organisation for deciding a course of action and, thus, restricts their freedom of action. Policy explains what a member should do rather than what he is doing. Policies, when enforced, permit prediction of roles with certainty. Since a policy provides guidelines to thinking in decision making, it follows that it must allow some discretion, otherwise it will become a rule.

2. Policy limits an area within which a decision is to be made and assures that decision will be consistent with and contributive to objectives. A policy tends to predecide issues, avoid repeated analysis, and give a unified structure to other types of plans, thus permitting managers to delegate authority and still retaining control of action. For example, if the organisation has framed a policy that higher positions in the organisation will be filled by internal promotion, the managers concerned can deal with the situation in this light whenever a vacancy at higher

level arises. Thus, organisation gets assurance that higher positions are filled by internal members without further control.

3. Policies are generally expressed in qualitative, conditional, or general way. The verbs most often used in stating policies are to maintain, to continue, to follow, to adhere, to provide, to assist, to assure, to employ, to make, to produce, or to be. Such prescriptions may be either explicit or these may be interpreted from the behaviour of organisation members, particularly at the top level. When such a behaviour is interpreted as policy guideline it is normally known as precedent, that is what has happened in the past on a particular issue if there is no clearly specified declaration.

4. Policy formulation is a function of all managers in the organisation because some form of guidelines for future course of action is required at every level. However, higher is the level of a manager, more important is his role in policy making. Similarly, policies may exist in all areas of the organisation from major organisational policies to minor policies applicable to the smallest segment of the organisation.

A policy is somewhat a permanent feature of an organisation. It being a standing plan provides guidelines to managerial decisions. Therefore, policies should be developed on a sound basis. If this is not done, managers have to make decisions again and again. However, what features constitute a sound policy cannot be prescribed universally because situations vary so greatly that an organisation may differ in respect of a policy formulation and implementation from others. However, the soundness of policy can be judged on the basis of following criteria.

1. Does it reflect present or desired organisational practices and behaviour?
2. Is it clear, definite, and explicit leaving no scope for misinterpretation?
3. Does it exist in the area critical to the success of the organisation?
4. Is it consistent with other policies and does it reflect the timing needed to accomplish the objectives?
5. Is it practical in a given existing or expected situation?

A sound policy will (1) specify more precisely how the decision will come – what is to be done, who is to do it, how it is to be done and when it is to be finished,(2) establish a follow-up mechanism to make sure that the decision intended will take place, and (3) lead to new strengths which can be used for decisions in future. Based on these questions and specifications, some major characteristics of a sound policy can be identified as follows:

1. **Relationship to Organisational Objectives:** A policy is formulated in the context of organisational objectives. Therefore, it tries to contribute towards the achievement of these objectives. Therefore, in formulation of a policy, those functions or activities which do not contribute to the achievement of objectives

should be eliminated. For example, if a policy of filling higher positions from within, produces hindrance in attracting talents at higher level but the organisation needs them, the policy can be changed because in the absence of suitable manpower, the organisation may not be able to achieve its objectives.

2. **Planned Formulation:** A policy must be the result of careful and planned formulation process rather than the result of opportunistic decisions made on the spur of the movement. Since policies are relatively permanent features of the organisation, *ad hocism* should be avoided because it is likely to create more confusion. It is true it is not possible to solve every problem in the organisation on the basis of policies because new situations may arise, however, for matters of recurring nature, there should be well-established policies.

3. **Fair Amount of Clarity:** As far as possible, policy should be clear and must not leave any scope for ambiguity. If there is a problem of misinterpretation, the organisation should provide the method for overcoming the ambiguity. Further, policy provides some discretion for managerial decisions but it should minimise the number of cases were decisions are based on personal judgement. If this happens frequently, there should be close scrutiny of the policy and suitable amendments should be made.

4. **Consistency:** The policy should provide consistency in the operation of organisational functions. Often the organisation formulates various functional areas and each function is related to other functions of the organisation. If the policy in one area is inconsistent with another area, there may be conflict resulting into inefficiency. This happens very frequently in functions. Therefore, the formulation of policies should be taken in an integrated way so that policies in each area contribute to other areas also.

5. **Balanced:** A sound policy maintains balance between stability and flexibility. On the one hand, a policy is a long-term proposition and it must provide stability so that members are well aware about what they are required to do in certain matters. On the other hand, the policy should not be so inflexible that it cannot be changed when the need arises. In a changed situation, the old policy becomes obsolete. Therefore, there should be a periodic review of policies and suitable changes should be incorporated from time to time. The changes may be in the form of addition, deflection, or substitution of the existing policy.

6. **Written:** A policy may be in the form a statement or it may be interpreted by the behaviour of the people at the top level. However, clearly-specified policy works better than the one which has to be interpreted by the organisation members. When the policy is in writing, it becomes more specific and clear. It creates an atmosphere in which individuals can take actions. A written policy is easier to communicate through the organisational manuals. However, written policy has certain disadvantages in the form of being flexible, too much emphasis on written words and their interpretation, and leakage of confidential policy. However, if the

policy has been formulated carefully, many of the dangers will be overcome. Of course, confidential policies cannot be made part of organisational manuals.

7. **Communication:** It is not just sufficient to formulate policies. Unless they are communicated property to the persons concerned, no meaningful purpose will be served. Therefore, a system should be developed to communicate the policies to them who are to make decisions in the light of those policies. While written policies can be communicated easily, problems exist for communicating unwritten ones. In such cases, there should be more frequent interaction between policy framers and policy implementations.

Strategic Business Unit

Strategic Business Unit (SBU) is 'any part of a business organisation which is treated separately for strategic management purposes'. When organisations face difficulty in managing divisional operations due to an increasing diversity, size and number of divisions, it becomes difficult for the top management to exercise strategic control. Strategic Business Unit (SBI) is a organisation of diversified businesses, multi-product, multi-service, multi-divisionalised firms. The head of each SBU is its chief executive. If the company is structured based on modern principles of organisation like, autonomy, responsibility and empowerment and corporate strategies encourage the SBU level Chief executives in formulating their strategies. SBU plays a vital role in strategic management. The chief of SBU performs the roles similar to those of managing director and attempts to achieve the best results in their business units within the facilities and resources provided, autonomy and freedom sanctioned and under the overall guidelines of the corporate objectives and policies. SBU is encouraged to start new ventures, or the SBU itself may be a new venture established within the present corporation.

DIMENSIONS OF STRATEGIC MANAGEMENT

- **CEO:** Chief Executive Officer plays key role in decision making. Strategic decisions are related with various functional levels of organisations. Hence, it is necessary that these decisions must be made in consultation with the CEO.
- **Budget:** Strategic decision making involves budget allocation i.e., resource allocation to various aspects of decision. Budget may be allocated to various factors of production.
- **Future Prosperity:** Strategic decisions are usually expected to have a significance on future prosperity of the organisation. This is because there is a long-term commitment. In case of absence of long-term commitment, the firm cannot achieve future development.
- **Competition-oriented:** Strategic decisions should keep in view of the competition existing in the market. Sometime firms has to face non-price competition.

- **Environment:** Business environment always is an influencing factor for decision making. There may be external or internal factors that influence business. Buyers, suppliers, government and competitors are likely to react in accordance with changes in environment. Thus, business also should act in the same passion.

- **Risk Bearing:** Strategic decisions mostly face the problem of risk. The decisions should be able to tackle the risk bearing capacity. Risk and uncertainty are two important aspects, which cannot be expected by businessman.

CLASSIFICATION OF STRATEGISTS

- CEO
- Board of Directors

CHIEF EXECUTIVE OFFICER

The CEO is the person responsible for the functioning of the entire organisation. The CEO has the responsibility for organisation building through organisational change. Organisational building strategies depend on the market opportunities, expansion and diversification. Organisational changes should be permanent, not situational.

CEO and degree of involvement in Strategic Management: Thomas L. Wheelmen and J. David Hunger propounded theory of degree of involvement and the role of CEO in decision making.

1. **Phantom:** CEO has no involvement in decision making. They never know what to do, if anything no degree of involvement.
2. **Rubber Stamp:** CEO will permit offers to make all decisions. It votes as officers recommend on action issues. It acts as mere rubber stamp.
3. **Nominal Participation:** CEO will formally review selected issues that officers bring to its attention. But they have nothing to do with policymaking with respect to the issues raised by officers. However, they can give some suggestions.
4. **Active Participation:** CEO approves, questions and makes final decisions on various strategies adopted by the organisation. Board will have active part and it performs fiscal and management audits also.
5. **Catalyst:** In this case, CEO takes the leading role in establishing and modifying policies, objectives, goals and strategies of the organisation. It may have active strategic management committee.

ROLE OF CEO: Mintzberg propounded the job of a top manager contains ten interrelated roles. The importance of each role is explained below:

1. **Figurehead:** CEO acts as legal and symbolic head, performs obligatory social, ceremonial, or legal duties (hosts retirement dinners, luncheons for employees, and plant dedications, attends civic affairs, signs contracts on behalf of firm).

2. **Leader:** CEO as a leader motivates, develops and guides subordinates, overseas staffing, training, and associated activities (introduced Management by Objectives (MBO), develops a challenging work climate, provides a sense of direction, acts as a role model).

3. **Liaison:** CEO maintains a network of contracts and information sources outside top management in order to obtain information and assistance.

4. **Monitor:** CEO seeks and obtains information in order to understand the corporation and its environments; acts as nerve centre for the corporation.

5. **Disseminator:** CEO transmits information to the rest of the top management team and other key people in the corporation.

6. **Spokesman:** CEO transmits information to key groups and people in the task environment, he prepares annual report to stockholders, talks to the chamber of commerce, states corporate policy to the media, participates in advertising campaigns, speaks before committees.

7. **Entrepreneur:** CEO searches the corporation and its environment for projects to improve products, processes, procedures and structures; then supervises the design and implementation.

8. **Negotiator:** CEO represents the corporation in negotiating important agreements, many speak directly with key representatives of groups in the task environment or work through a negotiator; negotiates disagreements with the heads.

9. **Resource Locator:** CEO is the key person to find resources for the organisation.

10. **Disturbance Handler:** CEO takes corrective action in times of disturbance or crisis.

BOARD OF DIRECTORS

'Board of Directors' play a vital role in managing the organisation. Board of directors represents the shareholders of the company. The functions and responsibilities of the board of directors are limited according to the Memorandum of Association, Articles of Association of the company. They are key persons in strategic decision making.

Responsibilities of Board of Directors

1. Preparation of organisation mission and specification of strategies to be adopted by the management.
2. To evaluate and influence management's proposal, decisions and actions.
3. To give advice and other suggestions as well as developing alternative strategies.
4. To monitor and regulate internal and external developments through the committees.

5. To alter the management on the new development and new entrants in the competitive market.
6. The board acts a vital and continual link between the company and external environment like governments, other companies, social and economic institutions, etc.
7. They will take active part in selection of top executives of the organisation.
8. Important financial decisions can also be taken by the Board of Directors.

FUNCTIONAL ASPECTS OF STRATEGIC MANAGEMENT

The following are the major benefits of strategic management. The benefits may be treated as functional aspects or merits or pros of strategic management.

1. **Decision Making:** CEO is the key man to take decisions. Thus, with the help of strategic management, CEO can select best strategy and sub-strategies. He can direct the management in a right manner.
2. **Achieving Performance:** The companies can fix production targets and productivity, with the help of strategic management.
3. **Growth:** Organisation always seeks to achieve growth. Profit maximisation, wealth maximisation will form part of formulation of strategies. Hence, strategic management helps the management for future growth.
4. **High Results:** Strategic management helps in determination for achievement of results which leads to growth. Every organisation always seeks to achieve high result. As low performing entities cannot survive in the competitive world.
5. **Reduction of Complexity:** Reduction of complexity in procedures result in achieving high result. Ultimately it leads to growth and good performance.
6. **Social Responsibility:** Social responsibility are expressed in terms of types of activities, number of days of service or financial contributions. These can be determined with the utility of strategic management.
7. **Customer Satisfaction:** By implementing strategic management process, the business entities can enhance their customer satisfaction. Goodwill may also be improved as a result of increased customer satisfacation.
8. **Development of Human Resources:** Every organisation will have a separate human resource department. It tries to concentrate on improving skills of manpower. Manpower planning and development is one of the key-factor of strategic management.
9. **Adoptability to Change:** The benefit of adoptability to change with minimum resistance is also likely to follow the uses of strategic management. Participative

process leads to greater awareness of the basis of choosing a particular option and the limits to available to alternatives.

10. **Cost Control:** To achieve more profits, organisation should concentrate on cost control and cost reduction techniques. Thus, cost control will be one of the important objective of the strategic management.

11. **Profitability:** Profitability can be expressed in terms of profits, return on investment, earnings per share, or profit-to-sales ratios. Strategic management will helps in enhancement of profitability of organisations.

12. **Ability to Compete:** Strategic management helps in analysing market. The organisation can able to increase sales, and it can achieve expected market share with the implementation of best strategies.

Dysfunctional aspects (or) demerits or (cons)

1. Strategic management process is costly exercise.
2. Its gestation period is very long.
3. Sometimes strategies may be failed, which leads to frustration.
4. Future uncertain, and risk is very high. Strategic management mostly depends on long-term results, which are uncertain and high risk-oriented.
5. Resistance to change by the employees.

FINANCIAL STRATEGIES

The firm can adopt a financial strategy, which matches the expected life of assets with the expected life of source of funds raised to finance assets. Thus, a ten-year loan may be raised to finance plant with an expected life of ten years; stock of goods to be sold in thirty days may be financed with a thirty-day commercial paper or a bank loan. The justification for the exact matching is that, since the purpose of financing is to pay for assets, the source of financing and the asset should be relinquished simultaneously. Using long-term financing for short-term assets is expensive, as funds will not be utilised for the full period. Similarly, financing long-term assets with short-term financing is costly as well as inconvenient as arrangement for the new short-term financing will have to be made on a continuing basis.

Matching Approach

When the firm follows matching approach (also known as hedging approach), long-term financing will be used to finance fixed assets and permanent current assets and short-term financing to finance temporary or variable current assets. However, it should be realised that exact matching is not possible because of the uncertainty about the expected lives of assets.

Different Financing Strategies

- **Long-term Financing:** This includes raising of share capital, debentures, long-term borrowings from financial institutions and making provision for reserves and surplus (retained earnings).
- **Short-term Financing:** The short-term financing is obtained for a period less than one year. It is arranged in advance from banks and other suppliers of short-term finance in the money market. Short-term finances include working capital funds from banks, public deposits, commercial paper, factoring of receivable, etc.
- **Spontaneous Financing:** Spontaneous financing refers to the automatic sources of short-term funds arising in the normal course of a business. Trade (suppliers) credit and outstanding expenses are examples of spontaneous financing. There is no explicit cost of spontaneous financing. A firm is expected to utilise these sources of finances to the fullest extent. The real choice of financing current assets, once the spontaneous sources of financing have been fully utilised, is between the long and short-term sources of finances.

Distinction between Short-term vs. Long-term Financing

A firm should decide whether or not it should use short-term financing. If short-term financing has to be used, the firm must determine its portion in total financing. This decision of the firm will be guided by the risk-return trade-off. Short-term financing may be preferred over long-term financing for two reasons: (i) the cost advantage and (ii) flexibility. But short-term financing is more risky than long-term financing. Short-term financing should generally be less costly than long-term financing. It has been found in developed countries, like USA, that the rate of interest is related to the maturity of debt. The relationship between the maturity of debt and its cost is called the term structure of interest rates. The curve, relating to the maturity of debt and interest rates is called the yield curve. The yield curve may assume any shape, but it is generally upward sloping. The justification for the higher cost of long-term financing can be found in the liquidity preference theory. This theory says that since lenders are risk averse, and risk generally increases with the length of lending time (because it is more difficult to forecast the more distant future), most lenders would prefer to make short-term loans. The only way to induce these lenders to lend for longer periods is to offer them higher rates of interest.

The cost of financing has an impact on the firm's return. Both short and long-term financing have a leveraging effect on shareholder's return. But the short-term financing ought to cost less than long-term financing; therefore, it gives relatively higher return to shareholders. It is noticeable that in India short-term loans cost more than long-term loans. Banks are the major suppliers of the working capital finance in India. Their rates of interest on working capital finance are quite high. The main source of long-term loans are financial institutions which till recently were not charging interest at differential rates. The prime rate of interest charged by financial institutions is lower than the rate charged by banks.

It is relatively easy to refund short-term funds when the need for funds diminishes. Long-term funds such as debenture loan or preference capital cannot be refunded before time. Thus, if a firm anticipates that its requirements for funds will diminish in near future, it would choose short-term funds.

FINANCIAL PLANNING

We may broadly define financial planning as a process of determining an individual's financial goals, purposes in life and life's priorities, and after considering his resources, risk profile and current lifestyle, to detail a balanced and realistic plan to meet those goals.

The above definition uses the individual's goals and purpose in life as strategic guideposts for mapping a course of action on 'what is needed to be done' to reach meaningful goals in meaningful ways for him. The goals and purposes in life are the reference points or outcomes to aim at when the financial plan is constructed. Alongside the data gathering exercise, the purpose of each goal is determined to ensure that the goal is meaningful in the context of the individual's situation. Through a process of careful analysis by an experienced financial planner, these goals are then subjected to a reality check by considering the individual's current and future resources available to achieve them. In the process, the constraints and obstacles to these goals are noted. The information will be used later to determine if there are sufficient resources available to get to these goals, and what other things need to be considered in the process. If the resources are insufficient or absent to meet any of the goals, the particular goal will be adjusted to a more realist level or is replaced with a new goal.

To plan for the future would usually require some forms of self-constrains in postponing some enjoyment today for the sake of the future. To be effective, the approach to financial planning should consider the individual's current lifestyle so that the 'pain' in postponing current pleasures is bearable over the term of the plan. It is in times where current sacrifices are involved that the strength of the plan's purpose for each goal is called upon to ensure that the pursuit of the goal will continue. The plan would consider the importance of each goal and prioritised them accordingly for taking action. It should be noted that many financial plans fail because these practical points were not sufficiently considered.

Scope of Financial Planning

The scope of financial planning would include the following:

- **Risk Management and Insurance Planning:** To make provision against cash flow risks through sound risk management and insurance techniques. The quantity of estimated risk is made through probability approach. The financial manager seeks the help of insurance advisor for insuring the cash inflows of the business.

- **Investment and Planning Issues:** Planning, creating and managing capital accumulation to generate future capital and cash flows for reinvestment and spending are major important issues in financial planning. Thus, capital budgeting, capital structure and cost of capital are three approaches for investment and planning decisions.
- **Tax Planning:** Planning for the reduction of tax liabilities and the freeing-up of cash flows for other purposes. Corporate tax planning is also playing a vital role in financial planning. Irregularities will lead to not only losses in cash inflows but also it leads to judicial problems.
- **Estate Planning:** This is nothing but planning for the creation, accumulation, conservation and distribution of assets. It also includes purchase of land, building, machinery and creation of goodwill, etc.

The Financial Planning Process

The financial planning process is generally accepted as a six-step process as follows:

Step 1: Setting Goals with the Client: This step (that is usually performed in conjunction with Step 2) is meant to identify where the client wants to go in terms of his finances and life.

Step 2: Gathering Relevant Information on the Client: This would include the qualitative and quantitive aspects of the client's financial and relevant non-financial situation.

Step 3: Analysing the Information: The information gathered is analysed so that the client's situation is properly understood. This includes checking whether there are sufficient resources to reach the client's goals and what those resources are.

Step 4: Constructing a Financial Plan: Based on the understanding of what the client wants in the future and his current financial status, a roadmap to the client goals is drawn to facilitate the achievements of those goals.

Step 5: Implementing the Strategies in the Plan: Guided by the financial plan, the strategies outlined in the plan is implemented using the resources allocated for the purpose.

Step 6: Monitoring Implementation and Reviewing the Plan: The implementation process is closely monitored to ensure it stays in alignment to the client's goals. Periodic reviews are undertaken to check for misalignment and changes in the client's situation. If there are any deviation or significant changes to the client's situation, the strategies and goals in the financial plan are revised accordingly.

Benefits of Financial Planning

- Helps monitor cash flows and reduces unnecessary expenditure.
- Enables maintenance of an optimum balance between income and expenses.

- Helps boost savings and create wealth.
- Helps reduce tax liability.
- Maximizes returns from investments.
- Creates wealth and ensures better wealth management to achieve life goals.
- Financially secures retirement life.
- Reviews insurance needs and therefore also ensures that dependants are financially secure in the unfortunate event of death or disability.
- Lastly, it also ensures that a will is made.

FUNCTIONS OF SFM

1. **Financial Analysis and Diagnosis:** SFM helps in examining financial health position of the organisation through different diagnostic tools like financial statement analysis, valuation of the equity and debt components of capital structure.
2. **Financial Planning and Forecasting:** As it was said earlier, financial planning and forecasting are two important dimensions of the SFM, which are helpful in overall financial development of the organisation.
3. **Financial Risk and Return Evaluation:** Risk and return are interdependent. Financial experts say that higher the risk leads to higher returns or higher losses. The quantum of risk bearing will influence the expected returns for the business entity.
4. **Financial Control through Optimising Techniques:** Optimisation means the least cost combination of inputs to get the best results. Several optimisation techniques like; capital rationing, sensitivity analysis, financial break-even analysis, etc., can be applied for financial control.
5. **Financial Resource Expansion Strategies:** Expanding the size and scale of business operations leads to expansion in the financial resources.
6. **Financial Restructuring and Re-engineering:** Corporate restructuring activities like; Mergers, acquisitions and takeover policies are important functions of SFM. Re-engineering is nothing but redesigning of financial instruments, capital structure and dividend policies of the organisation.
7. **Volume and Mix of Financing:** Volume refers to the amount of investment and mix refers to the proportion of equity and debt in the capital structure. By studying SFM, we can understand the optimal mix for the capital structure depending on the needs of organisation.

8. **Capital Budgeting using Risk and Probability Approach:** Investing techniques are also called as capital budgeting techniques. SFM deals with application of risk and probability for evaluating various projects for future investments.

9. **Decision Relating to Lease, Buy or Hire Purchase:** SFM deals with a comparative analysis of leasing, buying in instalments or hire-purchase system. This analysis is useful for investing decision of the organisation.

10. **Valuation of Firm:** SFM deals with study of valuing business firm. Thus, it studies about valuation of shares, bonds and goodwill.

11. **Disinvestment Policies:** This is one of the strategies of privatisation. By disinvesting the corporate entity under public sector will get more funds at the same time responsibility of the government will decreases accordingly.

12. **Distress Management and Turnaround Strategies:** SFM deals with financial distress management and turnaround strategies for revival of sick units.

13. **Liquidity Management through Working Capital:** Working capital is the primary source to meet day to day expenditure of the organisation. It is the excess of current assets over the current liabilities.

14. **Planning in Mergers, Acquisitions and Takeovers:** When competition is growing up, the finance manager has to think about various strategies of mergers, acquisitions and takeovers. SFM deals with various aspects of merger and acquisition strategies.

FACTORS TO BE CONSIDERED WHILE ESTIMATING FINANCIAL REQUIREMENTS

1. **Cost:** The cost of finance is an obvious consideration. It should be the minimum.

2. **Cost of Initial Promotional Outlays:** These include the cost of the development of a product or a process, the cost of market surveys, legal and incorporation expenditure, outlays on preliminary contract, if any, and compensation for promotion.

3. **Claim on Assets:** Borrowings may result in a charge on the assets and thus restrict their use. This may seriously impair the maneuverability of the enterprise.

4. **Current Assets:** Current asset needs should be assessed on the basis of estimated sales and production schedules or projections. Cost budgets and inventory estimates should be prepared and customer trade terms should be fixed.

5. **Distribution Outlays:** Distribution outlays should be estimated on the basis of the distribution system to be adopted by an enterprise. For this purpose, the advertising commission of the intermediaries, etc., should be taken into account.

6. **Fixed Asset Needs:** Fixed Asset needs should be based on estimates supplied by the production and engineering departments.

7. **Interest Payment:** Heavy interest charges are embarrassing and should be kept at the desired level.

8. **Margin of Safety:** Contingent funds should be provided for a margin of safety to take care of inaccurate projections or unforeseen events.

9. **Need for Additional Funds:** Financial forecasting involves the relation of sales to assets and liabilities. The financial manager should be able to anticipate the need for additional funds on the basis of projected income statements, projected balance sheet, cash budgets, statements of sources and uses of funds and such other tools of financial forecasting.

10. **Seasonality:** Financial requirements, influenced by seasonality or growth, cannot be easily anticipated. There are, moreover, unpredictable events strikes, product failure, changes in the supply price, changes in technology or consumer tastes-which significantly affect financial requirements.

SFM RELATION WITH OTHER SUBJECTS

Strategic Financial Management is closely linked with many other disciplines such as economics, accountancy, mathematics, statistics, operations research, psychology and organisational behaviour. Let us see these linkages in detail:

1. **SFM and Accountancy:** The accountant provides accounting information relating to costs, revenues, receivables, payable, profits/losses, etc. And this forms the basis for the finance manager to act upon. This forms authentic source of data about the performance of the firm. The main objective of accounting function is to record, classify and interpret the given accounting data.

2. **SFM and Economics:** SFM is the offshoot of economics, which deals with theoretical concepts, SFM is the application of these in the real life. In the presence of addressing various business problems, several empirically estimated functions such as demand for capital function, cost function, revenue function and so on are extensively used. Both are concerned with the problems of scarcity and resource allocation. If the economist is concerned with the study of 'markets', the business manager is interested in studying the impact of such markets on the performance of a given firm.

3. **SFM and Mathematics:** Business strategist is concerned with estimating and predicting the relevant economic factors for decision making and forward planning. In this process, he extensively makes use of the tools and techniques of mathematics such as algebra, calculus, exponentials, vectors, and input-output tables and such other. Mathematics facilitate derivation and exposition of economic analysis.

4. **SFM and Operations Research:** Decision making is the main focus of operations research. It emphasises solving the business problems. Hence, Operations Research is the tool for finding the solutions for many a business problem. 'Model building' is one area of common exercise. It is used to establish economic and logical relations ships among the given variables. The Operations Research models such as linear programming, queuing, transportation, optimisation techniques and so on, are extensively used in solving the business problems. Optimisation is an interesting word. It refers to both minimisation of costs and maximisation of revenues.

5. **SFM and Organisational Behaviour:** Organisational behaviour enables the business strategist to study and develop behavioural models of the firm integrating the manager's behaviour with that of the owner. This further analyses the economies' rationality of the firm in a focused way.

6. **SFM and Psychology:** Competitive business psychology is the basis on which strategic manager acts upon. Strategic finance manager has to study about rival reacts to a given change in business environment and its consequential effect on the business. Psychology contributes towards under-standing the behavioural implications, attitudes and motivations of each of the micro-economic variables such as consumer, supplier/seller, investor, worker or an employee.

7. **SFM and Statistics:** Statistics deals with different techniques useful to analyse the cause and effect relationships in a given variable or phenomenon. It also empowers the manager to deal with the situations of risk and uncertainly through its techniques such as probability. The business environment for the business economist is full of risk and uncertainty and he extensively makes use of the statistical techniques such as averages, measures of dispersion, correlation, regression, time series, interpolation, probability, and so on.

PROFIT MAXIMISATION VS. WEALTH MAXIMISATION

Meaning of Profit

In ordinary parlance, profit is the surplus of income over expenses of production according to businessman. It is the amount left with him after he has made payments for all factors and services used by him in the process of production. Profit maximisation is the process by which a firm determines the price and output level that returns the greatest profit. There are several approaches to this problem. The total revenue – total cost method relies on the fact that profit equals revenue minus cost, and the marginal revenue – marginal cost method is based on the fact that total profit in a perfectly competitive market reaches its maximum point where marginal revenue equals marginal cost.

Cost:

Any costs incurred by a firm may be classed into two groups: fixed cost and variable cost. Fixed costs are incurred by the business at any level of output, including none.

These may include equipment maintenance, rent, wages, and general upkeep. Variable costs change with the level of output, increasing as more product is generated. Materials consumed during production often have the largest impact on this category. Fixed cost and variable cost, combined, equal total cost.

Revenue:

Revenue is the total amount of money that flows into the firm. This can be from any source, including product sales, government subsidies, venture capital and personal funds.

IMPORTANT ISSUES IN PROFIT MAXIMISATION

- A firm is said to be making an economic profit when its average total cost is less than the price of the product at the profit-maximising output. The economic profit is equal to the quantity output multiplied by the difference between the average total cost and the price.
- A firm is said to be making a normal profit when its economic profit equals zero. This occurs where average total cost equals price at the profit-maximising output.
- A firm is said to be making a zero economic profit when its marginal revenue equals marginal cost.
- If the price is between average total cost and average variable cost at the profit-maximising output, then the firm is said to be in a loss-minimising condition. The firm should still continue to produce, however, since its loss would be larger if it was to stop producing. By continuing production, the firm can offset its variable cost and atleast part of its fixed cost, but by stopping completely it would lose equivalent of its entire fixed cost.
- If the price is below average variable cost at the profit-maximising output, the firm is said to be in shutdown. Losses are minimised by not producing at all, since any production would not generate returns significant enough to offset any fixed cost and part of the variable cost. By not producing, the firm loses only its fixed cost.

Meaning of Wealth

Wealth is nothing but aggregate amount of fixed and current assets of the organisation. Wealth includes land, building, factory, machinery, bank balance, shares, debentures, other forms of investments. For any organisation aggregate capital can also be treated as wealth. As we know that profit maximisation is fundamental objective of the business, wealth maximisation also one of the objectives of the business firm. Accumulated profits can be converted into sales maximisation or wealth maximisation. If the advertisement expenditure is increased, then it will help in increase of sales. If profits are converted into reserves, or purchase of new equipment or purchase of new machinery, it will be leading to wealth maximisation. Any businessman wants to rise in wealth of business, however if he neglects sales maximisation then it will hamper success of business. Profits vary from industry to industry and from businessman to businessman. The greater the risk and then the greater the uncertainty in business or industry, the greater are the opportunities for large profits. Profits are likely to be high in industries in which methods of production are constantly changing so that there is continuous adoption of new techniques.

Profit maximisation also depends on the achievement of sales targets. To achieve the expected targets, business firms will try to attract consumers by offering discounts, free-gifts, bundle-pack offers, etc. Sometimes prices may be reduced for a certain period of time to increase sales. In such cases, profits may be declined, however the firms will be able to compete with the rivals and elimination of rivals can be possible by practicing various sales strategies.

Wealth maximisation depends on investment decisions of the business. By taking best projects with the help of capital budgeting techniques like Net Present Value Method or Internal Rate of Return, the firm maximises its value of investment. The higher returns will give higher value to the organisation. The value of firm is also depends upon goodwill, quality of the product, and social commit of the firm. Hence, every business firm aims to achieve value or wealth maximisation as well as profit maximisation.

STRATEGIC FINANCIAL PLANNING

Integrating strategic and financial planning is the best way for health care organisations to ensure that they are spending money wisely. Too often, projects get approved only to be shelved because the money isn't available. This gatefold looks at the process of integrating strategic and financial planning and provides steps that will help hospitals combine these practices.

Objectives of Strategic and Financial Planning: The traditional role of strategic and financial planning must be incorporated into a combined process.

The traditional goals of the Strategic Planning Process

- Develop and implement a strategic plan that supports the organisation's mission, vision and values.
- Create organisational and business unit plans.
- Identify and evaluate new business opportunities.
- Provide training and education related to planning.
- Perform market assessments and forecasts.
- Reconcile the plan with capital and operational budgets, as well as with human resource and facility planning.
- Monitor plan implementation and measure results.

The traditional goals of the Financial Planning Process:

- Measure current performance.
- Compare the organisation's position against past organisational data and local, regional and national benchmarks.
- Make financial projections.
- Outline the organisation's financial requirements.
- Integrate the financial process with the strategic planning process.

How The Planning Process Works?: Integrating strategic and financial planning processes creates the essential link between organisational priorities and the deployment of resources. This overview is a consolidation and distillation of this process from a variety of sources. It is intended to guide organisations through the major steps in the integration process. The process typically varies from organisation to organisation but includes these major components.

1. Analytic Phase

Market Analysis: The market analysis provides an understanding of an organisation's financial strengths and weaknesses by providing local and national data for comparison. It helps the organisation predict market changes that will impact its strategic goals.

Internal Analysis: The internal analysis outlines an organisation's current performance and status of its workforce and patient population. When combined with the market analysis, organisations can compare the hospital's services with the needs of the community and determine the hospital's ability to grow.

Operational Assumptions: Operational assumptions include projections about needs within the service area, the ability to attract and retain physicians and nurses, as well as the impact of future clinical practices and technologies on the organisation.

Financial Assumptions: The financial assumptions serve as the financial framework for the operating budget and capital plan. At the project level, assumptions focus on the specific initiative. At the organisational level, assumptions are based on both external factors as well as internal factors, such as bad debt, collections, days-cash-on-hand and working capital.

2. Plan Development Phase

Identify Opportunities: Data from the internal and external analysis is combined with the assumptions to create a picture of current and future needs of the organisation to identify opportunities for growth and expansion.

Financial Projections: Examines how the combination of financial assumptions and internal operations will influence the availability of investment funds. For example, changes in interest rates can impact the sources and uses of capital. Changes in the marketplace and the organisation's fiscal situation may impact the ability of the organisation to finance its strategic plan.

Mission, Vision, Values: These key components of the strategic plan serve as the basis for prioritising opportunities. This ensures that all initiatives further the organisation's goals.

Prioritise Opportunities: Assessing opportunities and financial projections will help organisations prioritise projects based on financial viability, opportunity for growth and community need. Capital should be allocated to projects based on importance. Projects can be categorised as routine (maintenance and replacing equipment), mandated (a project that is required to meet regulations), and strategic (projects, such as adopting a new service line) to meet the long-term needs of the community and the organisation.

Test Viability: An interactive process that examines whether selected opportunities support the organisation's mission and will provide the projected financial, quality or operational returns. It also examines whether the organisation has the capital to finance the opportunity.

3. Implementation Phase

Operational Plan: This includes staffing, facility planning, process changes, technology planning and other nonfinancial activities necessary to implement the plan.

Financial Plans: Financial and capital plans identify both sources and uses of funds. This includes directions for capital allocation and spending, as well as the development of a time frame based on the needs of the operational plan.

Implement the Consolidated Plan: The implementation process for strategic initiatives must be outlined to ensure follow-through. Key players must be aware of their roles and responsibilities. Executives must assign accountability so plans are carried out effectively and set measurable goals to determine progress.

Ongoing Adjustments to Plan Evaluation: Results must be monitored continuously to ensure success. Key assumptions should be periodically reviewed to make sure they are on target. New threats and opportunities may also become apparent. The plan needs to be flexible to adapt to new opportunities.

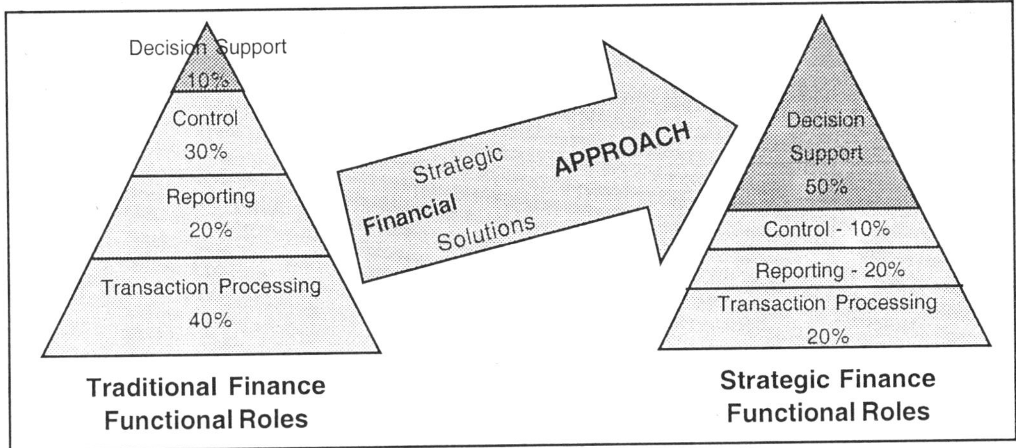

Fig. 1.3: Distinction between Traditional Finance and Strategic Finance

Source: strategicfinancialsolutions.net

Table 1.1: Distinction between Financial Management and Strategic Financial Management

	Financial Management (FM)		Strategic Financial Management (SFM)
1.	Central focus of FM is on various short -term and medium-term financial planning.	1.	SFM aims at long-term perspective as well as designing financial strategies to face the changing corporate business competition.
2.	FM is closely relating to both macro and micro-economics as it deals with budgeting, cash management, credit administration and working capital management.	2.	SFM is closely relating to business policy, strategic management and financial policy.
3.	Finance function covers four major decision making areas: a. financing decisions. b. investing decisions. c. dividend decisions. d. profitability decisions.	3.	SFM focuses on the following five major decision making areas: a. optimisation techniques for financing decision. b. corporate restructuring. c. financial reorganisation. d. disinvestment strategies. e. turnaround management.
4.	Financial management is middle-level function in the organisation structure.	4.	SFM is top-level function in the organisation structure.

CLOSING CASELET

SWARNA EARTH MOVERS LTD.

The Bengaluru-based SWARNA Earth Movers Ltd. (SEML), has consistently shown profits since its inception in 1984, showing an average growth of 14 per cent over the past decade in the 1990s. The objective of growth planning initiated by management of SEML early in 1998 was stated by its CMD as follows:

'The major challenge now before SEML is to emerge as a premier company in earth moving, mining, railway and defence equipment, qualify for ISO-9000 accreditation and the turnover target of ₹ 2,000 crores by the end of Ninth Plan period'. To start with, SEML took up for blue printing growth plans in its bread-and-butter earth moving and mining segments. It began working on expanding the range of its surface mining equipment and foraying into a host of underground mining equipment, like site discharge loaders, shuttle cars, root bolting equipment, in-pit crushers and blast-hole drills. This product range expansion was aimed at transforming SEML into a total mining solutions company. It also planned to turn out a range of track laying and maintenance equipment. The company actually set-up an application engineering cell for developing mining consultancy skills. Another aspect of SEML's growth plan related to overseas joint ventures. The company began exploring trough 'Stock-in-sell' experiments, taking equipment overseas and selling them first. The company planned to follow it up by assembling equipment overseas as a prelude to finally manufacturing them abroad. The markets in West Asia, Africa and Europe were identified for the experiments, the products to be 'Stock-in-sold' included in-house developed equipment such as B-35 dumpers and WL-720 wheel loaders. In order to gain greater acceptability in the international markets and finally secure ISO 9000 accredition, SEML put extra stress on quality. Doing away with the small quality set-ups within each division, the company established an independent quality division and put it in charge of a whole time director reporting directly to the CMD. Mr. Padmanabhan, Executive Director (Quality) stated, 'we have kicked off a full-scale quality audit in all our plants, and in the pipeline are intensive vendor-rating and vendor-education programmes'. SEML also planed opening customer service centres in all centres where at least one major SEML equipment-user was based, and aimed at assuring after sales service within 48 hours of a fault intimation.

The company had ability to financially support its forays. With a low equity base of ₹ 30 crores coupled with reserves of ₹ 320 crores, the margin of safety was quite appreciable. Besides, the replacement cost of SEML's gross block of ₹ 316 crores was estimated at ₹ 3,000 crores in 1998-99. However, the debt burden which stood at ₹ 518 crores was admitted heavy, and the interest was quite at 11 per cent of its turnover.

QUESTIONS

1. Analyse growth planning strategy of SEML.
2. Examine SEML's growth plan related to overseas joint ventures.
3. Evaluate the relationship between establishment of quality division and customer service centres and growth planning strategy of SEML.

KEYWORDS

1. **Corporate Strategy:** It is the way in which corporate endeavours to differentiate itself positively from its competitors, using its relative strengths to better satisfy customer needs.
2. **SBU:** Strategic Business Unit is 'any part of a business organisation which is treated separately for strategic management purposes'.
3. **Strategic Financial Management:** It involves various aspects of financial planning. [Financial planning is depending on two aspects] i.e., (i) Liquidity Planning and (ii) Profit Planning.
4. **Strategy:** It is nothing but the determination of the basic long-term goals and objectives of an enterprise, and the adoption of courses of action and the allocation of resources necessary for carrying out these goals.

SUMMARY

This chapter is divided into two sections: (a) the conceptual approach and (b) process of strategic management. Strategic Financial Management always concentrates on the anticipated aim. Future is always uncertain. Hence, strategic decisions are always incomplete and sometimes they have been based on false information. It may lead to further problems. Finance manager should always aim at achieving pre determined goal of the organisation. Further organisations have to work with brevity and variety. Thoughts should become actions. Actions will lead to results. Result-oriented action is the need of hour.

REVIEW QUESTIONS

1. Define 'Strategy' and explain different stages of strategic management process.
2. What is meant by the term 'Strategic Financial Management'? Explain its relation with other subjects.
3. Explain various functions of 'Strategic Financial Management'.
4. Explain important factors to be considered for financial estimation.

5. Distinguish between profit maximisation and wealth maximisation.
6. Distinguish between 'Financial Management' and 'Strategic Financial Management'

REFERENCES

1. Alexander W. Butler, Hess Cornaggia, Gustavo Grulon, James P. Weston, *'Corporate Financing Decisions and Managerial Market Timing'*, http://ssrn.com/abstract=1370403.
2. Ansof, H. Igor, *Corporate Strategy*, New York, McGraw-Hill, 1965.
3. Craig M. Lewis, Richard J. Rogalski and James K. Sewad, 'Industry Conditions, Growth Opportunities and Market Reactions to Convertible Debt Financing Decisions', http://ssrn.com/abstract=1618.
4. Gustave Grullon, Geroge Kanatas and Piyush Kumar, 'Financing Decisions and Advertising: An Empirical Study of Capital Structure and Product Market Competition', http://ssrn.com.
5. Jakhotiya G.P., *'Strategic Financial Management'*, Vikas Publications, New Delhi, 2007.
6. Sridhar A.N., *'Strategic Financial Management'*, SPD, New Delhi, 2008.

CHAPTER

2

STRATEGIC DECISION MAKING

CHAPTER OUTLINE

- Opening Caselet
- Introduction
- Steps for Strategic Decision Making Process
- Approaches to Strategic Decision Making
- Rationality in Decision Making
- Steps in the Rationale Model
- Classes of Decision Making
- Strategies for Profitability
- Decision Tree
- Problems and Solutions on Decision Tree
- Closing Caselet
- Summary
- Keywords
- Review Questions
- References

OPENING CASELET

Dinesh Patidar, 48, enjoys working on the R&D of submersible pumps and submersible motors. Though a commerce graduate, the MD of the Indore-based Shakti Pumps Ltd. (SPL) speaks the 'nuts and bolts' language on the manufacturing of submersible pumps. He has not only mastered the art of reverse engineering, but has been working on energy efficiency and innovating products that are now being shipped across geographies, to countries such as the US, South Africa, the Middle East Europe. However, this brand is not popular in other countries abroad. Today 62 per cent of the company's turnover of ₹ 132 crore (for June 2010) comes from exports to 50 odd companies.

In terms of numbers, SPL was small. Till, 2005, the company had barely touched ₹ 50 crore. However, in the past six years to 2010, SPL has reported a CAGR of 23 per cent in its top line to ₹ 132 crore. During the same period, the profits have moved at a faster clip too. While operating profit moved from ₹ 4.09 crores (2005) to ₹ 23.99 crores (2010) at a CAGR of 42 per cent, the net profit moved at a CAGR of 409 per cent to ₹ 11.19 crore. Currently the operating and net margins stand at 18.22 per cent respectively. Net worth also grew at 42 per cent CAGR. Enthused by this growth, the board has decided to issue bonus shares in a liberal ratio of 1:1.

Discuss strategic decision making issues in declaration of bonus shares by SPL.

Source: *Business India*, April 3, 2011.

(CAGR = Compounded Annual Growth Rate)

INTRODUCTION

Strategic Decision Making: Is to develop strategies by which an organisation will be able to achieve its objectives. The time horizon for strategic decisions, tends to be fairly long, so that fundamental shifts in the organisation may be made. Strategic decisions do not have to occur on a periodic, regular cycle as do management control activities. Future is always uncertain. Hence, strategic decisions are always incomplete and sometimes they have been based on false information. It may lead to further problems.

Decision Making: Is a means to an end. It entails identifying and choosing alternative solutions that lead to a desired state of affairs. The process begins with a problem and ends when a solution has been chosen. Decision making is one of the primary responsibilities of being a manager. The quality of a manager's decisions is important for two principal reasons. First, the quality of a manager's decisions directly affects his or her career opportunities, rewards, and job satisfaction. Second, managerial decisions contribute to the success or failure of an organisation.

A decision is the act of choosing among two or more options. Decision making is the process of thought and deliberation that leads to decision. It is important for managers to learn about good decision making for many reasons.

1. *'Every activity of management is based on decision'.* — *P.F. Drucker*
2. *'Decision making is the selection based on source criteria from two or more possible alternatives'.* — *George R. Terry*
3. *'A direction is the act of choice wherein an executive forms a conclusion about what must be done in a given situation. A decision represents behaviour chosen from a number of possible alternatives'.* — *D.E. McFarland*
4. *'Decision making' can be defined as the selection based on some criteria of one behaviour alternative from two or more possible alternatives. To decide means 'to cut off' or in practical content 'come to conclusion'.* — *R.S. Davar*
5. *'Decision making is the focal creative phychic event where knowledge, thoughts, feeling and imagination are fixed into action'.* — *G.L.S. Shackle*

Characteristics of Decision Making

Following are the important characteristics of decision making:

1. Decision making is based on rational thinking. The manager tries to force various possible effects of a decision on before deciding a particular one.
2. It involves the evaluation of various alternatives available. The selection of best alternative will be made only when pros and cons of all of them are discussed and evaluated.
3. It is a process of selecting the best from among alternatives available.

4. It involves certain commitment. Management is committed to every decision it takes.
5. Decision making is the end product because it is preceded by discussions and deliberations.
6. Decision making is aimed to achieve organisational goals.

Importance of Decision Making

According to Melvin T. Copland, 'Administration essentially is a decision making process and authority is responsible for making decisions and for ascertaining that the decisions made are carried out. In business, whether the enterprise be large or small changes in condition occur, shifts in personnel take place, unforseen contingencies arise Moreover, just to get wheels started and to keep them turning, decisions must be made'

At the heart of planning is decision making, i.e., the selection of a suitable course of action. It is an important function of management. Management without decisions is like a man without backbone. Nothing can be performed without taking decisions. Every aspect of management functions, such as planning, organisation, motivation and control is determined by decisions, the result of which the performance in the organisation. The days of 'hit and miss' methods in management are over, and have been replaced by new concepts and scientific techniques. Decision making is therefore, vital to all management activities. It helps to set definite objectives, prepare plans of action, determine organisational structure, motivate personnel and introduce innovations.

Further organisations have to work with brevity and variety. Thoughts should become actions. Actions will lead to results. Result-oriented action is the need of hour. Strategic manager should always aim at achieving pre-determined goal of the organisation. They can be somewhat irregular, although some strategic planning may be scheduled into the yearly planning and budgeting cycle. The following diagram explains the process of strategic decision making.

STEPS FOR STRATEGIC DECISION MAKING PROCESS

STEP-I — Recognising the Problem: The first step in the decision-making process is recognising situations in which a decision is needed because an opportunity, a problem or a crisis exists. In most cases, defining the problem is not an easy task. Opportunities and problems are not so obvious. What at times might appear to be the real problem might at best be simply the symptoms of the problems. Nibbling at the fringes of the problem, or treating only the symptoms of the problem, working on the wrong problem are wasteful efforts and may lead to the premature decision-making. Superficial disturbances can be misleading and fail to reveal underlying difficulties.

Management sees a clash of personalities while the real problem may be poor organisation structures. Management sees a problem of manufacturing costs and start a

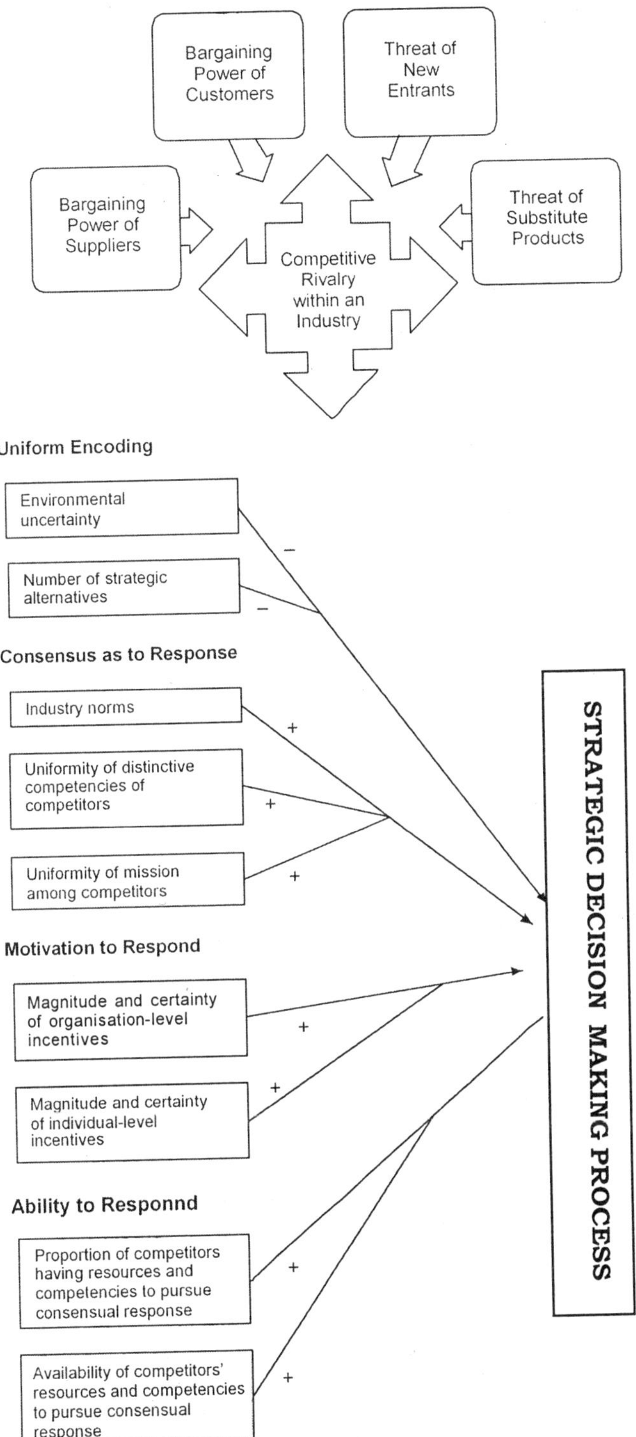

Rectangles indicate exogenous antecedents (James *et.al.,* 1985)

Figure 2.1: Strategic Decision Making Process

cost reduction drive, the real problem may be poor engineering design or poor sales planning. So apart from studying the symptoms, a manager may well try to find out the limiting factors before defining the problem. The critical factor analysis helps in finding out the difference between what is happening in a particular situation and what should be happening. The critical factor determines the gap between the desired and actual results. If a scooter is not operating because the spark plug needs replacement, the spark plug is the strategic factor. According to Barnard, the nature of the strategic factor will shift as the problem is defined correctly. After defining the problem, spark plug replacement, a new situation will arise where the new limiting factor will be obtaining the plug, or having money to buy the plug if it is available nearby and so on. Proper emphasis on all relevant factors will greatly help in defining the problem properly and it must be realised that problem is half solved when it is properly defined.

STEP-II — Analysing the Problem: In this stage, the decision maker gathers facts and looks for advice. He collects as many facts as he can and tries to separate facts from beliefs, opinions and preconceived notions. Each item is carefully evaluated, it is relatively weighted and its validity is judged. Irrelevant data and trivia will be discarded. The whole exercise helps in ensuring adequate background information and essential data relating to the problem defined. Earlier of course it is not possible to gain complete knowledge regarding problem. Certain intangible factors always force the manager to base his decisions on incomplete and coarse information. It is well-worth remembering that 'the best diagnostician is not the man who can spot early, and correct right away his own wrong diagnosis'. Knowing the extent of gap which has forced him to guess will help atleast in crystallising the problem correctly.

STEP-III — Generating Alternatives: Normally, a business problem can be solved in many ways. If there is only one alternative, no decision is required. But in any rational decision making process, the manager should not jump onto a single proposal without considering all the alternatives. At this stage, the decision maker searches for existing alternatives, modifies them, and design, customs or tailors alternatives as required. Existing ones are more reliable, easier to implement and available. If these alternatives are found unsuitable they can be made useful by modification. Totally unique alternatives are costly and time-consuming to create and often difficult to implement. Operating within these extremes (existing vs. unique alternatives) a manager may involve others in this exercise in order to devise possible courses of action. As pointed out by Koontz, the ability to develop alternatives is often as important as making a right decision among alternatives. Ingenuity research and creative imagination are required to make sure that the best alternatives are considered before a course of action is selected. Sometimes, taking no action would itself be sufficient. To take no action is a decision fully as much as to take specific action. To search for alternative calls for creative abilities on the part of managers. It helps in focusing adequate attention before it is finally resolved. Additionally, the availability of two or three good alternatives enables managers to fully test the soundness of each and every alternative before it is finally translated into practice. In the process of testing, if one decision were to fail, the next one can be pressed into service without difficulty.

STEP-IV — Evaluating Alternatives: The search for alternatives is not an unending process. The entire range of alternatives cannot be expressed in black and white as there is a cut-off point. Once, this point is reached as the decision-maker should weigh alternative solutions against one another. The problem effects of each alternative must be outlined unfortunately the consequences are always not clear. To reduce time and effort, the decision maker may well concentrate as really important facts of these alternative by applying the critical factor analysis. All pertinent facts must be collected. They must be classified, the pros and cons must be considered and the important facts must be distinguished from trivial facts. The basic purpose of evaluation should not be to find out one magic solution. The attempt should be to limit the alternatives to a manageable (two or three) and economically feasible number. Comparisons must be on the basis of values, the desirable and undesirable aspects in every alternative listed and the conflicting values resolved in some satisfactory manner. This requires subjective judgement. Experience, sometimes, may be the best teacher.

STEP-V — Choosing the Best Alternative: In this phase, the decision maker evaluates each alternative by judging it according to some criterion (profit, cost, product, quality etc.). According to Drucker, there are four criteria for picking the best among the possible solutions.

◇ **The Risk:** The manager has to weigh the risk of each course of action against the expected gains. He must decide as to how much risk he can take and find out the alternative that satisfies with this viewpoint.

◇ **Economy of Effect:** The alternative that will give the greatest output for the least input in terms of material and human resources is obviously the best one to be selected. Instead of picking an elephant gun to shoot sparrows, managers may well select the one that ensures efficient utilisation of scarce resources.

◇ **Timing:** If the situation has great urgency, the best alternative is one that warns the organisation about impending dangers. On the other hand, if consistent effort is needed, a low start that gears momentum may be preferable.

◇ **Limitation of Resources:** Physical, financial and human resources impose a limitation and must have to be considered by managers who implement the decision. Their vision, skill, understanding and competence, often determine how effectively the organisational efforts are carried out. If adequate resources are not currently available, the decision should give effect to their development or acquisition from outside sources in the next plan.

STEP-VI — Implementing and Verifying the Decision: Decision implementation is as important as decision formulation. A manager's decision is always a decision concerning what other people should do. So to avoid problems in implementation, he must communicate the decision, i.e., he must indicate as to what change in behaviour is expected, what action is expected, and so on. In addition, effective implementation depends on how people react to it. Gaining acceptance requires participation by operating people. The most appropriate stage for their involvement is that developing alternative solutions to the problem. At that point, they can contribute their ideas and suggestions. Decision implementation thus includes: Observing the decisions as it become operative, modifying it when necessary, coaching the people who implement it and perfecting it once it is in action. The process of decision is very important in the sense that it helps in highlighting the deviations and assists in taking rectificational actions in time.

APPROACHES TO STRATEGIC DECISION MAKING

The following are four important approaches to strategic decision making:

1. The Intuitive-Emotional Approach.
2. The Rational-Analytical Approach.
3. A Satisficing Approach.
4. Political Behavioural Approach.

1. The Intuitive-Emotional Approach

In this approach, decisions are based on intuition. Decision maker prefers habit or experience, relative thinking, and instinct using the unconscious cognitive process. The decision maker takes into account a number of alternatives into consideration, but simultaneously jumps one step in analysis and search to another and back again. The decision maker is normally an activist, fast mover and finds unique solutions to difficult problems.

2. The Rational-Analytical Approach

An intelligent and rational approach to decision-making is necessary in this approach. The decision maker makes the choice, in full awareness of all available feasible alternatives, to maximise advantages. The basic assumptions of this approach are:

(a) Decision maker is rational and unbiased.

(b) Decision maker has knowledge of all alternative solutions to existing problem.

(c) He can evaluate and rank based on the analysis of each alternative.

(d) He is self-disciplined person to choose best alternative.

3. A Satisficing Approach

Satisficing means choosing the first alternative that meets the decision maker's minimum standard of satisfaction, which is dependent on the current level of aspiration. Level of aspiration refers to the level of performance that a person expects to attain and it is determined by the person's prior success and failures. This approach is comparatively better than earlier approaches as pointed out here:

(a) Intuitive approach sometimes fails because of probability of risk.

(b) Rationality cannot be achieved by human being as he is being confined to his wants and desires. There are definite limits to human rationality.

Hence, the value of best previous alternative and current level of aspiration influence the value of alternative approach.

4. Political Behavioural Approach

Decision making in any organisation is influenced by several factors and political environment. Government policy will change in accordance with the changes in ruling political party. Government expects taxes from the people and business entities. Decisions of the organisation are influenced by the people, shareholders, competitors, suppliers and government. Decisions are made through mutual negotiations and consultation among all the stakeholders who affect and/or are affected by the decision.

Hence, decision maker must use political behavioural approach to balance through political compromise, the competing demands of different stakeholders in making decisions.

Types of Managerial Decisions

The managerial decisions can be classified as under:

1. Organisational and personal decisions.
2. Routine and strategic decisions.
3. Programmed and non-programmed decisions.
4. Policy and operative decisions.
5. Individual and group decisions.

1. **Organisational and Personal Decisions:** When a person takes a decision in the organisation as an executive, it will be an organisational decision. This decision will have its impact on the working of the organisation. The power to take organisational decisions can be delegated from a superior to the sub-ordinate.

   An executive can take also decisions about himself. Such decisions are also known as personal decisions. These generally affect the personal life of the decision maker. The power to take such decisions cannot be delegated to anybody else.

2. **Routine and Strategic Decisions:** Routine decisions are made repetitively following certain established rules, procedures, policies, etc. These are taken in context of day to day operations of the organisation. These decisions, do not require fresh information or discussions. Routine decisions are taken at middle and lower level management.

   Strategic dccisions are very important and are taken at top level management. They relate to policy matters and need the development and analysis of alternatives.

Strategic decisions influence organisational structure, objectives, working conditions, finances, etc. These decisions have long-term effects.

3. **Programmed and Non-programmed Decisions:** Programmed decisions are of routine nature and taken within the specified procedures. These decisions have short-term effect and are taken at lower level management. The decision to grant leave, make routine purchase, allow trade discounts, etc., are programmed decisions.

   Non-repetitive decisions are, on the other hand, non-programmed decisions. The need for such decisions arises due to specific circumstances. These decisions are taken at top level management. The opening of a new branch, introducing a new product, purchase of a new machinery are some of the examples of non-programmed decisions.

4. **Policy and Operative Decisions:** Policy decisions determine the basic policies of the organisation and are taken at top level management. The policies that are decided at the top become the basis for operative decisions. No decision can go beyond the policy framework of the organisation. These are important in nature and have long-term impact.

   Operative decisions, on the other hand, are less important and related with day-to-day operations of the business. These decisions are taken in the light of policies decided by the management. Middle and lower level management take these decisions since these involve actual execution and supervision. Whether to allow bonus to employers or not is a policy decision.

   Once it is decided to pay bonus then making calculations of payments to be made to different employees is an operative decision.

5. **Individual and Group Decisions:** This classification is based on the number of persons involved in decision making. If the decision is taken by one person, it is known as individual decision. In small concerns, only the owner takes all important decisions. Even in big concerns too, one person may be allowed to take decisions that are programmed and are of less importance.

   Group decisions are taken by a group of persons. The decisions of board of directors or of committes come under this category. These are generally, important decisions and relate to policy matters. The decisions are taken after a thorough decisions among persons who are assigned this work. The problem of delay in taking group decisions may create difficulties but otherwise these are well discussed decisions.

RATIONALITY IN DECISION MAKING

The concept of rationality is very important in decision making. Rationality implies the capacity for objective and intelligent action. A decision is said to be rational if appropriate means are chosen to achieve desired ends. According to Stenier, *et.al.*, *'rational business decision is one which effectively and efficiently assures the achievement of aims for which the means are selected'*. Rationality in Decision Making implies that the decision maker tries to maximise the values in a situation by choosing the most suitable course of action for achieving the goal. Rationality refers to the selection of preferred behaviour alternatives in terms of values where by the consequences of behaviour can be evaluated. The end means or value system approach to rationalist is faced with certain problems. *Firstly*, the ends to be attained are often completely or incorrectly stated. *Secondly*, in actual practices means can not be separated completely from ends. *Thirdly*, the means ends terminology obscures the role of the time element in decision making.

Simon has identified six descriptive models or rationality of choice behaviour. A decision is rational if it is oriented to the organisation's goals. It is consciously rational to the degree that the adjustmeant of means to ends is a conscious process. It is deliberately rational to the degree that the adjustment of means to ends has been deliberately brought about. It is objectively rational if infact it is the correct behaviour for maximising given values in a given situation. It is subjectively rational if it maximises attainment relative to the actual knowledge of subject.

STEPS IN THE RATIONAL MODEL

This model processes that managers use a rational, five-step sequence when making decision.

1. **Identifying the Problem:** Problem solving and decision making begin with the awareness that a problem exists. In other words, the first step in problem solving and decision making is identifying gap between desired and actual conditions. Being attentive to the environment helps the manager, identify problems.
2. **Generating Alternative Solutions:** In this stage, intellectually freewheeling aspect of decision making all kinds of possibilities are explored, even if they seem unrealistic. Often the difference between good and mediocre decision makers is that the former do not accept the first alternative they think of. Instead, they keep digging until they find the best solution.
3. **Evaluating Solution:** The next step involves comparing the relative value of the alternatives the problem solver examines the pros and cons of each one and considers the feasibility of each.
4. Selecting a solution.
5. Implementing and evaluating the solution.

CLASSES OF DECISION MAKING

1. Decisions under certainty
2. Decisions under risk
3. Decisions under uncertainty.

1. Decisions Under Certainty

A decision under certainty is one in which we know which state of nature will occur. Alternatively, we can think of it as a case with a single state of nature. Suppose, for example, in that morning we are deciding whether to take an umbrella to work and we know for sure that it will be raining when we leave work in the afternoon. The pay-off table for this problem, Fig. 2.2 is where ₹ 20 is the cost of having our suit cleaned if we get caught in the rain. It enters the table with a minus sign since it is a table of returns, obviously, the optimal decision is to take the umbrella.

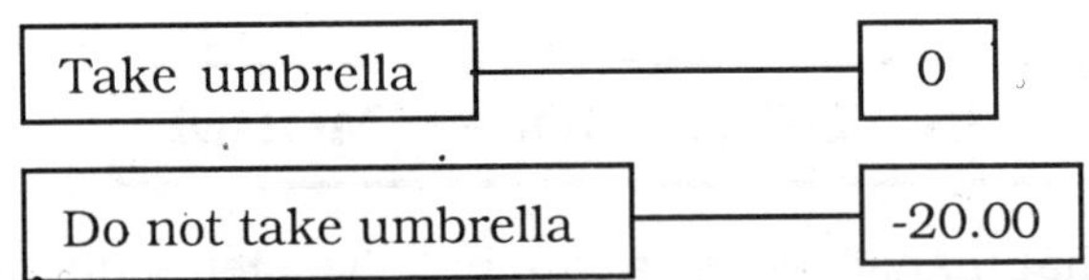

Fig. 2.2: Decisions under certainty

All linear programming models, integer programming models and many other deterministic models such as the EOQ model can be thought of as decisions against nature in which there is only one state of nature. This is so because we are sure (within the context of the model) what return we will get for each decision we make.

Conceptually, it is easy to solve a problem with one state of nature. We simply select the decision that yields the highest return. In practice, as opposed to 'in concept' finding such a decision may be another story.

2. Decisions Under Risk

A lack of certainty about future events is the characteristics of many if not most management decision problems. Decision theory provides alternative approaches to problems with less than complete certainty. One such approach is called 'decisions under risk'. In this context, the term risk has a restrictive and well-defined meaning. When we speaks of decisions under risk, we are referring a class of decision problems for which there is more than one state of nature and for which we make the assumption that the decision maker can arrive at a probability estimate for the occurrence for each of the various states of nature. Suppose, for example, that there are $m > 1$ state of nature, and Let P_j the probability estimate that state j will occur. We can then use equation to calculate ER_i, the expected return if we make decision i.

For this type of problem, management should then make the decision that maximises the expected return. In other words, i is the optimal decision where –

ER_i = maximum overall 1 of ER_i.

This concept can be understood by the following examples:

Rajesh buys Q papers from the delivery truck driver at the beginning of the day. During the day, he sells papers. How many he will sell is unknown in advance. At the end of the day, the papers are worthless. If he buys more than he sells, he loses the money associated with the left over papers. If he does not buy enough, he loses the potential profits from additional sales. He purchases each paper for ₹ 1 and sells it for ₹ 1.50.

In this problem, Rajesh assumes that any demand between 1 and 100 is equally likely. More specifically, state J be the event that demand is J items, he assumes that for each integer J, $1 \leq J \leq 100$, $P_J = 0.01$. For illustrative purposes and case of computation, suppose he has assumed, instead, the following probability distribution for demand:

P_o = Prob (demand = 0) = 1/10

P_1 = Prob (demand = 1) = 3/10

P_2 = Prob (demand = 2) = 4/10

P_3 = Prob (demand = 3) = 2/10

In this problem, each of the four different values for demand is a different state of nature and the number of papers ordered is the decision. The returns, or pay-offs, for this problem are shown in the table 1.

Table 1: Pay-off table (Net cash flows)

Decision	State of Nature (Demand)			
	0	1	2	3
0	0	0	0	0
1	-1	.50	.50	.50
2	-2	-.50	1	1
3	-3	-1.50	0	1.5

The entries in the Table 1 represent the net cash flow associated with each combination of number ordered and number demanded. These entries are calculated with the following formula:

Pay-off = ₹ 1.5 (Number of Paper Sold) - ₹ 1
(No. of papers ordered).

₹ 1.50 is the selling price and ₹ 1 is the purchase price. It is important to note that in this model, sales and demand need not be identical. Indeed, sales is the minimum of the two quantities (number demanded and number ordered). For example, when no papers are ordered, then clearly none can be sold, no matter how many are demanded. Thus, for all the entries in the first row the above expression for the pay-off gives ₹ 1.50(0) – ₹ 1(0) = 0. If one paper is ordered and none are demanded, then none are sold, the pay-off is ₹ 1.50(0) – ₹ 1(1) = ₹ 1, which is the first entry in row 2. However, if one paper is ordered and one or more are demanded, then exactly one is sold and the pay-off becomes ₹ 1.50(1) – ₹ 1(1) = – ₹ 50 and so on.

The first term is the return if we order 2 papers and zero are demanded multipled by the probability that 0 are demanded. The second term is the return if we order two papers and one is demanded (Table 1). The expected returns for all the decisions are calculated as follows:

Since ER1 is the largest of these four values, the optimal decision is to order one paper.

3. Decisions Under Uncertainty

When no historical data exist concerning the probabilities for the occurrence of the states of nature, the manager faces conditions of uncertainty. A number of different decision criteria have been proposed as possible bases for decisions under uncertainty including:

1. Maximin criterion (pessimistic): maximising the minimum possible pay-off.
2. Maximax criterion (optimistic): maximising the maximum possible pay-off.
3. Minimax criterion (regret): minimising the maximum possible regret to the decision maker.
4. Insufficient reason criterion: assuming equally likely possibilities for the occurrence of each possible state of nature.

As with conditions of certainty and risk, the first step in making decisions under conditions of uncertainty is to construct a conditional value pay-off table. The next step is to select and apply one of the above decision criteria. Using the conditional value pay-offs, we will illustrate the four criteria for decision making under conditions of uncertainty.

1. **The Maximin Criterion:** The maximin criterion simply maximises the minimum pay-offs given the various decisions that are possible. It is a simple two step process once the pay-off table has been formulated. The first step is to identify the minimum pay-off for each decision. The second step is to pick the largest minimum pay-off. *This concept can be understood by the following example.* President of a small manufacturing firm developed a new household gadget for roasting cheese and has obtained patent. Since he has developed the device on his own, he is offering to sell the patent rights for ₹ 50,00,000 or ₹ 25,00,000 plus a 2 percent royalty on total revenue. From our experience, we can state that the demand for the cheese roaster will be one of the three levels:

   (a) The cheese roaster will find no acceptance by the consumers and in this case the total investment in the patent will be lost, as will the ₹ 10,00,000 needed to develop and promote the product.

(b) The demand level possible is one of 20,000 units. The selling price of the cheese roaster is expected to be ₹ 2,000 and the variable cost (not including patent cost and development cost) is estimated to be approximately ₹ 1,200.

(c) The third level of demand is estimated to be 1,00,000 units.

Hence, analysing the three decisions:

d_1 = Buy patent rights outright for ₹ 50,00,000.

d_2 = Buy patent rights for ₹ 25,00,000 and agree to pay a 2 percent royalty.

d_a = Refuse to get involved in the cheese roaster product.

Next, we must define the various events or states of nature that affect the quality of the decision. In this problem, the states of nature correspond to the different levels of demand. Let-

S_1 = No demand for the cheese roaster.

S_2 = Demand of 20,000 units.

S_a = Demand of 1,00,000 units.

Since the decision is a financial one, it is necessary to compute the pay-offs given the different decisions we can make and the different states of nature.

For example, if we decide to buy the patent outright (d_1) and the demand is for 20,000 units (S_2), the pay-off or profit would be ₹ 4,00,00,000. These pay-offs are computed using the following formula:

Pay-off Revenue – Patent cost – Royalty – Variable cost – Development cost.

2. **The Maximax Criterion:** This criterion maximises the maximum pay-offs for the different decisions. We start by identifying the maximum pay-offs for each alternative decision. Then, the maximax decision is that decision which yields the largest maximum pay-off for the cheese roaster is to buy the patent right for ₹ 50,00,000 (d.). Hence, it can be stated that the maximax rule is an extremely optimistic criterion for choosing alternative decisions.

3. **The Minimax Regret Criterion:** This criterion involves the construction of an opportunity loss or regret matrix prior to applying the minimax rule. To construct an opportunity loss table, we must transform each element in the pay-off table an opportunity loss. The magnitude of the opportunity loss of a given element is the loss incurred by not selecting the optimal alternative decision given a state of nature. To convert a pay-off table to an opportunity loss table is a two-step integrative process. The first step is to find out the largest element in the first column. This element represents the best decision given a particular state of nature. The second step is to subtract each element in the column from the largest element to compute the opportunity loss. This two step process is repeated for each state of nature (each column is the pay-off table).

After the opportunity loss table is constructed, it is possible to apply type minimax regret criterion to determine the appropriate decisions. The minimax regret rule says to identify the maximum regret (opportunity loss) for each decision and then choose that decision with the smallest maximum regret.

4. **The Insufficient Reason Criterion:** The maximin criterion, the maximax criterion and minimax criterion assume that without any previous experience, it is not worth while to assign probabilities of occurrence for the various states of nature, they should assume that all are equally likely to occur. In other words, managers should assign equal probabilities (1/3) to each state of nature.

Different criteria result in different decisions. Each decision problem has uniquc data that lead to unique situations.

STRATEGIES FOR PROFITABILITY

In ordinary parlance, profit is the surplus of income over expenses of production according to businessman. It is the amount left with him after he has made payments for all factors services used by him in the process of production. Economists regard such profit as gross profit as distinct from pure profit it includes the following:

1. **Rent on Land:** This is implicit rent, if the businessman may have used his own land for erecting the factory. Had he hired from some other person, he would have paid its rent.
2. **Interest on Capital:** He may used his own capital in business. The implicit interest is again included in his gross profit.
3. **Wages of Management:** The businessman may have been busy in organising, co-ordinating and managing the entire business himself.
4. **Depreciation Charges:** During the process of production machinery and plants depreciate and become obsolete. Expenses incurred on their repairs and replacements are part of the cost of production. Hence, they should be excluded from gross profit for the purpose of calculating net profit.

Profit it reward for co-ordination, uncertainty bearing and rent of ability. We may conclude that economist's profit is quite distinct from a businessman's profit.

Nature of Profit

The nature of profit have ever been the most perplexed and troubled problems for economists. Professor Taussing's writing in the late 19th century referred to it as 'that mixed and vexed income'. It is a mixed income because it is made up of a number of sources and vexed because economists are unable to decide which source of profit to include or exclude.

Theories of Profit

(a) **Rent Theory of Profit:** This theory was first propounded by an American economists, Francis L. Walker. According to him, there was a good deal of similarity between rent and profit. Rent was the reward for the use of land while profit was the reward for the ability of the entrepreneur. Just as lands differ in fertility, entrepreneurs differ in business ability. Just as there is marginal land, there is marginal entrepreneur. The marginal entrepreneur secures only the wages of management, not profit.

(b) **Risk Theory of Profit:** This theory was propounded by an American economist, Prof. Hawley, in 1907. According to him, profit is the reward for risk-taking in business. As it is well-known, every business involves some risk or the other. Thus, higher the risk, the greater is the possibility of profit. The risk theory of profit is not considered satisfactory by critics. The main drawback of this theory is that it considers risk as the sole determinant of profit.

(c) **Uncertainty Bearing Theory of Profit:** This theory was first propounded by the American economist, Prof. Knight. According to Prof. Knight, profit is the reward of uncertainty bearing. Profit accrues to the entrepreneur, because he bears uncertainty in business. Prof. Knight divided risk under two heads: (i) foreseeable risk and (ii) unforeseeable risk or uncertainty. Unforeseeable risks also called non-insurable risk like competitive risk, technical risk, business cycle risk and risk of government intervention.

Dynamic Theory of Profit

This theory was first propounded by the J. B. Clark, who defined profit as the excess of prices of goods over their costs. According to Clark, profit arises due to dynamic changes in society or due to the fact that society is dynamic. The economic activities of the last year would be repeated this year without any change. There is, therefore, no risk of any kind for an entrepreneur in a static society. The prices of the goods in such a society would be equal to their costs of production. There would be no profit for the entrepreneur. According to Clark, five main changes are constantly taking place in society – (a) changes in the size of the population, (b) changes in the supply of capital, (c) changes in production techniques, (d) changes in the forms of industrial organisation and (e) changes in human wants.

Innovation Theory of Profit

This theory was propounded by Prof. Joseph A. Schumpeter. According to him, profit is the reward of innovation. He uses the term 'innovation' in a sense, wider than that of the changes mentioned by Clark. According to Schumpeter, innovations refer to all those changes in the production process, the objective of which is to reduce the cost of the commodity, and thus, cause a gap between the existing price of the commodity and its new cost.

The main motive for introducing innovations is the desire to earn profit. Profit is, therefore, the cause of innovations. It should be noted that a successful innovation results in the emergence of profit only for a temporary period. When an innovation comes to be known to other firms and is widely adopted by them, it ceases to yield profits.

Profit Planning

Profits vary from industry to industry and from businessman to businessman. The greater the risk and then the greater the uncertainty in business or industry, the greater are the opportunities for large profits. Profits are likely to be high in industries in which methods of production are constantly changing so that there is continuous adoption of new techniques.

The signs of healthy business include making a profit consistent with the various risks that it has to face. A firm is faced with a number of uncertainties. These uncertainties are created by the dynamic nature of consumer needs, the diverse nature of competition, the uncontrollable nature of most elements of cost and the continuous technological developments.

Measurement of Profit

Economic profit is quite different from accounting profit. Economic profit includes opportunity cost, which is not easily identifiable and measurable. On the other hand, the accounting costs, both direct and indirect are easily identified and recorded. There are three specific aspects of profit measurement where the use of accounting profit and of economic profit give different results.

1. **Depreciation:** An accountant measures the cost of depreciation by several methods like, Straight-line method, Diminishing-balance method, Annuity Method, and Service-unit Method. For economist, these methods are of no use. He looks at depreciation in terms of opportunity costs and uses the asset replacement costs rather than the original or historical costs of the asset. The replacement investment is needed to keep 'capital stock intact'. The opportunity costs of not taking timely replacement is increasing level and rate of depreciation and or obsolescence.

2. **Inventory Valuation:** This is another area of profit measurement where accounting conventions and economic concepts give different results. Inventory or stocks refer to goods in pipeline difference between production and consumption. When production exceeds consumption, the stocks pile up. Such inventory building or stock filing would have posted no problems of valuation, had prices remain constant. In reality, prices do not remain stable, materials costs change and, therefore, the valuation of stocks must change. The accountant uses some standard methods, *viz.*, FIFO, LIFO, weighted average, etc. The economist feels that the recorded value of business income in different periods may differ considerably depending upon the methods of valuation chosen. For a true measure of valuation, the net business income should be measured at constant prices.

3. **Unaccounted Value Changes:** There may be certain items of business expenditure which may not have any impact on current business income, but which may increase future income of the firm. The accountant does not consider the future value of the present expenditure on items like research and development, advertisement, recruitment of skillful managers, etc. In the process, the accountant may understate current profit and overstate future profit.

Reasons for Limiting Profit

1. **To Maintain Goodwill:** If the firm concentrates on the high profits, it has to loose confidence in the market.
2. **Avoiding High Taxation and Government Intervention:** Too much profit maximisation leads to high taxation and it attracts government intervention.
3. **To Avoid Business Risk:** High risk leads to higher profits as well as higher losses. To avoid such a business risk, the organisation has to limit its profits.
4. **Self-motivation:** Motivation of the entrepreneur also influences the limiting on profits.
5. **Liquidity Preference:** Liquidity preference leads to low profits. Low profit means lower prices and higher liquidity. Higher profit leads to higher prices and lesser the liquidity.
6. **Obstructing Potential Competition:** If the business entity wants obstruct competition, it has to sell at lower profits.
7. **Idealism:** Some organisations have the ideals like low profit at good quality of service. The idealist businessman sells goods at lowest profits.
8. **To Achieve Leadership in Market:** Leadership can be achieved only if there is competitive prices maintained by the organisation. Hence, the business entities will try to achieve leadership in the market by maintaining lower profits.
9. **To Survive in the Market:** If the competitors are selling at lower prices, then business entity has to reduce its prices and limit profit to survive in the market.
10. **To Face Stagnation:** If the firm faces the problem of stagnation, then it has to reduce prices. Thus, mobility of the products can be achieved by offering discounts, special gifts, etc.

DECISION TREE

One of the best ways to analyse a decision is to use a so-called decision tree. Decision trees depict, in the form of a 'tree', the decision points, chance events and probabilities involved in various courses that might be undertaken. A common problem occurs in business when a new product is introduced. Managers must decide whether to install expensive permanent equipment to ensure production at the lowest possible cost or to undertake cheaper, temporary tooling that will involve a higher manufacturing cost but lower capital investment and will result in smaller losses if the product does not sell as well as estimated.

Decision Tree Diagram

A decision tree represents another way to visualise the typical decision theory. There are four didactic or instructive parts to a decision tree: decisions modes (shown as squares in the figure), chance nodes (shown as circles), alternative branches (straight-lines that represent alternatives), and probabilistic branches (straight-lines that represent probabilities).

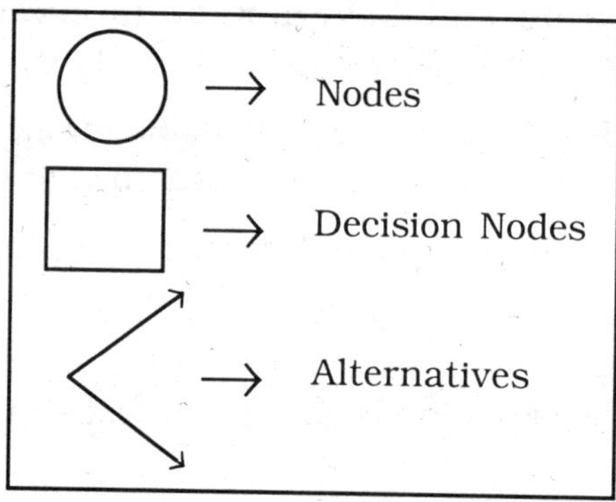

Fig. 2.3: Decision Tree Diagram

A decision node represents the choice between alternatives. From it, come alternative branches that show, or name, the choices. These branches often lead to chance nodes, which represent factors in the decision situation over which the decision-maker has no control. From these chance nodes come probabilistic branches that represent the actual or estimated numerical likelihood of various chances. Since the events, or states of nature, are mutually exclusive and exhaustive, the probabilities associated with each event must add to 1.

A decision must be made among several alternatives. One or more alternatives are associated with chance factors. These chances, however, can be assessed probabilistically. On the basis of evaluation at several stages, therefore, the decision maker can regard the alternatives rationally and choose the one most compatible with his ultimate goals.

Decision tree analysis has the following two major limitations:

1. For many complex decisions there are more than two feasible option at each decision juncture (in our example, adding new equipment and overtime), and there is an entire spectrum of chance events that could occur (including many different levels of sales increases and decreases). Theortically, all of these could be diagrammed, but the tree would quickly become unmanageable. Hence, simple

two-pronged models are the norm. In using them, however, managers should keep in mind the dangers of over-simplification.

2. The probability estimates used in the analysis are typically based on subjective judgement rather than on historical data. These estimates, therefore, are suspect. Their value however, lies in their relative not in their absolute accuracy. In assigning subjective probabilities, managers should feel confident that because of their experience and their knowledge of the situation, that they can quantify the relative likelihood of events and thereby assure a better decision than would be possible if each potential outcomes were arbitrarily assigned equal probability.

Despite these limitations, decision tree analysis can be very helpful to executives faced with complex decisions that will set-off a chain of future decisions. Decision tree analysis provides a structured methodology for examining the principal alternatives and their consequences. Ohio Edison used extensive decision tree analysis in selecting a technology for controlling particulate emissions at one of its coal fired power plants. Based on this analysis, electronic precipitators were chosen over fabric fibres, and the company reportedly saved a million dollars a year over the life of the precipitators.

PROBLEMS AND SOLUTIONS ON DECISION TREE

Problem 1:

ABC Ltd has an investment proposal, requiring an outlay of ₹ 20,00,000 at present. The following are expected cash thus and their probabilities.

Year 1		**Year 2**			
		If CFAT is 14,00,000		**If CFAT of 1st year is = 10,00,000**	
CFAT	**Probability**	**CFAT**	**Probability**	**CFAT**	**Probability**
14,00,000	0.2	8,00,000	0.25	9,00,000	0.4
10,00,000	0.4	7,50,000	0.45	8,00,000	0.3
11,00,000	0.2	9,50,000	0.30	10,00,000	0.2

Year 2 If CFAT of Year 1 is 11,00,000		
CFAT	**Probability**	**CFAT = Cash Flows After Taxes**
11,00,000	0.15	
9,00,000	0.15	
8,00,000	0.60	

It was observed that probability of required outlay for project varies as per following data

If Project	1 is accepted	₹ 19,00,000	0.6
	2 is accepted:	₹ 21,00,000	0.4

Questions:

You are required to draw decision - tree Diagram.

Solution:

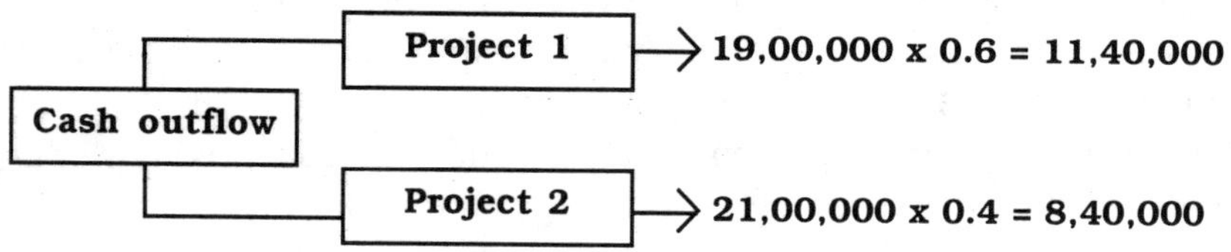

Cash Flows after Taxes

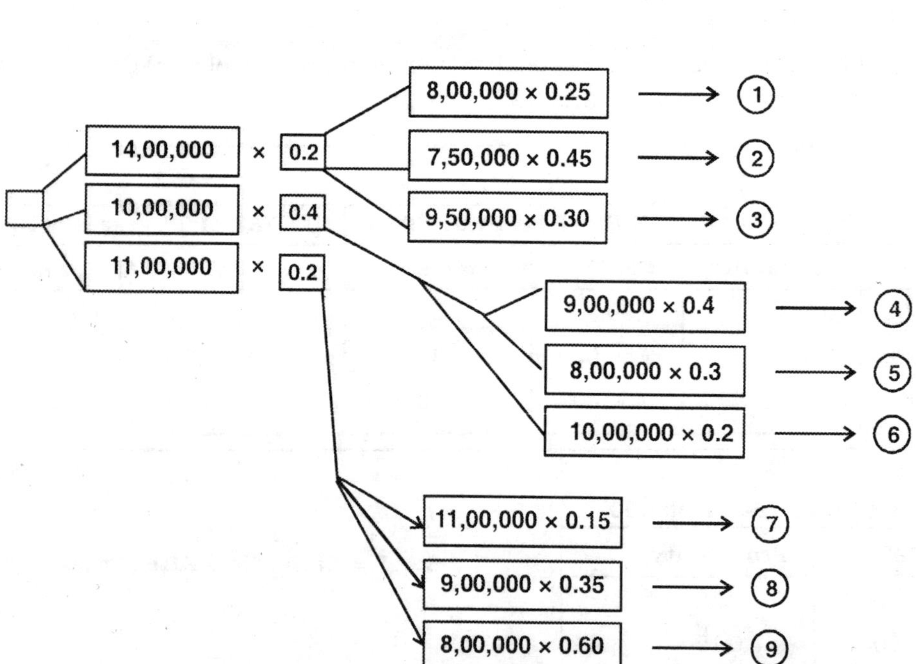

If Project-1 is accepted

(CFAT)

Path	Cash Flows		Project 1 outflows	PVF–PVCO NPV
1.	2,80,000 + 2,00,000 = 4,00,000	-	11,40,000	(7,40,000)
2.	2,80,000 + 3,37,500 = 7,37,500	-	11,40,000	(40,25,000)
3.	2,80,000 + 2,85,000 = 5,65,000	-	11,40,000	(5,75,000)
4.	4,00,000 + 3,60,000 = 7,60,000	-	11,40,000	(3,80,000)
5.	4,00,000 + 2,40,000 = 6,40,000	-	11,40,000	(5,00,000)
6.	4,00,000 + 2,00,000 = 6,00,000	-	11,40,000	(5,40,000)
7.	2,20,000 + 1,65,000 = 3,85,000	-	11,40,000	(7,55,000)
8.	2,20,000 + 2,25,000 = 4,45,000	-	11,40,000	(6,95,000)
9.	2,20,000 + 4,80,000 = 7,00,000	-	11,40,000	(4,40,000)

All NPV's are < 0 Hence This project is rejected.

Similarly cash outflows for project 2 can be calculated.

Problem 2:

Viswa Ltd., wants to expand its plant capacity. The plant is expected to cost ₹ 6,00,000/- you are required to calculate expected net present value, if the desired rate is 10 percent Another consideration without expansion is repair on improvement it costs ₹ 4,00,000/. If expansion cost is ₹ 10,00,000 find NPV.

With Expansion CFAT	Without Expansion CFAT	Probabilities with Expansion	Probabilities without Expansion
₹	₹		
13,00,000	12,00,000	0.25	0.3
15,00,000	12,00,000	0.35	0.2
21,00,000	14,50,000	0.40	0.5

Solution:

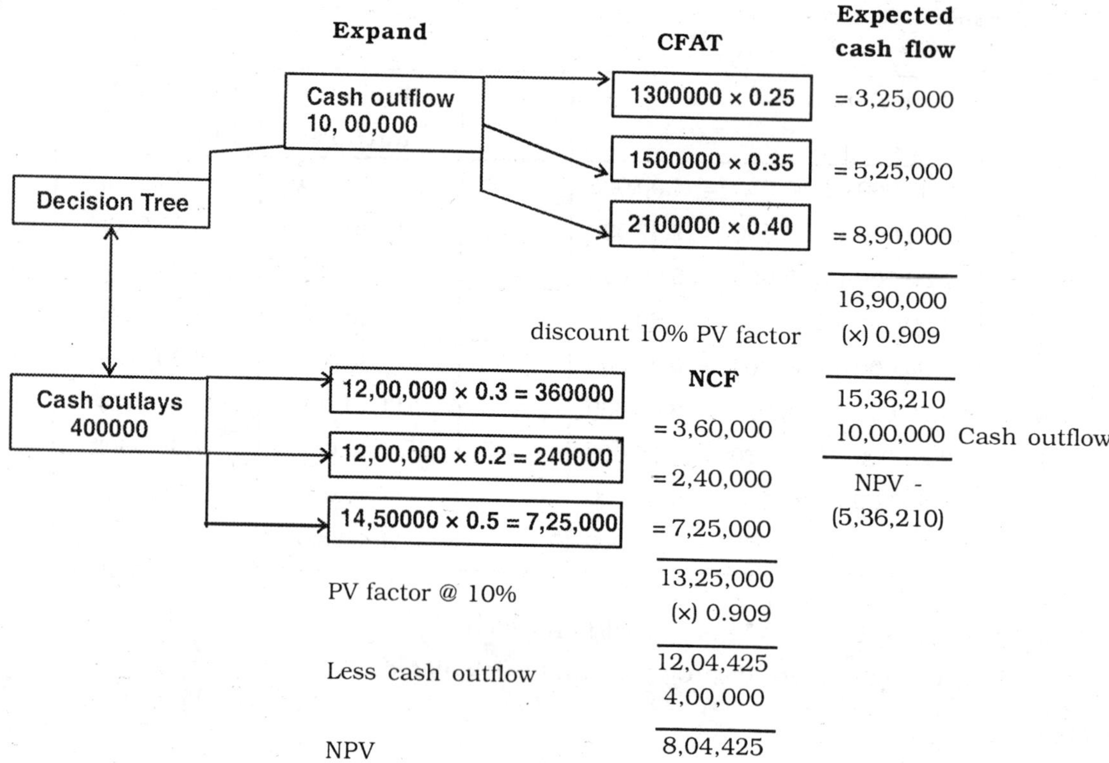

NOTE: NPV of second option is greater than first option. Hence, the company need not go on expansion.

Joint Probability Approach

Problem 3:

Suchitra Corp. Ltd's after tax cash flow, are dependent on first year performance as per following data

If CFAT1 = 80,000 year 2		**If CFAT1 = 1,50,000 year 2**		**If CFAT1 = 1,00,000 year 2**	
CFAT2	Probability	CFAT2	Probability	CFAT2	Probability
15,000	0.4	40,000	0.1	45,000	0.8
20,000	0.4	45,000	0.3	25,000	0.1
25,000	0.2	60,000	0.6	50,000	0.1

Expected Probability of CFAT, is as follows

$CFAT_1$	Probability
80,000	0.4
1,50,000	0.3
1,00,000	0.2

The project requires an initial investments of ₹ 1,00,000 Risk – free rate of capital is 12 percent.

Solution:

Time 0	Year 1	Year 2	Path	NPV @ 12%	Joint Probablity	Expected NPV
		0.4 → 15,000	1	-16,605	0.16	-2,656.80
	80000	0.4 → 20,000	2	-12,620	0.16	-2,019.20
		0.2 → 25,000	3	-8,635	0.16	-1,381.60
		0.1 → 40,000	4	65,830	0.03	1,974.90
-100000	150000	0.3 → 45,000	5	69,815	0.09	6,253.35
		0.6 → 60,000	6	81,770	0.18	14,718.60
		0.8 × 45,000	7	25,165	0.16	4,026.4
	100000	0.1 × 25,000	8	9,225	0.02	184.50
		0.1 × 30,000	9	29,150	0.02	583

Working Notes

NPV@12% - Calculation

Path 1

Cash Flows

80,000 × (PVF @ 12%, 1) + 15,000 x (PVF@12%,2)

(80,000 × 0.893) + (15,000 × 0.797)

Cash Flows = 71,440 + 11,955 = 83,395

Less Investment -1,00,000

-16,605

Joint probability of path 1

0.4 × 0.4 = 0.16

Path	Cash Flows Year 1	PV Factor	Year 2	PV Factor	Total PVCF	NPV (TPVCF - CO)
1	80,000	0.893	15,000	0.797	83,395	(16,605)
2	80,000	0.893	20,000	0.797	87,380	(12,620)
3	1,50,000	0.893	25,000	0.797	91,365	(8,635)
4	1,50,000	0.893	40,000	0.797	1,65,830	65,830
5	1,50,000	0.893	45,000	0.797	1,69,815	69,815
6	1,50,000	0.893	60,000	0.797	1,81,770	81,770
7	1,00,000	0.893	45,000	0.797	1,25,165	25,165
8	1,00,000	0.893	25,000	0.797	1,69,225	9,225
9	1,00,000	0.893	50,000	0.797	1,29,150	29,150

Steps for Joint Probability Approach

Step 1 : Draw Decision Tree diagram using given data.

Step 2 : Calculate 'Net present value' of cash flow with given discount rate on specified period.

Step 3 : Calculate joint probability of cash flows of each path.

Step 4 : Multiply joint probabilities with NPV at given discount rate.

Step 5 : Calculate cumulative value of all expected cash flows in all the paths.

CLOSING CASELET

Volkswagen India

Volkswagen Group India is a part of Volkswagen AG, which is globally represented by 9 brands- Audi, Bentley, Bugatti, Lamborghini, Scania, Seat, Skoda, Volkswagen Commercial Vehicles (Volkswagen Nutzfahrzeuge) and Volkswagen Passenger Cars. The product range extends from low-consumption small cars to luxury class vehicles and trucks. The Group operates 60 production plants around the world. In total more than 3,70,000 employees produce more than 26,600 vehicles or are involved in vehicle-related services each working day. With its headquarters in Pune, Maharashtra (India), the Volkswagen Group is represented by three brands in India: Volkswagen, Audi and Skoda. The Volkswagen Group is completing 10 years of its India journey which began with the entry of the Skoda brand in 2001, Audi brand and Volkswagen brand in 2007. Each brand has its own character and operates as an independent entity in the market. The highest volume brand of the Group is Volkswagen. Europe's most successful car brand has made successful inroads into the Indian market. Volkswagen presents itself in a variety of segments as a premium manufacturer of high-volume models. As a first step, the Volkswagen brand launched the globally successful Passat in 2007. To expand its portfolio and cater to the mid segment, Volkswagen launched one of the brand's bestselling models, the Jetta, in India in July 2008. Both the sedans are being assembled locally. The iconic New Beetle and the high-end SUV Touareg were introduced in December 2009. Also available is the high-end automobile Phaeton.

From December 12, 2009 the new Pune plant has started rolling-out the hatchback version of the Volkswagen Polo.The made-in-India Polo was presented to the general public for the very first time at the Auto Expo 2010. The launch of this premium hatchback in March, brought access to one of the Indian passenger car segments with the highest-volume unit sales. Skoda entered the Indian market in 2001. Its plant in Aurangabad, which assembles a total of eight models including the Audi A6 and Audi A4 as well as the Volkswagen Passat and Volkswagen Jetta, has been instrumental in this achievement. For Indian customers, the name of Skoda stands for high-quality, robust yet affordable cars in the compact, lower mid-size and mid-size ranges. In terms of models, the Skoda product offering in India ranges from the Fabia through the Octavia, the Laura to the Superb. Skoda lifted the veil,off its international bestseller SUV Yeti for the first time in India at the Auto Expo 2010. In the period between January 2009 and December 2009, the three brands of the Volkswagen Group have together sold around 19,000 vehicles in India, an increase of 1.4 percent over 2008 in a year marked by recession in the auto industry.

A crucial element of the Volkswagen's strategy is to establish a long-term presence in India is the Group's production facility near Pune in the Chakan Industrial Park. The investment with a total sum of around INR 3,800 crore (580 million Euros) is the biggest investment of a German company realised in India so far. The plant, one of the most modern in the Volkswagen Group has a high level of vertical integration – not least attributable to the high share of local suppliers. The recruitment is of some 2,500 employees at the end of 2010, primarily from the region itself. With the investment, the vertical integration of suppliers and the employment of people Volkswagen will thus demonstrate its commitment to the new site. Simultaneously Volkswagen contributes to a positive development of the economy of the region and of Maharashtra at the same time.

Source: http://www.volkswagen.co.in/en/volkswagen_world/volkswagen_india.html

Discuss the strategic decisions of Volkswagen India.

SUMMARY

This chapter focuses on strategic decision making and profitability of the corporate entity. It also focuses on difference between the economic and accounting profit. The purpose of strategic decision making is to develop strategies by which an organisation will be able to achieve its objectives. The time horizon for strategic decisions tends to be fairly long, so that fundamental shifts in the organisation may be made. Strategic decisions do not have to occur on a periodic, regular cycle as do management control activities. Future is always uncertain. Hence, strategic decisions are always incomplete and sometimes they have been based on false information. It may lead to further problems.

A business entity is always profit motivated. Profit seeking is the motive force of any business undertaking. In practice, most of firms have many goals of primary importance other than profit. Hence, it has to keep in view of other factors besides aiming at maximising profits.

KEYWORDS

- **Decision Making:** Decision making is the focal creative physhic event where knowledge, thoughts, feeling and imagination are fixed into action.
- **Depreciation:** An accountant measures the cost of depreciation by several methods like, straight-line method, diminishing balance method, annuity method, service unit method.
- **Economic Profit:** Economic profit includes opportunity cost, which is not easily identifiable and measurable, on the other hand, the accounting costs, both direct and indirect are easily identified and recorded.
- **Expansion Strategies:** These are contradictory to stability strategies. Stability aims at consistency where as growth requires dynamism. It aims to take challenging tasks for the development.
- **Inventory Valuation:** Inventory or stocks refer to goods in pipeline difference between production and consumption. When production exceeds consumption, the stocks pile up.
- **Retrenchment Strategy:** It is a strategic option which involves reduction of any existing product or service line alongwith the level of objectives set below the past achievement is known as retrenchment strategy.
- **Decision Making:** Is the vehicle of carrying managerial work load and discharging the managerial responsibilities. Elucidate the statement and examine the significance of national decision making in management. Discuss the steps necessary in managerial decision making.

REVIEW QUESTIONS

1. 'Management means making decisions and executions thereof,' Do you agree? Describe the essential steps in the process of decision making.
2. What do you understand by decision making? Discuss the various types of decisions managers take in an organisation.

3. Explain the concept of rationality in decision making. What are the limits of rationality in decision making?
4. What do you understand by decision making? Discuss the various classes of decision making.
5. Write brief note on the followings:
   (a) Decisions under certainty.
   (b) Decisions under risk.
   (c) Decisions under uncertainty.
6. What do you understand by decision tree? Discuss the importance and implications of decision tree analysis.

REFERENCES

1. Ansof, H. Igor, *'Corporate Strategy'*, New York, McGraw-Hill, 1965.
2. Azhar Kazmi, *'Business Policy and Strategic Management'*, Tata McGraw-Hill, New Delhi, 2009.
3. Jakhotiya G.P., *'Strategic Financial Management'*, Vikas Publications, New Delhi, 2007.
4. James C. Van Horne, *'Financial Management and Policy'*, Pearson, New Delhi, 2008.
5. Sridhar A.N., *'Strategic Financial Management'*, SPD, New Delhi, 2008.

ഇഗ ഇഗ ഇഗ

CHAPTER

3

STRATEGIES FOR PROJECT FINANCING

CHAPTER OUTLINE

- Opening Caselet
- Introduction
- Specification of Project
- Various Definitions of Project Management
- Essentials of a Good Project
- Roles and Responsibilities of a Project Manager
- Project Finance
- Sources of Project Finance
- Estimation of Cost of a Project and Production
- PERT
- PERT Conventions
- Network Techniques
- PERT-NETWORK Analysis - Steps
- Closing Caselet
- Summary
- Practical Problems Solutions
- Keywords
- Review Questions
- References

OPENING CASELET

PROJECT PLANNING FOR A REAL ESTATE BUSINESS

MSN Real Estate provides high-quality, comfortable rental units in Eugene and other areas of Oregon. MSN's apartment units offer state-of-the-art living conditions reflective of the rapid advancements in technology and a growing need for quality housing. Our company is dedicated to a hassle free living environment in which our tenants can enjoy all of the benefits of safe, attractive, and inviting units. Unlike many other realty companies that are solely concerned with turning profits, our primary objective at MSN is to maintain the highest level of customer satisfaction that is achievable. Tenant safety, happiness, and comfort are our main goals. MSN maintains competitive market prices, while working toward expanding the number of units owned, and increasing total profits earned. Within the company we will strive to work as a cohesive, harmonious unit focused on exemplifying our mission. Just as customer satisfaction is an intricate part of MSN's success, so is employee satisfaction. That is why the founders of MSN Real Estate believe that employee satisfaction will make the company a success and will be the key to their longevity. Initial focus will be to buy and develop existing apartment complexes. We will modify and remodel the acquired real estate so as to meet MSN standards and increase long-term assets and income. Housing units will predominantly be located in the University neighborhood targeting both students and professionals. MSN fosters the ideals of the importance of tenant needs along with healthy and understanding relationships and a professional commitment to satisfaction. The following table provides financial requirements of the company.

Start-up Funding

Start-up expenses to fund	$91,560
Start-up assets to fund	$1,243,330
Total funding required	$1,334,890
Assets	
Non-cash assets from start-up	$132,000
Cash requirements from start-up	$1,111,330
Additional cash raised	$0
Cash balance on starting date	$1,111,330
Total assets	$1,243,330

Liabilities and Capital

Liabilities	
Current borrowing	\$5,000
Long-term liabilities	\$1,080,000
Accounts payable (Outstanding bills)	\$3,890
Other current liabilities (Interest-free)	\$0
Total liabilities	\$1,088,890

Capital

Planned investment	
Menashe	\$23,000
Koach	\$23,000
Investors	\$200,000
Additional investment requirement	\$0
Total planned investment	\$246,000
Loss at start-up (Start-up expenses)	(\$91,560)
Total capital	\$154,440
Total capital and liabilities	\$1,243,330
Total funding	\$1,334,890

Read more: *http://www.bplans.com/real_estate_management_business_plan/strategy_and_implementation_summary_fc.cfm#ixzz16AcKbczP*

- Analyse financial requirements of the real estate business project.

INTRODUCTION

A project is a group of unique, inter-related activities that are planned and executed in a certain sequence to create a unique product or service, within a specific timeframe, budget and the client's specifications. Some of the characteristics of the tasks that qualify to be a project are: uniqueness, specificity of goal, sequence of activities, specified time and interrelatedness. Projects are carried out under many resource constraints and their success depends on the ability of the manager to manage these constraints effectively. Project management is the application of the knowledge, skills, tools and techniques to project activities in order to meet or exceed stakeholder needs and expectations.

Every project has a set of activities that are unique, which means it is the first time that an organisation handles that type of activity. These activities do not repeat in the project under similar circumstances i.e., there will be something different in every activity or even if the activity is repeated, the variables influencing it change every time.

SPECIFICATION OF PROJECT

A specification is the definition of a project: a statement of the problem, not the solution. Normally, the specification contains errors, ambiguities, and mis-understandings. The outcome of this deliberation should be a *written* definition of what is required, by when; and this must be *agreed* by all involved.

The *agreement* upon a *written* specification has several benefits:

- The clarity will reveal misunderstandings.
- The completeness will remove contradictory assumptions.
- The rigour of the analysis will expose technical and practical details.
- The agreement forces all concerned to actually read and think about the details.

The work on the specification can be seen as the first stage of quality assurance since you are looking for and countering problems in the very foundation of the project — from this perspective the creation of the specification clearly merits a large investment of time.

The places to look for errors in a specification are:

- **The Global Context:** It often focuses too narrowly on the work of one team and fails to consider how it fits into the larger picture. Some of the work given to you may actually be undone or duplicated by others. Some of the proposed work may be incompatible with that of others; it might be just plain barmy in the larger context.
- **The Interfaces:** Between your team and both its customers and suppliers, there are interfaces. At these points something gets transferred. Exactly what, how and when should be discussed and agreed from the very beginning. Never assume a

common understanding, because you will be wrong. All it takes for your habitual understandings to evaporate is the arrival of one new member, in either of the teams. Define and agree your interfaces and maintain a friendly contact throughout the project.

- **Time Scales:** It always underestimates the time involved for work. If there are no time scales in the specification, you can assume that one will be imposed upon

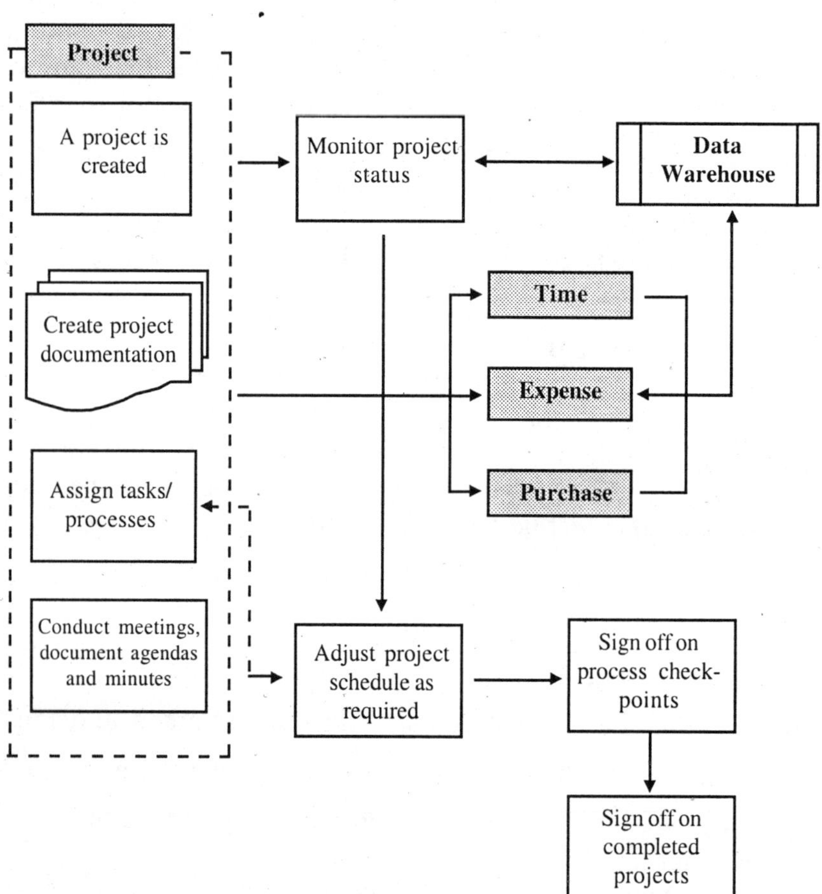

Figure 3.1: Stages of Project Specification

you. You must add realistic dates. The detail should include a precise understanding of the extent of any intermediate stages of the task, particularly those that have to be delivered.

- **External Dependencies:** Your work may depend upon that of others. Make this very clear so that these people too will receive warning of your needs. Highlight the effect that problems with these would have upon your project so that everyone is quite clear about their importance. To be sure, contact these people yourself and ask if they are able to fulfill the assumptions in your specification.

VARIOUS DEFINITIONS OF PROJECT MANAGEMENT

- Project management is the application of knowledge, skills, tools and techniques to a broad range of activities in order to meet the requirements of the particular project. A project is a temporary endeavor undertaken to achieve a particular aim. Project management knowledge and practices are best described in terms of their component processes. These processes can be placed into five process groups: Initiating, Planning, Executing, Controlling and Closing.

  scrc.ncsu.edu/public/DEFINITIONS/Pper cent20-per cent20R.html

- The leadership role which plans, budgets, co-ordinates, monitors and controls the operational contributions of property professionals, and others, in a project involving the development of land in accordance with a client's objectives in terms of quality, cost and time.

  narains.com/glossary.htm

- A controlled process of initiating, planning, executing and closing down a project.

  www.cbu.edu/~lschmitt/I351/glossary.htm

- Both a process and set of tools and techniques concerned with defining the project's goal, planning all the work to reach the goal, leading the project and support teams, monitoring progress, and seeing to it that the project is completed in a satisfactory way.

  www.shapetomorrow.com/resources/p.html

- The application of modern management techniques and systems to the execution of a project from start to finish, to achieve predetermined objectives of scope, quality, time and cost to the equal satisfaction of those involved.

  oit.osu.edu/projmanage/glossary.html

- Project management is concerned with the overall planning and co-ordination of a project from inception to completion aimed at meeting the client's requirements and ensuring completion on time, within cost and to required quality standards. Project management is typically carried out either by a private consultant or an employee of the project client.

  www.ecbp.org/glossary.htm

- Manages the production of projects with schedules and tasks associated with the project. It often involves detailed expertise in many of the following areas: planning, cost management, contract negotiations/procurement, technical writing (proposals, etc.), research, technical development, information/computer management, business development, corporate/administrative management, time management, and others.

  www.organized-living.com/industryterms.html

- The methods and disciplines used to define goals, plan and monitor tasks and resources, identify and resolve issues, and control costs and budgets for a specific project.

  www.homercomputer.com.au/homer_software_guide/glossary.htm

- The action of managing a project. It can involve many activities, from scheduling to communication. Project Management in TOC is outcome-based as opposed to activity-based, and TPACC software is an ideal tool used to measure the progress toward the financial outcome.

  www.tpacc.com/knowledge_base_dictionary.htm

- Approach used to manage work with the constraints of time, cost and performance targets.

  www.mccombs.utexas.edu/faculty/Linda.Bailey/glossary.htm

- This is managing the resources needed to ensure that a project is finished on time and within budget and to the satisfaction of the end user. Project managers use tools such as PERT and Gantt charts for scheduling all the tasks that need to be completed. They are conscious of managing time, scope and resources for a project. To reduce time to complete a project the manager might decide to employ more workers which would increase costs.

  michaelmnz.tripod.com/dictionary.htm

- The planning, control and co-ordination of all aspects of a project, and the motivation of all those involved in it, in order to achieve the project objectives.

  www.ams.mod.uk/ams/content/docs/ils/ils_web/glossary.htm

- Project management is the discipline of defining and achieving targets while optimising the use of resources (time, money, people, space, etc.). Thus, it could be classified into several models: time, cost, scope, and intangibles.

  en.wikipedia.org/wiki/Project_management

ESSENTIALS OF A GOOD PROJECT

1. A project should be based on objectives of business.
2. A project should be able to relate the objectives to physical factors and company personnel.
3. It must be prepared on facts and sound judgement.
4. It should be able to expect uncertainties in the future.
5. A good project must be in conformity with the government rules.
6. A business project should be made in accordance with the ethics and social responsibility of business.
7. It should be easy to understand and simple to follow.

8. It must be able to assist and help to superior policies.
9. A project should be preferably written and understandable.
10. It should be feasible for implementation.
11. A good project can be easily communicable to all categories.
12. A flexible and stable project is good for organisation.
13. It can be supplementary to overall corporate planning.
14. It should be able to comprehensive by approach to achieve organisational goals.
15. It should be able to help in planned development of organisation.

ROLES AND RESPONSIBILITIES OF A PROJECT MANAGER

According to Project Management Institute (PMI): 'Project Management is the application of knowledge, skills, tools and techniques to project activities in order to meet or exceed stakeholders' needs and expectations'.

Project Management is quite often the province and responsibility of an individual project manager. This individual seldom participates directly in the activities that produce the end result, but rather strives to maintain the progress and productive mutual interaction of various parties in such a way that overall risk of failure is reduced.

A project manager is often a client representative and has to determine and implement the exact needs of the client based on knowledge of the firm he/she is representing. The ability to adapt to the various internal procedures of the contracting party, and to form close links with the nominated representatives, is essential in ensuring that the key issues of cost, time, quality and above all client satisfaction, can be realised. Any type of product or service – buildings, vehicles, electronics, computer software, financial services, etc. – may have its implementation overseen by a project manager and its operations by a product manager.

The project manager needs to be an HRD expert who can motivate the workforce by training and promoting leadership among them, and boost their morale by incentives and promotions. He has to be conversant with the principles of organisation, and be a good judge of people who has the ability to place the right man in the right job at the right time.

Social Issues: A project can only be successful when there is no conflict between the management and the local populace. Right from the acquisition of the project land to recruitment to organisation to infrastructural facilities, the management has to interact with the social fabric of the locale. It can only ensure a smooth functioning at the project site if there is a 'co-operational', and not a 'confrontational' environment. The management can display its cordiality to the locals by, for instance, recruiting 'The sons of the soil' in the workforce, which will not only be conducive to reciprocal cordiality of the populace, but might actually make good business sense in employing labour that is familiar with the locale and the conditions prevalent at the projcct site.

The various steps in financial feasibility of a project is given in the following flow chart:

FLOW CHART FOR PROJECT FEASIBILITY

Estimate Total Costs
↓
Estimate Financing Needs
↓
Prepare Pro forma Income Statement
↓
Prepare Cash Flow Projections
↓
Prepare Pro forma Balance Sheet
↓
Evaluate Project Feasibility

Does Project Satisfy Investment Decision Criteria?

NO → Terminate

YES → Analyses Projections of Operating Conditions

NO → Necessary

YES → Conduct Sensitivity Analysis
↓
Risk Analysis
↓
YES
Conduct Risk Analysis

Is Project Feasible ?

NO → Terminate

YES → Prepare Investment Proposal

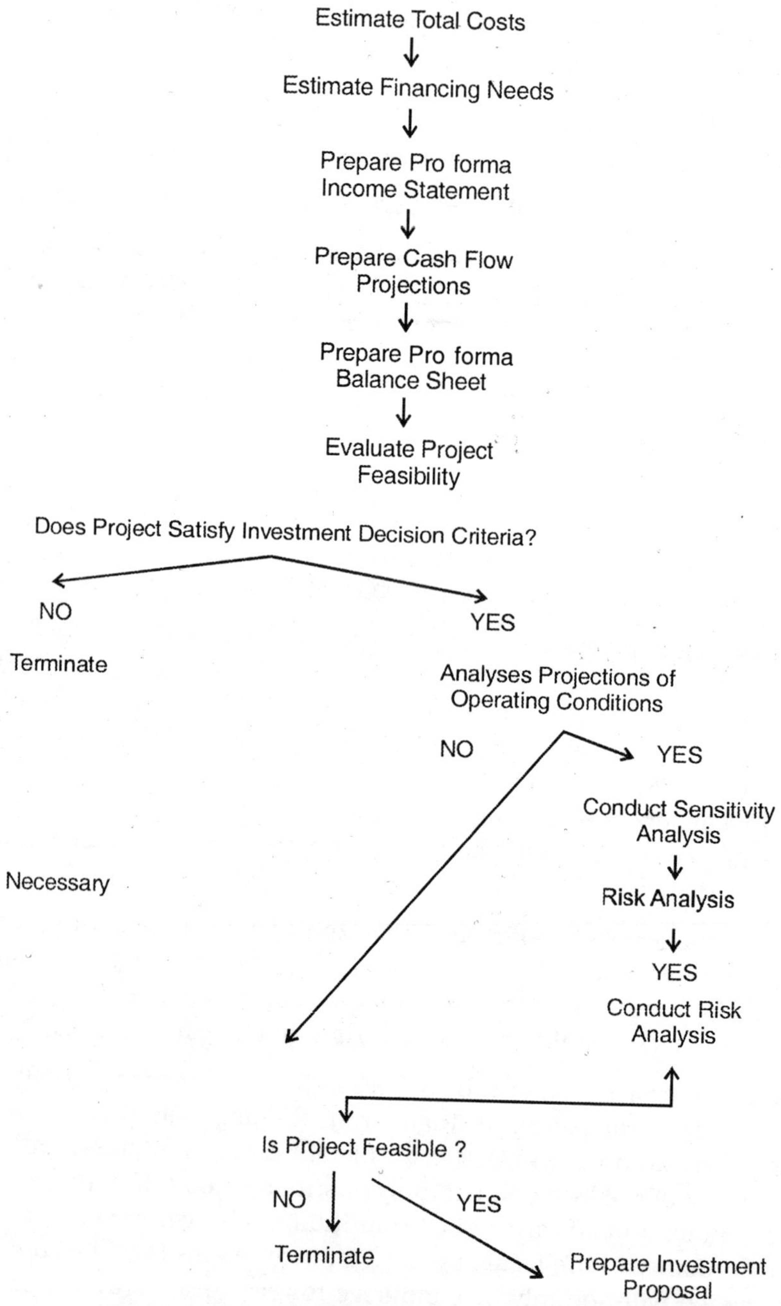

Figure 3.2: Flow Chart for Project Feasibility

PROJECT FINANCE

'Project Finance' has two dimensions *viz.*, (i) Cost estimation and (ii) Identifying sources of finance. Thus any project has to be assessed with regard to its financial feasibility measured in terms of costs and benefits. While defining the costs and benefits of a project, various projections have to be made, starting with the cost of project and ending with the preparation of the pro forma balance sheet. Based on the data derived from these projections, various appraisal criteria are used to assess the financial feasibility of the project. If the project is found to be technically feasible, commercially viable and financially sound, the final investment proposal is prepared by the company assimilating all these factors for presentation to the Board of Director, Financial institutions, etc. This is the first step in conducting financial analysis and should be done with great care as all the other projections are based on this.

Estimation of Bank Finance and Margin Money

1. **Estimation of the Current Assets Required to be Held by the Company:** The estimate is generally based on the experience of similar units. Raw material stocks are estimated in terms of number of months consumption while finished goods and work-in-process are estimated in terms of so many months costs of production. The estimate of debtors is based on the sales estimate and the credit period proposed to be allowed by the unit.
2. **Reduce the Margin Money Required to be Brought in by the Promoter from the Current Assets:** Banks normally insist that at least 25 per cent of the current assets have to be financed by units through long-term funds. Therefore, 25 per cent of the current assets have to be included in the project cost. The margin money included in the cost of capital for Mini garments is ₹ 22.12 lakh. The margin money included in the cost of capital is generally based on the estimate of working capital for the second year of operations.
3. **Reduce the Current Liabilities Other than Bank Finance Presently Sought from the Remaining Amount:** The current liabilities such as trade credit, wages and salaries payable and other outstanding expenses have to be reduced from the current assets after netting out for margin money. This is because these liabilities are short-term funds which can be used by the unit to finance its current assets. The same cannot again be funded by the bank.

SOURCES OF PROJECT FINANCE

Once the cost of the project has been estimated, the next typical step is to find how best to finance it. The means of finance and the financing mix chosen are bound to have a far reaching effect on the profitability and also the risk associated with the project. Therefore, all the available avenues should be evaluated and the means and pattern of financing should be fixed carefully. The financing pattern of the companies mentioned in the previous section is given below.

1. Equity Capital

Equity capital is the capital contributed by the owners of a company. A part of the equity capital is brought in by the promoters while the rest is issued to the public.

Equity may also be raised though the issue of Global Depository Receipts (GDRs). GDRs are negotiable instruments issued by a depository bank which entitles the holder to the number of equity shares specified in the receipt. The shares are denominated in the currency of the country to which the issuing company belongs and can be subscribed through the currency of the investor or the US dollar. The company issues the shares to be depository bank which in turn issues the GDRs to the investors against the shares held by it. The issuing company receives funds in foreign currency.

Sometimes financial institutions may subscribe to a part of the equity capital through firm allotments. In addition, reservations may also be made to the employees of the company and the promoter companies as also to mutual funds and NRIs. The regulatory requirements relating to issue of equity share, preference share, and debentures including right and bonus issues have been given in the Appendix I to this chapter. Apart from the regulatory requirements, the extent of control desired by the promoter and that allowed by the financial institutions, the lending norms of financial institutions which have been given in Appendix III and the listing requirements of the stock exchanges should be kept in view while deciding the amount of equity to be brought in by the promoter and that to be raised through the public issues.

2. Preference Capital

Preference capital is a hybrid between the equity capital and debt capital. While the claim of the preference shareholders is just above the equityholders, it is subordinate to the claims of all other stakeholders of the company. The dividend on preference shares, which is paid at a fixed per centage of the face value of the shares, is not a tax deductible expense. However, the companies act requires that the preference shares have to be redeemed within a maximum time period of 20 years, which alongwith the fixed nature of the dividend gives them the character of debt. These shares are issued when the promoters want to raise the net worth of the company without diluting their stake to meet the requirements of the financial institutions as the institutions consider preference shares as a part of the net worth.

There are many variations of the preference shares such as the cumulating of the dividend payable when the profits are inadequate, participation in profits if the equity dividends exceed a certain per centage, etc.

3. Debenture Capital

Debenture capital is debt raised through the issue of debentures. Based on whether they are convertible into equity shares or not, debentures may be fully convertible, partly convertible or non-convertible. Debentures may be secured by a charge on the assets of the company or may be unsecured. There is no restriction in the period of maturity for which debentures can be issued, though generally the period of maturity varies between five and ten years. Interest on debentures, like on any other debt, is tax deductible. The amount to be raised though debentures should be decided keeping in view the amount of finance available from the institutions and the security available.

When convertible debentures are issued in Euromarkets to raise debt in foreign currency, they are called Euro Convertible Bonds. The ECBs carry an option to the holder to get them converted into equity shares at a ratio specified at the time of issue.

4. Term Loans

Financial institutions and commercial banks extend terms loans with a repayment period ranging generally between eight and fifteen years. The loans are available for setting up new projects and also for expansion and renovation. The loans are secured by a first charge on the assets financed and a second charge on all other assets of the firm. Term loans are allowed in both rupees and foreign currency, Foreign currency loans are availed of to meet the cost of imported equipment, cost of technology and know-how, etc, for which payment may have to be made in foreign currency. The loan account is maintained in foreign currency and the interests then prevailing. Term loans, both in rupees and foreign currency and the interest and installments are converted into rupees at the time of repayment at the rates then prevailing. Term loans, both in rupees and foreign currencies available from non-banking financial companies also. But generally, the limitation is that the NBFCs do not finance the entire project, but limit themselves to the items they believe are relatively safe to finance and also charge a rate higher than the financial institutions. Foreign currency term loans amy also be obtained directly from overseas lenders if the borrower has a high credit rating.

5. Deferred Credit

Suppliers of equipment often allow the buyer to pay in installments. The period over which the installments are spread over and the finance charges depend on the credit standing of the buyer, the value of the equipment and the demand for the equipment in the market.

6. Bill Rediscounting Scheme

The scheme has been introduced by the IDBI to encourage the sale of indigenous capital equipment on a deferred payment basis.

7. Seed Capital Assistance

Seed capital assistance is provided to small and medium ventures made generally by first generation entrepreneurs who are technically qualified, but do not have sufficient resources to augment the resources brought in by them at very low rates of interest.

8. Unsecured Loans

When promoters are unwilling or unable to bring in equity to the extent wanted by the financial institutions, they extend unsecured loans to the venture. Such unsecured loans, which do not carry any interest, may also be extended by friends and relatives of the promotes and cannot be withdrawn without the permission of the lending institutions.

9. Deposits

Public deposits are also unsecured, and can be raised by the firm subject to the rules made by the central government and RBI in this regard.

10. Leasing and Hire Purchase

As already mentioned, non-banking financial companies finance only a part of the project, and rarely the entire project, unlike the FIs. Therefore, the willingness of the financial institutions to let a third company finance a part of the project should be kept in mind while deciding on the financing mix. Comparison of: The finance charges demanded by the hire purchase company (or the finance charge implicit in the lease) with the cost of funds from other sources, and the outflow on hire payments or lease rentals with the expected cash inflows should be done to decide on which source of finance to choose.

11. Availability of Investment Subsidy

The backward areas have been further divided into the following three categories depending on the degree of backwardness.

Category A : No industry districts plus special regions.

Category B : Districts currently eligible for investment subsidy from the central government minus districts included in category 'A'.

Category C : Existing concession finance[1] districts minus those included in categories 'A' and 'B'.

---

1. It may be noted that investment subsidy whether provided by the central or state government is a source of financing the project cost. Concession finance implies giving of term loans at concessional interest rates and may or may not be accompanied by an increase in the repayment period.

The central subsidy applicable to industrial projects in these districts was as follows:

Category A : 25 per cent of the fixed capital investment subject to a maximum of ₹ 25 lakh.

Category B : 15 per cent of the capital investment subject to a maximum of ₹ 15 lakh.

Category C : 10 per cent of the fixed capital investment subject to a maximum of ₹ 10 lakh.

The above schemes of central subsidy were discontinued with effect from 1st October, 1988. However, the financial institutions agreed to continue with the scheme of confessional finance for projects in backward areas. For this purpose, the financial institutions would follow the same classification of districts as was used in the central subsidy scheme.

12. State Investment Subsidy

The state governments also offer subsidy to promote wide spread dispersal of industries within their states. The districts notified for state investment subsidy generally differ from those covered under the central subsidy scheme. The state subsidies vary between 5 per cent to 25 per cent of the fixed capital investment in the project, subject to a ceiling varying between ₹ 5 lakh and ₹ 25 lakh depending on the location.

Sales Tax Deferments/Exemptions: To promote rapid industrialisation, depending upon the location of the industrial undertaking, the states offers the incentive of extending interest free long-term sales tax deferments and sales tax exemptions. Under the sales tax deferment scheme, sales tax against the sale of finished goods need not be paid for periods ranging between five to twelve years and this deferred liability of sales tax is repayable free of interest over a period of five to twelve years depending on the location of industrial undertaking. During the deferment period, the money that would be normally paid as sales tax is ploughed back into business to provide the increased requirements of margin for working capital or towards financing the deferred capital expenditure. Under the sales tax exemption scheme, payment of sales tax is exempted against raw materials, consumables, packing and processing materials from within the state which are utilised for the purposes of manufacturing goods. The period of exemption varies between three to nine years depending upon the location of the industrial undertaking.

Income Tax Benefits: The projects are offered incentives by granting exemptions under section 10A, etc., of the Income Tax Act if the projects are set up in free zones.

ESTIMATION OF COST OF PROJECT AND PRODUCTION

1. Land, Building and Civil Works

The costs under this head can be segregated into two groups: (i) main factory building and (ii) allied civil work like administrative block, storage space for raw materials and civil works for utilities, security gates and structures and miscellaneous civil works not included in the above heads. The areas of the building for factory and other purposes are worked out depending upon the plant layout and manpower requirement. These areas are then multiplied with the constructions cost per unit area for that respective type of building. The sum of these will give the cost of building and civil works. Generally, current cost of building materials and construction charges are used for projects with a relatively shorter implementation period, say upto one year. In case of projects with a longer implementation schedule, an allowance is added to the current cost estimates equal to the latest available annual inflation rate for civil works multiplied by the number of the years of implementation period. The cost of buildings and civil works in case of Mini Garments Limited was estimated to be ₹ 50 Lakh.

The elements of cost which go in for determining the cost of land and the site development are-

(i) Basic cost of land.

(ii) Conveyance charges and other allied charges.

(iii) Levelling of the plot.

(iv) Laying of the internal roads.

(v) Laying of the approach roads.

(vi) Construction of the boundary walls.

(vii) Construction of the main gate.

(viii) Tube-well digging cost.

2. Plant and Machinery

The calculation of the cost of plant and machinery needs segregation of the entire plant, machinery and equipment into imported and indigenous categories and also into those in respect of which firms orders have been placed and are yet to be placed. Quotations are examined to analyse the cost estimates and if the quotations are old and latest estimates are not available, suitable escalation in the cost estimates, based on the validity of the quotations, is provided. In case of large projects, provision for escalation is made by adding the latest figures of annual inflation for machinery multiplied by the length of the delivery period. Thus, the cost of the plant and machinery is done by adding the costs of all items of plant and machinery. In case of imported equipment, the price is converted into rupee equivalent. The component of custom duty at the prevailing rate should be taken into consideration while assessing the final costs of the plant and machinery.

The total cost of plant and machinery is calculated as follows:

Basic cost of indigenous machines (a)

Basic cost of imported plant and machinery (b)

Custom duty on the imported plant and machinery (c) Basic Cost : (a) + (b) + (c) —— A

Excise (normally 15 per cent of basic cost) —— B

Sales Tax ——— C

Octroi, freight, transportation, loading ,unloading, cleaning and forwarding charges (say 4 per cent of basic cost) ——— D

Erection charges (generally 5-10 per cent of basic cost) —— E

TOTAL COST: A + B + C + D + E

3. Miscellaneous Fixed Assets

There are others items of machinery, which do not form part of the direct manufacturing process and are called miscellaneous fixed assets or utilities. These may differ from project to project. Common to most projects are DG set, boiler, piping, meters, etc.; laboratory equipment, testing equipment, transformer, furniture, office equipment, cables, etc. Sometimes expenses incurred for patents, licenses, payments in respect of trademarks, etc.; are also included under this head. The provision of these assets is determined depending upon their need and justification. Adequate provision for escalation charges is made in the light of escalation clauses, if any, in the quotations or by adding an allowance at the latest rate of annual inflation on various equipment multiplied by the delivery period.

4. Pre-operative Expenses

The expenses incurred till the date of commencement of commercial production are included under this head. Pre-operative expenses incurred upto the point of time the plant and machinery are ready for use are capitalised by apportioning them to depreciable fixed assets in proportion to their book values. The pre-operative expenses for Mini Garments Limited was estimated to be ₹ 18 lakh including interest on term loan (of ₹ 100 lakh, as shown in means of financing) during construction period of 6 months. The interest on term loan for those 6 months at the rate of 18 per cent was calculated as: 100* 18/100* 6/12 = 9 lakh.

Broadly speaking pre-operative expenses comprises as follows:

- Promotional expenses.
- Organisational and training costs.
- Rent, rates and taxes.
- Travelling expenses.
- Postage, telegrams and telephone expenses.
- Printing and stationery expenses.
- Advertisement expenses.
- Guarantee commission.
- Insurance during construction.
- Interest during construction period, etc.

5. Provision for Contingencies

Over and above the escalation under various items of cost on the basis of latest available rate of inflation, contingency provision is made on the basis of projects implementation schedule. Escalation may arise due to minor changes in the specifications of the buildings, plant and machinery, which result in the increase of costs. Contingency for price escalation can be provided by analysing each and every item of the cost of the project. For this purpose, costs can be divided into firm and non-firm costs, where firm costs are those which are already procured, or there is reasonable possibility of the items being procured within the provisions made at the time of appraisal. Firm costs have less possibility of variation as compared to non-firm costs. So, it does not call for provisions for escalation.

6. Preliminary Expenses

Preliminary and capital issue expenses include cost of preparation of feasibility report,. project reports conducting market survey or any other survey necessary for the project, legal charges for drafting agreements, memorandum and articles of association, capital issue, underwriting commission, brokerage, charges for drafting, printing and issue of prospectus, share certificates, etc.

7. Technical Know-how Fees

The technical know-how and engineering fees include know-how fees, expenses on foreign technicians, training of Indian technicians within the country and abroad as also any royalty and compensation if payable. A through scrutiny should be done with regard to the precise scope and cost of know-how and constancy services. To avoid overcharging by the consultant, three or four consultants are approached, their experience is examined and the relatives' fees are compared. While estimating know-how and consultancy fees, government guidelines, range of services rendered by the consultant, guarantees offered, risks shared, etc, are examined. If the royalty or fees for know- how is payable in lump sum at the beginning of the project, it is considered to be a part of the cost of the project. On the other hand, if it is payable periodically, whether or not based on sales, it is considered as an operating cost.

PROGRAM EVALUATION REVIEW TECHNIQUE (PERT)

The Program Evaluation and Review Technique (PERT) is a model for project management invented by United States Department of Defense's US Navy Special Projects Office in 1958 as part of the Polaris mobile submarine-launched ballistic missile project. This project was a direct response to the Sputnik crisis. PERT is basically a method for analysing the tasks involved in completing a given project, especially the time needed to complete each task, and identifying the minimum time needed to complete the total project. It was able to incorporate uncertainty in the sense that it was possible to schedule a project not knowing precisely the details and durations of all the activities. Though every company now has its own 'project model' of some kind, they all resemble PERT in some respect. Only the DuPont corporation's critical path method was invented at roughly the same time as PERT.

It is well-known that management of any project involves the activities of planning, co-ordination, monitoring, control and review of the performance of a number of inter-related tasks with limited resources. Apart from studying the inter-relations, the project manager has to know the consequences of the deviations from the initial plan in order to take appropriate corrective measures on the effect of delay in one task on the other tasks. Project managers are compelled to look for dependable dynanlic planning, scheduling, control and monitoring devices.

PERT CONVENTIONS

- A PERT chart is a tool that facilitates decision making; a PERT chart does not make decisions.
- A PERT chart displays interconnected events (each of which is an important milestone), conventionally represented as numbered circles.
- The first draft of a PERT chart will number its events sequentially in 10s (10, 20, 30, etc.) to allow the later insertion of additional events.
- Two consecutive events in a PERT chart are linked by activities, which are conventionally represented as arrows in the diagram above.
- The events are presented in a logical sequence and no activity can commence until its immediately preceding event is completed.
- The planner decides which milestones should be PERT events and also decides their 'proper' sequence.
- A PERT chart may have multiple pages with many sub-tasks.

Requisites of PERT

The requisites of PERT are important if the system is to be used effectively in Project Management. These are detailed here under:

- The project goal needs to be clearly and unambiguously identified; all the individual tasks in a given programme need to be visualised in a logical manner, creating a work-break structure.
- These are put in a network flow diagram, which is comprised of events and activities; the duration of an activity, except in a time-scale network, is not represented by the length of the line.
- An activity succeeding an event cannot occur until all activities leading to it are accomplished.

- All activity paths need to be completed by appropriate events, and a description of each activity needs to be written above the arrow linking the events. Emphasis is laid on defining events and activities with precision so that there is no difficulty in monitoring actual accomplishments.

Benefit of PERT

PERT is particularly suited to the uncertain Indian conditions for R&D because of the following reasons:

- PERT gives management the ability to plan the best possible use of resources to achieve a given goal within the overall time and cost limitations. It enables the project executives to manage a variety of programmes as opposed to repetitive production situations; it helps the project manager to handle the uncertainties involved in programming where no standard time data are available; it utilises the time network analysis as a base method of approach to determine manpower, material, machinery and capital requirements. The use of PERT needs a clear definition of goals for proper communication at all levels: the feedback and review of the different stages of the project helps the management to take corrective measures and formulate strategies for allocating the limited resources in case of emergencies.
- PERT is an effective mechanism for planning, scheduling and co-ordinating the different activities in project buying. The tenders for many public sector projects insist on PERT network charts to be submitted along with the quotations.
- PERT is useful for balance sheet preparation, annual shutdown and overhauls to identify the critical activities, it is particularly useful in construction and R&D projects because it makes room for uncertainties associated with futuristic decisions on project planning. It not only helps the management in deciding when to initiate the follow-up and provide the materials, but also gives an estimate of the consequences of not meeting such demands. Thus, it helps avoid last minute delays, and panic buying resulting in cost overruns. Because of the logical interrelationships between the planned elements, the project can think of alternative vendors.
- PERT enables the optimum utilisation of the resources by their transfer from the slack to busy segments in the network in order to accomplish the stipulated goal. It is useful for pre-crisis planning and buying when the force major clauses are operative because the responsibilities to project executives are allocated well in advance to tackle such emergencies. The summation of manpower data in PERT.

Implementing PERT

The first step to scheduling the project is to determine the tasks that the project requires and the order in which they must be completed. The order may be easy to record for some tasks (i.e., When building a house, the land must be graded before the foundation can be laid) while difficult for others (There are two areas that need to be graded, but there are only enough bulldozers to do one). Additionally, the time estimates usually reflect the normal, non-rushed time. Many times, the time required to execute the task can be reduced for an additional cost or a reduction in the quality.

In the following example, there are seven tasks, labeled *a* through *g*. Some tasks can be done concurrently (*a* and *b*) while others cannot be done until their predecessor task is complete (*c* cannot begin until *a* is complete). Additionally, each task has three time estimates: the optimistic time estimate *(a)*, the most likely or normal time estimate *(m)*, and the pessimistic time estimate *(b)*, The expected time (T_E) is computed using the formula (a + 4m + b)/6.

NETWORK TECHNIQUES

Network techniques are primarily used in project management, particularly in dealing with non-repetitive operations. They are improvements of the earlier Gantt charts with an attempt to study the effect of inter-relations. The network specifically deals with these situations. Network techniques provide the help a manager needs, when he is defining the complex relationship that exists in 'sequencing' and 'time' between many jobs and planned elements of work. Thereafter, during the execution of the project, the inevitable slippages from the planned schedule occur. Network analysis enables the project manager to determine the importance of these deviations by taking the most cost-effective measures after adequate monitoring, evaluation and control.

A network is an arrow diagram, which is a graphic representation of the project plan. It depicts the logical sequence of the various elements for work, in relation to each other, that must be accomplished before a project can be completed. Any network consists of events and activities. For this purpose, it is necessary to divide the project into clearly defined major components, and to recognize the events that mark the start and completion of each activity. This is called work break structure, which enables to achieve project completion at different levels.

Concept of Event

An event is an occurrence at a point of time marking the commencement or completion of one or more activities. Since it is instant in time, no time element is ascribed to it. The symbol for an event is a circle. Major events are described by squares or rectangles. The events are numbered logically, head events having a higher number than the tail events. The event numbers are inscribed inside the circle. An event is considered to have occurred when all the activities leading to it are completed. An event is:

(a) The start or completion of a task/job.

(b) A significant point or milestone in a project, and

(c) Consumes, in itself, no time or resources.

It is represented by a circle or a rectangle. Examples of events are finishing the compilation of a project report, completion of auditing of accounts, commencing the docking of a space ship, approval of a house loan, completion of digging a borewell, etc.

Definition of Activity

An activity represents a clearly defined project element, work, job or task, which forms an integral part of a project and needs time and resources for carrying out. It is accepted, conventionally, that an activity is any function that takes place between events, whether work is involved or not, e.g., awaiting approval of a loan, setting and hardening of concrete, etc. These represent periods of idleness and involve only the passage of time with no actual work being carried out; but, nonetheless, these are activities. The symbol for an activity is an arrow. The tail of the arrow is its start, and the head is its completion. It always lies between two events. Activity is designated by the tail and head event numbers. The length or the scope of an arrow is not significant. Hence, an activity is the actual performance of a task and is represented by an arrow. It consumes time and resources. Activity is always between two events and can be spotted only once in the network diagram. Examples of activity are compilation of detailed project report, auditing of accounts, docking a spaceship, waiting for the approval of a loan, conducting a wedding, digging a borewell, etc.

Dummy Activity

Dummy activities may have to be introduced in network to keep the logic correct and to keep the designation of each activity unique or different from others, for the purpose of recognition. A dummy activity requires neither time nor resources, although it is dealt in the same manner as an activity. It is known as zero time activity. Imagine four jobs — A, B, C and D in the midst of a network. The sequence is that job B can be done only after completion of job A, and job D can be done after both the jobs A and C have been completed. For its representation in the network, there are the following three possible ways.

Numbering of Events

For the purpose of scheduling the project and analysing the network, it is necessary that every event is numbered so that the activities can be identified. By convention, networks are drawn with progress flowing from left to right and events numbered such that the number allocated to the start event of an activity is lower than the end event. If these conventions are followed, as a matter of general policy, it is not necessary to number the events in strict sequence.

Controlling

Controlling is viewing the physical progress of the project against the schedule and taking corrective actions when necessary. Deviations always occur from the original plan. If the deviations from plan are so large that they cannot be corrected, then it calls for preplanning the project to take account of the changed circumstances. Once the network has been completed, it is possible to assign details of duration, cost and resources to each activity, and to examine, schedule and control the rate of progress, costs and allocation of resources. The main advantage of network analysis is the logic and discipline it brings to bear on planning and control functions.

PERT NETWORK ANALYSIS — STEPS

(a) Clearly defining the goal of the project.

(b) Obtaining a work-break structure to a set of individual jobs, and arranging them in a logical fashion.

(c) Estimating the job duration, making provisions for optimistic and pessimistic schedules.

(d) Identifying the resource requirement constraints.

(e) Locating the schedule of dates for each activity by planning a detailed control structure,

(f) Preparing project control systems and identifying the requirements of progress reports for different levels of management.

(g) Developing the critical path and slack times.

(h) Crashing the time-optimum cost levels on the basis of costs.

(i) Updating the network continuously by systematised methods, and

(j) Monitoring, evaluating and reviewing the network constantly.

CLOSING CASELET

Draw the network diagram for the following problem and indicate a sequence of plans that the company should want to consider in making a time-cost trade-off. The company is not interested in reducing the project duration below 29 days. Start with the plan that has the longest duration.

Activity	Preceding Activity	Time (Days)		Cost (₹)	
		Regular Program	Crash Program	Regular Program	Crash Program
A	-	10	9	5,000	5,200
B	-	14	11	3,500	3,950
C	A	8	7	4,000	4,100
D	A	7	2	2,100	3,600
E	B	5	3	2,500	3,000
F	B	10	7	2,250	3,750
G	C	9	9	5,000	5,000
H	D, E	11	9	3,850	5,250
I	G, H	5	3	2,375	3,575

SUMMARY

A project is a group of unique, interrelated activities that are planned and executed in a certain sequence to create a unique product or service, within a specific timeframe, budget and the client's specifications. Some of the characteristics of the tasks that qualify to be a project are: uniqueness, specificity of goal, sequence of activities, specified time and interrelatedness. Projects are carried out under many resource constraints like time, cost and material resources. Their success depends on the ability of the manager to manage these constraints effectively. Project management is the application of the knowledge, skills, tools and techniques to project activities in order to meet or exceed stakeholder needs and expectations.

PRACTICAL PROBLEMS AND SOLUTIONS

Problem 1

Find optimal cost schedule for the completion of the project subject to following data.

Job	Normal		Crash	
	Time (Days)	Cost (₹)	Time (Days)	Cost (₹)
1 - 2	12	600	10	1000
2 - 3	10	250	8	350
2 - 4	8	800	6	950
3 - 5	09	1100	09	1400
3 - 6	8	950	6	1100
5 - 6	0	0	0	0
3 - 7	8	850	5	950
6 - 7	6	650	4	750
4 - 6	8	800	6	1200

Solution:

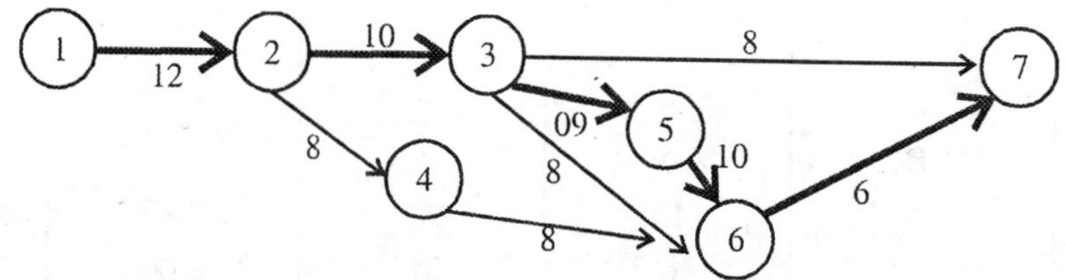

Step 1: Draw network diagram using given data.

Critical Path

Step 2 : Calculate duration of each path.

Path	duration		Days
1-2-3-7 :	12+10+8	=	30
1-2-4-6-7 :	12+8+8+6	=	34
1-2-3-5-6-7 :	12+10+9+6	=	39 critical
1-2-3-6-7 :	12+10+8+6	=	36

Step 3: Calculate cost slope $= \dfrac{\text{Crash cost} - \text{Normal cost}}{\text{Normal time} - \text{Crash time}}$

Calculation of Cost Slope

Job	Crash cost	Normal		
		Cost		Slope
1 - 2	1000	600	=	400(12-10) = 200
2 - 3	350	250	=	100 / (10-8) = 50
2 - 4	950	800	=	150 / (8-6) = 75
3 - 5	1400	1100	=	300 / (11-10) = 300
3 - 6	1100	950	=	150 / (8-6) = 75
3 - 7	950	850	=	100 / (8-5) = 33.3
6 - 7	750	650	=	100 / (6-4) = 50
4 - 6	1200	800	=	400 / (8-6) = 200

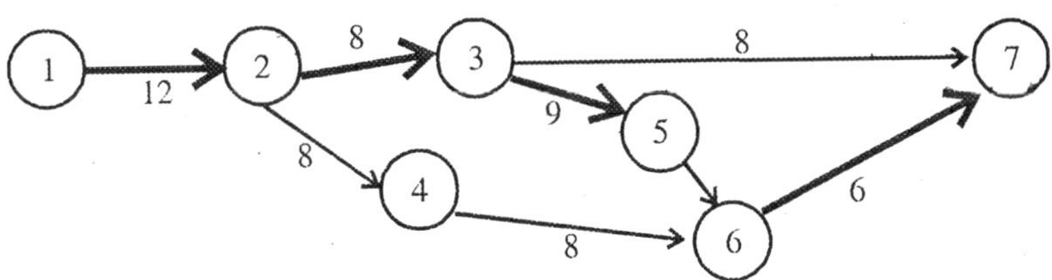

Step 4: On the Critical path, job (2-3) has the cheapest cost slope i.e., ₹ 50/- we can reduce 2 days of total duration.

Path	Duration		Days
1-2-3-7	12+8+8	=	28
1-2-4-67	12+8+8+6	=	34
1-2-3-5-6-7	12+8+9+6	=	35 critical
1-2-3-6-7	12+8+8+6	=	34

Steps 5: Now, activity 6-7 can be reduced by 2 days.

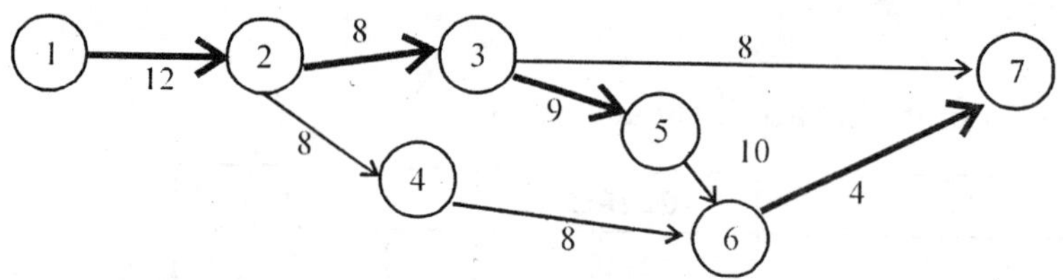

PATH	Duration		Days
1-2-3-7	12+8+8	=	28
1-2-4-6-7	12+8+8+4	=	32
1-2-3-5-6-7	12+8+9+4	=	33 critical
1-2-3-6-7	12+8+8+4	=	32

Step 6: Last, 3-5 Activity is reduced by one day.

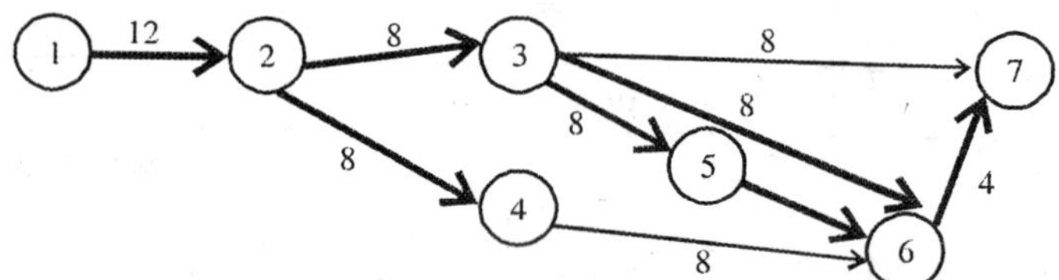

PATH	Duration	Days
1-2-3-7 :	12+8+8 =	28
1-2-4-6-7 :	12+8+8+4 =	32
1-2-3-5-6-7 :	12+8+8+0+4 =	32
1-2-3-6-7 :	12+8+8+4 =	32 critical

Step 7: Project cost calculation

	Normal Time	Cost	Total Cost
1-2	12	600	7200
2-4	8	800	6400
4-6	8	800	6400
6-7	4	650	2600
			22600
Crashing Cost			1500*
			24100
Total cost of the project optimal cost schedule			

Note: * Activity 6-7 is reduced by 2 days @ ₹ 750/-

Problem 2

A Project schedule is given below. Draw a network diagram.

Activity	Time	Activity	Time
1 - 2	6	3 - 4	7
1 - 4	5	5 - 6	8
2 - 3	3	5 - 7	3
2 - 5	2	7 - 8	2

Use dummy lines for finalization of network

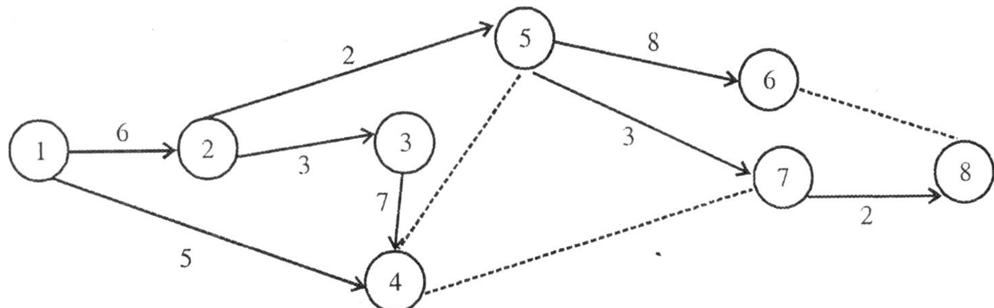

Problem 3

[Activity on Arc Model]

Job	Duration	Job	Duration
A	10	G	6
B	6	H	11
C	11	I	7
D	9	J	8
E	7	K	11
F	9	L	5
		M	12

Constraints:

(1) A, B are start Jobs

(2] A controls C, E

(3] B controls D, F

(4] G depends A, E

(5] C controls I

(6] H depends on F

(7) I controls J, K

(8) L depends on H, K

(9) J controls M

NETWORK DIAGRAM

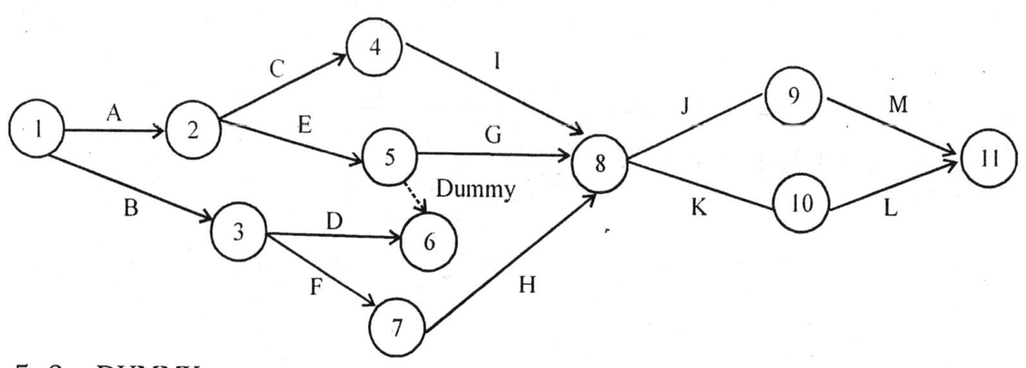

5- 6 DUMMY

Problem 4

Calculation of standard deviation

$$\tau = \sqrt{\left(\frac{tp - to}{6}\right)^2}$$

Task	to	tp	tm	te	(tp-to)	$\left(\frac{tp-to}{6}\right)^2$
A	6	12	9	9	6	(1)
B	18	20	16	17	2	(1/9)
C	24	36	30	30	12	(4)
D	12	18	15	15	6	(1)
E	12	24	18	18	12	(4)
F	6	14	10	10	8	(4/3)2
G	8	12	9	7	6	(1)
H	8	14	11	11	6	(1)

Working Notes

Calculation of expected time each task

$$\text{Task A} = \frac{6 + (4 \times 9) + 11}{6} = \frac{6 + 36 + 12}{6} = 9$$

$$\text{Task B} = \frac{18 + (4 \times 16) + 21}{6} = \frac{18 + 64 + 20}{6} = 17$$

$$\text{Task C} = \frac{24 + (4 \times 30) + 36}{6} = \frac{24 + 120 + 36}{6} = 30$$

$$\text{Task D} = \frac{12 + (4 \times 15) + 18}{6} = \frac{12 + 60 + 18}{6} = 15$$

$$\text{Task E} = \frac{12 + (4 \times 18) + 24}{6} = \frac{12 + 72 + 24}{6} = 18$$

$$\text{Task F} = \frac{6 + (4 \times 10) + 14}{6} = \frac{6 + 40 + 14}{6} = 10$$

Problem 5

A Project is represented by the network shown below and has the following data.

Task: :	A	B	C	D	E	F	G	H
Least time :	6	18	24	12	12	6	6	18
Greatest time :	12	210	36	18	24	14	12	14
Host Likely time :	9	16	30	15	18	10	9	11

Constraints

(1) A is start job

(2) A controls B & C

(3) C controls D & E

(4) F depends C & D

(5) G depends C & E

(6) G controls H

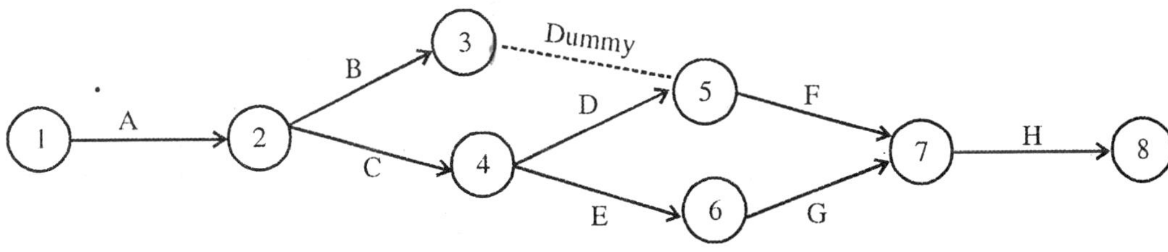

3 - 5 DUMMY

Calculation of Expected Time

$$te = \frac{to + 4tm + tp}{6}$$

to = optimistic time

tm = most likely time

tp = pessimists time

$$\text{Task G} = \frac{6 + (4 \times 9) + 12}{6} = \frac{6 + 36 + 12}{6} = 7$$

$$\text{Task H} = \frac{8 + (4 \times 11) + 14}{6} = \frac{8 + 44 + 14}{6} = 11$$

Calculation of probability of completion of project within specified period.

Problems 6

From the following network diagram find the probability of completion of project within 25 days. If standard deviation for 22 days is 7.779

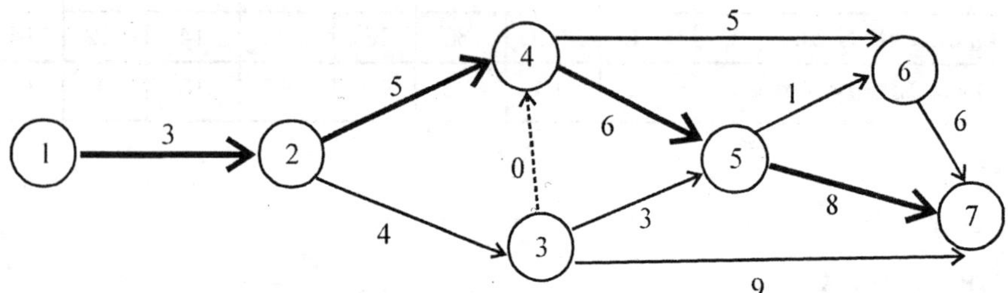

Solution:

Step 1: Find critical path after calculation of duration of each path

Path	Duration
1-2-4-6-7 :	3+5+5+6 = 19
1-2-3-7 :	3+4+9 = 16
1-2-4-5-7 :	3+5+6+8 = 22 critical
1-2-3-5-6-7 :	3+4+3+1+6 = 17

Step 2: Using 'Z' test, we can find probability of completion of project within 25 days.

$$Z = \frac{25 - 22}{\sqrt{7.779}} = 1.08$$

$$\phi(1.08) = 0.3599$$

$$P(t \leq 25) = P(2 \leq 1.08) = 0.5 + \Phi(1.08)$$

$$= 0.5 + 0.3599 = 0.8599$$

Using standard normal distribution table, the probability of completion of project is 85.99 per cent.

KEYWORDS

1. **A PERT Activity:** Is the actual performance of a task. It consumes time, it requires resources and it can be understood as representing the time, effort, and resources required to move from one event to another.
2. **A PERT Event:** Is a point that marks the start or completion of one tasks. It consumes no time, and uses no resources.
3. **A Predecessor Event:** An event that immediately precedes some other event without any other events intervening. It may be the consequence of more than one activity.
4. **A Successor Event:** An event that immediately follows some other event without any other events intervening. It may be the consequence of more than one activity.
5. **Critical Path:** The longest pathway taken from the initial event to the terminal event. It determines the total calendar time required for the project; and, therefore, any time delays along the critical path will delay the reaching of the terminal event by at least the same amount.
6. **Expected Time (T_E):** The best estimate of the time required to accomplish a task, assuming everything proceeds as normal.
7. **Lag Time:** The earliest time by which a *successor event* can follow a specific PERT event.
8. **Lead Time:** The time by which a *predecessor event* must be completed in order to allow sufficient time for the activities that must elapse before a specific PERT event is reached to be completed.
9. **Most Likely Time (M):** The best estimate of the time required to accomplish a task, assuming everything proceeds as normal.
10. **Optimistic Time (O):** The minimum possible time required to accomplish a task, assuming everything proceeds better than is normally expected.
11. **Pessimistic Time (P):** The maximum possible time required to accomplish a task, assuming everything goes wrong (but excluding major catastrophes).
12. **Project Life Cycle:** Project life cycle is a collection of generally sequential project phases. The number of project phases is determined by the control needs of the project organisation.
13. **Project Manager:** A project manager is often a client representative and has to determine and implement the exact needs of the client based on knowledge of the firm he/she is representing.

14. **Project:** A project is a group of unique, interrelated activities that are planned and executed in a certain sequence to create a unique product or service, within a specific timeframe, budget and the client's specifications.

15. **Slack:** The slack of an event is a measure of the excess time and resources available in achieving this event. Positive slack would indicate *ahead of schedule*; negative slack would indicate *behind schedule*; and zero slack would indicate *on schedule*.

REVIEW QUESTIONS

1. Write various definitions of project management.
2. What are the essentials of a good project?
3. Explain the role and responsibilites of a project manager.
4. The following table gives the activities in a project and their duration. Draw a Network diagram to find critical path.

Activity	Duration
1-2	15
1-3	25
1-4	14
2-4	21
2-5	10
3-6	15
4-6	13
5-7	25
6-7	22
6-8	17
7-8	10
8-9	9

5. The following table gives the activities in a construction project and their duration. Draw a network diagram to find critical path.

Activity	Preceding Activity	Duration
1-2	-	15
1-3	-	25
2-3	1-2	10
2-4	1-2	12
3-4	1-3, 2-3	10
4-5	2-4, 3-4	15

REFERENCES

1. *Project Management* — Harvey Maylor — MacMillan India Ltd.
2. *Project Management* – S. Chowdary- Tata Mcgraw-Hill Publishing
3. *Project Management — Principles and Techniques* — B.B. Goel — Deep & Deep Publications Pvt. Ltd.
4. *Project Planning, Analysis, Selection Implementation and Review* — Prasanna Chandra, Tata McGraw-Hill Publishing Co. Ltd.
5. *Project Management — A Systems Approach to Planning, Scheduling and Controlling* — Harlold Kerzner, CBS Publishers and Distributors, New Delhi.
6. *Project Management — Strategic Financial Planning Evaluation and Control* — Bhavesh M.Patel — Vikas Publishing House Pvt. Ltd., New Delhi.
7. *Total Project Management* — P.K. Joy – Macmillan India Ltd.

ജ്ഞ ജ്ഞ ജ്ഞ

CHAPTER

4

Financial Feasibility and Competence Diagnosis

CHAPTER OUTLINE

- Opening Caselet
- Introduction
- Environmental Scanning and Appraisal
- Economic Feasibility Study
- Technical Feasibility Study
- Cultural Feasibility Study
- Legal Feasibility Study
- Marketing Feasibility Study
- Competence Diagnosis
- Stages of Development
- Michael Porter's Model of Forces of Competition
- Competitive Advantage
- Strategic Alternatives
- Summary
- Closing Caselet
- Keywords
- Review Questions
- References

OPENING CASELET

GEOGRAPHICAL SPREAD

Infrastructure Leasing and Financial Services Ltd. (IL&FS), will be the new promoter of the Hyderabad-based Maytas Infras Ltd., following the recent orders passed by the Company Law Board (CLB), which has also allowed IL&FS to nominate its managing director Hari Sankarna, joint managing director Arun K Saha, President and CEO Karunakaran Ramchand, and chairman Ravi Parthasarathy, on the board of the severely impaired entity.

In mid-2007, when Chennai-based Zylog Systems Ltd (ZSL) — a Tier-II software services and solutions provider — approached the capital market to raise ₹ 126 crore to put up off-shore development centres, besides setting aside a corpus for merger and acquisition activity.

Sesharthnam, CEO and his team have lapped up three more companies — PEQ Consulting, Fairfaz Consulting and the Dubai-based Ducontt. PEQ, the $2.5 million acquisition, is an infrastructure management company rendering information technology services in the managed services space. Its core focus is automotive industry and it derives 85 per cent of its revenue from this vertical with client spread over the US and Canada.

ZSL started off in 1996, providing services such as application development and maintenance, enterprise infrastructure management and quality assurance and testing to clients mainly in the US. Besides this, it has product platforms for seamless integration of various software, application for its telecom, manufacturing and banking clientele.

Additionally, Zylog gets revenues from partnering system integrators/solution providers, independent software vendors and value-based sellers. While banking, finance telecom and insurance were its key operational verticals, over the years, the company has moved to a broader canvass, encompassing retail, manufacturing and health care verticals, also in new countries across North America, APAC and Europe.

Though ZSL has reported good numbers, it hasn't found any takers. In this report on the company., Sanjeev Hota of Reliance Money comment that, at the current growth rates, the company will join the ₹ 1,000 crore league by March 2010. And, with profits close to ₹ 140 crores, the EPS is projected to touch ₹ 89 crores.

Source: *Business India,* December 27, 2009.

INTRODUCTION

This chapter is divided into two sections: (a) Financial Feasibility Study (b) Competence Diagnosis, which is further divided into two section *viz.*, (i) Core Competence and (ii) Strategic Alternatives.

Financial feasibility estimates the financial capacity of business entity. Short and long-term investment decisions will be made after the study of financial feasibility. A feasibility study is a preliminary study undertaken to determine and document a project's viability. The results of this study are used to make a decision whether to proceed with the project, or table it. If it indeed leads to a project being approved, it will — before the real work of the proposed project starts — be used to ascertain the likelihood of the project's success. It is an analysis of possible alternative solutions to a problem and a recommendation on the best alternative. It, for example, can decide whether an order processing be carried out by a new system more efficiently than the previous one.

Important Considerations

- **Volume and Mix of Financing:** The amount of capital required for the organisation and capital structure, i.e., equity and debt component will be determined.
- **Financial Risk:** Without risk there is no business. Hence, financial risk analysis is important for financial planning.
- **Financial Return Evaluation:** Return is associated with probability of risk. Hence, there is risk-return relation which must be kept in mind while preparing financial plans.
- **Resource Allocation:** Investing decision is nothing but allocation of resources to various accounts. Strategic financial management always considers resource allocation as an important concept.
- **Financial Control:** Control and implementation of finance of the organisation is a crucial consideration in strategic finance.

ENVIRONMENTAL SCANNING AND APPRAISAL

Environment means the surrounding under which someone or something exists and the aggregate of all conditions events and influences that surround and affect it. The environment influences an organisation in many ways, it understanding is of crucial importance. Environment may be broadly categorized into two types:

(1) External Environment

(2) Internal Environment

1. External Environment

It includes all the factors outside organisation which provide opportunities or threats to the organisation. It may be social, cultural, political, economical, market, technological environment.

2. Internal Environment

This environment in which an organisation exists. It refers to all the factors within an organisation which impart strengths or cause weaknesses of a strategic nature.

Environmental analysis is nothing but identifying opportunities and threats affecting their business. In other words environmental analysis is nothing but SWOT Strengths, Weaknesses, Opportunities and Threats — analysis. Strategic management needs environmental analysis and appraisal. Environment may be broadly classified into two types *viz.*, (1) Internal Environment and (2) External environment or both may be called as 'Environment in General'. This General environment has different dimensions, as mentioned below:

ECONOMIC FEASIBILITY STUDY

This involves questions such as whether the firm can afford to build the system, whether its benefits should substantially exceed its costs, and whether the project has higher priority and profits than other projects that might use the same resources. This also includes whether the project is in the condition to fulfill all the eligibility criteria and the responsibility of both sides in case there are two parties involved in performing any project. Economic environment refers to all those economic factors which have a bearing on the functioning of business, like — economic policies, economic systems and economic reforms. Economic environment mostly influences business sector. Indian economic environment is influenced by several factors, which are mentioned below:

1. Industrial policy
2. Public sector
3. Private sector
4. Liberalization, privatization and globalization
5. Foreign trade policies
6. Per capita income levels of consumers
7. Financial sectors

TECHNICAL FEASIBILITY STUDY

Technological environment is prevailing even before evolution of computers. The concept of computerization and its application to decision making process is a recent phenomenon, and it is also called as user-machine system. It implies that some tasks are best performed by humans, while others are best done by machine. The user of an technological environment, is any person responsible for entering input data, instructing the system, or utilising the information output of the system. Hence, this system is useful to solve many problems of the organisation. User-machine interaction is facilitated by operations in which the user's input-output device (usually a visual display unit) is connected to the computer. This involves questions such as whether the technology needed for the system exists, how difficult it will be to build, and whether the firm has enough experience using that technology. The assessment is based on an outline design of system requirements in terms of Input, Output, Fields, Programs and Procedures. This can be qualified in terms of volumes of data, trends, frequency of updating etc., in order to give an introduction to the technical system.

CULTURAL FEASIBILITY STUDY

In this stage, the project's alternatives are evaluated for their impact on the local and general culture. For example, environmental factors need to be considered and cultural environment refers to the influence exercised by certain factors which are beyond the company's gate. Such factors include people's attitude to work and wealth, role of family, marriage, religion and education, ethical issues and social responsiveness of business. Social and cultural environment is highly relevant for a business unit as the variety of goods it produces, the type of employees it gets, and its obligation to society depend on the cultural milieu in which the business operates. Social and cultural environment is man-made. Man has created the social and cultural environment by using the natural environment with skill and culture. He has exploited natural resources in some regions of the world and developed a cultural environment, while in some other regions natural resources have not been exploited.

LEGAL FEASIBILITY STUDY

Not necessarily last, but all projects must face legal scrutiny. When an organisation either has legal council on staff or on retainer, such reviews are typically standard. However, any project may face legal issues after completion too. The Government of India is now implementing several law for the monitoring and regulating business and industries. For example:

- **Acts:** (a) Monopolies and Restrictive Trade Practices Act, (b) Companies Act, (c) Industrial Regulation Act, (d) Income Tax Act, (e) Sales Tax Act, etc.
- **Policies Like:** Industrial policy, EXIM policy, Fiscal policy, Banking policy, Monetary policy etc.,

MARKETING FEASIBILITY STUDY

This will include analysis of single and multi-dimensional market forces that could affect the commercial.In common parlance, the term 'competitive environment' means a particular place or locality, where goods are bought and sold. In economics, competition refers to a complex set of activities by which potential buyers and potential sellers are brought into close contact with each together and the price as well as the output is determined. A market system by which buyers and sellers bargain for the price of a product, settle the price and transact their business — buy and sell a product. Personal contact between the buyers and sellers is not necessary. In some cases, e.g., forward sale and purchase, even immediate transfer of ownership of goods is not necessary. Market does not necessarily mean a place. The market for a commodity may be local, regional, national or international. It is important to note that a market is established irrespective of time and place, whenever two groups of transactors (buyers and sellers) are there to undertake exchange transactions. Competitive markets exist in every economy, so long as two or more individuals are willing to undertake exchange transactions. Further, an economy, particularly, the capitalist economy cannot function without markets. Truly, speaking, the whole rationality of the capitalist economy is deeply rooted in the price or market mechanism. The consumers exercise their free choice in the market and the producers take decisions about the allocation of resources including time among competing ends in response to market demand. Decision making by the producers will become irrational.

Important Elements

The following are the important elements of competitive environment:

1. Seller and buyer agree to transact at a particular price of a product.
2. Nature of the commodity is known to both parties.
3. Price of the product is determined under conditions of the market.
4. Competition depends on the increase in the buyers and sellers.
5. If there is increase in number of buyers, price will increase and it is treated as Seller's market.
6. If there is increase in number of sellers, price will decrease, it is treated as Buyer's market.
7. Free communication between the buyers and sellers.
8. Size of the market is not restricted, it may be in a certain city, a region, a country or even the entire world.
9. Product is homogenous in case of perfect competition, and the product may be differentiated in case of other markets.

Competition can be classified into two broad categories

(1) Perfect Competition, and

(2) Imperfect Competition

Further imperfect competition can be classified into four categories like:

(a) Monopoly

(b) Duopoly

(c) Oligopoly, and

(d) Monopolistic

COMPETENCE DIAGNOSIS

Core competence is communication and involvement and commitment to working across organisational boundaries. It involves different people and different functions. The skills of individuals and organisation together treated as core competence. It never diminishes and perishes like physical assets. It is way managing organisation and enhances everyday when the intellectuals are working together for the development of organisation. It is based on preparation of competitive agenda and action plan. Core competence can be developed through continuous interaction among employees with their leaders and managers. In other words, core competence means a creative corporate thinking for building competencies in different ways among the employees.

Definition:

Prahlad and Hamel define 'Core Competence' as: 'Core competence is the collective learning in the organisation, especially how to coordinate diverse production skills and integrate multiple streams of technologies'.

Identification of Core Competence

1. **Ability to Market:** Core competence provides access to a wide variety of markets. If any organisation identifies its core competence as preparation of electronic goods, it can prepare computers, televisions and other electronic media. So that it can enter wide variety of market of electronic devices.

2. **Contribution:** By identifying core competence company can contribute significantly for the development of product design. This will be giving more benefits to the organisation.

3. **Imitation:** Core competition cannot be imitated by others. It is very difficult to duplicate the strategies adopted by one organisation. Because there will be differences in core competencies of each organisation.

Significance

Core competence provides strength to the organisation. It gives stability and sustainable development. Core competence improves the ability of the organisation to compete in business competition. It plays a significant role for the following benefits:

1. Cost reduction
2. Increase in the profitability
3. Enhance competition
4. Improving skills of the organisation
5. Diversification of products
6. Change in strategies
7. Improvement in managerial skills
8. Quick adaptability to the changing world.

STAGES OF DEVELOPMENT

1. **First Stage:** In the first stage organisation will have limited products and markets. Core competence leads to identification of its rivals in the markets and analyzing strengths of the organisation.
2. **Second Stage:** In this stage organisation moves to divisionalised structure and diversified products besides markets. Core competency refers to the ability of the organisation to diversify strategies, products and markets.
3. **Third Stage:** In the third stage organisation will have a comprehensive analysis. SWOT analysis gives a clear picture to top level management. At this stage organisations will conceptualise new needs and invest new products and markets. Core competence here refers to the ability to take fast decisions.

DEVELOPMENT OF COMPETITIVE ADVANTAGE

1. Competitive advantage can be developed through continuous interaction among employees.
2. Competitive advantage means building competencies in different ways among the employees.
3. It is a communication and involvement and commitment to working across organisational boundaries.
4. It involves development of strengths in different functional areas of management.
5. The skills of top levels and organisation together are treated as competitive advantage.

6. It is a way of managing organisation and enhances the chances for the development of the organisation.
7. It is based on analysis of competitive strengths and action plan.

MICHAEL PORTER MODEL OF FORCES OF COMPETITION

Competitive forces are the force which can create competition among the corporate entities. There are several forces in the competitive situation of corporate entity. These forces lead to complex situation in decision making. Michael Porter states that a corporation is most concerned with the intensity of competition within its industry. The level of intensity is determined by basic competitive forces like Buyers, Substitutes, Suppliers, Potential entrants, other Stakeholders.

1. **Potential New Entrants:** Every corporate entity is facing problem of threat of new entrants in the market. It should consider and have a watch on the new entrants in the market. The threat of entry depends on the presence of entry barriers and the reaction that can be expected from existing competitors. There are several entry barriers like product differentiation, capital requirements, cost of production, etc.
2. **Buyers:** Buyers play a vital role in the competitive forces. Bargaining power of buyers and purchasing power are important considerations in determining competition. Buyers affect an industry through their ability to force down prices, bargain for higher quality or more services.
3. **Suppliers:** Bargaining power of suppliers and competition among suppliers are also important influencing factors in competition. Rivalry among existing firms should also be considered. Suppliers have the ability to raise prices or reduce the quality of purchased goods and services.
4. **Substitutes:** A substitute product may have the quality of satisfying nature, but it will be in different form. Each product or service will have substitute products or services. Hence, substitutes will become a competitive force in the industry. For example tea and coffee. If there is increase in price of tea, there will be demand for coffee and *vice-versa*.
5. **Rivals:** Rivalry among different entities will be forming as a competitive force. As per Michael Porter analysis, corporate entities are mutually dependent. A competitive move by one firm can be expected to have a noticeable effect on its competitors. For example, Pepsi and Thumbs up, Horlicks and Complan, Polo and Minto are different rivals in the same consumer products market.
6. **Stakeholders:** The stakeholders in the corporate entity can also create a competition among different entities. For example, creditors, debtors, government, trade associations, shareholders and trade unions. The importance of the stakeholders varies according the nature of the industry.

Offensive and Defensive Strategies or Tactics

Competitive strategies are tools to face different competitive situations created by various competitive forces in the market. There are two main categories of competitive strategies they are: Offensive and Defensive strategies. Offensive strategy usually takes place in an established competitor's market location. Defensive strategy usually takes place in the firm's own current market position.

Offensive Strategies: The following are important offensive strategies:

1. **Frontal Assault:** In this category a corporate entity faces direct attacks or attacks another entity directly. It requires huge resources and abilities. The attacking organisation requires tackling the other organisation in all aspects like pricing policy, promotional strategy and all other aspects.
2. **Bypass Attack:** This is indirect method of attack. In this method a new product is offered to reduce demand for the existing product of the competitor. Hence, the competitor will lose command over the market.
3. **Encirclement:** This is like frontal assault, the organisation will have wide variety of products. For example: Netscape and Microsoft are two competitors. Even Microsoft organisation is entering very late in the market, it could dominate Netscape.
4. **Guerilla Warfare:** This model is small, intermittent assaults on different market segments held by the competitor. By using this model new firms can gain short-term benefits. But in the long-run they cannot be successful.

Defensive Strategies: Defensive strategies will reduce short-term profitability of the entities to gain long-term profitability. Defensive strategies aim to lower the probability of attack to less threatening avenues or lessen the intensity of an attack.

Some Examples of Defensive Strategies

1. Increase the size of organisation to get benefits of economies of scale.
2. Limit outside access to facilities and personnel.
3. Block channel access by signing exclusive agreements with distributors.
4. Agreement with suppliers for obtaining exclusive contracts.
5. Offer full line of products.

Differentiation

Differentiation means 'the strategy of meeting customer needs, tastes and preferences by production of different products. In other words product differentiation is the best strategy to meet customers' satisfaction.

For Example:

* **Television** – There are different products available like Black & White, Colour, Flat screen, Digital sound, Different screen sizes, etc.

* **Soaps** – Even small product like soap also has different fragrances like rose, saffron, sandal, milk, baby soaps, beauty soaps, etc.

COMPETITIVE ADVANTAGE

Competitive advantage results when more customers become strongly attached to the products of the organisation. Competitive advantage helps a firm in a specific and limited way and it also provides competitive strengths to the firm in a given business or product. Competitive advantage can be easily imitated. Competitive advantage does not necessarily imply core competence whereas core competence implies competitive advantages. Competitive advantage accrues from the functional strength.

Differentiation and Competitive Advantage

Differentiation can be used as strategy to achieve competitive advantage. Differentiator's products will be attracted by more customers. Differentiation erects entry barriers in the form of customer loyalty and uniqueness that newcomers find hard to overcome. Differentiation helps a company in finding solution to threats from substitutes. It also provides some buffer against rival's strategies.

Differentiation and Market Focus

Differentiated products should be marketed and advertised properly. It should be communicated to all customers about the brands, features and specifications of different products. The following are important aspects of differentiation:

1. **Quantitative Differentiation:** Making differences in quantities like size, weight, appearance, etc.
2. **Qualitative Differentiation:** Improvement in quality of the product.
3. **Service Differentiation:** Providing different qualities of service to different products
4. **Taste Differences:** Making changes in tastes.
5. **Value Addition to the Product:** Giving free products with the existing products.
6. **Discounts:** Announcement of discounts for different products.
7. **Prizes, Offers:** Special draws, prizes and offers will attract more customers.

STRATEGIC ALTERNATIVES

Strategy is that set of managerial decisions and actions that determines the long-run performance of a corporation. It includes environmental observation, strategic planning, formulation, implementation, evaluation and control. Development of organisation completely rests on the efficiency of the decision makers. They have to be decisions, based on present policies for achievement of future goals. Strategic planning always concentrates on the anticipated aim. Future is always uncertain. Hence, strategic decisions are always incomplete and sometimes they have been based on false information. It may lead to further problems. Strategy should always aim at achieving pre-determined goal of the organisation. Further organisations have to work with brevity and variety. Actions will lead to results. Result-oriented action is the need of hour.

There are four important areas of strategies; these may also be called as strategic alternatives.

(a) Stability Strategies

(b) Growth or Expansion Strategies

(c) Retrenchment Strategies

(d) Combination or Mixed Strategies

(a) Stability Strategies

Any business organisation should try for the stability. To achieve stability, the organisation should try to improve its skills. Continuing in the same business with the same objectives can be treated as stability strategy. In other words, stability is nothing but the consistency of the business policies to achieve goals. There will be no change in the attitude of the management.

Steps for Stability Strategy

These strategies aim at stability by causing the companies to marginally improve their performance or, atleast, letting them remain in the highly competitive market. The essence of these strategies is not to do nothing, but try to do something for survival in the market. The following are the important steps to be adopted as a part of stability strategies.

- Management should concentrate on consistency of policies and objectives.
- It should try to maintain present market share.
- It should aim to improve efficiency of functional areas.
- Providing special service to potential customers.
- Providing better after-sales service to attract more customers.
- Improving quality of the product.
- Producing different accessories for existing products.
- Try to maintaining and developing competitive advantages.

(b) Growth or Expansion Strategies

Expansion or growth strategies are contradictory to stability strategies. Stability aims at consistency where as growth requires dynamism. It aims to take challenging tasks for the development. Diversification of business, changes in the objectives, planning for growth of business are important aspects of these strategies. Aiming for increase in market shares, holding the relative position of the business are some of the adoptable strategies. These strategies can be followed when an organisation substantially broadens the scope of its customers.

Growth or expansion strategy is to attract all classes of customers i.e., poor, middle and rich customers. It may be aimed to attract irrespective size of the purchases made by customers *viz.*, huge investors and small investors. The company may move to different directions and it may alter its objectives and goals of the business.

Steps for Growth or Expansion Strategy

- **Diversification of Products:** Launching different product lines can be treated as one of the expansion strategy.
- **Diversification of Area of Market:** Market segmentation is an important criterion in this regard. Expansion to south Indian market or north Indian market, etc.
- **Increasing Market Share:** The Company may establish new machinery so that it can produce more goods to capture more shares in the market.
- **Increase in Objectives and Policies:** The corporate entity may increase its objectives and diversify its policies to make expansion of its business.
- **Applying Different Strategies for Different Types of Markets:** Some markets may be slow-moving, medium and some may behave as fast-moving. Hence, the corporate entity has to adopt different strategies for different types of markets.

Different Expansion or Growth Strategies

1. Internal Growth Strategy
2. Diversification Strategy
   - (a) Horizontal Diversification
     - (i) Concentric Diversification
     - (ii) Conglomerate Diversification
   - (b) Vertical Diversification
     - (i) Forward Integration
     - (ii) Backward Integration
3. Mergers and Takeovers
4. Joint Ventures

(c) Retrenchment Strategies

Retrenchment strategy is a strategic option which involves reduction of any existing product or service line along with the level of objectives set below the past achievement is known as retrenchment strategy. It is a defensive strategy adopted as a reaction to parting problems stemming from the either internal mismanagement, unanticipated actions by competitors or changes in market coordination. This may be used as short-run business policy to whether a strong and survive in the face of economic recession, financial stringency or poor performance, it is adopted out of necessity, not by deliberate choice.

Steps for Retrenchment Strategy

1. Analysing performance of units or segments of the organisation.
2. Dropping or retrenching such units in case of poor performance which continued to be a drag on total performance.
3. Examining problems existing in the market.
4. Identifying rivals in the competitive market conditions.
5. When there are unanticipated problems in the product market, the management may be under pressure to improve performance by all means including cutback of operations.
6. To improve the profitability of investments which give higher returns, some of the existing investments may be shed and resources, thus, released utilized for increased profitability and growth.

(d) Combination or Mixed Strategies

A combination strategy is one in which there is conscious use of different strategies for different units or divisions at the same time or sequential use of different strategies over time. It is nothing but combination of two or more basic strategic elements at the same time in the organisation is called 'mixed strategy'. Combination strategy is a mixture of stability, expansion and retrenchment strategies. Combination strategy is the result of a serious attempt on the part of strategies to take into account the variety of environmental and organisational factors that affect the process of strategy formulation; complex situations generally require complex solutions. These strategies are solutions that strategists have to offer when faced with the problems of business.

Steps for Combination Strategy

1. Identification and analysis of business problems.
2. Selection of different elements from different strategies like stability, growth, retrenchment, to solve business problems.

3. Implementation of mixed or combination strategies.
4. Evaluation of the implemented strategies

Factors Involved in Strategic Forecasting

1. **Time Factor:** Forecasting may be done for short-term or long-term. Short term forecasting is generally taken for one year while long-term forecasting covering a period of 5, 10 or 20 year period.
2. **Level Factor:** Strategic forecasting may be undertaken at three different levels.
   (a) **Macro Level:** It is concerned with business conditions over the whole economy.
   (b) **Industry Level:** Prepared by different industries.
   (c) **Firm-level:** Firm-level forecasting is the most important from managerial view point.
3. **General or Specific Purpose Factor:** The firm may find either general or specific forecasting or both useful according to its requirement.
4. **Product:** Forecasting varies according to the type of product i.e., new product or existing product or well established product.
5. **Nature of the Product:** Goods can be classified into (i) consumer goods and (ii) producer goods. Business for a product will be mainly dependent on nature of the product. Forecasting methods for producer goods and consumer goods will be different accordingly.
6. **Competition:** While making forecasting, market situation and the product position in particular market should be analysed.
7. **Consumer Behaviour:** What people think about the future, their own personal prospects and about products and brands are vital factors for firm and industries.

Advantages

The following are the merits or benefits or advantages derived from strategic forecasting business for a product.

1. **Analysing Business:** Business analysis is first and foremost application of strategic forecasting. Price of a product is the key factor which influences business for the product. Apart from price, there are several other factors also influence business for the product like income, taste, preferences, consumer behaviour, etc. Strategic forecasting will considers all the factors influencing business for the product, to estimate future business for the product.
2. **Estimation of Supply:** By making strategic forecasting of a business, one can understand the needs of business. One can estimate the required raw-materials, finished goods etc, by identifying the suppliers who can supply qualitative products at competitive prices.

3. **Capital Outlay:** Capital outlay is nothing but ascertaining the investment requirements for the organisation. Strategic forecasting includes the responsibility of determining capital requirements for business.

4. **Market Conditions:** Several market conditions like monopoly, oligopoly, monopolistic competitions, are existing in the market. Competitive market conditions are varying according to the product nature and number of sellers existing in the market. Thus forecasting will be useful to examine the market conditions to suggest for pricing decisions.

5. **Price of a Product:** Cost-Volume-Profit analysis, i.e., C.V.P analysis is an important tool to analyse cost to determine target profit for the organisation. Cost behaviour study is the important factor in this regard. The firm can be able to decide appropriate price for the product on the basis of forecasting.

6. **Advertising Policy:** Forecasting helps the management and it has to act as adviser to the management. It can advise about advertising policy, as it is necessary product promotion.

7. **Market Segmentation:** The strategist can be adviser to the marketing department. He can take active part in decisions relating to marketing issues like market segmentation, product mix, product line and determination of decisions like product addition, deletion – can also be taken with the help of business estimator.

8. **Feasibility Report:** The reports of forecasting helps in preparation of feasibility reports. These reports can be classified into three types i.e., Technical feasibility, Operational feasibility, Economic feasibility. Organisation can take important decisions by studying these feasibility reports.

9. **Helping in Profit Policymaking:** The reports of forecasting also helps in making profit policies of the organisation. As stated earlier C.V.P. analysis is a useful tool in determining profit policy.

10. **Production Scheduling:** Scheduling is fixation of time boundaries. Thus production budgets and time-frame for production will be determined on the basis of strategic forecasting.

11. **Cost Reduction:** As the production is predetermined on the basis of strategic forecasting, there will be control over the cost of production. Hence, wastage can be avoided.

12. **Inventory Control:** Inventory or Stock of materials can also be planned according to Production Planning and Control (PPC) methods. It helps in under or over inventory levels.

13. **Setting Sales Targets:** Strategic forecasting helps in determining sales targets of the organisation. Each sales executive has to achieve his assigned tasks as determined by forecasting department.

14. **Planning Manpower Requirements:** Manpower requirements for the organisation, i.e., sales staff, production staff, administration staff etc., can be determined using strategic forecasting technique.

SUMMARY

This chapter deals with financial feasibility and competence diagnosis. Financial feasibility study includes environmental scanning and diagnosis for strategic financing activities of the firm. Hence, the feasibility study of marketing, economic, technical, cultural and schedules are also needed in this regard. Core competence helps a firm in a far-reaching and multi-faceted manner and it also helps the firm to play in a variety of business or products. Competitive advantage can be easily imitated whereas core competence cannot be imitated.

CLOSING CASELET

BHARTI-WARID DEAL

Bharti Airtel has been trying to expand its footprint overseas for the past couple of years. Bharti is all set to snap up Warid Telecom, Bangladesh's fourth largest telecom operator.

Sunil Bharti Mittal, CEO, Bharti Enterprises, was recently in Bangladesh to discuss the deal with the country's telecom regulatory body, Bangladesh Telecommunications Regulatory Commission (BTRC). The clearance from BTRC will see Bharti picking up a 70 per cent in Warid for $300 million. As per the telecom laws in Bangladesh, BTRC will receive 5.5 per cent of the total deal amount.

While 30 per cent of the stake in Warid will be held by Abu Dhabi Group, Bharti is expected to invest over $1 billion in the Bangladesh teleco in the coming years. The Bharti-Warid deal is also expected to provide a strong fillip to investment and trade between India and Bangladesh.

Warid has operations in Uganda, Pakistan and Congo. Through the deal, Bharti has become the first Indian telecom operator to enter Bangladesh. It will compete against the state-run Teletalk, the Bangladesh-Singapore Joint Venture Citycell, Grameenphone which is a Bangladesh-Norway Joint Venture; and Japan-Malaysia Joint venture is AKTEL. Bharti's move to enter a foreign market had been long anticipated.

Bangladesh subscriber base has seen a significant jump, increasing from 2 lakh in 2001 to more than 50 million in 2009. the low telecom density, in a country with a population of the 150 million, promises to increase the subscriber base to 70 million by 2011.

Questions

- Discuss pros and cons in the Bharti-Warid deal.

Source: *Business India,* Jan., 24, 2010.

KEYWORDS

1. **Corporate Strategy:** It is the way in which corporate endeavours to differentiate itself positively from its competitors, using its relative strengths to better satisfy customer needs.
2. **SBU:** Strategic Business Unit is 'any part of a business organisation which is treated separately for strategic management purposes'.
3. **Strategic Financial Management:** It involves various aspects of financial planning. Financial planning is depending on two aspects i.e., (i) Liquidity Planning and (ii) Profit Planning.
4. **Strategy:** It is nothing but the determination of the basic long-term goals and objectives of an enterprise, and the adoption of courses of action and the allocation of resources necessary for carrying out these goals.

REVIEW QUESTIONS

1. Define 'Feasibility Study' and explain various types of feasibility study.
2. What do you understand by environmental diagnosis?
3. Examine the importance of competitive diagnosis.
4. Explain various stages of strategic development.
5. What are the various strategic alternatives available to a corporate entity?

REFERENCES

1. Ansof, H. Igor, *Corporate Strategy,* New York, McGraw-Hill, 1965.
2. Azhar Kazmi, *Business Policy and Srategic Management,* Tata McGraw-Hill, New Delhi, 2009.
3. Jakhotiya G.P., *Strategic Financial Management,* Vikas Publications, New Delhi, 2007
4. James C. Van Horne, *Financial Management and Policy,* Pearson, New Delhi, 2008.
5. Sridhar A.N., *Strategic Financial Management,* SPD, New Delhi, 2008.

ꕤ ꕤ ꕤ

CHAPTER

5

FINANCIAL RISK AND RETURN EVALUATION

CHAPTER OUTLINE

- Opening Caselet
- Risk
- Risk Return Trade-off
- Risk and Uncertainty
- Types of Risk
- Causes of Risk and Uncertainty
- Risk Adjusted Discount Rates
- Project's Impact on Corporate Risk
- Sensitivity Analysis
- Simulation Approach
- Scenario Analysis
- Practical Problems
- Sensitivity Analysis Problems
- Closing Caselet
- Summary
- Keywords
- Review Questions
- References

OPENING CASELET

The Ram & Co., is analysing two mutually exclusive proposals, each costing ₹ 30,00,000 and having a five-year expected life. Each project will have expected cash flows which will increase by ₹ 5,00,000, each year after the first year, and will not have any value after the fifth year. The first year possible net cash inflows for project-1 are ₹ 1,00,000, ₹ 1,40,000, ₹ 1,60,000 with associated probabilities of 25, 50 and 25. The first year possible net cash inflows for project-2 are ₹ 4,00,000, ₹ 1,20,000 and ₹ 2,50,000 with associated probabilities of 20, 50 and 30 project-1 is considered less risky and can be evaluated at 8 per cent, while project-2 is more risky and can be evaluated at 10 per cent rate of discount. Which project should be chosen?

RISK

Risk is inherent in almost every business decision. It is vital in Capital Budgeting decisions as they involve costs and benefits extending over a long period of time during which many things can change in unanticipated ways. For the sake of expository convenience, we assumed so far that all investments being considered for inclusion in the capital budget had the same risk as those of the existing investments of the firm. Hence, the average cost of capital was used for evaluating every project. Investment proposals, however, differ in risk. A research and development project may be more risky than an expansion project and the latter tends to be more risky than a replacement project. In view of such differences, variations in risk need to be evaluated explicitly in capital investment appraisal. Risk analysis is one of the most complex and slippery aspects of capital budgeting. Many different techniques have been suggested and no single technique can be deemed as best in all situations.

Sources of Risk

The first step in risk analysis is to uncover the major factors that contribute to the risk of the investment. Four main factors that contribute to the variability of results of a particular investment are cost of project, reinvestment of cash flows, variability of cash flows and the life of the project.

(a) Size of the Investment: A large project involving greater investments entails more risk than the small project because in case of failure of the large project the company will have to suffer considerably greater loss and it may be forced to liquidation. Furthermore, cost of a project in many cases is known in advance. There is always the chance that the actual cost will vary from the original estimate. One can never foresee exactly what the construction, debugging, design and developmental costs will be. Rather than being satisfied with a single estimate it seems more realistic to MBA-Finance Strategic specify a range of costs and the probability of occurrence of each value within the range. The less confidence the decision-maker has in his estimates, the wider will be the range.

(b) **Re-investment of Cash Flows:** Whether a company should accept a project that offers a 20 per cent return for 2 years or one that offers 16 per cent return for 3 years would depend upon the rate of return available for reinvesting the proceeds from the 20 per cent 2-year period. The danger that the company will not be able to return funds as they become available is a continuing risk in managing fixed assets and cash flows.

(c) **Variability of Cash Flows:** It may not be an easy job to forecast the likely returns from a project. Instead of basing investment decision on a single estimate of cash flow it would be desirable to have range of estimates.

(d) **Life of the Project:** Life of a project can never be determined precisely. The production manager should base the investment decision on the range of life of the project.

RISK RETURN TRADE-OFF

In capital budgeting decisions, a project's risk can be looked at three levels. First, there is the standing alone risk, which is a project's risk ignoring the fact that much of this risk will diversified away as the project is combined with the firm's other projects and assets. Besides this, there is a conflict between long and short-term financing. Short-term financing is less expensive than long-term financing, but, at the same time, short-term financing involves greater risk than long-term financing. The choice between long and short-term financing involves a trade-off between risk and return.

The relative liquidity of the firm's assets structure is measured by current assets to fixed assets (or current assets to total assets) ratio. The greater this ratio, the less risky as well as less profitable will be the firm and *vice versa.* Similarly the relative liquidity of the firm's financial structure can be measured by the short-term financing to total financing ratio. The lower this ratio, the less risky as well as profitable will be the firm and vice-versa. In shaping its working capital policy, the firm should keep in mind these two dimensions-relative asset liquidity (level of current assets) and relative financing liquidity (level of short-term financing (or low level of short-term financing). Such policy will be will not be risky at all but would be less profitable. An aggressive firm, on the other hand, would combine low level of current assets with a low level of long-term financing (or high level of short-term financing). This firm will have high profitability and high risk. In fact the firm may follow a conservative financing policy to counter its relatively liquid assets structure in practice. (See Graph 5.1 and 5.2)

Graph 5.1: Risk Return Trade-off

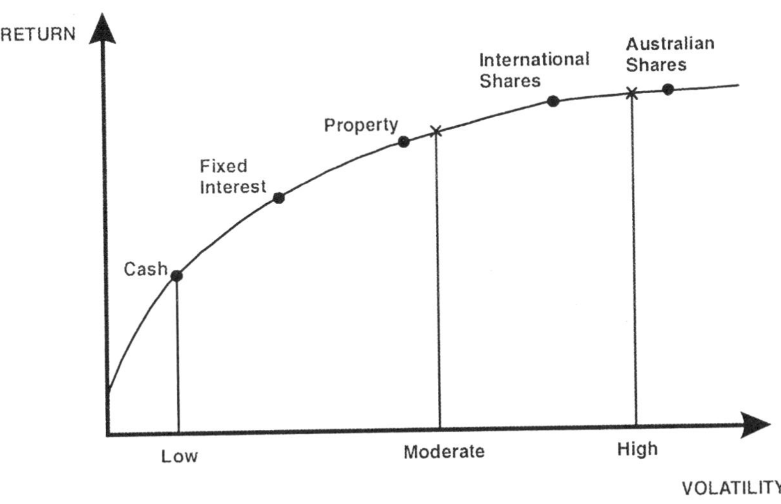

Risk Return Anlysis of Investment Avenues

Type of Asset	Exp. R of R*	Risk Level
1. Bank accounts	2.5-3%	No risk of deposit loss. Inflation risk.
2. Money market deposit accounts	3.5-4%	No risk of deposit loss. Rates geared to inflation.
3. Money market funds	4.5-5%	Very little. Rates vary with inflation.
4. Special 6-month certificates	5%	Early withdrawals subject to penalty. Rates geared to expected inflation.
5. High quality corporate bonds	8-8.25%	Very little if held to maturity. Rate geared to expected long run inflation rate.
6. Diversified portfolios	9%	Moderate to substantial. In any one year, the actual return could be negative. Diversified portfolios have at times lost 25% or more of their actual value.
7. Diversified portfolios of risky stocks such as aggressive growth mutual funds.	9-10%	Substantial. Diversified portfolios have at times lost 50% or more of their actual value.
8. Real estate	Similar to common stocks	Cannot be sold quickly. Hard to diversify. Good inflation hedge if bought at reasonable price levels for long-term investors.
9. Gold	Unpredictable	Substantial. Believed to be a hedge against hyperinflation. Can help to balance a diversified portfolio.

*Expected Rate of Return

Graph 5.2: Risk Return Comparison

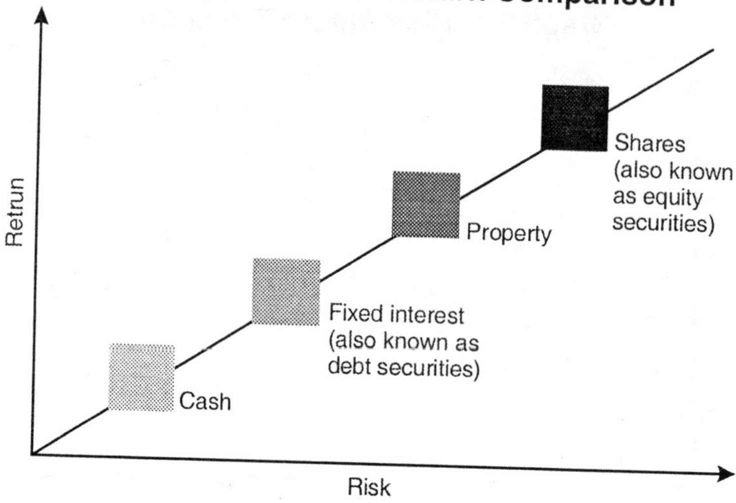

RISK AND UNCERTAINTY

Risk refers to the set of unique consequences for a given decision which can be assigned probabilities, while uncertainty implies that it is not fully possibly to identify outcomes or to assign probabilities. Perhaps the worst forms of uncertainty are the unknown unknowns-outcomes from events that we did not even consider. The most obvious example of risk is the one in six chance of obtaining a six from a sing die. For most investment decisions, however, empirical experience is hard to find. Managers are then forced to estimate probabilities where objective statistical evidence is not available. A manager with little prior experience of launching a particular product in a new market can still subjectively assess the risks involved based on the information available to him or her. Because subjective probabilities may be applied to investment decisions in a manner similar to objective probabilities, the distinction between risk and uncertainty is not critical in practice, and the two terms are often used interchangeably.

Risk — postulates that the decision maker is aware of all possible future states of the economy, business and so on, which may occur and thereby affect relevant decision parameters and is able to place a probability on the value of occurrence of each of these states. Uncertainty — postulates that the decision maker may or may not be aware of all the possible states that affect the decision and may or may not be able to place a probability distribution on the occurrence of each. The classical distinction between risk and uncertainty is that an element or analysis involves risk of the probabilities of the alternative, possible outcomes are known, while it is characterized by uncertainty if the frequency distribution of the possible outcomes is not known.

TYPES OF RISKS

1. **Business Risk:** The variability in operating cash flows or profits before interest. A firm's business risk depends, in large measure, on the underlying economic environment within which it operates. But variability in operating cash flows can be heavily affected by the cost structure of the business, often termed as operating gearing.

2. **Financial Risk:** This is the risk, over and above business risk, which results from the use of debt capital. Financial gearing is increased by issuing more debt, thereby incurring more fixed-interest charges and increasing the variability is net earnings.

3. **Portfolio or Market Risk:** The variability in shareholders' returns. Investors can significantly reduce their variability in earnings by holding carefully selected investment portfolios. This is sometimes called 'relevant risk', because only this element of risk should be considered by a well-diversified shareholder.

CAUSES FOR RISK AND UNCERTAINTY

1. Insufficient number of similar investments.
2. Bias in the data and its assessment.
3. Changing external environment, invalidating past experience.
4. Misinterpretation of data.
5. Errors of analysis.
6. Managerial talent availability and emphasis.
7. Salvageabilty of investment.
8. Obsolescence of plant and machinery.

RISK ADJUSTED DISCOUNT RATES

A finance manager being risk averter when given choice between two projects promising the same rate of return but different in risk would prefer the one with the least perceived risk. He will require compensation for bearing risk so that overall value of the company remains unaffected by assumption of the risky project. There are several methods of adjusting risk in investment decisions, which can be classified broadly in two groups, *viz.*, formal and informal methods.

Formal Method

Among the formal methods of adjusting risk in capital budgeting decisions, the most popular ones are:

1. Risk Adjusted Discount Rates
   (a) Risk Adjusted Net Present Value (NPV)
   (b) Risk Adjusted Internal Rate of Return (IRR)
   (c) Modified IRR
2. Certainty Equivalent Approach
3. Probability Distribution
4. Decision Tree Approach

1. (a) Risk Adjusted Net Present Value (NPV): Risk is an important element in virtually all investment decisions. Because most people in business are risk-averse, preferring less risk to more, the identification, measurement and where possible, reduction of risk should be a central feature in the decision-making process. The NPV formula can be adjusted to consider risk. Adjustment of the cash flows is achieved by the Certainty Equivalent (CE) method. The risk adjusted discount rate increases the risk-premium for higher-risk projects.

(b) Risk Adjusted Internal Rate of Return (IRR): The IRR is the discount rate which equates the aggregate present value of CFAT (Cash flows After Taxes) with the aggregate present value of cash outflows of a project. The project will be accepted only if IRR exceeds the required rate of return.The following steps are taken in determining IRR when CFAT is annuity:

1. Determine the payback period of the proposed investment.
2. Present Value factor of annuity (see in Present Value tables)
3. Find P.V. factor or discount factor using above data.
4. Use IRR formula to find actual rate of interest where NPV is equal to zero.

(c) Modified Internal Rate of Return (MIRR): MIRR is that rate of return, which, when the initial outlay is compared with the terminal value of project's net cash flows reinvested at the cost of capital, gives an NPV of Zero. This involves a two-stage process:

1. Calculate the terminal value of the project by compounding forward all interim cash flows at the cost of capital to the end of project.
2. Find that rate of interest which equates the terminal value with the initial cost.

2. Certainty Equivalent Approach: While using the certainty equivalent approach, the risk-free discount rate may be easily approximated (may be, for instance, by the interest rate on government bonds) but difficulties may arise in determining the trade-off between risk and return for the purpose of converting a particular distribution of NPV into its certainty equivalent. Under this method, adjusting cash inflows rather than adjusting the discount rate compensates risk element. The expected uncertain cash flow of each year are modified by multiplying them with what is known as 'certainty equivalent coefficient' (CEO) to remove the element of uncertainty. This coefficient is determined by management's preferences with respect to risk. For example, assume that the expected cash flow from an investment at the end of the first year is ₹ 10,000 and that the management ranked this investment on par with another alternative investment with a certain cash flow of ₹ 7,000, then ₹ 7,000 is certainty equivalent of the risky cash flows of ₹ 10,000. the ratio 7,000/10,000 = 0.7 is called the certainty equivalent coefficient for the period. The value of certainty equivalent coefficient usually ranges between 0 and 1. A value of 1 implies that the cash flow is certain or the management is risk-neutral. In industrial situations, however, cash flows are generally uncertain and managements usually risk-averse. Hence, the certainty equivalent coefficients are typically less than 1.

The certainty equivalent method is conceptually superior to the risk-adjusted discount rate method because it does not assume that risk increase with time at a constant rate. Each year's certainty equivalent coefficient is based on the level or risk characterizing its cash flow. Despite its conceptual soundness it is not as popular as the risk-adjusted rate method. This is perhaps because it is inconvenient and difficult to specify a series of certainty equivalent coefficients but seemingly simple to adjust the discount rate. Notwithstanding this practical difficulty, the merits of the certainty equivalent method must not be ignored. The certainty equivalent approach can be summarized as follows:

Step 1: Risk is removed from the cash flows by substituting certainty equivalent cash flow for the risky cash flows. If the equivalent coefficient **(_t)** is given, this is done by multiplying each risky cash flow by the appropriate **_t** value.

Step 2: The riskless cash flows are then discounted back to the present at the riskless rate of interest.

Step 3: The normal capital budgeting criteria are then applied, except in the case of the internal rate of return criterion, where the project's internal rate of return is compared with the risk-free rate of interest rather than the firm's required rate of return.

Informal Method

This is the most common method of adjusting risk. The finance manager recognizes that some projects are more riskier than others. He also finds that riskier projects would yield more than what risk free or less risky projects promise. To choose a project carrying greater risk as against the less risky one, the finance manager decides on subjective basis (by using his discretion), the margin of difference in rate of return of both types of projects. The manner of fixing the standard is strictly internal known to the finance manager himself and is not specified. The use of the risk-adjusted discount rates is on the notion that the investors expect higher returns for more risky projects.

Statistical Distribution Approach

In this approach, the degree of risk associated with a project is sought to be measured in terms of the variance (or standard deviation) of the NPV distribution, and the investment decisions are taken considering the expected (mean) value, and its standard deviation, of the net present value distribution. This information about the project risk may also be usefully employed for calculating certainty-equivalent for the uncertain returns from the investment proposal, as also it is a major factor in calculating the size of the risk-adjusted discount rate to use. The derivation of the probabilistic information about investment proposals owes its origin to the work of Frederick Hillier. In this method of considering risky investment proposals, the net cash flow from an investment in each period is viewed as a random variable which can assume any one of the possible values. The method requires that probability distribution of cash flows for each of the years be obtained and considered. Using the cash-flow distribution, the expected value of the NPV distribution and its variance are calculated in the first instance.

Variance of NPV

In the discussion on the variance of the NPV distribution, Hillier has given an analysis of three cases. In the first case, the cash flows between different periods are assumed to be independent of one another. This is to say; the cash flows of one period are not related to the cash flows of another period. In the second case, the cash flows between different periods are assumed to be perfectly correlated. The third case deals with the mixed situation in which a part of the flows are perfectly correlated and part are independent. Obviously, when we consider more than two periods of time, the cash flows cannot all be perfectly negatively correlated with each other. This explains why Hillier's analysis is restricted to the case of positive correlation. Now, we consider the three cases in turn:

(a) **Independent Net Cash Flows:** When net cash flows for the various years are independent of each other, then the calculation of the variance of the distribution of cash flow becomes a difficult tasks. This is because independence substantially increases the number of possible outcomes. To illustrate, suppose a project has a life of 3 years and in each of the years, there are four cash flow values possible with some given probabilities. Under the assumption of independence, a total of $4 \times 4 \times 4 = 64$ combinations are possible. The probability of occurrence of each of the combination is given by the product of the probabilities of the particular cash flow values of different years entering into that combination. For this probability distribution, we can find the present values of each of the possible cash flow streams (64 in our example) and determine the expected value and the variance of present values in the usual way.

(b) **Perfectly Correlated Cash Flows:** The assumption of perfect correlation between the cash flows of the successive years implies, technically, that if random factors cause a cash flow Cj (for the jth year) to deviate from its mean value by a standard deviations, the same factors will cause the cash flow Ck (for the kth year) to deviate from its own mean in the same direction by a standard deviations.

(c) **Mixed Case:** There are very few investments for which the net cash flows are either completely independent or perfectly correlated. Closer to the reality is the 'mixed' case in cash flows is partially dependent and partially independent. To understand this situation, consider a very simple case where a company is contemplating to introduce a new product, whose life is expected to be only three years. The market acceptance of the product may be unsatisfactory, satisfactory, or excellent. How the product will be accepted in the first year will determine how it will be accepted in the second years. In this respect, it is case of dependence. Also, the product sales are influenced by general economic conditions, which may be poor, good, or excellent. However, economic conditions in one year do not affect the economic conditions in the next year. From this standpoint, it is a case of independence. For the mixed case as well, all possible combinations of the cash flows are obtained and their joint probabilities calculated. The present value of each of the cash flow streams is then calculated and we can get the mean and the standard deviation as usual.

Once the expected net present value and its standard deviation (from variance) value are obtained, the riskiness of the project can be measured. The standard deviation is a measure of absolute amount of risk associated with a given project. While it is a useful measure for the purpose of risk evaluation, it is not suitable when comparative riskiness of the projects is to be considered. In order to compare the various projects, we should compute their respective coefficients of variation.

PROJECT'S IMPACT ON CORPORATE RISK

(i) **Sensitivity Analysis:** It is aimed to identify the impact on Net Present Value (NPV) of changes to key assumptions. Sensitivity analysis provides the decision maker with answers to a whole range of 'what if' questions. For example, what is the NPV, if selling prices rises by 15 per cent? Or what is the level of sales revenues required to break-even in net present value terms?

(ii) **Scenario Analysis:** While Sensitivity analysis only considers the effects of changes in key variables one at a time. Scenario analysis seeks to establish 'worst' and 'best' scenarios so that the whole range of possible outcomes can be considered.

(iii) **Simulation:** Simulation is a more sophisticated approach, which captures the essential characteristics of the investment which are subject to uncertainty.

SENSITIVITY ANALYSIS

In the evaluation of an investment project, we work with the forecasts of cash flows. orecasted cash flow depends on the expected revenue and costs. Further, expected revenue a function of sales volume and unit selling price. Similarly, sales volume depends on the market size and the firm's market share. Costs include variable costs, which depend on sales volume and unit variable cost and fixed costs. Costs include variable costs, which depend on sale volume, and unit variable cost and fixed cost. The net present value or the internal rate of return of a project is determined by analyzing the after-tax cash flows arrived at by combining forecasts of various variables. It is difficult to arrive at an accurate and unbiased forecast of each variable. We can't be certain about the outcome of any of these variables. The reliability of the NPV or Internal Rate of Return (IRR), we can work out how much difference it makes if any of these forecasts goes wrong. We can change each of the forecast, on at a time, to atleast three values: Pessimistic, Expected, and Optimistic. The NPV of the project is recalculated under these different assumptions. This method of recalculating NPV or IRR by changing each forecast is called **'Sensitivity analysis'.**

Sensitivity Analysis is a way of analyzing change in the project's NPV (or IRR) for a given change in one of the variables. It indicates how sensitive a project's NPV (or IRR) is to changes in particular variables. The more sensitive the NPV, the more critical is the variable. The following three steps are involved in the use of sensitivity analysis:

- Identification of all those variables, which have an influence on the project's NPV (or IRR).
- Definition of the underlying (mathematical) relationship between the variables.
- Analysis of the impact of the change in each of the variables on the project's NPV.

The decision maker, while performing sensitivity analysis, computes the project's NPV (or IRR) for each forecast under three assumptions:

(a) pessimistic, (b) expected, and (c) optimistic. It allows him to ask 'what if'questions. For example, what (is the NPV) if the volume increases or decreases? What (is the NPV) if variable cost or fixed cost increases or decreases? What (is the NPV) if the selling price increases or decreases? What (is the NPV) if the project is delayed or outlay escalates or the project's life is more or less than anticipated? A whole range of question can be answered with the help of sensitivity analysis. It examines the sensitivity of the variables underlying the computation of NPV or IRR, rather than attempting to quantify risk. It can be applied to any variable, which is an input for the after-tax cash flows.

Let us consider an example.

Example:

A company is considering an investment proposal to install new milling controls at a cost of ₹ 50,000. The facility has a life expectancy of 5 yrs and no salvage value. The tax rate is 35 per cent. Assume the firm uses straight line depreciation and the same is allowed for tax purposes. The estimated Cash Flows before Depreciation and Tax (CFBDT) from the investment proposal are as follows:

Year	CFBDT (₹)
1	10,000
2	10,692
3	12,769
4	13,462
5	20,385

Compute the following:

(1) Payback period

(2) Average rate of return,

(3) Internal rate of return,

(4) Net present value at 10 per cent discount rate,

(5) Profitability index at 10 per cent discount rate.

Solution:

Year	CFBDT (₹)	Depreciation (₹ 50,000/5)	PBT (2 – 3) (₹)	Taxes (0.35) (₹)	EAT (4 – 5) (₹)	CFAT (6 + 3) (₹)
1	2	3	4	5	6	7
1	10,000	10,000	Nil	Nil	Nil	10,000
2	10,692	10,000	692	242	450	10,450
3	12,769	10,000	2,769	969	1,800	11,800
4	13,462	10,000	3,462	1,212	2,250	12,250
5	20,385	10,000	10,385	3,635	6,750	16,750
					11,250	61,250

1. Payback period:

Year	CFAT (₹)	Cumulative CFAT (₹)
1	10,000	10,000
2	10,450	20,450
3	11,800	32,250
4	12,250	44,500
5	16,750	61,250

The recovery of the investment falls between the 4th and 5th years. Therefore, the PB is 4 years plus a fraction of the 5th year. The fractional value = ₹ 5,500/₹ 16,750 = 0.328. Thus, the PB is 4.328 years.

2. Average Rate of Return (ARR) = $\frac{\text{Average income}}{\text{Average investment}} \times 100$

$$= \frac{₹12{,}250 \times 100}{₹25{,}000} = 9 \text{ per cent}$$

3. Internal Rate of Return (IRR)

$$₹50{,}000 = \frac{₹10{,}000}{(1+r)1} + \frac{₹10{,}450}{(1+r)2} + \frac{₹11{,}800}{(1+r)3} + \frac{₹12{,}250}{(1+r)4} + \frac{₹16{,}750}{(1+r)5}$$

The fake payback period = 4.0816 (₹ 50,000/₹ 12,250). From table below, the value closest to the fake payback period of 4.0816 against 5 years is 4.100 against 7 per cent since the actual cash flow stream in the initial years is slightly below the average cash flow string the IRR is likely to be lower than 7 per cent. Let us try with 6 per cent.

Year	CFAT	PV Factor		Total PV (₹)	
	(₹)	(0.06)	(0.07)	(0.06)	(0.07)
1	10,000	0.943	0.935	9,430	9,350
2	10,450	0.890	0.873	9,300	9,123
3	11,800	0.840	0.816	9,912	9,629
4	12,250	0.792	0.763	9,702	9,347
5	16,750	0.747	0.713	12,512	11,942
Total PV				50,856	49,391
Less: Initial Outlay				50,000	50,000
NPV				+ 856	– 609

IRR = 6+ [NPV@6%/NPV@6% – PV@7%] (7 – 6)

The IRR is between 6 and 7 per cent. By interpolation, IRR = 6.6 per cent.

4. NPV

Year	CFAT (₹)	PV Factor (0.10)	Total PV (₹)
1	10,000	0.909	9,090
2	10,450	0.826	8,632
3	11,800	0.751	8,862
4	12,250	0.663	8,367

5	16,750	0.621	10,401
Total PV			45,352
Less: Initial Outlay			50,000
NPV			4,468

5. Profitability Index (PI) $= \dfrac{\text{PV of Cash inflows}}{\text{PV of Cash outflows}} = \dfrac{₹\,45,352}{₹\,50,000} = 0.907$

SIMULATION APPROACH

David B.Hertz was the first authority that proposed the use of the simulation approach to secure the expected return and dispersion on this expected return for an investment proposal. He took an example of medium size industrial chemical company, which was contemplating a $ 10 million extension to its processing plant. The estimated service life of the facility was 10 years, the engineers expected to be able to utilise 2,50,000 tons of proceed material worth $510 per ton at an average processing cost of 435 per ton. The company was interested to know the return likely to be fetched by the project and the risks involved in it. In order to undertake risk analysis Hertz isolated nine basic economic values, *viz.*, market size, selling price, market growth rate, share of market, initial cost of investment residual value of investment after taxes, useful life of facilities, operating costs and fixed costs. The first four variables were categorised under the heading of market analysis, the next two were grouped under the category investment cost analysis and the last three variables were regarded as part of operating costs. After identifying the nine factors, probability distribution were assigned to each of these factors on the basis of the management's assessment of the probable outcomes so as to know the possible range of values for each factor, the average and some ideas as to the likelihood that the variable possible values will be repeated.

The next step followed by Hertz was to determine the returns that will result from random combination of factors involved. For this purpose, simulation trials were undertaken with the help of computer. To show how this trial was made, he took the following example. Suppose we have a wheel, as in roulette, with the numbers from 0-15 representing one price for the product or material, the numbers 16 to 30 representing a second price, the numbers 31 to 45 a third price, and so on. For each of these segments one would have a different range of expected market volumes: e.g., $150,000 – $200,000 for the first, $100,000 - $150,000 for the second, $75,000 – $100,000 for the third and so forth. Now suppose that we spin the wheel and the ball falls in 37. This would mean that we pick a sales volume in the $75,000 – $100,000 range. If the ball goes in 11, we have a different price and we turn to the $ 150,000 – $200,000 range for a sales volume. Fortunately, this type of operation can be carried out on computer in a much more efficient manner. Simulation trials will have to be undertaken for the other eight variables.

When trial values for market variables and operating and fixed costs are combined, we shall be able to calculate the annual earnings. If these trail values are combined with trial values for the required investment, the useful life and the residual value of the project, we shall have sufficient information to compute the return on investment for that trial run. In this way the computer simulates trial values for each of the nine factors and then computes the return on investment based upon the values simulated. The above process is repeated a number of times and each time we shall get a combination of values for the nine factors and the returns on investment for the combination. When the trial is repeated times without number, the rates of return can be presented in the form of frequency distribution, on the basis of which an expected return, standard deviation and coefficient of variation can be calculated. By comparing the probability distribution of rates of return for one proposed with that of the other, the management can evaluate the respective merits of different risky investments. Thus, simulation method allows the management to discriminate between measures of expected return based on weighted probabilities of all possible returns, variability of return and risks.

In considering risky investments, we can also use simulation to approximate the expected value of net present value, the expected value of internal rate of return, or the expected value of profitability index and the dispersion about the expected value. By simulation we mean testing the possible results of an investment proposal before it is accepted. The testing itself is based on a model coupled with probabilistic information. Probability distributions are assigned to each of these factors based on management's assessment of the probable outcomes. Thus, the possible outcomes are charted for each factor according to their probability of occurrence. Once the probability distributions are determined, the next step is to determine the internal rate of return (or net present value calculated at the risk-free rate) that will result from a random combination of the nine factors just listed.

Steps in Simulation Approach

1. List all the basic economic variables that will affect the outcome of the decision.
2. Estimate the range of variables for each of these variables that are subject to uncertainty.
3. State in equation from the economic or accounting relationships that connect the basic variables to the final outcome on which the decision will be based.
4. With the aid of computer randomly select a specific value for each basic variable according to the chances this value has of actually turning up in the future. Given these specific values, use the equation in step 3 to calculate the resulting outcome.
5. Repeat this process to define and evaluate the probability of the occurrence of each possible rate of return. Since there are literally millions of possible combinations of values, we need to test the likelihood that various specific returns on the investment will occur.

SCENARIO ANALYSIS

The simple sensitivity analysis assumes that the variables are independent. In practice, the variables will be interrelated. One way out is to analyse the impact of alternative combinations of variables. The decision-maker can develop some plausible scenarios. For example, it may be possible to increase volume to 12,50,000 units (25 per cent increase) if the company reduces unit selling price to ₹ 13.50 (10 per cent reduction), resorts to aggressive advertisement campaign, thereby increasing unit variable cost to ₹ 7.10 (5 per cent increase) and fixed cost to ₹ 44,00,000 (10 per cent increase). The following table shows that this scenario generates a positive NPV of ₹ 27,01,000. More plausible scenarios could be thought out and analysed to arrive at a final judgment about the project.

Scenario Analysis

Variables	Actual	Expected Scenario Assumptions
1. Volume (units '000)	1,000	1,250
2. Price (₹)	15.0	13.5
3. Unit variable cost (₹)	6.75	7.1
4. Fixed cost (₹ '000)	4,000	4,400
5. NPV (₹ '000)	4,829	2,901

NPV calculation for scenario:

$$NPV = ((1250\,(13.5 - 7.1) - 4400)\ 0.65 \times 4.5638 + 2{,}222) - 10{,}000$$

$$= 10{,}679 + 2{,}222 - 10{,}000 = 2{,}901$$

PRACTICAL PROBLEMS

1. The financial manager of a Food processing company is considering the installation of a plant costing ₹ 1 crore to increase its processing capacity. The expected values of the underlying variables are given in the following tables provides the project's after-tax cash flows over its expected life of 7 years. Depreciation will be 20 per cent on written down value. Cost of capital is 12 per cent and tax of the company is 35 per cent. The capacity of the machine 2000 units annually. Each unit sales value ₹ 15,000/-. Variable cost per unit is ₹ 3,000 and annual fixed costs are ₹ 15 lakhs.

Year	**1**	**2**	**3**	**4**	**5**	**6**	**7**
Capacity utilisation	60	60	75	80	100	100	80
Sales promotion expenses (₹ in lakhs)	20	20	15	15	15	15	15

2. Find the return, sample mean and sample variance for the Copper price in percentage for each year:

Year	Copper price Cents per Pound
1	49.65
2	49.85
3	49.70
4	51.25
5	51.10
6	53.30
7	54.20
8	55.10
9	54.90
10	55.65

Hint: R (t) = {Price (t + 1)/Price t} – 1

3. Calculate standard deviation and expected return.

Returns	Probability
20	0.15
21	0.20
22	0.50
23	0.10
24	0.05

4. Andhra Sugars had acquired 5 years ago a machine for ₹ 3,00,000. The current net salvage value of machine is ₹ 60,000, it is expected to last another 3 years and provide net cash inflows of ₹ 70,000, ₹ 6,000 and ₹ 50,000. The salvage value of the machine after 3 years is estimated as ₹ 40,000. A technologically superior design is available now. The new machine will cost ₹ 4,00,000 and have a life of 5 years. It will provide annual net cash inflows of ₹ 1,50,000, ₹ 1,30,000, ₹ 1,20,000, ₹ 1,00,000 and ₹ 80,000. It is also expected that the new machine will have a net salvage value of ₹ 20,000 after 5 years. The required rate of return is 10 per cent. Should the firm replace of machine now or after three years?

5. Bright company is considering a project which has an estimated site 4 years. The cost of the project is ₹ 10,000 and the possible cash flows are given below: The cash flows of various years are independent and the risk-free discount rate (Post-Tax) is 6 per cent required.

   (a) What is the net present value?

   (b) If the NPV is approximately normally distributed, what is the probability that NPV will be zero or less?

   (c) What is the probability the NPV will exceed ₹ 10,000?

   (d) What is the probability that profitability index will be greater than 1.2?

Year 1		Year 2		Year 3		Year 4	
Cash Flow	Probability	Cash Flow	Probability	Cash Flow	Probability	Cash Flow	Probability
2,000	.2	3,000	.4	4,000	.3	2,000	.2
3,000	.5	4,000	.3	5,000	.5	3,000	.4
4,000	.3	5,000	.3	6,000	.2	4,000	.4

6. A company is considering the following investment projects.

Cash Flows (₹)

Projects	CO	C1	C2	C3
A	10000	+10000		
B	10000	+7500	+7500	
C	10000	+2000	+4000	+12000
D	10000	+10000	+3000	+3000

Rank the projects according to payback. ARR assumes discount rates of 10 per cent and 30 per cent. If the projects are independent, which one should be accepted? If the projects are mutually exclusive, which is the best project.

7. Data relating to three investment projects are given below:

	A	B	C
Investment	₹ 30,000	₹ 20,000	₹ 50,000
Useful life	10 Yrs	4 Yrs	20 Yrs
Annual cash savings	₹ 6,207	₹ 7,725	₹ 9,341

Rank the projects according to their attractiveness using the:

(a) Payback period.

(b) IRR

(c) NPV using 14 per cent cost of capital.

8. A company is considering two mutually exclusive projects, namely X and Y each involving a cost of ₹ 30,000. The expected life of the projects is 5 years for which the cash flows after tax (CFAT) are given below:

Decide which project should be selected by computing.

(i) Net Present Value, and

(ii) Internal Rate of Return.

Year	Project 'X' (₹)	Project 'Y' (₹)
1	10,000	5,000
2	10,000	5,000
3	10,000	10,000
4	10,000	20,000
5	10,000	10,000

The required rate of return of the company is 15%.

9. XYZ Ltd. wants to purchase a plant for its expanding operations. The desired plant is available at ₹ 10 lakhs. The expected earnings before depreciation and taxes (EBDT) during its 5 years economic useful life are as shown in table

Year	EBDT (₹)
1	3,50,000
2	3,80,000
3	4,00,000
4	3,25,000
5	2,50,000

The rate of inflation during the period is expected to be 8 per cent and the stated EBDT are also expected to grow at this rate of inflation. The management policy of the firm is to evaluate its capital budgeting proposal by using cost of capital in real terms at 10 per cent.

10. S.L. and Company has ₹ 2,00,000 to invest. The following proposals are under consideration. The cost of capital for the company is estimated to be 15 per cent.

Project	Initial Outlay (₹)	Annual Cash flow (₹)	Life of the Project
A	1,00,000	25,000	10
B	70,000	20,000	8
C	30,000	6,000	20
D	50,000	15,000	10
E	50,000	12,000	20

Rank the projects on the basis of: (a) NPV method, (b) profitability index method and (c) post payback profitability method. Present value of annuity ₹ 1 received in steady stream discounted at 15 per cent.

8 years	4.6586
10 years	5.1790
20 years	6.3345.

11. A company is considering the proposal of buying one of the two machines for the production of a new product. Each machine requires an initial investment of ₹ 50,000 and is expected to have an useful life of 4 years. Both the sellers have guaranteed that after the expiry of the useful life, they will buy back the machines at ₹ 5,000. The management of the company uses certainity equivalent approach to evaluate risky investments. The company's risk adjusted discount rate is 16 per cent and the risk-free rate is 10 per cent. The expected values of net cash flows (CFAT) with their respective Certainty Equivalents (CE) are:

Year	Machine A CFAT (₹)	CE	Machine B CFAT (₹)	CE
1	30,000	0.8	18,000	0.9
2	30,000	0.7	36,000	0.8
3	30,000	0.6	24,000	0.7
4	30,000	0.5	32,000	0.4

Which machine should be purchased by the company?

12. Standard Pharma is considering an investment in a formulation that requires an initial investment of ₹ 2,40,000 with a projected after-tax cash inflow generated over the next 3 years as follows:

Annual cash flow	Probability of cash flow year		
(₹)	1	2	3
40,000	0.10	0.20	0.30
80,000	0.30	0.40	0.40
1,20,000	0.20	0.30	0.10
1,60,000	0.40	0.10	0.20

Assume that probability distributions are independent and the after tax risk-free rate is 6 per cent. Calculate:

(a) The expected NPV of the project.

(b) Standard deviation of the expected NPV.

(c) The probability that the NPV will be zero or less.

(d) The probability that the NPV will be greater than zero, and

(e) The probability that the NPV will be greater than the expected value.

13. The Desert Products Ltd. is considering six investment proposals of similar risk, for which the funds available are limited. The projects are independent and have the following initial investment and present values of cash inflows associated with them:

Project	Investment	PV
A	6,00,000	8,40,000
B	3,20,000	4,80,000
C	2,00,000	3,00,000
D	1,60,000	2,56,000
E	80,000	1,40,000
F	40,000	76,000

(a) Compute the profitability index and NPV for each project.

(b) Under capital rationing which projects should be selected, assuming a total budget of ₹ 10,00,000/-.

(c) Which projects should be selected if the total budget is ₹ 6,00,000/-?

14. The Ram & Co. is analysing two mutually exclusive proposals, each costing ₹ 30,00,000 and having a five-year expected life. Each project will have expected cash flows which will increase by ₹ 5,00,000, each year after the first year, and will not have any value after the fifth year. The first year possible net cash inflows for project-1 are ₹ 1,00,000, ₹ 1,40,000, ₹ 160,000 with associated probabilities of 25, 50 and 25. the first year possible net cash inflows for project-2 are ₹ 4,00,000, ₹ 120,000 and ₹ 2,50,000 with associated probabilities of 20, 50 and 30 project-1 is considered less risky and can be evaluated at 8 per cent, while project-2 is more risky and can be evaluated at 10 per cent rate of discount. Which project should be chosen?

15. Determine the Risk Adjusted Net Present Value of the following projects:

	A	B	C
Net cash outlays (₹)	1,00,000	1,20,000	2,10,000
Project life (years)	5	5	5
Annual cash inflow (₹)	30,000	42,000	70,000
Coefficient of Variation	0.4	0.8	1.2

The company selects the risk adjusted rate of discount on the basis of the Coefficient of Variation:

Cefficient of Variation	Risk adjusted rate of discount	Present value factor 1 to 5 year at risk adjusted rate of discount
0.0	10%	3.791
0.4	12%	3.605
0.8	14%	3.433
1.2	16%	3.274
1.6	18%	3.127
2.0	22%	2.864
More than 20	25%	2.689

SENSITIVITY ANALYSIS PROBLEMS

16. X Ltd., is considering a project with the following cash flows: (₹)

Year	Purchase of Plant	Running Cost	Savings
0	-7000		
1		2,000	6,000
2		2,500	7,000

The cost of capital is 8 per cent. Measure the sensitivity of the project to changes in the plant value, running costs, and savings (considering one factor at a time) such that net present values becomes zero. Which factor is most sensitive to affect the acceptability of the project?

17. The following forecast are made about a proposal which is being evaluated by a firm.

Initial Outlay ₹ 12,000 — Cash Inflows ₹ 4,500 (Annual)

Life 4 years — Ke 14%

PVAF(14% 4y) =2.9137 — PVAF(14% 3y) =2.3216

Analyze the sensitivity of different variables with respect to the NPV.

18. MN Integrated Ltd., is considering a proposal for which the following relevant information is provided:

Cost of the project ₹ 30,000

Life of the project 5 years

Annual Sales at ₹ 30/- each 1,400 uints

Variable cost per unit ₹ 20/-

Fixed Cost ₹ 3,000/-

Depreciation ₹ 2,000/-

It is estimated that following variables may take the values given hereunder for different economic situations:

	Pessimistic	Optimistic
No. of units sold	800	1800
Selling price	₹ 20	₹ 20
Variable cost per unit	₹ 15	₹ 4

Given the tax rate 50 per cent and cost of capital 10 per cent, analyse the sensitivity of the NPV of the proposal with respect to

(1) Number of Units Sold.

(2) Selling Price, and

(3) Variable Cost Per Unit.

CLOSING CASELET

* From the following table, find the expected net present value using scenario analysis. The situations are assumed based on present trend in the market.

Variables	Actual	Scenario assumptions			
		Option 1	Option 2	Option 3	Option 4
Sales volume units	10000	10% increase	20% increase	15% decrease	25% decrease
Selling price	₹ 70	5% decrease	10% decrease	10% increase	15% increase
Variable cost per unit	₹ 40	12% increase	14% increase	10% decrease	15% decrease
Fixed cost	4000	5000	3500	4500	5500

You are required to calculate:

1. Expected sales
2. Break even point
3. Profit at each option
4. Net present value if the investment is ₹ 2,00,000 and expected rate of return is 10 per cent.

SUMMARY

This chapter is intended to examine the importance of the study of risk, types of risk and risk adjusted discounting techniques. This also deals with various approaches to risk analysis like sensitivity analysis and simulation method. Risk is inherent in almost every business decision. A research and development project may be more risky than an expansion project and the latter tends to be more risky than a replacement project. In view of such differences, variations in risk need to be evaluated explicitly in capital investment appraisal. Risk analysis is one of the most complex and slippery aspects of capital budgeting. Many different techniques have been suggested and no single technique can be deemed as best in all situations.

KEYWORDS

1. **Business Risk:** The potential variability in firm's earnings before interest and taxes resulting from the nature of the firm's business endeavours.
2. **Certainty Equivalent:** A ratio of certain cash flow and the expected value of a risky cash flow between which the decision-maker is indifferent.
3. **Discount Rate:** The rate at which cash flows are discounted. This rate may be taken as the required rate of return on capital, or the cost of capital.

4. **Financial Risk:** The added variability in earnings available to a firm's shareholders and the additional risk of insolvency caused by the use of financing sources that require a fixed return.
5. **Mutually Exclusive Projects:** A situation in which the acceptance of one investment proposal leaves out the acceptance of another proposal.
6. **Net Present Value:** A method of evaluation consisting of comparing the present value of all net cash flows (discounted by cost of capital as the interest rate) to the initial investment cost.
7. **Risk:** Refers to a situation in which there are several possible outcomes, each outcome occurring with a probability that is known to the decisionmaker.
8. **Risk Adjusted Discount Rate:** Sum of risk-free interest rate and a risk premium. The former is often taken as the interest rate on government securities. The risk premium is what the decision-maker subjectively considers as the additional return necessary to compensate for additional risk.
9. **Uncertainty:** Refers to situations in which there are several possible outcomes of an action whose probabilities are either not known or are not meaningful.

REVIEW QUESTIONS

1. What do you understand by the term 'risk return trade-off?
2. Distinguish between risk and uncertainty.
3. Explain various approaches to risk analysis.
4. What is 'Simulation approach'?
5. What is 'Sensitivity analysis'? Explain with suitable example.
6. What are the various techniques of risk adjusted discounting methods.

REFERENCES

1. Alexander W. Butler, Hess Cornaggia, Gustavo Grulon, James P. Weston, 'Corporate Financing Decisions and Managerial Market Timing, http://ssrn.com/abstract=1370403.
2. Ansof, H. Igor, *Corporate Strategy*, New York, McGraw-Hill, 1965.
3. Craig M. Lewis, Richard J. Rogalski and James K. Sewad , 'Industry Conditions, Growth Opportunities and Market Reactions to Convertible Debt Financing Decisions', http://ssrn.com/abstract=1618.
4. Gustave Grullon, Geroge Kanatas and Piyush Kumar, Financing Decisions and Advertising: An Empirical Study of Capital Structure and Product Market Competition, http://ssrn.com.
5. Jakhotiya G.P., *Strategic Financial Management*, Vikas Publications, New Delhi, 2007.
6. Sridhar A.N., *Strategic Financial Management*, SPD, New Delhi, 2008.

CHAPTER

6

STRATEGIES OF BUSINESS VALUATION

CHAPTER OUTLINE

- Opening Caselet
- Introduction
- Theories of Valuation of a Firm
- Valuation Methods
- Valuation of Securities
- Bonds or Fixed Income Securities
- Valuation of Goodwill
- Formulae for Valuation of Goodwill
- Valuation of Merged Firm
- Accounting Standard 14 (AS 14): Accounting for Amalgamation
- Appendix
- Closing Caselet
- Summary
- Keywords
- Review Questions
- References

OPENING CASELET

DC Ltd., is proposing to acquire the AB Ltd. The valuation is expected to be based on the recommendation of the auditors. Purchase consideration is to be discharged in the form of equity shares issued by DC Ltd., which has paid up equity capital of ₹ 100 lakhs at share price of ₹ 100 each. In the secondary market, during the last six months, the highest and lowest prices are ₹ 340 and ₹ 230. The exchange price can be determined at the average of the market price during the last six months. It is expected that the cash flows for the year 2011 is ₹ 25,00,000 and it is also estimated that there will be 20 per cent growth rate in the cash flows of the business. The required rate of return is 9 per cent. The balance sheet of DC Ltd., as 31-3-2011, is given below:

SOURCES	₹
Equity Share capital 1.5 lakhs shares of ₹ 100 each	1,50,00,000
Long-term liabilities	75,00,000
Short-term liabilities	25,00,000
Total	**2,50,00,000**
APPLICATION	
Fixed Assets	1,75,00,000
Current Assets	75,00,000
Total	**2,50,00,000**

Analyse the balance sheet and find the total value of the business using (a) present value of expected cash flows and (b) number of shares to be issued by DC Ltd.

INTRODUCTION

Corporate entity valuation becomes necessary when there is a proposal for a takeover, merger or acquisition of another corporate entity. The concept of valuation is at the heart of strategic financial management with a well established market in the asset concerned, and if the asset is fairly homogenous, valuation is relatively simple. So long as the market can be accepted as being reasonably efficient, then the market price can be trusted as a fair assessment of value.

Value is defined as: (a) The worth, desirability, or utility of a thing, or the qualities on which these depend, (b) Worth as estimated, (c) The amount for which a thing can be exchanged in the market, (d) Purchasing power and (e) Estimate the value of, appraise (professionally). The economic theory of value tells that the value of any asset is the sum of discounted benefits expected from owning it. The historical information found on a corporation's financial statements represents only the company's financial position at some time in the past. No matter how strict accounting practices were adhered to, they can never fully represent the actual value of the firm and its components. Investors trying to place a value on a firm must be aware and take into account the discrepancies between what a firm is worth on paper and what is really worth in the market. Suppose a company buys an asset and records its value according to Generally Accepted Accounting Principles (GAAP)[1] as the total amount of money paid for the asset. Essentially, the book value of the asset is the price paid and using a depreciation schedule, the asset will lose value over time until it reaches the end of the schedule and the asset is no longer counted as an asset on the company's books. This procedure may be a fair way to value an asset from an accounting point of view but the reality is that there can be major discrepancies between book value and market values.

The total value of a corporation is the sum of the market values of its assets. However, financial statements only report book values. The longer an asset is held, the greater the chance that the book value of an asset differs from its market value. These values can also diverge because of other economic issues outside the control of the corporation. Given this information, it is clear that the total value of a firm should never be estimated as the total value of the book values of its assets found on the firm's financial statements. Global/corporate investors have become highly demanding and are extremely focused on maximizing corporate value. The list of investors includes high net worth individuals, pension and hedge funds, and investment companies. They no longer remain passive investors but are keen followers of a company's strategies and actions aimed at maximizing and protecting the value of their investments. The following entities may require valuation to be carried out:

1. A buyer or a seller
2. A lender
3. An intermediary like an agent, a broker
4. Regulatory authorities such as tax authorities, revenue authorities
5. General public.

If the market values of a firm's assets and liabilities could be easily confirmed, then the residual, which represents the value of stockholders, would be an accurate measure of a firm's value. The lack of accurate market values make investors seek other methods of determining the total value of a corporation. The best estimate of a firm's value is based on stock price for which shares of the company are selling in a stock market. In fact, a very accurate measure is to simply find the product of the price of a share of stock and the number of shares outstanding. This value takes into account more than just the book values of a firm; it includes market, economic, and currency conditions. The stock price of a firm will fluctuate to account for new information, such as the decisions of the

1. GAAP: Generally Accepted Accounting Principles: See Appendix

company's managers. According to Institute of Cost and Works Accountants of India (ICWAI), 'Investors in shares and companies seeking to make acquisitions need to know how much a company is worth and how much to pay for their investment'.

NEED FOR DETERMINATION OF 'VALUE'

1. **Portfolio Management/Transactions:** A transaction of sale or purchase, i.e., whenever an investment or disinvestment is made. Transaction appraisals include acquisitions, mergers, leveraged buy-outs, initial public offerings, ESOPs, buy-sell agreements, sales of interest, going public, going private, and many other engagements.
2. **Mergers and Acquisition:** Valuation becomes important for both the parties – for the acquirer to decide on a fair market value of the target organisation and for the target organisation to arrive at a reasonable for itself to enable acceptance or rejection of the offer being made.
3. **Corporate Finance:** The desire to know intrinsic worth and enhance value is important, as financial management itself is defined as 'maximisation of corporate value'. A proper valuation will help in linking the value of a firm to its financial decisions such as capital structure, financing mix, dividend policy, recapitalisation and so on.
4. **Resolve Disputes Among Stakeholders/Litigation:** Divorce, bankruptcy, breach of contract, dissenting shareholder and minority oppression cases, economic damages computations, ownership disputes, and other cases.
5. **Taxes (or Estate Planning):** Including gift and estate taxes, estate planning, family limited partnerships, *ad valorem* taxation, and other tax-related reasons.

Misconceptions about Valuation:

There are a number of misconceptions about valuation and some of them are given below:

1. **Myth 1:** A valuation is an objective search for 'true' value.

   Truth 1.1: All valuations are biased. The only questions are how much and in which direction.

   Truth 1.2: The direction and magnitude of the bias in your valuation is directly proportional to who pays you and how much you are paid.
2. **Myth 2:** A good valuation provides a precise estimate of value.

   Truth 2.1: There are no precise valuations.

   Truth 2.2: The payoff to valuation is greatest when valuation is least precise.
3. **Myth 3:** The more quantitative a model, the better the valuation.

Truth 3.1: One's understanding of a valuation model is inversely proportional to the number of inputs required for the model.

Truth 3.2: Simpler valuation models do much better than complex ones.

4. **Myth 4:** Valuing a private business should only be done when the business is ready to be sold or a lender requires a valuation as part of its due diligence process.

   Truth 4.1: Although the above situations require valuations to be carried out, effective planning for ownership transition requires a regular valuation of the business.

5. **Myth 5:** Businesses in an industry always sell for x times the annual revenue (the revenue multiple). So why should valuation of the business be done by an external valuer?

   Truth 5.1: While median multiple values are commonly used as a rule of thumb, they do not represent the revenue multiple for any actual transaction.

6. **Myth 6:** The business should be atleast worth equivalent to what a competitor sold his business for recently.

   Truth 6.1: What happened a few months ago is not really relevant to what something is worth today.

   Truth 6.2: What a business is worth today depends on three factors: (1) how much cash it generates today? (2) expected growth in cash in the foreseeable future; and (3) the return buyers require on their investment in the business. Therefore, unless a firm's cash flows and growth prospects are very similar to the competitor firm, that firm's revenue multiple is irrelevant to valuing the firm. Also, the current value of the business is likely to be different than a few months ago because economic conditions may have changed.

7. **Myth 7:** How much a business is worth depends on what the valuation is used for?

   Truth 7.1: The value of a business in its fair market values, i.e., what a willing buyer will pay a willing seller when each is fully informed and under no pressure to transact.

8. **Myth 8:** The business loses money, so it is not worth much.

   Truth 8.1: While most private businesses may appear to lose money, the cash a business generates determines the value of the business. Quantifying the size of discretionary expenses is often a critical determinant of the firm's value.

Enterprise value = Equity value + market value of debt + minority interest + pension and other similar provisions + other claims.

Since the book values found on a firm's financial statements provide an inaccurate measure of a corporation's value, investors look for estimates of the firm's market values of both assets and liabilities. The best estimate of a company's worth can be found in its stock price which is influenced by all available information affecting the firm. Using this information, investors can also better estimate the market values of both assets and liabilities to obtain a more complete picture of a company's health and future profitability. Different approaches may be required when valuing whole companies from those appropriate to valuing part shares of companies.

THEORIES OF VALUATION OF A FIRM

There are three important theories of capital structure in valuing a firm: (1) Net Income Approach (NI). (2) Net Operating Income Approach (NOI) and (3) Traditional Approach.

1. **Net Income Approach (NI):** According to NI approach, capital structure is relevant, as a change in it will lead to a corresponding change in the cost of capital and the total value of the firm. The core of this approach is that, as the degree of leverage increases, the ratio of less expensive source of funds (debt) in the capital structure increases while that of equity (involving higher cost) decreases. In fact, a change in leverage amounts to substitution of a less costly source in place of a more costly source. With a judicious mixture of debt and equity, a firm can, according to NI approach, evolve an optimum capital structure at which the cost of capital would be the lowest, and the value of the firm would be the highest. The following table indicates total value of firm under Net Income approach.

Total Value of the Firm (Net Income Approach)

1.	Net Operating Income (Earning Before Interest and Taxes or EBIT).
2.	*Less:* Interest (I) = B × Ki
3.	Earnings available to Equity Share holders (NI) = (1) _ (2)
4.	Equity Capitalization rate (Ke)
5.	Market value of equity (S) = (3)/(4) or NI/Ke
6.	Market value of debt (B) = I/Ki
7.	Total market value of firm or V = (5) + (6) or S + B
8.	Overall cost of capital, Ko = EBIT/V or (1)/(7)
	Ki – Cost of Debt or Interest rate
	Ke – Cost of Equity or Capitalisation rate or Dividend rate

Example:

Find the value of the firm using the following data, given that debt is ₹ 2,00,000, Interest rate is 12 per cent and Equity Capitalisation rate (Ke) is 15 per cent and net operating income is ₹ 2,00,000 compute the total value of the company and the overall cost of capital using Net Income approach.

1.	Net Operating Income (Earning Before Interest and Taxes or EBIT):	**₹ 2,00,000**
2.	*Less:* Interest (I) = B × Ki Interest rate is 12% on 20,00,000	24,000
3.	Earnings available to Equity Shareholders (NI) = (1) _ (2):	1,76,000
4.	Equity Capitalization rate (Ke)	**15%**
5.	Market value of equity (S) = (3)/(4) or NI/Ke = **?**	176000/0.15 = 1173333.33
6.	Market value of Debt (B) = I/Ki = **?**	2,00,000
7.	Total Market value of firm or V = (5) + (6) or S + B = **?**	11933333.33
8.	Overall cost of capital, Ko = EBIT/ V or (1)/(7) = **?**	200000/11933333 = 0.16

2. **Net Operating Income Approach (NOI):** The NOI approach is diametrically opposite to the NI approach. The essence of this approach is that capital structure is totally irrelevant. A change in leverage will not cause any change in the cost of capital and value of the firm. The main thrust of the argument of NOI is that an increase in the proportion of debt in the capital structure would lead to an increase in the financial risk of the shareholders. To compensate for the increased risk, the shareholders would require a higher rate of return on their investment. The increase in the cost of equity would match the savings in the lower cost of debt, according to NOI, has two elements: (i) explicit, represented by the rate of interest, and (ii) implicit, the increase in the cost of equity capital caused by an increase in the degree of leverage. As a result, the advantage associated with the use of the relatively less expensive debt in terms of the explicit cost of equity capital. Therefore, the real cost of debt and equity are to be the same. The following table indicates the process of valuation under NOI approach.

Total Value of the Firm (Net Operating Income Approach)

1.	Net Operating Income (Earning Before Interest and Taxes or EBIT)
2.	Overall Cost of Capital, Ko
3.	Total Market Value of firm or V = EBIT/Ko {OR} (1)/(2)
4.	Market Value of Debt (B)
5.	Market Value of Equity (S) = V – B {OR} (3)/(4)
6.	Equity Capitalization Rate (Ke) = (EBIT – I)/(V – B)
	Ki – Cost of Debt or Interest Rate
	Ke – Cost of Equity or Capitalization Rate or Dividend Rate

Example:

Find the value of the firm using the following data, given that debt is ₹ 2,00,000, Interest rate is 12 per cent and overall cost of capital (Ko) is 15 per cent and net operating income is ₹ 2,00,000, compute the total value of the company and the overall cost of capital using **Net Operating Income Approach.**

1. Net Operating Income (Earning Before Interest and Taxes or EBIT):	₹ 2,00,000
2. Overall cost of capital, Ko	0.15
3. Total Market value of firm or V = EBIT/Ko {OR} (1)/(2)	2,00,000/0.15 = 1333333.33
4. Market value of Debt (B)	2,00,000
5. Market value of equity (S) = V – B {OR} (3)/(4)	1133333.33
6. Equity Capitalisation rate (Ke) = (EBIT – I)/(V – B)	176000/1133333.33 = 0.155

3. **Modigliani Miller Approach (MM approach):** This is identical with Net Operating Income approach if taxes are ignored. When taxes assumed to exist, it is similar to the net income approach. In the absence of taxes:

   - The theory proves that the cost of capital is not affected by any changes in the capital structure. The debt-equity mix is irrelevant in the determination of the total value of firm.
   - The theory emphasizes the fact that a firm's operating income is a determinant of its total value.
   - The theory propounds that beyond a certain limit of debt, the cost of debt increases (due to increased financial risk) but the cost equity falls thereby again balancing the two costs.
   - In the opinion of Modigiolani and Miller, two identical firms in all respects except their capital structure cannot have different market values or cost of capital because of arbitrage process.
   - In case two identical firms except for their capital structure have different market values or cost of capital, arbitrage will take place and the investors will engage in 'personal leverage' (i.e., they will buy equity of the other company in preference to the company having lesser value) as against the 'corporate leverage' and this will again render the two firms to have the same total value.

Assumptions

1. Capital markets are perfect. Information is cost less and readily available to all investors, there are no transaction costs, and all securities are infinitely divisible.

2. The average expected future operating earnings of a firm are represented by a subjective random variable.
3. Firms can be categorised in to equivalent return classes. All firms within the class have the same degree of business risk.
4. The absence of corporate income taxes is assumed.

Value Maximising Capital Structure

(a) Market value of levered firm =

Market value of un-levered firm – Present Value of (Tax shield + Bankruptcy costs + agency cost) Or

(b) $V_L = V_U + D_t$

VALUATION METHODS

The finance manager uses the following valuation methods, *viz.*, (a) Conventional valuation method, (b) Present-value method and (c) Revenue multiplier method.

A. Conventional Valuation Method: This is based on the expected increase in the initial investment that could be sold out to a third party or through public offering via the exit route. Price-Earning ratio is calculated on the maturing date, multiplying the earning level post-tax effect by P/E ratio on the future maturity date arrives at valuation of investment at a future date. This method does not take into account the stream of cash flows beginning from the date of investment till the date of liquidity of investment.

B. Present-value Method: This method takes into account the stream of earnings generated during the entire period of the investment from the date of initial investment till date of maturity at a presumed discounted rate. This method is popularly known as 'First Chicago Method'. Three alternative scenarios styled as 'success', 'survival' and 'failure' are assumed for the entire maturing period of the project that are discounted by a uniform discount rate to arrive at the present value of investment. Each scenario is assigned a probability figure. Probability figures are based on many factors, which affect the earning stream: price of raw material, price of finished good, marketing factors. The product is multiplied by respective probability figures to arrive at expected value in each scenario. The total of these scenarios gives the expected present value of the company. Based on such value the venture capitalist makes his investment.

C. Revenue Multiplier Method: Revenue multiplier is an assumed factor used to estimate the value of an enterprise. By multiplying the annual estimated sales by such factor, the valuation figure is derived. This method is based on sales income and not on earning. Assuming the absence of profit in the early stage of a project, the method is useful for valuation at the early stages.

The Multiplier (M) is obtained by using the following equation.

$$M = \frac{(1+g)n(e)(PE)}{(1)+dn}$$

where,

M = Multiplier.

g = Growth rate.

n = Number of years between initial investment and exit date.

e = Expected profit margin (post tax) percentage at the exit date.

PE = Expected price earning ratio at the exit date.

d = Appropriate discount rate for venture capital investment and undertaking risk.

Valuation, (V) is obtained by using the following equation:

$$V = \frac{R(1+g)n(a)(PE)}{(1)+dn}$$

Utilisation of earlier investment is an important part of investigation that would reveal the ability of management to economically and efficiently utilise funds.

APPROACHES TO VALUATION

1. Discounted Cash Flow Valuation Approach (DCF): This approach is also known as the Income approach, where the value is determined by calculating the net present value of the stream of benefits generated by the business or the asset. Thus, the DCF approach equals the enterprise value to all future cash flows discounted to the present using the appropriate cost of capital.

In Discounted Cash Flow (DCF) valuation, the value of an asset is the present value of the expected cash flows on the asset. The basic premise in DCF is that every asset has an intrinsic value that can be estimated, based upon its characteristics in terms of cash flows, growth and risk. Though the DCF Valuation is one of the three approaches to Valuation, it is essential to understand the fundamentals of this approach, as the DCF method finds application in the use of the other two approaches also. The DCF model is the most widely used standalone valuation model.

Discounted Cash Flow (DCF) Analysis:

To use DCF valuation, we need to estimate the following:

1. The life of the asset.
2. The cash flows during the life of the asset.
3. The discount rate to apply to these cash flows to get present value.

The Present Value of an asset is arrived at by determining the present values of all expected future cash flows from the use of the asset. Mathematically,

Value = CF1/(1+r) 1 + CF2/(1+ r)2 + ...+ CFn/(1+ r)n

where,

CFi= Expected Future Net Cash Flow during period i.

n = Life of the asset.

r = Rate of discount.

The expected future net cash flow is defined as after-tax cash flow from operations on an invested capital basis (excluding the impact of debt service) less the sum of net changes in working capital and new investments in capital assets. The discount rate should reflect the risk of the estimated cash flows. The rate will be higher for high risk projects as compared to lower rates for safe or less risky investments. The Weighted Average Cost of Capital (WACC) is used as the discount rate. The cost of capital with which the cash flows are discounted should reflect the risk inherent in the future cash flows.

The WACC is calculated using the following formula:

WACC = [(E/(D+E) × CE] + [(D/(D+E) × CD × (1-T)]

where E is the market value of equity, D is the market value of debt, CE is the cost of equity, CD is the cost of debt and T is the tax rate. The first step in determining WACC is the assessment of capital structure, i.e., how a company has financed its operations. It can thus be seen that the company's net cash flows are projected for a number of years and then discounted to present value using the WACC. The expected cash flows earned beyond the projection period are capitalised into a terminal value and added to the value of the projected cash flows for a total value indication.

1. Steps in DCF Valuation: The steps in valuing a company using DCF are given below:

1. Determine the time horizon for specific forecasts:

   Consider economic and business cycles, positive and negative growth.

2. Forecast operating cash flows: Determine value drivers, estimate historic, current and future ratios, decide on cash/investment policy.

3. Determine residual value: Decide on residual value methodology, estimate growth rate in perpetuity.

4. Estimate WACC: Estimate cost of equity and debt, the debt-equity ratio.

5. Discount cash flows: Determine enterprise value and equity value, conduct sensitivity analysis.

6. Prepare related financial statements.

2. Relative Valuation: This is **also known as the market approach**. In this approach, value is determined by comparing the subject company or asset with other companies or assets in the same industry, of the same size, and/or within the same region, based on common variables such as earnings, sales, cash flows, etc. The Profit multiples often used are: (a) Earnings before interest tax depreciation and amortisation (EBITDA), (b) Earnings before interest and tax (EBIT), (c) Profits before tax, and (d) Profits after tax.

Historic, current and forecast profits/earnings are used as multiples from the quoted sector and actual transactions in the sector.

3. Contingent Claim Valuation: This approach uses the option pricing models to estimate the value of assets.

4. Asset-based Approach: A fourth approach called asset-based approach is also touted as another approach to valuation. The valuation here is simply the difference between the assets and liabilities taken from the balance sheet, adjusted for certain accounting principles. Two methods are used here:

(a) The liquidation value, which is the sum of estimated sale values of the assets owned by a company.

(b) Replacement Cost: The current cost of replacing all the assets of a company. However, the asset-based approach is not an alternative to the first three approaches, as this approach itself uses one of the three approaches to determine the values. This approach is commonly used by property and investment companies, to cross check for asset based trading companies such as hotels and property developers, underperforming trading companies with strong asset base (market value vs. existing use), and to work out break – up valuations.

5. Economic Value Added (EVA): This analysis is based on the premise that shareholder value is created by earning a return in excess of the company's cost of capital. EVA is calculated by subtracting a capital charge (invested capital x WACC) from the company's Net Operating Profit After Taxes (NOPAT). If the EVA is positive, shareholder value has increased. Therefore, increasing the company's future EVA is key to creating shareholder value. An EVA model normally includes an analysis of the company's historical EVA performance and projected future EVA under various assumptions. By changing the assumptions, such as for revenue growth and operating margins, management can see the effects of certain value improvement initiatives.

A simple illustration is given below:

- NOPAT = \$15,000
- Invested capital = \$50,000
- WACC = 12%
- EVA = NOPAT – (Invested capital × WACC)

$= \$15{,}000 - (\$50{,}000 \times 12\%)$

$= \$9{,}000$

6. Performance-based Compensation: This effective tool for motivating employees aligns their interests with the shareholders. For example, establish a base level of compensation plus a bonus pool tied to certain EVA targets. A minimum level of EVA is required for any bonus to apply, and the pool increases based on how much actual EVA exceeds the minimum threshold. By tying compensation to certain performance metrics, such as EVA or EVA improvement, employees have a sense of ownership and strong incentives to help achieve the company's value creation goals. Numerous criteria and performance metrics can be used in setting up a performance based compensation plan. However, to be effective, the performance criteria must be achievable, measurable and clearly communicated to the employees intended to be impacted by it. Regular feedback and information reporting procedures should be established that will help employees monitor their progress for meeting the performance goals throughout the year.

ADJUSTMENTS FOR VALUATION PURPOSES

A number of adjustments are required from the account statements of the company to be valued, and these are listed below:

1. **Income Statement**
   - Excess compensation
   - Excess fringe benefits
   - Inventory accumulation
   - Bad debts
   - Depreciation
   - Extraordinary write-offs
   - Corporate income taxes
2. **Balance Sheet**
   - Inventory
   - Bad debts
   - Fixed asset appreciation/depreciation
   - Patent, franchises, goodwill, and other intangibles
   - Investment in affiliates
   - Future royalties
   - Low cost debt service
   - Tax loss carry forwards

3. General Accounting Policies

- Overhead allocations
- Installment sales
- Deferred compensation
- Pension and profit sharing
- Foreign exchange
- Consolidation
- Depreciation
- Inventories
- Accounts receivable
- Research and development
- Income tax deferrals
- Marketable securities
- Contingencies
  - (a) Unknown law suit potential (product liability)
  - (b) Management or employment contracts
  - (c) Ownership restrictions

VALUATION OF SECURITIES

The primary focus of valuation is to determine if a share is over-priced, under-priced, or fairly priced at any given market price. Based on the valuation one can decide either to purchase or sell his shares in the stock market accordingly. Market price is volatile and its fluctuations are caused by different factors like rumors, inflation, political scenario, government policies, industrial policies, changing technology, etc.

VALUE-PRICE RELATIONSHIP

Present value, also known as intrinsic value or economic value, determines price. Value of a security is a fundamental variable and depends on its promised return, risk and the discount rate, which tend to change over time. Thus, security prices may rise or fall with buying and selling pressures respectively assuming supply of securities does not change and this may affect capital gains and hence returns expected. Consequently, estimates of future income will have to revise and values reworked. An increase in risk would raise the discount rate and lower value. It would then seem to be a continuous exercise.

VALUATION OF PREFERENCE SHARES

Preference shares are considered as a perpetual security but these are convertible, callable, redeemable and other similar features which enable issuers to terminate them within a finite time horizon. In the case of redeemable preference shares, legal mandates require creation of redemption sinking funds and their earmarked investments to ensure funds for repayment. Preference dividends are specified like bonds. This has to be done because they rank prior to equity shares for dividends. The value of preference share is determined on the basis of dividend and the required rate of return appropriate for the perpetuity.

VALUATION OF EQUITY SHARES

Valuation of equity shares is based on dividend valuation models with zero growth, constant growth, and super-normal growth assumptions are found useful for the practicing security analysts and the investors. The discount rate in all these models is the required rate of return of the investor appropriately adjusted for the time value of money and riskiness of returns. The price-earnings approach to valuation uses current earnings as the basis for determining normal price-earnings as the basis for determining normal price-earning ratios and calculating actual price-earning ratios. It may be noted that prevent values which form the numerator of normal price-earnings ration are based on future estimates of cash flows and these are linked upto current earnings through varying growth assumptions.

BONDS OR FIXED INCOME SECURITIES

Debt securities issued by government and quasi-government organisations, and private business firms are fixed-income securities. Bonds and debentures are the most common examples. The intrinsic value of a bond or debenture is equal to the present value of its expected cash flows. The coupon interest payments, and the principal repayment are known and the present value is determined by discounting these future payments from the issuer at an appropriate discount rate or market yield.

1. Current Yield: Current yield is the ratio between stated interest per year and current market price of the bond. For example, if a 15 per cent ₹ 200 debenture is current selling for ₹ 220 the annual current yield would be 13.64 per cent (i.e., 30/220 × 100). Current yield does not account for the difference between the purchase price of the bond or debenture and its maturity value.

2. Yield-to-Maturity (YTM): This is the most widely used measure of return on fixed income securities. It may be defined as the indicated (promised) compounded rate of return an investor will receive from a bond purchased at the current market price and held to maturity. Computing YTM involves equating the current market price of a bond with the discounted value of future interest payments and the terminal principal repayment; thus YTM equates the two values, *viz.*, and the market price of a bond with the discounted value of future payments including the principal repayment.

VALUATION OF GOODWILL

Goodwill is the value of the reputation of a business house in respect of the profits expected in future over and above the normal level of profits earned by undertakings belonging to the same class of business. In otherwords, goodwill is the present value of a firm's anticipated super normal earnings. The term super-normal earnings means the excess of earnings attributable to operating tangible and intangible assets (other than goodwill) over and above the normal rate of return earned by representative firms in the same industry. It is observed that when a man pays for goodwill, he pays for something which places him in the position of being able to earn more money than he would be able to by his own unaided efforts. Goodwill is an intangible asset but not a fictitious one.

Factors Affecting the Value of Goodwill

Value of goodwill depends upon the capacity of the business to earn excess profits. Therefore, all such factors which help in increasing the profitability of business will also affect this value of goodwill. This will depend on the following factors.

1. **Reputation of Management/Owners:** A business managed by persons of high integrity and efficiency will have higher profitability and will have more value for its goodwill.
2. **Location of Business:** A favourable location of the business helps to a great extent in attracting customers, leads to greater profitability and thus goodwill.
3. **Prior Entry in the Business:** A business older in age will have more goodwill since it is better known to the customers.
4. **Nature of Business:** A business dealing in goods of a monopolistic type or goods having a stable demand will have a higher value of goodwill as compared to others.
5. **Other Factors:** The reputation of the goods dealt in or the quality of service rendered, the patents, copywrite or trademarks owned by the firm have an effect on its value of goodwill.

Need for Valuing Goodwill

The necessity for the valuation of goodwill in a firm arises in the following circumstances:

(a) Where the profit sharing ratio amongst the partners is changed.

(b) When a new partner is admitted.

(c) When a partner retires or dies.

(d) When the business is sold, and

(e) When a firm is amalgamated with another firm.

Methods of Valuation of Goodwill

Following are the different methods of valuing goodwill:

(i) Average Profit Method: Goodwill is sometimes valued on the basis of a certain number of years' purchase of the average profits of the past few years. While calculating average profits for the purposes of valuation of goodwill certain adjustments are made, which are as follows:

(a) All actual expenses and losses not likely to occur in the future are added back to profits.

(b) Expenses and losses expected to be borne in future are deducted from such profits.

(c) All profits likely to accrue in the future are added, and

(d) Even actual profits not likely to reccur in future are deducted.

After having adjusted profit in the light of future possibilities, average profits are estimated and then the value of goodwill is calculated, i.e., the average profits are ascertained then it is multiplied by a particular number, say 3 or 4, representing the number of years' purchase. This method has nothing to recommend itself since goodwill is attached to profits over and above what one can earn by starting a new business or by normal business engaged in the same line of activity, and not to total profits. It ignores the amount of capital employed for earning the profit. However, it is usual to adopt this method for valuing the goodwill of the practice of a professional person such as a chartered accountant or a doctor.

(ii) Super Profit Method: In this case the future maintainable profits of the firm are compared with the normal profits for the firm. Normal earnings of a business can be judged only in the light of normal rate of earning and the capital employed in the business. Hence, this method of valuing goodwill would require the following information:

(a) A normal rate of return for representative firms in the industry.

(b) The fair value of capital employed.

(c) Estimated future maintainable profits.

The normal rate of earning is that rate of earning which investors in general expect on their investments in the particular type of industry. Normal rate of earning depends upon the risk attached to the investment, bank rate, market need and the period of investment. Capital employed may be expressed as aggregate of share capital and reserves less the amount of non-trading assets such as investments. The capital employed may also be ascertained by adding up the present values of trading assets and deducting all liabilities. Super profit is the simple difference between future maintainable operating profit and normal profit. There are three methods of calculating goodwill based on super profit:

(a) Purchase of super profit: As per this method, value of goodwill be obtained by multiplying super profit by a certain number of years.

(b) Annuity method: Goodwill according to the annuity method is the present value of a terminal annuity of super profit for a reasonable period during which the super profit is likely to occur. It is calculated as:

Super profit × Annuity rate

(c) Capitalisation of super profit: In this method, the value of goodwill is arrived at by capitalising the super profit at the normal rate of return. It is calculated as:

Normal rate of return= Super profit × 100

(iii) Capitalisation Method: The capitalisation of profit method values goodwill at the excess of capital that should have been employed for earning the average profit over the capital which has been actually employed. In this method the value of whole business is found by using the formula:

Normal rate of return= Average profit × 100

From this figure, the net assets (excluding goodwill) of the firm are deducted and the resultant value will be the goodwill.

Accounting Treatment

Para 16 read with para 36 of the Accounting Standard-10 (AS-10) — 'Accounting for Fixed Assets' states that goodwill should be recorded in the books of account only when some consideration in money or money's worth has been paid for it. Whenever a business is acquired for a price (payable in cash or in shares or otherwise) which is in excess of the value of the net assets of the business taken over, the excess should be treated as goodwill. For example, when a partnership firm of X and Y purchases the net assets of Z amounting to ₹ 6,00,000 for ₹ 6,50,000 in cash, the additional payment of ₹ 50,000 is a payment for goodwill in cash. It is a case of purchased goodwill (an asset) and can be recorded in the books of account of X and Y. Therefore, only purchased goodwill should be recorded in the books of account whether the payment is made directly in cash or money's worth. When no payment is made for the purchase of goodwill, it is a case of internally generated goodwill or inherent goodwill. For instance, in the event of reconstitution of the firm as a result of admission, retirement, death or change in profit sharing ratio, goodwill of the firm is evaluated. In such cases, the value of goodwill should not be brought into books of account as it is an inherent or self generated goodwill and no money or money's worth has been paid for it. Then goodwill should be calculated as per any of the methods stated above and adjusted through the capital accounts of the partners. Hence no goodwill account should be raised in the books of account on reconstitution of the firm or change in the profit sharing ratio among the partners.

Therefore, it is stated that the internally generated or inherent goodwill should not be raised in the books of account. Instead it should be treated through the capital accounts of the concerned partners. In no case, the goodwill raised should be shown in the balance sheet.

FORMULAE FOR VALUATION OF GOODWILL

Points to be considered while Calculation of FMP

1. Only profit of those years with normal activity to be considered (years of abnormal activity excluded).
2. Profits – Operating profits (non-operating items excluded but if they are recurring to be included).
3. Income from Trade Investment only to be considered (NTI not to be considered).
4. Fluctuating Profits – Simple Average.
5. Profits with a trend – Weighted Average.
6. If fixed asset is revalued – ignore p/l on revaluation, if other assets (liab) – consider.
7. But consider additinal depreciation on the revaluation of Fixed Assets.

Points to be considered while calculating Capital Employed

Capital Employed = Total Assets (excl. Fictitious Assets and non trade Assets and GW) Less: Outside liabilities

1. Unproductive assets excluded.
2. Assets @ FV.
3. Only purchased GW to be considered.
4. Patents/Trademarks/Licenses/FV.
5. Trade Investment/FV.
6. Non-trade investment – ignore.
7. Stock, Drs, Loans and Adv – Realisable/recoverable value.
8. Liabilities – at redemption amounts.
9. Do not deduct Pref Cap and proposed dividend.
10. Borrowing relating to pur. of NTI not to be deducted.
11. Workmen Compensation Fund is not outsider liability.
12. Alternatives for CE.

    (a) CCE - Closing capital employed _ (preferred).

(b) ACE – Avg capital employed (opg+clg/2) (Used in SP method where past profits are considered).

(c) Avg. Capital = Closing capital - half profits after tax.

Points to be Considered while Calculating

1. Bank rate + Risk Premium
2. NRR= EY= EPS/MPS *100

Super Profits Method

1. Compute Normal Profits (NP) = CE × NRR
2. Determine Super profits (SP) = FMP – NP
3. Compute GW = SP × NYP

Capitalisation Method

1. Compute NCE = FMP/NRR × 100
2. GW = NCE – Actual Capital Employed

Leverage Effect on Goodwill

Shareholder's fund approach:

1. Actual Capital Employed = Equity + Pref + R/S (or Total assets (excl. fictitious) Less: Outsiders liabilities)
2. FMP = EBIT – Int – Tax i.e., EAT

Long-term Fund Approach

1. Actual Capital Employed = Capital Employed under above method+ long-term loans.
2. FMP = EBIT – Tax (Interest is not deductible).

If goodwill calculated under SHF approach is more than LTF approach, then its' a positive leverage effect otherwise *vice versa.*

Goodwill represents the difference between the overall business valuation, which is arrived at on the foregoing basis, and the aggregate book value of the individual net assets carried in the balance sheet.

The answers to the following questions will impact on the value of goodwill:

- Is the goodwill of the business to be valued:
  - As on the outright sale of just the fees, or the goodwill of the business as a growing concern, to a willing buyer, or
  - As if there were a continuation of the partnership business, with the remaining partners acquiring the goodwill, or
  - By an incoming partner who would be acquiring a minority share?

- Can the fees be serviced from locations over a wide area, without the probable loss of clients?
- Is there a higher density of established practices in the immediate area, tending to increase demand?
- Is there a prohibitively high contingent liability in the office lease?
- Is the existing payroll cost high, with a heavy contingent liability in staff contracts?
- Are key members of staff under non-competition contracts?
- What is the size of the client profile?
- Are value added services, such as Financial Services, currently offered, giving scope for further development?
- What are the charge our rates like, compared with the norm for the area?
- Does the summary of the time records show significant under recoveries?
- Have there been any PI claims or late filing penalties?
- Have there been any recent JMU visits? What was the outcome?
- What payment period is the vendor looking for?
- Will there be a 'clawback' clause in the agreement, over how many years?
- Will a heavy investment be required in computerisation and upgrading systems?

VALUATION OF MERGED FIRM

Mergers and acquisitions involve share stocks of different companies, and their exchange for suitable consideration. Acquiring the shares of another company entitles one to get the dividend accruing on the same, or the capital gains by selling the shares when the prices are higher than what was paid for. Value of the shares/stocks of a company is determined by factors such as:

- Present dividend returns
- Likely future returns and risk of these future returns
- Present profitability
- Potential growth rate.

Thus, the valuation for merger and acquisition involves evaluation of the associated risks and the potential growth rate of the firm and its earnings. The valuation procedure follows a rigorous analysis similar to the one followed for other capital budgeting decisions. It is central to the merger process. Fundamentally firms should merge only if the value to the shareholders will be enhanced. Target firms usually justify resisting hostile mergers by claiming that a proposed merger undervalues the potential of the firm. According to

Weston and Weaver (2002) 'this analysis and valuation becomes even more complex in stock-for-stock transactions, where bidders must analyse how much of the combined company will be owned by bidder and target shareholders'.

Valuation of Target Company: The principal incentive for a merger is that the business value of the combined business is expected to be greater than the sum of the independent business values of the merging entities. The difference between the combined value and the sum of the values of individual companies is the synergy gain attributable to the M&A transaction. Hence,

Value of acquirer + Standalone value of Target + Value of Synergy = Combined Value. There is also a cost attached to an acquisition.

The cost of acquisition is the price premium paid over the market value plus other costs of integration.

Therefore, the net gain is the value of synergy minus premium paid.

Example:

Suppose VA = ₹ 200, VB = ₹ 50 and VAB = ₹ 300, where VA and VB are the values of companies A and B before merger respectively and VAB is the combined value after merger. Therefore, Synergy = VAB – (VA + VB) = ₹ 50.

If the premium is ₹ 20, Net gain from merger of A and B will be ₹ 30 (i.e., ₹ 50 – ₹ 20).

1. **Income Approach:** Under this approach two primary used methods to value a business interest include:
   (a) Discounted Cash Flow Method
   (b) Capitalized Cash Flow Method

Each of these methods depend on the present value of an enterprise's future cash flows.

A. Discounted Cash Flow Technique: The Discounted Cash flow valuation is based upon the notion that the value of an asset is the present value of the expected cash flows on that asset, discounted at a rate that reflects the riskiness of those cash flows. The nature of the cash flows will depend upon the asset: dividends for an equity share, coupons and redemption value for bonds and the post tax cash flows for a project. The steps involved in valuation under this method are as under:

Step I: Estimate free cash flows available to all the suppliers of the capital *viz.*, equity holders, preference investors and the providers of debt.

Step II: Estimate a suitable Discount Rate for acquisition, which is normally represented by weighted average of the costs of all sources of capital, which are based on the market value of each of the components of the capital.

Step III: Cash flows computed in Step I are discounted at the rate arrived at in Step II.

Step IV: Estimate the Terminal Value of the business, which is the present value of cash flows occurring after the forecast period.

TV = CFt (1+ g)/k – g

where CFt is the cash flow in last year,

g is constant growth rate and

k is the discount rate.

Step V: Add the present value of free cash flows as arrived at in Step III and the Terminal Value as arrived at in Step IV.

Step VI: This will give the value of firm.

Step VII: Subtract the value of debt and other obligations assumed by the acquirer to arrive at the value of equity.

B. Capitalised Cash Flow Technique: The capitalised cash flow technique of income approach is the abbreviated version of discounted cash flow technique where the growth rate (g) and the discount rate (k) are assumed to remain constant in perpetuity. This model is represented as under:

Value of Firm = Net cash flow in year one/(k – g).

C. Market Approach: The market approach to business valuation has its origin in the economic principle of substitution which says, 'Buyers would not pay more for an item than the price at which they can obtain an equally desirable substitute'. The market price of the stocks of publicly traded companies engaged in the same or similar line of business can be a valid indicator of value when the transactions in which stocks are traded are sufficiently similar to permit a meaningful comparison. The difficulty lies in identifying public companies that are sufficiently comparable to the subject company for this purpose. Suppose a company operating in the same industry as ABC with comparable size and other situations has been sold at ₹ 500 crores in last week provides a good measurement for valuation of business. Considering the circumstances, value of the business of ABC should be around ₹ 500 crores under market approach.

D. Assets Approach: The first step in using the assets approach is to obtain a balance sheet as close as possible to the valuation date. Each recorded asset including intangible assets must be identified, examined and adjusted to fair market value. Now all liabilities are to be subtracted, again at fair market value, from the value of assets derived as above to reach at the fair market value of equity of the business. It is important to note here that any unrecorded assets or liabilities should also be considered while arriving at the value of business by the assets approach. None of the above methods is the best or none of them is the worst but each one has its own advantages and view points different from others. All these methods should be used in combinations to arrive at proper valuation of the business.

ACCOUNTING STANDARD 14 (AS 14): ACCOUNTING FOR AMALGAMATION

The following are the salient features of accounting standard (As 14) issued by the Institute of Chartered Accountants of India. This standard has come into effect in respect of accounting periods commencing on or after 1.4.1995. This standard is mandatory in nature. 'Accounting for Amalgamations' deals with the accounting to be made in the books of Transferee Company. This AS is applicable where the acquired company is dissolved and its separate entity ceased to exist and the purchasing company continues the business of acquired company.

As per AS-14 there are two types of amalgamations:

(a) Amalgamation in the nature of purchase and

(b) Amalgamation in the nature of merger.

An amalgamation will be in the nature of purchase if any of the conditions regarding amalgamation in the nature of merger is not satisfied. An amalgamation is in the nature of merger if all the conditions as prescribed in AS-14 for it are satisfied.

A. **Accounting Treatment for Amalgamation in the Nature of Merger:** In preparing the balance sheet of transferee company after amalgamation, all the assets and liabilities of the transferor and transferee company will be added line by line except share capital. The difference between the purchase consideration paid by the transferee company to the transferor company and the share capital of the transferor company should be adjusted with reserves.

B. **Accounting Treatment for Amalgamation in the Nature of Purchase:** In the books of the transferee company assets and liabilities (except fictitious assets and reserves and surplus) shall be recorded at the value at which they are taken over by the transferee company from the transferor company.

   If the purchase consideration exceeds the net assets taken over (Net Assets = Agreed value of assets less agreed value of liabilities), the difference will be debited to goodwill account which is to be amortised over a reasonable period of time generally not exceeding five years and if reverse is the case then the difference is credited to Capital Reserve.

Definitions:

The following terms are used in this statement with meanings specified:

- Amalgamation: It means an amalgamation pursuant to the provisions of the Companies Act, 1956 or any other statute which may be applicable to companies.
- Tansferor company means the company which is amalgamated into another company.

- Transferee company means the company into which a transferor company is amalgamated.
- Reserve means that portion of earnings, receipts or other surplus of an enterprise (whether capital or revenue) appropriated by the management for a general or a specific purpose other than a provision for depreciation or diminution in the value of assets or for a known liability.
- Fair value is the amount for which an asset could be exchanged between a knowledgeable, willing buyer and knowledgeable, willing seller in an arm's length transaction.
- If the purchase consideration is more than the share capital of the transferor company, then the excess shall be debited to reserves, if reverse is the case, then credited to reserves.

APPENDIX

GENERALLY ACCEPTED ACCOUNTING PRINCIPLES (GAAP)

INTRODUCTION

The common set of accounting principles, standards and procedures that companies use to compile their financial statements. GAAP are a combination of authoritative standards (set by policy boards) and simply the commonly accepted ways of recording and reporting accounting information. GAAP are imposed on companies so that investors have a minimum level of consistency in the financial statements they use when analysing companies for investment purposes. GAAP cover such things as revenue recognition, balance sheet item classification and outstanding share measurements. Companies are expected to follow GAAP rules when reporting their financial data via financial statements. If a financial statement is not prepared using GAAP principles, be very wary! That said, keep in mind that GAAP is only a set of standards. There is plenty of room within GAAP for unscrupulous accountants to distort figures. So, even when a company uses GAAP, you still need to scrutinise its financial statements.

PRINCIPLES

Principles derive from tradition, such as the concept of matching. In any report of financial statements (audit, compilation, review, etc.), the preparer/auditor must indicate to the reader whether or not the information contained within the statements complies with GAAP.

- **Principle of Regularity:** Regularity can be defined as conformity to enforced rules and laws. This principle is also known as the Principle of Consistency.
- **Principle of Sincerity:** According to this principle, the accounting unit should reflect in good faith the reality of the company's financial status.

- **Principle of the Permanence of Methods:** This principle aims at allowing the coherence and comparison of the financial information published by the company.
- **Principle of Non-compensation:** One should show the full details of the financial information and not seek to compensate a debt with an asset, a revenue with an expense, etc.
- **Principle of Prudence:** This principle aims at showing the reality as one should not try to make things look prettier than they are. Typically, a revenue should be recorded only when it is *certain* and a provision should be entered for an expense which is *probable*.
- **Principle of Continuity:** When stating financial information, one should assume that the business will not be interrupted. This principle mitigates the principle of prudence: assets do not have to be accounted at their disposable value, but it is accepted that they are at their historical value.
- **Principle of Periodicity:** Each accounting entry should be allocated to a given period, and split accordingly if it covers several periods. If a client pre-pays a subscription (or lease, etc.), the given revenue should be split to the entire time-span and not counted for entirely on the date of the transaction.

These principles variously called accounting concepts and conventions are commonly referred to as the conceptual framework of accounting. The Federal Accounting Standards Board was entrusted with the task of developing a conceptual framework of accounting which is defined as 'a constitution, a coherent system of inter-related objectives and fundamentals that can lead to consistent standards and that prescribes the nature. Function and limits of financial accounting and financial statements'. It has published its Statement of Financial Accounting Concepts (SFAC) in November 1978. What the board has done is a codification of principles that have been in -existence and followed for several years. These principles have been developed over a long period by accountants, academician's regulatory bodies and legislation. Accountants are familiar with these core principles and they are taken for granted. It is only the beginner to the subject who needs to be told about these principles.

In this sub-set comes, for example 'the money measurement concept'. As per this, accounting records only transactions which can be measured in terms of money. This sets the scope as well as the limitation of financial accounting. For example, financial accounting. However important they may be but it does not consider non-financial aspects, such as quitting of an able CEO or the competition the firm is facing or the best industrial relations that the firm enjoys. Example of another core principle is 'the cost concept. As per this, an asset is ordinarily recorded at the price at which it is required. The asset may subsequently undergo change in its value with the passage of time. Therefore, the assets appear at their cost rather than their worth.

The second sub-set is the principles that govern the detailed practices and procedures in the preparation of financial statements. For example, on what basis inventory is to be valued, how should depreciation be determined, what principles to be followed in translating foreign currency transactions, what procedures are to be followed in valuing fixed assets. Like this, there are several aspects where the preparation of account can differ from an enterprise to enterprise and also within the same enterprise over a period of time.

GENERALLY ACCEPTED ACCOUNTING PRINCIPLES

Financial statements, in every country, are prepared in accordance with the accounting principles generally followed in each country. Hence, they are called by the name 'Generally Accepted Accounting Principles' briefly called GAAP. GAAP evolved gradually and informally, over a period of time, but their consolidation, refinement and further development are now vested in specially constituted rule making bodies in which broad representation is given to professional accounting bodies, academicians, regulatory authorities etc. In US, for example, Federal Accounting Standards Board (FASB) was created in 1972 with the support of major professional bodies and financial executives. This body makes major pronouncements called Statements of Financial Accounting Standards (SFASs) from time to time. The Securities and Exchange Commission (SEC), which has been given the power by the statute to determine the measurement rules for financial statements to be provided to shareholders, currently depends on FASB to work out detailed rules that become GAAP. Statutory auditors are also required to ensure the compliance with GAAP and report to shareholders if there is non-compliance. GAAP, therefore are the guidelines for preparing financial statements and in fact the reporting standards of financial statements to external users. The accounting profession has played a great role in developing GAAP that are generally accepted and universally practiced.

It should, however, be noted that GAAP differ from country to country. There are gaps between one country and another. This is mainly because of legislative requirements of each country. There are also other reasons, like the local accounting practices, custom, usage and business environment peculiar to each country. Some of the Indian companies like ICICI and Infosys have recently started preparing the accounts in accordance with US GAAP as well. This is because these companies got listed on New York Stock Exchange and NASDAQ respectively and as per the requirements of SEC, the accounts will have to conform to US GAAP. Moreover, US GAAP are considered as a benchmark for financial reporting. Naturally, income measured as per US GAAP will be less than income measures as per Indian GAAP. In general, US GAAP are more exacting in nature, than Indian GAAP. Some of the significant requirements of US GAAP which are not found in India, are listed below:

1. Provision to be made for deferred taxes.
2. Compulsory consolidation of the accounts of subsidiary concerns.
3. Application of 'equity accounting method' for investments in 'associated companies'.
4. Dividends on redeemable preference shares are a charge to profits and not an appropriation as is the practice in India.
5. Amortisation of stock-based compensation.

NEED FOR GAAP

Financial statements are to be prepared in accordance with GAAP. This is because, if each and every organisation were to adopt its own principles in the preparation of accounts, it will lead to a welter of confusion. Such financial statements will have low acceptability as it will be difficult to understand them without knowing the basis of preparing such financial statements. It can also lead to wrong use by the users of financial statements. Such statements do not serve the purpose of inter-firm or inter-period comparisons. Therefore, there is pressure to comply with GAAP in the preparation of financial statements. Public auditors are required to ensure such compliance and report to the users in case of non-compliance. Observance of GAAP ensures the using of a standard language which every user of such statements can understand in correct perspective.

However, the observance of GAAP does not mean absolute rigidity. There is latitude for the accountants to select alternate policies. Sometimes the standard gives the choice to the accountant. As for example, in the matter of inventory valuation the accountant may follow FIFO or Weighted Average Method. Given the current state of knowledge it is not possible to say that given a particular situation only one accounting treatment is appropriate. Usually the Accounting Standards Committee selects one possible treatment from many as the best practice to be followed by the companies. Where the company feels the standard treatment recommended is not appropriate. It is free to depart from that treatment. But the published accountants should disclose such a departure and in many cases. The impact of such departure on profit measurement. There are also critics of the standardisation brought about by GAAP. In the longer run such standardisation may hinder experimentation and progress. The accountants may stick to GAAP blindly rather than experimenting with alternative approaches. They confine to the learning of rules rather than expanding the frontiers of knowledge. Therefore GAAP must he considered valid only at a point of time. They should change as a result of further developments in the subject. Such developments can result in making an earlier principle wrong and such a principle should be weeded out.

ESSENTIAL REQUISITES OF ACCOUNTING PRINCIPLES

Accounting principles to secure general acceptance must have three attributes *viz*, relevance, objectivity and feasibility. A principle is said to have relevance if it results in more meaningful and useful information about the enterprise to the users. It is said to be objective when the information furnished is not influenced by the bias or personal judgement of those furnishing the same. It is said to be objective when it is solidly supported by facts. A principle is said to be feasible when the adoption does not create problems of collecting information or increase the cost.

Normally all the three features are found in the principles. But, in some cases an optimum balance of the three is struck for adopting a particular rule as an accounting principle. In some cases even a sacrifice of one in favour of another becomes necessary. For example the cost principle followed for recording assets is not useful to the readers as it does not represent its market value. However the adoption of market price will introduce bias and in some cases it may not be feasible as well.

It is important that the information contained in financial reports be both highly reliable and clearly understood. Also, it is important to prepare financial information in a manner that facilitates proper comparisons with past years' reports and with financial information of other enterprises. Therefore, we need a body of broad concepts as well as detailed practices to guide business enterprises in preparing financial reports that will be useful for making decisions. The set of conventions, rules, and procedures necessary to define accepted accounting practice at a particular time is referred to as Generally Accepted Accounting Principles (GAAP). GAAP represents the fundamental positions that have been generally agreed upon, often tacitly, by accountants and encompasses contemporary permissible accounting practice. Unlike the laws of physics or chemistry, accounting principles and practices are not the product of any laboratory research.

INSTITUTIONS THAT INFLUENCE INDIAN GAAP

Many institutions influence the accounting practices followed in preparation and presentation of financial reports by business enterprises in India. These include the Institute of Chartered Accountants of India (ICAI), the Department of Company Affairs (DCA), the Securities and Exchange Board of India (SEBI), the Central Board of Direct Taxes (CBDT), the Reserve Bank of India (RBI), and the Comptroller and Auditor General (CAG) of India. There are also international organisations that take a keen interest in accounting and reporting.

THE INSTITUTE OF CHARTERED ACCOUNTANTS OF INDIA (ICAI)

The Institute of Chartered Accountants of India (ICAI) is constituted under the Chartered Accountants Act, 1949 and is responsible for regulating the profession of chartered accountants. It has played a leading role in developing accounting and reporting practices and has issued many recommendations dealing with a variety of accounting matters. Like its counterparts in the United States and the United Kingdom, ICAI has no legal powers to enforce compliance with its recommendations. Nevertheless, its views on accounting have the weight of professional opinion and hence a significant persuasive influence on accounting practices.

DEPARTMENT OF COMPANY AFFAIRS (DCA)

Department of Company affairs (DCA), Government of India, is concerned with administration of the Companies Act, which lays down the form and content of financial reports of companies. It articulates the government's views on financial reporting and accounting requirements. In the past, barring a few occasional interventions, DCA has kept a low profile in accounting matters. It seems that the DCA would play a key role in the evolution of accounting with the likely establishment of a National Advisory Committee on Accounting Standards in the near future.

SECURITIES AND EXCHANGE BOARD OF INDIA (SEBI)

SEBI is a regulatory agency established by Parliament 'to protect the interests of investors in securities and to promote the development of, and to regulate, the securities market'. SEBI has successfully overhauled the type and amount of information provided in the prospectus at the time of issue of any security to the public. It has an interest in ensuring adequate, true and fair disclosure of financial information and has stated that it would work with ICAI and others on improving the standards of financial reporting. In recent years, SEBI has assumed an active role for itself in corporate disclosure by making it mandatory for companies listed in a stock exchange to publish cash flow statements and quarterly financial statements.

INCOME TAX AUTHORITIES

Income tax authorities including the Central Board of Direct Taxes (CBDT) of the Government of India, Commissioners of Income Tax, and income tax officers, enforce the Income Tax Act that authorises the levy and collection of income tax. The law, contains detailed provisions for determining taxable income. These provisions are interpreted and administered by the Income Tax Department. Income tax is an important outgo for many business enterprises and they attempt to minimise it by taking advantage of tax rules. A business enterprise may choose to follow an accounting practice which is specified in the tax law to reduce its income tax expense. In a few cases, the accounting practices specified by the tax law must be followed. Good tax accounting is not necessarily good financial accounting. Nevertheless, tax rules constitute one of the strongest influences on accounting practice. The Government of India can prescribe accounting rules for tax purposes.

RESERVE BANK OF INDIA (RBI)

Reserve Bank of India (RBI), the central bank of the country, regulates the functioning of the financial sector in India. It has an interest in financial reporting by financial institutions. RBI specifies accounting and reporting requirements for banks and finance companies. For example, in 1992, RBI laid down detailed rules for income recognition and provisioning of bad debts broadly in line with international practices.

COMPTROLLER AND AUDITOR GENERAL OF INDIA (CAG)

Comptroller and Auditor General of India (CAG) is the constitutional functionary appointed by the President of India to audit the accounts of government organisations. The CAG office reviews the financial statements of a number of government departments and public enterprises and sends its observations to the Parliament. The advice of CAG on accounting matters is generally accepted by government organisations.

INTERNATIONAL ORGANISATIONS

The globalisation of capital markets in recent years has given rise to demands for comparable financial information. The International Accounting Standards Committee

(IASC) works for the improvement and harmonisation of financial reporting, primarily through the development and publication of International Accounting Standards. As on January 1, 1999, the IASC has issued 29 standards. There are 142 member professional accountancy bodies (including ICAI) in 102 countries in the IASC. ICAI tries to formulate national accounting standards in tune with the IASC's standards to the extent possible. The International Federation of Accountants (IFAC), whose members are the same as IASC's, is primarily concerned with bringing about greater international harmony in matters such as education, ethics, and auditing practices. Other international groups that take a keen interest in accounting and reporting include the United Nations Inter-governmental Working Group on International Standards of Accounting and Reporting, the Organisation for Economic Co-operation and Development, the International Organisation of Securities Commissions (IOSCO), and the European Community, and their views may have an impact on financial reporting of foreign enterprises operating in India.

Financial Accounting Standards Board (FASB):

Realising the need to reform the APB, leaders in the accounting profession appointed a Study Group on the Establishment of Accounting Principles (commonly known as the Wheat Committee for its chair Francis Wheat). This group determined that the APB must be dissolved and a new standard-setting structure be created. This structure is composed of three organisations: the Financial Accounting Foundation (FAF, it selects members of the FASB, funds and oversees their activities), the Financial Accounting Standards Advisory Council (FASAC), and the major operating organisation in this structure the Financial Accounting Standards Board (FASB). FASB has 4 major types of publications:

1. **Statements of Financial Accounting Standards** – the most authoritative GAAP setting publications.
2. **Statements of Financial Accounting Concepts** – first issued in 1978. They are part of the FASB's conceptual framework project and set forth fundamental objectives and concepts that the FASB use in developing future standards.
3. **Interpretations** – modify or extend existing standards.
4. **Technical Bulletins** – guidelines on applying standards, interpretations, and opinions. Usually solves some very specific accounting issue that will not have a significant, lasting effect.

In 1984 the FASB created the Emerging Issues Task Force (EITF) which deals with new and unusual financial transactions that have the potential to become common (e.g., accounting for Internet-based companies). It acts more like a problem filter for the FASB - the EITF deals with short-term, quickly resolvable issues, leaving long-term, more pervasive problems for the FASB.

Governmental Accounting Standards Board (GASB)

Created in 1984, the GASB addresses state and local government reporting issues. Its structure is similar to that of the FASB's.

Influential Organisations: (e.g., American Accounting Association, Institute of Management Accountants, Financial Executives Institute).

Other Influential Organisations: The Government Finance Officer's Association (GFOA) also influences financial policies for governments. Disagreements between the GFOA and GASB are rare, but can continue for many years.

DIFFERENCES IN VALUATION DISCLOSURES: FRS, IFRS, IAS

The following paragraphs focuses the most fundamental differences between UK Financial Reporting Standards (FRS) and the International Financial Reporting Standards (IFRS) and International Accounting Standards (IAS).

Stock Valuation

Under SSAP 9 *Stocks and long-term contracts* a company can adopt the 'last-in first-out' method of stock valuation (often referred to as the 'LIFO' method). However, under the provisions of IAS 2 Inventories this method of stock valuation is not permitted.

Intangible Assets – Amortisation vs. Impairment

In UK GAAP, FRS 10 *Goodwill and intangibles* allows an entity to amortise goodwill over its expected useful life if that expected useful life is less than twenty years. There is a rebuttable presumption whereby an entity may consider the life of the goodwill to be more than twenty years. However, where an entity states that goodwill is deemed longer than twenty years, the directors have to undertake an 'impairment' review at the end of the first full financial year following the initial recognition of the goodwill or intangible asset and in other periods, where events or changes in circumstances indicate that its carrying value may not be recoverable in full.

Under the provisions of IAS 38 *Intangible assets* amortisation is prohibited and the directors must undertake an impairment review on an annual basis. This links into IAS 36 *Impairment of assets*.

Cash Flow Statements

Under FRS 1 *Cash flow statements* cash flows of an entity prepared under UK GAAP are prepared under eight headings – *operating activities, returns on investments and servicing of finance etc.* IAS 7 *Cash flow statements* require cash flows to be reported under three headings: operating activities, investing activities and financing activities.

Another notable feature under IAS 7 is that the 'reconciliation of movements in cash flows to movements in net debt' is not required.

The cash flow statement under IFRS is a mandatory primary financial statement, whereas in UK GAAP most 'small' companies are exempt under FRS 1 from the requirement to prepare a cash flow statement.

Operating Profit

Under FRS 3 *Reporting financial performance* the FRS requires an entity to report 'operating profit'. Under IAS 1, *Presentation of financial statements* this is not required, though an entity may choose to do so.

Changes in Accounting Policy

Under IAS 8 *Accounting policies*, changes in accounting estimates and errors a company can only change its accounting policies if it results in the financial statements giving more 'relevant and reliable' information. Under FRS 18 *Accounting policies* management must review their accounting policies to ensure they remain the most appropriate to its particular circumstances for the purposes of giving a 'true and fair' view. Note the differences between the IFRS objective of 'relevant and reliable' and UK GAAP 'true and fair'.

Construction Contracts

Under IAS 11 *Construction contracts* an entity can apply the 'percentage of completion' method if the outcome of the contract can be reliably estimated. Under the provisions of SSAP 9 *Stocks and long-term contracts* this task force abstract takes a more prudent approach and recognises 'prudently' calculated profit only if the outcome of the contract can be reliably estimated.

However, both IAS 11 and SSAP 9 take the same stance that where a contract is making-loss losses are recognised in the statement of comprehensive income (income statement)/profit and loss account as soon as they arise.

Deferred Tax

Under the provisions of FRS 19 *Deferred taxation* a company can choose to 'discount' its deferred tax to present day values – though it has to be said that this is rarely done in practice. Under the provisions of IAS 12 *Income taxes*, a company cannot discount its deferred tax to present day values.

Another notable difference in deferred tax is that FRS 19 recognises deferred tax as 'timing differences'. Under IAS 12, deferred tax is recognised on the basis of 'taxable temporary differences'.

Fixed Assets (Non-current Assets)

Under IAS 16 Property plant and equipment, assets 'held for sale', 'biological assets' related to agricultural activity and 'exploration and evaluation assets' are specifically excluded from IAS 16. They are, instead, covered under IFRS 5 Non-current assets held for sale and discontinued operations, IAS 41 Agriculture and IFRS 6 Exploration for and evaluation of mineral resources respectively.

Such assets identified above which are not covered by IAS 16 do, however, fall under the scope in UK GAAP of FRS 15 Tangible fixed assets.

It is to be noted that 'investment properties' are excluded specifically from both standards (IAS 16 and FRS 15), being dealt with under the provisions of IAS 40 Investment properties and SSAP 19 *Accounting for investment properties* respectively.

Related Party Transactions

Under IAS 24 *Related party disclosures* there is no exemption to report related parties if this conflicts with the entity's 'duties of confidentiality'. There is an exemption under FRS 8 where such disclosure would conflict with the reporting entity's duties of confidentiality arising by operation of law.

Consolidation

Under FRS 2 *Accounting for subsidiary undertakings*, a parent does not consolidate where there are severe long-term restrictions over the assets or management of the subsidiary undertaking. IAS 27 *Consolidated and separate financial statements* does not have such exclusion.

Investment Properties

Under IAS 40 *Investment properties*, an entity can choose between the fair value model and depreciated cost model for valuation of its investment properties. SSAP 19 *Investment properties* does not allow the depreciated cost model for such properties.

Agriculture

This follows on from the issues touched on in Fixed Assets (Non-current assets) above. There is no UK equivalent standard for agriculture but there is under IFRS by virtue of IAS 41 *Agriculture*.

Fixed Assets (Non-current Assets) Held for Sale

Again, there is no 'specific' standard which deals with assets held for sale or discontinued operations. In UK GAAP, these are dealt with under FRS 3 *Reporting financial performance*. However, the international regime deals with these under separate accounting standard, IFRS 5 *Non-current assets held for sale and discontinued operations.*

Employee Benefits

Actuarial gains and losses are recognised in the Statement of Recognised Gains and Losses (STRGL) in the UK under FRS 17 *Retirement benefits*. IAS 19 *Employee benefits* offers a choice. These can either be recognised in the statement of comprehensive income (income statement); usually over a period representing the average working lives of the employees participating in the defined benefit scheme. Alternatively, an entity can recognise actuarial gains and losses in full as and when they arise, outside profit or loss, in a Statement of Recognised Income and Expenses (SRIE). This is very similar to the provisions of FRS 17 *Retirement benefits* mentioned above.

CLOSING CASELET

Camera Ltd is proposing to acquire the Bus Ltd. The valuation is expected to be based on the recommendation of the auditors. Purchase consideration is to be discharged in the form of equity shares issued by Camera Ltd which has paid up equity capital of ₹ 50 lakhs at share price of ₹ 50 each. In the secondary market, during the last six months, the highest and lowest prices are ₹ 140 and ₹ 70. The exchange price can be determined at the average of the market price during the last six months. It is expected that the cash flows for the year 2011 is ₹ 15,00,000 and it is also estimated that there will be 12 per cent growth rate in the cash flows of the business. The required rate of return is 11 per cent. The balance sheet of Camera Ltd. as 31-3-2011, is given below:

SOURCES	₹
Equity Share capital	75,00,000
1.5 lakhs shares of ₹ 50 each	
Long-term liabilities	25,00,000
Short-term liabilities	5,00,000
Total	**1,05,00,000**
APPLICATION	
Fixed Assets	75,00,000
Current Assets	30,00,000
Total	**1,05,00,000**

Analyse the balance sheet and find the total value of the business using (a) present value of expected cash flows and (b) number of shares to be issued by the acquiring company.

SUMMARY

This lesson deals with theories of valuation of a firm like: net income approach and net operating income approach and MM approach, and various valuation methods viz., conventional value method, present value method, revenue multiplier method. In the economic sense, the value of corporate entity depends on the discounted benefits expected from owning of an asset. The total value of a corporate entity or corporation is the sum of the market values of its assets. However, financial statements report only book values. This lesson also focuses on valuation of merged firm besides a brief discussion on accounting standard 14 pronounced by Institute of Chartered Accountants of India.

KEYWORDS

1. **Value of Corporate Entity:** Sum of market value of all assets of the entity.
2. **Present Value:** Discounted value of expected cash flows.
3. **Current Yield:** The ratio between stated interest per year and current market price.
4. **YTM:** Yield to maturity, this is equating the current market price of a bond with the discounted value of future interest payments and the terminal principal repayment.
5. **Goodwill:** It is the value of reputation of business house in respect of the profits expected in future over and above the normal level of profits earned by undertakings belonging to same class of business.

REVIEW QUESTIONS

1. Explain various valuation methods of corporate entity?
2. How do you evaluate securities, bonds and goodwill of a corporate entity?

REFERENCES

1. Andrade, Mitchell & Stafford, New Evidence and Perspectives on Mergers, *15, Journal of Economic Perspectives*, 103, (Spring 2001).
2. Anuraag Saxena and Naresh Grandly, (2001). "Alternative for Payments in M&A Deals. A Strategic Evaluation of the Choices at Hand", *The Management Accountant*, 36.11, 864-866.
3. Jarrell & Poulsen, The Returns to Acquiring Firms in Tender Offers: Evidence from Three Decades, 12 *Financial Management*, 18 (1989).
4. Jensen, Takeovers: Their Causes and Consequences, *Journal of Economic Perspectives*, 21 (Winter 1988).
5. Loughran & Vijh, *Do Long-term Shareholders Benefit from Corporate Acquisitions?*

CHAPTER

7

STRATEGIES OF CORPORATE RESTRUCTURING

CHAPTER OUTLINE

- ✧ Opening Caselet
- ✧ Introduction
- ✧ Different Forms of Corporate Restructuring
- ✧ Strategies of Corporate Restructuring
- ✧ Merger Strategies
- ✧ Mergers and Acquisitions in India
- ✧ Tax Consolidation
- ✧ Merger and Acquisitions in Banking Sector
- ✧ Different Types of Mergers
- ✧ Financial Conglomerates
- ✧ Managerial Conglomerate
- ✧ Congeneric Merger
- ✧ Merger Procedure
- ✧ Acquisition
- ✧ Advantages of Mergers and Acquisitions
- ✧ Take-over Strategies
- ✧ Take-over Defenses
- ✧ Leveraged Case-Outs (LCO)
- ✧ Coercive Offers and Defense
- ✧ Problems and Solutions
- ✧ Practice Problems
- ✧ Closing Caselet
- ✧ Summary
- ✧ Keywords
- ✧ Review Questions
- ✧ References

OPENING CASELET

RELIANCE INDUSTRIES HIRES MCKINSEY FOR CORPORATE RESTRUCTURING

India's largest corporate, Reliance Industries has hired business consultancy firm McKinsey to advice it on a business transformation plan which would catapult the company's enteprise value by another $ 80 billion in the next 10 years. RIL will also take help from its independent director and former dean of Kellogg's management school Dipak Jain to chart out the new business reorganisation plan. ET now has learnt from three independent sources that the new corporate structure would lead to changes in the top management team. Though the current core team of Chairman Mukesh Ambani comprising of Manoj Modi, PMS Prasad and Kamal Nanavati will remain untouched, a few new faces will be hired to head new economy businesses like telecom, retail and financial services. RIL has already sounded off head hunting firms to poach talent from rival companies. On the Bombay Stock Exchange, RIL's stock was trading at ₹ 1,021.70, up by over 1 per cent since previous close. RIL is working in a plan to make a foray into new growth areas. The plan includes merger and acquisitions apart from setting up new businesses. In the last one year, Reliance has made some big ticket acquisitions in the United States to buy stake in shale gas assets.

In India, Reliance bought 14.8 per cent stake in Oberoi Hotels and spent ₹ 4,500 crore in taking over Infotel Broadband to launch 4G telecom services in the country. The company recently sold 30 per cent stake in its Krishna Godavari based gas assets for $7.2 billion to BP. The new corporate restructuring is expected to enable RIL transform itself into one of the world's biggest conglomerates. Last year, Mukesh Ambani's RIL and younger brother's Anil Dhirubhai Ambani Group (ADAG) dropped the earlier non-compete agreement and signed a new non-compete agreement. After this, RIL has been looking for opportunities in power sector across generation, transmission and distribution.

The company is currently looking for strategic partners, such as service providers, infrastructure providers, device manufacturers and other participants to expand its infocomm business. Last month, RIL also announced to establish a joint venture with US-based investment and technology development firm DE Shaw group to build financial services business in India. ADAG is already present in telecom, power and financial services. RIL's main businesses under older Ambani brother have been exploration and production of oil and gas, petroleum refining and marketing, petrochemicals, textiles, retail and special economic zones. RIL has now become the world's largest producer of polyester yarn and fibre, is among the world's top ten producers of various petrochemicals and is the largest producer of gas in India.

(***Source:*** **Ruchita Saxena, ET Now** Apr 13, 2011, 06.24pm IST)

INTRODUCTION

Corporate Restructuring covers all aspects of the functioning of a work organisation. It examines the process of top level decision making, the manner of communication of decisions and the procedure for the implementation of management decisions at the operational level. It looks into the process of monitoring of results achieved. Corporate restructuring is necessary when a company needs to improve its efficiency and profitability and it requires expert corporate management. A corporate restructuring strategy involves the dismantling and rebuilding of areas within an organisation that need special attention from the management and CEO. The process of corporate restructuring often occurs after buy-outs, corporate acquisitions, takeovers or bankruptcy. It can involve a significant movement of an organisation's liabilities or assets.

Corporate Restructuring[1] is necessary when a company needs to improve its efficiency and profitability and it requires expert corporate management. A corporate restructuring strategy involves the dismantling and rebuilding of areas within an organisation that need special attention from the management and CEO. The process of corporate restructuring often occurs after buy-outs, corporate acquisitions, takeovers or bankruptcy. It can involve a significant movement of an organisation's liabilities or assets.

Meaning of Corporate Restructuring

Corporate restructuring is all about creating value. Of course, most of the daily decisions that you will make as professional managers or investors will have an impact on value. Sometimes, however, the value of an enterprise falls significantly short of where it could be. In other words, a company can find itself facing a large 'value gap'. The size of a value gap can be huge for larger companies it can be billions of dollars.

Value Gaps can Arise for a Variety of Reasons, Including

- Poor management
- Emergence of new strategic opportunities
- Failure of the capital markets to recognize (i.e., market inefficiency)
- Increased competition
- Macro-economic shocks
- Changes in technology, taxes or regulation.

In order to close the value gap, a firm will generally have to renegotiate the contracts, commitments, claims, obligations, and promises both written and unwritten that it has entered into with its various constituencies. In other words, it will have to re-slice the corporate pie. This process of renegotiation and 'recontracting' is the central focus of the course.

The course also emphasises that choosing the right restructuring approach often requires managers to understand the fundamental business and strategic problems facing

1. Gilson, *Creating Value through Corporate Restructuring: Case Studies in Bankruptcies, Buyouts, and Breakups* (John-Wiley & Sons, 2001).

their companies. Corporate restructuring almost always requires managers to enact fundamental, sometimes radical, changes in the firms' operations, assets, and corporate strategy. One cannot constructively think about re-slicing the corporate pie without also addressing the firms underlying real business problems. In other words, restructuring the right hand side of the balance sheet generally cannot be accomplished without also restructuring the left hand side.

The number of economic claimholders that one has to deal with in a restructuring situation is typically very large. The list includes creditors, shareholders, suppliers, managers, customers, employees (both active and retired), companies, governments, regulators, and the communities in which the firm operates. Each of these groups has its own objectives, and faces its own set or constraints; often one group's interest directly conflict with those of some other group(s). Managers' ability to create value in a restructuring situation often depends on their ability to understand, and balance, the competing interests of these multiple constituencies. The following diagram depicts merger and acquisition advisory which is part of corporate restructuring policy.

Objectives of Corporate Restructuring

1. Evaluation of current endowments and performance.
2. Fine tuning of available skills, technology and plant.
3. Assessment of changes in business environment.
4. Identification of new business opportunities.
5. Securing of a competitive edge for the corporation.

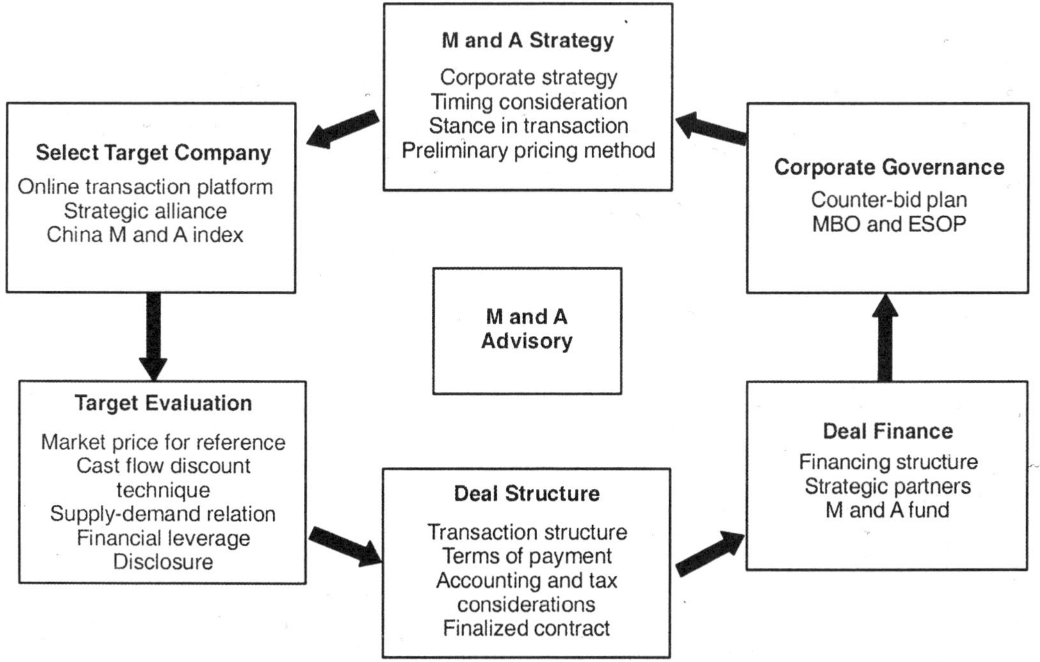

DIFFERENT FORMS OF CORPORATE RESTRUCTURING

Corporate restructuring covers all aspects of the functioning of a work organisation. It examines the process of top level decision making, the manner of communication of decisions and the procedure for the implementation of management decisions at the operational level. It looks into the process of monitoring of results achieved. Corporate restructuring plays a vital role in financial management of any business entity. Top level management will take necessary decision with regard to structural changes in the organisation. The broad categorisation of corporate restructuring is: (1) Expansion, (2) Sell-offs and (3) Changes in ownership and control. Corporate restructuring covers all aspects of the functioning of a work organisation. It examines the process of top level decision making, the manner of communication of decisions and the procedure for the implementation of management decisions at the operational level. It looks into the process of monitoring of results achieved.

STRATEGIES OF CORPORATE RESTRUCTURING

A. Expansion Strategies	B. Reorgansiation Strategies/ Sell-offs	C. Financial Engineering Strategies	D. Governance and Control Strategies
1. Alliances	1. Divestitures	1. ESOP	1. Compensation Arrangements
2. Franchising	2. Equity Carve-outs	2. Exchange	2. Premium Buyback-Green mail
3. Investment	3. Going Public	3. LBO	3. Proxy Contest
4. Joint Ventures	4. Privatisation	4. Leveraged Recapitalis-ation	4. Take-over Defences
5. Mergers	5. Spin-offs and Split-ups	5. Share Repurchase	
6. Purchase of Divisions of Business Unit	6. Tracking Stock		
7. Supplier Network			
8. Tender Offer			

(A) Expansion Strategies

1. **Alliances:** This is more informal interbusiness relations.
2. **Franchising:** Contracts for the use of name, reputation, business format.

3. **Investments:** A stake, but not control in another organisation.
4. **Joint Ventures:** Private sector and public sector may make an Memorandum of Understanding (MOU) to start any new venture. A joint collaboration will be called Joint Venture.
5. **Mergers:** In this case, two organisations will merge and form as a one organisation. There are various forms of mergers like vertical merger, horizontal merger and financial conglomerate. Example: Hewlett Packard (HP) and Compaq.
6. **Purchase of Division/Business Unit:** In this process, the organisation may try to purchase a business unit or a division of any other organisation. Hence, there will be expansion of the business.
7. **Supplier Network:** It is a long-term co-operative relationships.
8. **Tender Offers:** A method of making a take-over via a direct offer to target firm shareholders.

(B) Reorganisation Strategies/Sell-offs

1. **Divestitures:** A sale of a segment of a company to a third party. The divestiture by a seller generally represents focusing on a narrower core of activities. The buying firm seeks to strengthen its strategic programs.
2. **Equity Carve-outs:** A public sale of a portion of a segment equity. In an equity carve-out, a company sells upto 20 per cent of the stock of a segment, for instance the equity carve-out of General Motor and DuPont in the year 1998.
3. **Going Public:** Going public means issuing shares to public.
4. **Privatisation:** It means handing over the ownership to private managers.
5. **Spin-offs and Split-ups:** If the organisation is not able to continue in the business, it may take the decision to sell-off. The sell-off process may be taken in the two forms either divestitures or spin-offs and split-ups. Spin-offs are best when the main business of the company is not likely to make substantial contribution to the segment.
6. **Tracking Stock:** A separate class of common stock that tracks the performance of a segment. This is similar to spin-off in that financial result of the parent and the tracking stock companies are reported separately. But in the tracking stock relationship, the board of the parent continues to control the activities of the tracking segment. Management compensation can be based on performance of the tracking stock company and its stock price behaviour.

(C) Financial Engineering Strategies

1. **ESOP:** A defined contribution pension plan designed to invest primarily in the stock of the employer firm.

2. **Exchange Offers:** The right option or option to exchange one class of a security for another, for example, exchange between equity shares and debt.

3. **Leverage Buy Out (LBO):** By adopting the LBO method, the organisation will have financial advantage.

4. **Leveraged Recapitalisations:** A large increase in the leverage ratio to finance the return of cash to shareholders.

5. **Share Repurchases:** To increase share of management, the organisation may buy-back the issues shares.

(D) Governance and Control Strategies

1. **Compensation Arrangements:** Payment forms to align interests of managers, owners and employees.

2. **Premium Buybacks-green Mail:** The repurchase of specified shares, usually from a party seeking to take-over a firm.

3. **Proxy Contest:** An attempt by a dissident group of shareholders to gain representation on a firm's board of directors.

4. **Take-over Defences:** This decision is useful to taking of entire business of other organisation. Loss-making units may be handed over to profit-oriented units. Example: Oriental Bank of Commerce has taken over Global Trust Bank.

MERGER STRATEGIES

A merger occurs when two or more firms are combined and the resulting firm maintains the identity of one of the firms usually, the assets and liabilities of the smaller firms are merged into those of the larger firms. The three main merger types are horizontal, vertical and conglomerate. An affirmative rationale can be made for each.

Merger is a financial tool that is used for enhancing long-term profitability by expanding their operations. Mergers occur when the merging companies have their mutual consent as different from acquisitions, which can take the form of a hostile take-over. The business laws in US vary across states and hence the companies have limited options to protect themselves from hostile take-overs. One way a company can protect itself from hostile take-overs is by planning shareholders' rights, which is alternatively known as, poison pill. If we trace back to history, it is observed that very few mergers have actually added to the share value of the acquiring company. Corporate mergers may promote monopolistic practices by reducing costs, taxes, etc. Such activities may go against public welfare. Hence, mergers are regulated supervised by the government, for instance, in US any merger requires the prior approval of the Federal Trade Commission and the Department of Justice. In US regulations on mergers began with the Sherman Act in

1890. Mergers may be horizontal, vertical, conglomerate or congeneric, depending on the nature of the merging companies.

In today's dynamic business world, Mergers & Acquisitions (M&As) are becoming a common and regular feature for majority of corporate houses. This article throws light on various implications and aspects connected with a Merger & Acquisition transaction. A merger is said to occur when two or more business combine into one. This can happen through absorption of an existing company by another. In a consolidation, which is a form of merger, a new company is formed to takeover existing business of two or more companies. In India, mergers are called amalgamations in legal parlance. The acquisition refers to the acquisition of controlling interest in an existing company. A take-over is same as acquisition, except that a take-over has a flavour of hostility in majority of cases. For this reason, the company taken-over is usually called the target company and the acquirer is called the predator. The mergers are different from acquisitions in the sense that acquisitions generally do not involve liquidation of the target company.

The common objective of both the parties in a M&A transaction is to seek synergy in operating economies by combining their resources and efforts. Now, we shall see the reasons for M&A from the perspective of both, the buyer company as well as the seller company.

Genesis of Mergers and Acquisitions

- **First Wave Mergers:** The first wave mergers commenced from 1897 to 1904. During this phase merger occurred between companies, which enjoyed monopoly over their lines of production like railroads, electricity, etc., the first wave mergers that occurred during the aforesaid time period were mostly horizontal mergers that took place between heavy manufacturing industries.
- **End of First Wave Mergers:** Majority of the mergers that were conceived during the 1st phase ended in failure since they could not achieve the desired efficiency. The failure was fuelled by the slowdown of the economy in 1903, followed by the stock market crash of 1904. The legal framework was not supportive either. The Supreme Court passed the mandate that the anticompetitive mergers could be halted using the Sherman Act.
- **Second Wave Mergers:** The second wave mergers that took place from 1916 to 1929, focused on the mergers between oligopolies, rather than monopolies as in the previous phase. The economic boom that followed the post world war I gave rise to these mergers. Technological developments like the development of railroads and transportation by motor vehicles provided the necessary infrastructure for such mergers or acquisitions to take place. The government policy encouraged firms to work in unison. This policy was implemented in the 1920s.

  The 2nd wave mergers that took place were mainly horizontal or conglomerate in nature. The industries that went for merger during this phase were producers of primary metals, food products, petroleum products, transportation equipments and chemicals. The investments banks played a pivotal role in facilitating the mergers and acquisitions.

- **Third Wave Mergers:** The mergers that took place during this period (1965-69) were mainly conglomerate mergers. Mergers were inspired by high stock prices, interest rates and strict enforcement of antitrust laws. The bidder firms in the third wave merger were smaller than the target firm. Mergers were financed from equities; the investment banks no longer played an important role. The third wave merger ended with the plan of the Attorney General to split conglomerates in 1968. It was also due to the poor performance of the conglomerates. Some mergers in the 1970s, have set precedence. The most prominent ones were the INCO-ESB merger; United Technologies and OTIS Elevator Merger are the merger between Colt Industries and Garlock Industries.

- **Fourth Wave Mergers:** The fourth wave merger that started from 1981 and ended by 1989 was characterised by acquisition targets that were much larger in size as compared to the third wave mergers. Mergers took place between the oil and gas industries, pharmaceutical industries, banking and airline industries. Foreign take-overs became common with most of them being hostile takeovers. The fourth wave mergers ended with anti take-over laws, Financial Institutions Reform and the Gulf War.

- **Fifth Wave Mergers:** The fifth wave merger (1992-2000) was inspired by globalisation, stock market boom and deregulation. The 5th wave merger took place mainly in the banking and telecommunications industries. They were mostly equity financed rather than debt financed. The mergers were driven long-term rather than short-term profit motives. The 5th wave merger ended with the burst in the stock market bubble.

  Hence, we may conclude that the evolution of mergers and acquisitions has been long drawn. Many economic factors have contributed its development. There are several other factors that have impeded their growth. As long as economic units of production exist mergers and acquisitions would continue for an ever-expanding economy. Trend essentially refers to the observed long-term movement in a time series data. Trend estimates are seasonally adjusted through an averaging process. Merger and acquisition trends provide an idea about the market movements.

Global Merger and Acquisition Trends for 2006 and 2007, were marked by a spate of mergers and acquisitions all over the globe in both developing and developed countries. The general trend was that, there was a decline in the number of public sector undertakings along with a hike in the number of private sector enterprises. This was due to the fact that many public sector organisations worldwide were either acquired by large private sector enterprises or merged with them. The explanation to this merger and acquisition trend as observed in 2006 and 2007, lay in the robust growth recorded by the Private Equity Funds. The other factors propelling this trend were the emphasis on short-term earnings growth and the strict regulatory structure of public sector enterprises.

This merger and acquisition trend towards increased privatisation of public sector holdings was observed in Europe, Brazil, North America, and China. Europe in that period hosted a strong investment market, which catered to the public to private sector transition of companies.

For Europe the general prediction was that of a high transactional demand related to private equity. Analysts observed that certain European markets were characterised by different financial advantages and tax structures. Western European nations possessed well oiled legal machinery and conducive investment climates. In particular Britain exhibited a strong market for public to private investments. After the accession of nations like Poland, Czech Republic and Hungary into the EU, a section of European funds for private equity were seen to be abstaining from applying the 'emerging market discount' for investment in those nations. Equity investment in Brazil turned attractive with the program called Novo Mercado. Brazilian pension funds turned out to be a prime investment force. Their bankruptcy code got a revision. The elected government was supportive of a free market structure. In North America domestic dealings in M&A executed by private equity investors of USA displayed a robust international component. The observed trend was that a majority of the funds wanted to secure off-shore partners for distribution, contract manufacturing or joint ventures.This kind of cross-border transactions entailed a careful planning for tax obligations arising out of fund repatriation.

Global leveraged buyouts figures for 2006, were above US$ 800 billion. This was more than twice the comparable figure for 2005. It constituted around 20 per cent of US international mergers and acquisitions. However, even then it was not a significant component of the world equity and debt market. In 2006, North America saw vigorous leveraged buyout activities, which amounted to half of the world activity in that field. Europe witnessed a fairly heightened activity in the arena of leveraged buyouts; while Asia had a relatively slow increase. France, Netherlands, and Germany were the biggest European buyout markets in 2006.

MERGERS AND ACQUISITIONS IN INDIA

The process of mergers and acquisitions has gained substantial importance in today's corporate world. This process is extensively used for restructuring the business organisations. In India, the concept of mergers and acquisitions was initiated by the government bodies. Some well known financial organisations also took the necessary initiatives to restructure the corporate sector of India by adopting the mergers and acquisitions policies. The Indian economic reform since 1991 has opened up a whole lot of challenges both in the domestic and international spheres. The increased competition in the global market has prompted the Indian companies to go for mergers and acquisitions as an important strategic choice. The trends of mergers and acquisitions in India have changed over the years. The immediate effects of the mergers and acquisitions have also been diverse across the various sectors of the Indian economy.

Mergers and Acquisitions Across Indian Sectors

Among the different Indian sectors that have resorted to mergers and acquisitions in recent times, telecom, finance, FMCG, construction materials, automobile industry and steel industry are worth mentioning. With the increasing number of Indian companies opting for mergers and acquisitions, India is now one of the leading nations in the world in terms of mergers and acquisitions.

The merger and acquisition business deals in India amounted to $40 billion during the initial 2 months in the year 2007. The total estimated value of mergers and acquisitions in India for 2007, was greater than $100 billion. It is twice the amount of mergers and acquisitions in 2006.

Mergers and Acquisitions in India: The Latest Trends

Till recent past, the incidence of Indian entrepreneurs acquiring foreign enterprises was not so common. The situation has undergone a sea change in the last couple of years. Acquisition of foreign companies by the Indian businesses has been the latest trend in the Indian corporate sector.

There are different factors that played their parts in facilitating the mergers and acquisitions in India. Favorable government policies, buoyancy in economy, additional liquidity in the corporate sector, and dynamic attitudes of the Indian entrepreneurs are the key factors behind the changing trends of mergers and acquisitions in India.

The Indian IT and ITES sectors have already proved their potential in the global market. The other Indian sectors are also following the same trend. The increased participation of the Indian companies in the global corporate sector has further facilitated the merger and acquisition activities in India.

Major Mergers and Acquisitions in India

Recently the Indian companies have undertaken some important acquisitions. Some of those are as follows:

Hindalco acquired Canada based Novelis. The deal involved transaction of $5,982 million. Tata Steel acquired Corus Group plc. The acquisition deal amounted to $12,000 million. Dr. Reddy's Labs acquired Betapharm through a deal worth of $597 million. Ranbaxy Labs acquired Terapia SA. The deal amounted to $324 million. Suzlon Energy acquired Hansen Group through a deal of $565 million. The acquisition of Daewoo Electronics Corp. by Videocon involved transaction of $729 million. HPCL acquired Kenya Petroleum Refinery Ltd. The deal amounted to $500 million. VSNL acquired Teleglobe through a deal of $239 million. When it comes to mergers and acquisitions deals in India, the total number was 287 from the month of January to May in 2007. It has involved monetary transaction of US $47.37 billion. Out of these 287 merger and acquisition deals, there have been 102 cross country deals with a total valuation of US $28.19 billion.

REASONS

1. An opportunity for achieving faster growth.
2. Obtaining tax concessions.
3. Eliminating competition.
4. Achieving diversification with minimum cost.
5. Improving corporate image and business value.
6. Gaining access to management or technical talent

Why Companies go for Sale or Offer themselves for Sale?

1. Declining earnings and profitability.
2. To raise funds for more promising lines of business.
3. Desire to maximise growth.
4. Give itself the benefit of image of larger company.
5. Lack of adequate management or technical skills.

Procedural aspects under the Companies Act, 1956: The procedure for putting through a M&A transaction under the Companies Act, 1956, is very tedious and a lot of time is consumed in completion of the process. Sections 391 to 396 deal with the procedure, powers of the court and allied matters. The basic difference between a court merger and an acquisition is that the transferor company will be dissolved in case of a merger, whereas in case of acquisition the transferor company continues to exist.

TAX CONSOLIDATION

Tax consolidation is a regime adopted in the tax or revenue legislation of a number of countries which treats a group of wholly-owned or majority-owned companies and other entities (such as trusts and partnerships) as a single entity for tax purposes. This generally means that the head entity of the group is responsible for all or most of the group's tax obligations (such as paying tax and lodging tax returns). The aim of a tax consolidation regime is to reduce administrative costs for government revenue departments and reduce compliance costs for corporate tax-payers. However, consolidation regimes can include onerous rules and regulations.

Reasons for Consolidating

1. If there are losses in the group companies which you wish to absorb.
2. If there are dividends you wish to declare but do not have sufficient imputation credits in the particular company.

3. If there are assets that you wish to transfer between companies without triggering capital gains tax.
4. You have bought shares in a subsidiary instead of the assets of the business, and wish to name the assets of the company so that depreciation can be calculated thereon.

Consolidation is an all or nothing event — once decision to consolidate has been made, companies are irrevocably bound, and only by having a less than 100 per cent interest in a subsidiary, can it be left out of the consolidation. When subsidiaries are bought for share value rather than outright purchase of assets, a regime called allocalble cost amount is in force to transform the amount paid for the shares into depreciable and other assets. Likewise, when a company is sold for the value of its shares, the reverse of allocable cost amount takes place to extract the assets from the consolidation.

Current losses have no problem in being absorbed by current profits in the other companies but losses brought into the consolidation can pose a problem for amount allowed to be written-off in each year, called the available fraction. The reason for this is otherwise companies with big losses could be bought to offset current tax liabilities, and there is a calculation based on the overall size of the group and the size of the purchased loss, to limit the amount that can be written-off each year. That is not to say that the whole loss might not be allowed, it will, but only a percentage of it can be written-off each year.

In a consolidation, all imputation credits and losses float to the top company and there is no need to declare individual dividends from the discrete companies in order for the head company to pay franked dividends, and only one dividend is declared which is from the head company. Fixed trusts and 100 per cent partnerships can be members of a consolidated group, but the head company must be company and cannot be a trust or partnership.

Implications under the Income Tax Act, 1961

Tax implications can be understood from the following three perspectives:

(a) Tax concessions to the Amalgamated (Buyer) Company.

(b) Tax concessions to the Amalgamating (Seller) Company.

(c) Tax concessions to the shareholders of an Amalgamating Company.

Tax Concessions to the Amalgamated Company

- If the amalgamating company has incurred any expenditure eligible for deduction under sections 35(5), 35A(6), 35AB(3), 35ABB, 35D, 35DD, 35DDA, 35E and/or 36(1)(ix), prior to its amalgamation with the amalgamated company as per Section 2(1B) of the Act and if the amalgamated company is an Indian company, then the benefit of the aforesaid sections shall be available to the amalgamated company, in the manner it would be available to the amalgamating company had there been no amalgamation.

- Also under section 72A of the Act, the amalgamated company is entitled to carry forward the unabsorbed depreciation and unabsorbed accumulated business losses of the amalgamating company provided certain conditions are fulfilled.
- The CBDT is expected to reckon on the possibility of extending the benefits of section 72A to M&As in the financial sector. Currently, the benefits of this section are applicable to manufacturing sector only.
- Any transfer of capital assets, in the scheme of amalgamation, by an amalgamating company to an Indian amalgamated company is not treated as transfer under section 47(vi) of the Act and so no capital gain tax is attracted in the hands of the amalgamating company. When the shareholder of an amalgamating company transfers shares held by him in the amalgamating company in consideration of allotment of shares in amalgamated company in the scheme of amalgamation, then such transfer of shares in not considered as transfer under section 47(vii) of the Act and consequently, no capital gain is attracted in the hands of the shareholder of amalgamating company. The above are only few out of the various tax concessions available to the aforementioned categories of the assesses due to M&A transaction.

MERGERS AND ACQUISITIONS IN BANKING SECTOR

Dario Focareli *et.al.*, (1999)[2] studies about banking industry in Italy. He mentions that Italian market is similar to other main European countries. He states that the banking industry is consolidating at an accelerating pace, yet no conclusive results have emerged on the benefits of mergers and acquisitions. We analyse the Italian market, which is similar to other main European countries. By considering both acquisitions (i.e., the purchase of the majority of voting shares) and mergers, they evidence the motives and results of each type of deal. Mergers seek to improve income from services, but the increase is offset by higher staff costs; return on equity improves because of a decrease in capital. Acquisitions aim to restructure the loan portfolio of the acquired bank; improved lending policies result in higher profits.

Bhatnagar, R.G. (2001)[3] pointed out that the urge to merge is overwhelming in the corporate sector in the context of globalisation. However, size base mergers need not be the best of strategies especially in the banking sector. A cost cut strategy is a better option. The author remarked that bank mergers in India might facilitate compliance with the stipulation of dilution of the promoters stake to 40 per cent. Deeksha Verma (2001)[4] in her study stated that Indian banking system has decisively entered the consolidation phase through mergers. The merger of UTI bank with Global Trust Bank enhanced the branch network to 158, most of them in metro and urban areas. The

2. Dario Forcarelli, Fabio Panetta and Carmello Salleo (1999), 'Why do Banks Merge?', Banca d' Italia, Research Department. This Paper is Submitted to Bank of Italy.
3. Bhatnagar, R.G., (2001), "Banking too Much on Mergers", *Professional Banker*, 1.3, pp. 39-40.
4. Deeksha Verma (2001), "Banking on Merger", *Professional Banker*, 1.3, pp. 36-38.

challenges in future will be in the form of integration of work culture and higher exposure of Global Trust Bank to sensitive sector financing.

According to Sangita Mehta (2001),[5] in the study of major financial institutions of India like IDBI, IFCI and ICICI etc., are in a restructuring phase. These institutions are shunned by the bourses because of the problems of rising non-performing assets and high fund costs. The author pointed out that Government interference and disparity in pay scales are the hindering factors towards restructuring. Giridharan R. (2001)[6] points out the possible causes for the explosive spurt in mergers that have rocked the banking industry. The author elaborated the risk associated with mergers and remarks that the success or otherwise of mergers would depend on the success of the measures discussed in the article.

Anurag Saxena and Naresh Grandhy (2001)[7] proposes to demystify the strategic intent behind each of the modes of payment in M&A deals. The issues including Indian legal framework, the tax and accounting implications have also been discussed. The authors attempt to deal with quantifying the financial risk involved in such deals.

RECENT MERGERS, ACQUISITIONS

USA

Unilever offers $1.8 billion for Sara Lee personal care operations.

Posted: Fri., Sep 25, 2009. 3:27 p.m. IST.

The Hague: Anglo-Dutch food and cosmetics giant Unilever said on Friday it had made a binding offer of •1.28 billion ($1.83 billion) for the personal care operations of US giant Sara Lee Corp. 'Personal Care is a strategic category and a key growth driver for Unilever,' Chief Executive Paul Polman said. 'This transaction builds on our portfolio in Western Europe and also in Asia. The Sara Lee brands enjoy strong consumer recognition, offer significant growth potential and are an excellent fit with Unilever's existing business.'

The Sara Lee business posted sales of more than •750 million in the 12 months to June 2009, with earnings before interest, depreciation and amortisation of •128 million, according to a Unilever statement.

INDIA

Mumbai: Tube Investments of India Ltd., a maker of steel products, plans to buy companies locally or overseas by the end of March to benefit from spending on infrastructure in the world's second fastest growing economy.

'We are looking at companies that have technologies we don't have,' Managing Director L. Ramkumar said in a telephone interview on Tuesday. 'The growth in infrastructure will require some chains, tubes, boilers, those kinds of things'.

5. Sangita Mehta (2001), "The Writing on the Wall", *Professional Banker*, 1.6, pp. 40-41.
6. Giridaran. R. (2001). "Mergers — The Emerging Reality", *IBA Bulletin*, pp. 32-34.
7. Anuraag Saxena and Naresh Grandly. (2001), "Alternative for Payments in M&A Deals — A Strategic Evaluation of the Choices at Hand", *The Management Accountant*, 36.11, pp. 864-866.

India needs $1.7 trillion (₹ 81.94 trillion) for roads, utilities, railways and other large projects in the next decade to boost growth, Goldman Sachs said on 16 September.

'Tube Investments may spend about ₹ 140 crore this year to boost production capacity, which doesn't including buying companies', Ramkumar said.

'The budget for acquisitions will be known when we decide. We have scope for leverage without fuss,' Ramkumar said. 'We are looking at options in all areas'. He declined to say whether Tube Investments is in negotiations to buy any companies.

Shares in Tube Investments, have more than doubled this year, compared with an 80 per cent increase in the Bombay Stock Exchange BSE 500 index. Toyota Motor Corp. bought a 1.5 per cent stake in the company on 14 September, according to Bombay Stock Exchange data.

'Business has been better than our expectations in the first and the second quarters,' Ramkumar said. 'If the current trend continues over the next two quarters, this could well be one of our best years'.

He declined to forecast sales or profit growth in the 12 months ending 31 March.

"Tube Investments, which gets almost half of its income from bicycles, parts and electronic scooters and about a quarter from formed metal products, including doors for Tata Motors Ltd.'s Nano, won't be expanding in the automotive sector,' Ramkumar said.

'It is going to be more of the non-auto sector that will drive growth,' he said. 'Auto companies want more for less all the time. Over the next two to three years, we'd like to reduce it by 10% to 15 per cent'.

Tube Investments is part of the Murugappa group, a privately held investment company that has holdings in financial services, agro-industry and other businesses.

Following are some of the important mergers and acquisitions that took place in the banking sector of the United States:

S.No.	Acquiring Bank	Merged Bank	New Bank
1.	Amsouth Bank Corporation	Regions Financial Corporation	Regions Financial Corporation
2.	Bank One	J.P. Morgan Chase and Company	J.P. Morgan Chase and Company
3.	Chase Manhattan Corporation	J.P. Morgan Chase and Company	J.P. Morgan Chase and Company
4.	Dime Bancorp, Inc.	Washington Murtual	Washington Murtual
5.	Fifth Third Bancorp	Old Kent Financial	Fifth Third Bancorp
6.	Fifth Union Corpo-ration	Wachovia Corporation	Wachovia Corporation
7.	Firstar Corporation	U.S. Bancrop	U.S. Bancrop
8.	Fleet Boston Financial Corporation	Bank of America Corporation	Bank of America Corporation

9.	Golden State Bancorp	Citigroup INC	Citigroup INC.
10.	Hibernia National Bank Sun Trust	National Commerce Financial	Sun Trust
11.	LaSalle Bank	Bank of America	Bank of America
12.	MBNA Corporation	Bank of America	Bank of America Card Services
13.	Summit Bancorp	Fleet Boston Financial Corporation	Fleet Boston Financial Corporation

DIFFERENT TYPES OF MERGERS

1. **Horizontal Merger:** These provide economies of scale. A horizontal merger involves two firm operating and competing the same kind of business activity. Thus, the acquisition in 1987, of American Motars by Chrysel represented a horizontal combination or merger. Forming a larger firm may have the benefit of economies of scale. Horizontal mergers are regulated by the government for their potential negative effect on competition. The number of firms in an industry is decreased by horizontal mergers and this may make it easier for the industry members to collude for monopoly profit.
2. **Vertical Merger:** Vertical mergers occurs between in different stages of production operation. In the oil industry, for example, distinctions are made between exploration and production, refining and marketing to the ultimate consumer. In pharmaceutical industry, one could distinguish between research and the development of new drugs, the production of drugs and the marketing of drug products through retail drug stores. Technological economies can be achieved and cost-efficiencies also can be achieved with the help of vertical mergers.
3. **Conglomerate Merger:** This type of merger involve firms engaged in unrelated types of business activity. Thus, the merger between Mobil and Montgomoery Ward was generally regarded as a conglomerate merger. Among conglomerate mergers, three types have been distinguished:
   - Product-extension mergers broaden the product lines of firms. These are mergers between the firms in related business activities and may also be called 'concentric' mergers.
   - A geographic market-extension merger involves two firms whose operations have been conducted in non-overlapping geographic areas.
   - Finally, the other conglomerate mergers which are often referred to as pure conglomerate mergers involving unrelated business activities.

FINANCIAL CONGLOMERATES

These provide a flow of funds to each segment of their operations, exercise control, and are the ultimate financial risk takers. In theory, financial conglomerates undertakes strategic planning but do not participate in operating decisions.

Economic Functions of Financial Conglomerates:

- It improves risk/return ratio through diversification.
- It avoids 'gambler's skin' (an adverse run of losses which might cause bankruptcy). If the losses can be covered by avoiding gambler's skin, the financial conglomerate maintains the availability of an economic activity with long-run value.
- A third are of potential contributions by financial conglomerates derives from their establishing programs of financial planning and control.
- A fourth benefit also results from financial planning and control. If management does not perform effectively but the productivity of assets in the market is favourable, the management is changed.
- Fifth, in the financial planning and control process, distinction is made between performance based on underlying potentials in the product-market area and results related to managerial performance.

MANAGERIAL CONGLOMERATE

This carries the attributes of financial conglomerate still further. By providing managerial counsel and interactions on decisions, managerial conglomerate increase the potential for improving performance.

CONGENERIC MERGER

A congeneric merger is achieved by acquiring a firm that is in the same general industry but neither in the same line of business nor a supplier or customer. An example is the merger of a machine-tool manufacturer with the manufacturer of industrial conveyor systems. The benefit of this type of merger is the resulting ability to use the same sales and distribution channels to reach customers of both businesses.

Other types of mergers:

- Negotiated Merger
- Tender Offer
- Hostile Takeover bid
- Arranged Mergers

MERGER PROCEDURE

1. Search for a target company.
2. Primary investigation about target firm.
3. Financial Analysis based on financial statements.
4. Industry Analysis to assess the present and future position.
5. Management Analysis to assess the standing of the present management of target firm.
6. Economic Analysis: to assess the competitive condition, cyclical variations.
7. Marketing Analysis to assess the present and future market shares, product life cycle and marketing strategies.
8. Engineering Analysis to examine the production capacity, research and development facilities and operating economies etc.
9. Selecting merger strategy:
   (a) Tender offer (or)
   (b) Negotiated deal (or)
   (c) Hostile take-over bid.

ACQUISITION

It includes takeovers also. In general, acquisition refers to the acquiring of ownership right in the property and assets. It denotes a situation when one company acquires ownership in the assets, and to control of monies of another company. The other company of which the control is so acquired, remains a separate company and is not liquidated but there is a change in control. Acquisition results when one company purchases the controlling interest in the share capital of another existing company in any of the following ways:

- By entering into an agreement with a person or persons holding controlling interest in other company.
- By subscribing new shares being issued by other company.
- By purchasing shares of the other company at a stock exchange and
- By making an offer to buy the shares of other company, to the existing shareholders of that company.

ADVANTAGES OF MERGERS AND ACQUISITIONS

1. Combined company can develop new customers, new relationships and make regular follow-up with clients.
2. Cost control, cost reduction and reduction in overhead costs can be possible with the merger/acquisition activity.
3. Diversification products, markets and customers is possible.
4. It can acquire talent for fast-moving trends in the industry.
5. It can develop new products to reach customers demand.
6. It can prevent competition in the market.
7. Market expansion is easy so as to achieve more market share and profit.
8. New company acquires capabilities in the competitive industrial environment.
9. New company can achieve all benefits of economies of scale.
10. New company can develop a new strategic vision for achieving long-run goals.
11. New managerial skills can be acquired after merger.
12. Technology, quality and service aspects can be improved.

TAKE-OVER STRATEGIES

A take-over generally involves the acquisition of a certain block of equity capital of a company which enables the acquirer to exercise control over the affairs of the company. In theory, the acquirer must buy more than 50 per cent of the paid-up equity of the acquired company to enjoy complete control. Harris and Raviv (1988) focus on the effect of financial leverage on the take-over methods (proxy fights versus tender offers) and their price effects. The basic idea is that incumbent management of a take-over target can affect the type of take-over attempt and its probability of success by choosing the fraction 'a' of the firm's equity to be held by the management. The change on the fraction 'a' is affected by the amount of debt issued.

The management's strategy is based on a trade-off between the potential gain in firm value due to an improvement in management through take-over and the loss of personal benefits derived from being in control of the firm. In the model, increases in debt increase 'a', but reduced the expected benefits of control by increasing the bankruptcy probability, by increasing monitoring activity by creditors and by reducing the discretion of incumbents in allocating cash flows. It is assumed that if no benefit is outstanding, the benefits of control are sufficiently large in relation to the gain in equity value from better management that the incumbent prefers always to vote for itself. In the model, all parties know that either the incumbent or the rival is best able to manage the firm, but are uncertain about identity of the better team.

Friendly vs. Hostile Bids

According to Berkovitch and Khanna (1988), in their model, a merger is a bargaining game between the managements of target and acquiring firms, while a tender offer is an auction in which acquirers arrive sequentially and compete for the target. The acquiring firm prefers a merger over a public tender offer because a merger is assumed to be a private negotiation whereas a tender offer releases more information on the targets and results in an auction.

In equilibrium, there is a unique level of synergy gains below which the acquiring firm makes only a merger attempt, as it expects to lose in a public auction. The target management is given a golden parachute contract and there by encouraged to force the acquirer into making a tender offer wherever possible.

TAKE-OVER DEFENSES

Defenses can take the form of general wall building to make the firm less attractive to raiders or more difficult to take-over and thus, discourage any offers being made. These include asset and ownership restructuring, anti-take-over charter amendments, adoption of poison pill rights plans, and so forth. Defensive actions are also taken in response to explicit threats ranging from early intelligence that a 'raider' or any acquirer has been accumulating the firm's stock to an open tender offer.

Financial Defensive Measures

It is possible to identify the characteristics that make a firm a desirable candidate for acquisition from the acquirer's point of view. The factors that make a firm valuenerable to a take-over include:

- A low stock price in relation to the replacement cost of assets on their potential earning power.
- A highly liquid balance sheet with large amounts of excess cash, a valuable securities portfolio, and significant unused debt capacity.
- Good cash flow relative to current stock prices.
- Subsidiaries or properties which could be sold off without significantly impairing cash flow.
- Relatively small stockholdings under the control of incumbent management.

LEVERAGED CASH-OUTS (LCO)

LCO has been implemented in response to a takeover bid. All firms that used an LCO have also made charter amendments such as super majority voting or adopting poison pill voting plans. LCO is also called leveraged recapitalisation. In a typical recapitalisation, outside shareholders receive a large one-time cash dividend and insiders and employee benefit plans receive new shares instead of the cash dividend. The cash dividend is financed mostly by newly borrowed funds, both senior bank debt and mezzamine debt (subordinated debentures). As a result, the firm's leverage is increased to an 'abnormally' high level and this would discourage take-over attempts financed mainly by borrowing against the firm's own assets. The proportional equity ownership of management also significantly rises through the recapitalisation. In many cases, new shares, called 'stubs' are issued to replace the old shares. The firm's shares continue to be publicly traded. This appears to be one reason why LCO's are generally implemented by firms larger than those involved in LBO's (Leveraged Buy-Outs).

Golden Parachutes

These refer to separation provisions of an employment contract that compensate managers for the loss of their jobs under a change-of-control clause. The provision usually calls for a lump-sum payment or payment over a specified contract has been increasingly used even by the largest Fortune 500 firms as M&A activity has intensified in 1980s and these firms have become susceptible to hostile take-over. By the mid-1980s, about 25 per cent of the Fortune 500 firms had adopted golden parachute features in their employment contracts for top managers.

The majority view on golden parachutes is that these control related contracts help reduce the conflict interest between shareholders and managers in change-of-control situations. Excessive use of golden parachutes appears to be infrequent and the new tax law now imposes specific limits.

Poison Put

Corporate bond quality often deteriorates following the issues's leveraged buy-out or other forms of control change. Since 1986, some new bond issues have provided their holders with poison put convenants as protections from the risk of take-over related credit deterioration of the issues. The exercise price of the put option is usually set at 100 or 101 per cent of the bonds face amount. Exercise of the put after an unfriendly take-over can be very costly to the bidder even when it can easily finance the required funds. Sometimes, the put will improve worthless and impose no cost to the bidder. This will be in case if the bond price prior to the exercise price and is still higher after the take-over and the resulting deterioration in its quality.

COERCIVE OFFERS AND DEFENSE

Front-end Loading in Tender Offers

The pressure or 'Coercion' to tender arises when take-over bid is front-end loaded, that is, when the offer price is greater than the price of any unpurchased shares. When a bid is front-end loaded, individual shareholders will have the incentive to tender to receive the higher-front-end price. It is obvious that front-end loading occurs in two-tier offers. Further, it is commonly believed that partial and any-or-all offers are also front-end loaded. In a two-tier offer, the bidder offers a first-tier price for a specified maximum number of shares that it would accept and announces at the same time its intention to acquire in a follow-up merger the remaining shares at a second-tier price.

Poison Pill Defense

A controversial but popular defense mechanism against hostile take-over bids is the creation of securities called Poison pills. These securities provide their holders with special rights exercisable only after some time (for example, ten days) following the occurrence of a triggering event such as a tender offer for control or the accumulation of a specific percentage of target shares these rights take several forms but all make it difficult or costly to acquire control of the issuer, or the target firm. They economically, 'poison' the would-be acquirer if swallowed. Poison pills are generally adopted by the board of directors without shareholder approval. Usually, the rights provided by a poison pill plan can be attended quickly by the board or redeemed by the firm any-time before they become exercisable following the occurrence of triggering event.

Types of Poison Pill Plan

Since the first poison pill plan was introduced in late 1982, about 380 firms had adopted variants of (Poison pill) right plan by December, 1986. Both Malatests and Walking Ryngaert identify and characterise five main types of Poison Pill Plans.

1. **Original or Preferred Stock Plans:** Dividends of preferred stock convertible into common, if a trigger point reached can exercise put for cash at highest price paid during post year, if a merger, can convert into common stock of acquirer.
2. **Flip-over Plans:** Rights are call on the (target) firm's stock far out of the money, (a) in a merger in which acquirer survives flip-over to permit call on acquirer stock price deep in the money, i.e., allow big discount, (b) in a merger in which target survives, become flip-in.
3. **Ownership Flip-in Plans:** At trigger point, rights flip-in to permit call on target stock at price deep in the money, but acquirer's rights are void.
4. **Back-end Rights Plan:** At a trigger point, rights plus stock of target can be put at a value greater than current market, in effect, sets a minimum take-over price.
5. **Voting Plans:** Issues preferred stocks with super majority voting rights to target's shareholders at trigger point acquirer's preferred loses voting rights.

Poison Pills are also classified into:

- Discriminatory Poison Pill
- Non-discriminatory Poison Pill

Discriminatory Poison Pill

Empirical evidence indicates that the 'discriminatory poison pills', some defensive adjustment in asset and ownership structure, and targeted share re-purchases have negative effects on stock prices and reduce the success rate of takeover bids. Negative effects do not appear to be limited to those defensive measures that will not have shareholder approval.

Non-discriminatory Poison Pill

Mostly flip-over plans, and the other types of anti-take-over mergers including anti-greenmail amendments do not show clearly negative effects on stock prices. However this does not necessarily imply that they cannot be harmful to shareholders. Because they may signal an increased likelihood of a take-over bid or because they may not be viewed as an effective defensive by the market. Unlike most defensive actions taken in reaction to explicit take-over attempts, leveraged cash-outs show no negative effect on shareholder wealth.

FORMULAE

Valuation by P/E Ratio

- P/E Ratio = Market Price per Share/Net Earnings after Tax per share

Exchange Ratio using P/E Approach

- Exchange Ratio = P/E of acquiring firm/P/E of takeover firm.
- Exchange Ratio using EPS:
- Exchange Ratio = EPS of acquiring firm/EPS of takeover firm.
- Exchange Ratio using Market Value Per Share: (MVPS).
- Exchange Ratio = MVPS of acquiring firm/ MVPS of takeover firm.
- Market Value Per Share = P/E ratio x Earning Per Share (EPS).

Value Created by Merger

- Net Economic Advantage = Economic Advantage – Cost of Merging.

Effect of Merger on EPS (Combined EPS):

- EAT a + EAT t
- Combined EPS = Na + Nt
- EAT a = Earning after taxes of acquiring firm
- EAT t = Earning after taxes of takeover firm
- Na = Number of shares of acquiring firm
- Nt = Number of shares of takeover firm

Determination of Market Value of Merged Firm

- Vm = EPSm × P/E A
- Vm = Market value of merged firm
- EPS m = Combined EPS after merger
- P/E A = Price-earning ratio of acquiring firm

Total gain from Merger

- Total gain = Vm – (Va + Vt)
- Va = EPSa x P/E a
- Vt = EPSt x P/E t

Va: Value of acquiring firm or bidder

Vt: Value of target company or taken firm

Vm: Value of merged company or newly formed company

Equations:

1. **Basic Valuation Model**

   PV = [CF1/(1 + r)] + [CF2/(1 + r)] + ...+ [CFn/(1 + r)]

2. **Valuation of fixed income certificates**

   PV = [C/(1 + r)t + TV/(1 + r)n]

   C = Coupon or interest payments per time period

   TV = Terminal value

   R = Discount rate or Market yield

   n = Number of years

3. **Yield to Maturity [YTM]**

   MP = [C/(1+ YTM)t + TV/(1 + YTMr)n]

4. **Valuation of Preference Shares**

   Vp = [C/(1+ Kp)1 + C/(1+ Kp)2 ...] = C/Kp

5. **Valuation of Equity Shares**

   (a) Zero growth case:

   Ve = [D0/(1+ Ke) + D1/(1+ Ke)1 + ...] = D/Ke

   (b) Constant growth case:

   Ve = D/Ke – g

Ke = Cost of equity

G = Growth rate

PROBLEMS AND SOLUTIONS

1. Yax Ltd., is considering the acquisition of Singh Ltd. with stock. The following information is given in this context.

Particulars	Yax Ltd.,	Singh Ltd.,
Earnings (₹ lakhs)	9,000	2,000
Equity Shares (₹ lakhs)	3,000	1,000
EPS	₹ 3	₹ 2
PE ratio	12	8

Yax Ltd., plans to offer a premium of 25 per cent over the market price of Singh Ltd.'s stock.

(a) What is the ratio of exchange of stock and how many new shares will be issued?

(b) What are earnings per share for the surviving company immediately following merger?

Solution:

Particulars	Yax Ltd.	Singh Ltd.
EPS	₹ 3	₹ 2
PE ratio	12	8
Market Price = PE × EPS	36	16

(a) What is the ratio of exchange of stock and how many new shares will be issued?

1. Offer to Singh Ltd., in Yax Ltd. (including the premium) = ₹ 16 × 1.25 = ₹ 20
2. Exchange Ratio = 20/36 = 0.56 share of Yax Ltd.
3. Number of new shares issued = 2,000 × 0.56 = 1,120 (lakh)

(b) EPS after Merger

Particulars	Yax Ltd.	Singh Ltd.	After Merger
Earnings (₹ lakhs)	9,000	2,000	11,000*
Equity Shares (₹ lakhs)	3,000	1,000	4,120**
EPS	₹ 3	₹ 2	2.67
PE Ratio	12	8	—

* Earnings after merger = Yax Ltd. earnings 9,000 + Singh Ltd. earnings 2,000 = 11,000

** New Shares after merger = Shares of Yax Ltd. 3,000 + Share issued to Singh Ltd. 1,120.

2. Anand Ltd., is considering merger with Akash Ltd., There are no gains from merging. Complete the following table if Anand Ltd., wishes an EPS of ₹ 3.50 after the merger.

Particulars	Anand Ltd.	Akash Ltd.	After Merger
Earnings (₹)	12,00,000	2,00,000	?
Equity Shares (₹)	4,00,000	1,00,000	?
EPS	₹ 3	₹ 2	₹ 3.50
PE Ratio	11	6	?
Market Price	?	?	?

(a) Complete the above table.

(b) Calculate exchange ratio?

(c) What is the cost of merger to Anand Ltd.?

Solution:

Particulars	Anand Ltd.	Akash Ltd.	After Merger
Earnings (₹)	12,00,000	2,00,000	14,00,000
Equity Shares (₹)	4,00,000	1,00,000	14,00,000/3.50 = 4,00,000
EPS	₹ 3	₹ 2	₹ 3.50
PE Ratio	11	6	36/3.5 = 10.29
Market Price	11 × 3 = 33	2 × 6 = 12	1,44,00,000/4,00,000 = 36
Total Market Value	4,00,000 × 33 = 1,32,00,000	1,00,000 × 12 = 1,32,00,000	1,44,00,000 12,00,000

Formulae:

1. No. of Shares after Merger = Total Earnings/Required EPS.
2. Total Market Value = Market Price × No. of Shares
3. Market Price after Merger = Total market value after merger/No. of shares after merger.
4. PE Ratio after Merger = Market price after merger/required EPS.

PRACTICE PROBLEMS

1. A Ltd is considering takeover of B Ltd., and C Ltd., The financial data for three companies are as follows:

Details	Equity Share Capital of ₹ 10 each (₹/Million)	Earnings (₹/Million)	Market Price of each share (₹)
A Ltd	450	90	60
B Ltd	180	18	37
C Ltd	90	18	46

Calculate (a) Price-Earning Exchange Ratios and (b) EPS of A Ltd after the acquisition of B Ltd and C Ltd separately. Will you recommend the merger of either/both of the companies? Justify your answer

2. Axis Ltd is considering the acquisition of Xerox Ltd. Their financial data at the time of acquisition is as follows:

Details	Axis Ltd.	Xerox Ltd.
Net Profit After Taxes	30,00,000	6,00,000
No. of Shares	6,00,000	2,50,000
EPS	₹ 5/-	₹ 2.40/-
Market Price Per Share	₹ 75/-	₹ 24/-

Assuming that the net profit(after tax) of the two companies would remain the same after amalgamation i.e., ₹ 36 lakhs. Explain the effect on EPS of the total merged company, under each of the following situations:

(a) Axis Ltd offers to pay ₹ 30 per share to the shareholders of Xerox Ltd.

(b) Axis Ltd offers to pay ₹ 40 per share to the shareholders of Xerox Ltd.

The amount in the both cases is to be paid in the form of shares of Axis Ltd.

3. Krishna Ltd. is studying the possible acquisition of Rama Ltd. by way of merger. The following data available in respect of the companies:

Particulars	Krishna Ltd.	Rama Ltd.
Earnings after tax (₹)	80,00,000	24,00,000
No. of equity shares	16,00,000	4,00,000
Market value per share (₹)	200	160

(a) If the merger goes through by exchange of equity and the exchange ratio is based on the current market price. What is the new earnings per share for Krishna Ltd.

(b) Rama Ltd. wants to be sure the earnings available to its shareholders will not be diminished by the merger. What should be the exchange ratio in that case?

4. Akash Ltd is considering takeover of Bandan Ltd and Caring Ltd. The financial data for three companies are as follows:

Particulars	Akash Ltd.	Bandan Ltd.	Caring Ltd.
Equity Share Capital of ₹ 10 each (₹/Million)	225	90	45
Earnings (₹/Million)	45	9	9
Market Price of each share (₹)	30	18.50	23

Calculate (a) Price-Earning Exchange Ratios and (b) EPS of Akaash Ltd after the acquisition of Bandan Ltd and Caring Ltd separately. Will you recommend the merger of either/both of the companies? Justify your answer.

5. Harsha Ltd is considering the acquisition of Santosh Ltd. Their financial data at the time of acquisition is as follows:

Details	No. of Shares	EPS	Market Price Per share
Harsha	16,00,000	₹ 15/-	₹ 65/-
Santosh	12,50,000	₹ 12.40/-	₹ 44/-

Assuming that the net profit(after tax) of the two companies would remain the same after amalgamation. Explain the effect on EPS of the total merged company, under each of the following situations:

(1) Harsha Ltd offers to pay ₹ 30 per share to the shareholders of Santosh Ltd.

(2) Harsha Ltd offers to pay ₹ 40 per share to the shareholders of Santosh Ltd.

The amount in the both cases is to be paid in the form of shares of A Ltd.

6. Suraj Ltd. is studying the possible acquisition of Chandra Ltd. by way of merger. The following data available in respect of the companies:

Particulars	Suraj Ltd.	Chandra Ltd.
Earnings after tax (₹)	40,00,000	12,00,000
No. of equity shares	8,00,000	2,00,000
Market value per share (₹)	100	80

(a) If the merger goes through by exchange of equity and the exchange ratio is based on the current market price. What is the new earnings per share for Suraj Ltd.

(b) Chandra Ltd. wants to be sure the earnings available to its shareholders will not be diminished by the merger. What should be the exchange ratio in that case?

7. The Chetana Enterprises is determined to report earnings per share of ₹ 2.67. It therefore acquires the Wiswa Company. You are given the following facts:

	Chetana Enterprises	Wiswa Co.	Merged Firm
Earnings per share	₹ 2.00	₹ 2.50	₹ 2.67
Price per share	₹ 40.00	₹ 25.00	?
P/E Ratio	20	10	?
Number of Shares	1,00,000	2,00,000	?
Total Earnings	₹ 2,00,000	₹ 5,00,000	?
Total market value	₹ 40,00,000	₹ 50,00,000	?

There are no gains from merging. In exchange for Wiswa Co. shares, Cehtana Enterprises issues enough of its own shares to ensure its ₹ 2.67 earnings per share objective.

(a) Complete the above table for the merged firm.

(b) How many shares of Chetana Enterprises are exchanged for each share of Wiswa Co.?

8. Rama company is considering the acquisition of Krishna company with exchange of its shares. The financial data is as follows:

	Rama Co.	Krishna Co.
Present earnings	₹ 8 lakhs	₹ 6 lakhs
Equity shares (at ₹ 10 each)	2 lakhs	3 lakhs
EPS	₹ 4	₹ 2
Price earning ratio	15	10
MPS	₹ 60	₹ 20

Krishna company expects are offer of 125 per cent of its market price from Rama Company.

(a) What is the exchange ratio of shares?

(b) What is the surviving company's EPS? Assume that 15 per cent synergy benefits.

(c) If the price earning ratio after merger is 20 times, what is the surviving company's MPS?

9. Royal Industries Limited (RIL) is considering a take-over of Supreme Industries Limited (SIL). The earnings, number of outstanding equity shares and P/E ratios of the two companies is as follows:

Particulars	RIL	SIL
Earnings after taxes	₹ 20,00,000	₹ 10,00,000
No. of equity shares Outstanding	10,00,000	10,00,000
P/E ratios (times)	10	5

(a) What is the market value of each company before merger?

(b) Assume that the management of RIL estimates that the shareholders of SIL, will accept an offer of one share of RIL for four shares of SIL. If there are no synergic effects, what is the market value of the post-merger RIL? What is the new price per share? Are the shareholders of RIL better or worse-off than they were before the merger?

(c) Assume because of synergistic effects, the management of RIL estimates that the earnings will increase by 10 per cent, what is the new post-merger EPS and price per share?

CLOSING CASELET

WARNER MUSIC GROUP PLANS MODEST RESTRUCTURING

Now officially under new ownership, the Warner Music Group plans to achieve cost savings between $50-65 million over the next 27 months. The company plans to achieve those saving through 'certain planned corporate restructuring initiatives,' according to documentation provided to bond holders, which eventually will be filed with the SEC. While that may seem like the Warner Music Group is headed for a big downsizing, contrast that plan with Terra Firma's cost saving agenda after it acquired EMI in 2007. Back then, it charged EMI management with realising 200 million pounds ($324 million) in overall savings, and it achieved 80 million pounds ($130 million) to 100 million pounds ($162 million) of that in the first year alone, according to the Maltby Report for the period ended March 31, 2008.

Warner Music/Access Industries Deal Is A Win For Both

Moreover, not all of the WMG savings will come from restructuring, as the document says it also expects to realise savings simply from the shift from being a public-traded company to now being privately-held and due to reduced expenses related to finance, legal and information technology. Of course, if WMG is successful in winning the ongoing auction for EMI, discussion about the planned $65 million in savings will be moot because that discussion will shift to a completely different dimension. In other moves, while WMG envisioned raising $695 million in senior subordinated bonds, and $200 million in holding company notes, and $150 million in additional senior secured debt; in the actual offering, the company sold $765 million in senior subordinated bonds and $150 million in holding company notes; and the $150 million in senior secured bonds. The bondholders of the $1.1 billion in senior secured bonds issued by WMG prior to its latest acquisition waived the requirement to redeem those debentures, so those bonds are still outstanding. That means WMG's debt now has total debt of $2.165 billion. Based on interest rates reported by Debtwire of 11.5-11.75 for the $765 million notes, 13.25 per cent – 13.5 per cent for the holding company notes and 9.5 per cent for the secured bonds, Billboard estimates that WMG will have about $227 million in debt service, versus $195 million in interest payments made it its most recent fiscal year, according to its 10-K. In fact, because of its ability to sell more than expected senior-secured bond notes carrying 11.5 per cent – 11.75 per cent interest payments, it was able to reduce its expected offering of the more expensive holding notes from $200 million to $150 million, which allowed WMG to shave about $7 million from its interest payments. In yet another move to ensure liquidity, WMG has tapped Credit Suisse to provide a $60 million revolving credit facility, also secured like the bonds by WMG's U.S. assets.

Getting back to EMI, while the New York Post reported that an amendment to the bond offering documentation includes a financial covenant stating that if it makes a media company acquisition of more than $1 billion, its debt-to earnings before interest, taxes depreciation and amortization cannot exceed 4.6-to-1. That story went onto report that Anthony Canale of Covenant Review said that as it stands now, WMG cannot buy EMI. That's because WMG currently has total senior debt of $2.015 billion (not including the holding company debt) and adjusted EBITDA of $424 million, which means the ration stands at nearly 4.74-to-1, exceeding the 4.6-to-1 ratio in the covenant. Moreover, Canale himself said many factors that could allow WMG to make such an acquisition, since whatever EBITDA EMI brings to the table would also be included in the equation; as would any incremental EBITDA realised from cost savings through consolidating the two companies. Also it would depend on how much new senior debt was used to finance the deal, he said. Consequently, if WMG won the auction by bidding, say, $3 billion and putting up $1 billion in equity and raised $2 billion in debt, you would have to see how it would impact the formula. In its last Maltby report for the fiscal year ended March 31, 2010, EMI reported 334 million pounds in EBITDA, which at that time converted to $503 million to OANDA.com.

So in this proposed scenario, with $4.015 billion in debt and $927 million in EBITDA, the ratio would stand at 4.33 times to one, so WMG would be in compliance with the covenant and could make such an acquisition. Also revealed in the bond documentation, WMG says it has a huge catalog of music videos, album art, lyrics and unreleased be sides that it plans to exploit so that those assets can be fully monitised.

(***Source:*** http://www.billboard.biz/bbbiz/industry/record-labels/warner-music-group-plans-modest-restructuring-1005290292.story)

SUMMARY

This lesson intends to study various issues of corporate restructuring and different forms of restructuring. It examines the process of top level decision making. This is necessary when a company needs to improve its efficiency and profitability and it requires expert corporate management. There are various strategies of restructuring a corporate entity like expansion strategies, reorganisation strategies, financial engineering strategies and control strategies.

A merger occurs when two or more firms are combined and the resulting firm maintains the identity of one of the firms. Acquisition refers to the acquiring of ownership right in the property and assets. Take-over generally involves the acquisition of a certain block of equity capital of a company which enables the acquirer control over the affairs of the company. This lesson focuses on recent mergers in banking sector.

KEYWORDS

- **Asset Stripping:** When a company acquires another and sells it in parts expecting that the funds generated would match the costs of acquisition, it is known as asset stripping.
- **Black Knight:** The company that makes a hostile take-over is known as the Black Knight.
- **Dawn Raid:** This is a process of buying shares of the target company with the expectation that the market prices may fall till the acquisition is completed.
- **Demerger or Spin-off:** During the process of corporate restructuring, a part of the company may break-up and set-up as a new company and this is known as demerger. Zeneca and Argos are good examples in this regard that split from ICI and American Tobacco respectively.
- **Carve-out:** This is a case of selling a small portion of the company as an Initial Public Offering.
- **Green-mail:** Green-mail is a situation where the target company purchases back its own shares from the bidding company at a higher price.
- **Grey-knight:** A grey-knight is a company that takes-over another company and its intentions are not clear.
- **Hostile Take-over:** Hostile bids occur when acquisitions take place without the consent of the directors of the target company. This confrontation on the part of the directors of the target company may be short-lived and the hostile take-over may end up being friendly. Most American and British companies like the phenomenon of hostile take-overs while there is some more which do not like such unfriendly take-overs.
- **Macaroni Defense:** Macaroni Defense is a strategy that is taken-up to prevent any hostile take-overs. The issue of bonds that can be redeemed at a higher price if the company is taken-over does this.
- **Management Buy In:** When a company is purchased and the investors bring in their managers to control the company, it is known as management buy-out.

- **Management Buy-Out:** In a management buy-out, the managers of a company purchases it with support from venture capitalists.
- **Poison Pill Or Suicide Pill Defense:** This is a strategy that is taken by the company to make itself less appealing for a hostile take-over. The bondholders are given the right to redeem their bonds at a premium should a take-over occur.

REVIEW QUESTIONS

1. What is meant by 'Corporate Restructuring'? Explain various methods of corporate restructuring strategies.
2. Distinguish between 'Hostile Merger' and 'Friendly Merger'.
3. Explain the 'Accounting Standard -14' of ICAI. What are the various definitions pronounced in it?
4. Explain the recent trends in mergers of banking sector.

REFERENCES

1. Andrade, Mitchell & Stafford, "New Evidence and Perspectives on Mergers", 15, *Journal of Economic Perspectives* 103 (Spring 2001), esp. Table 3.
2. Anuraag Saxena and Naresh Grandly. (2001). "Alternative for Payments in M&A Deals. A Strategic Evaluation of the Choices at Hand", *The Management Accountant,* 36.11, 864-866.
3. Bhatnagar, R.G. (2001) "Banking too Much on Mergers", *Professional Banker,* 1.3, 39- 40.
4. Dario Forcarelli, Fabio Panetta and Carmello Salleo (1999), "Why do Banks Merge?", Banca d' Italia, Research Department. This Paper is Submitted to Bank of Italy.
5. Deeksha Verma, (2001). "Banking on Merger", *Professional Banker,* 1.3, 36-38.
6. Gilson, *"Creating Value Through Corporate Restructuring: Case Studies in Bankruptcies, Buyouts, and Breakups"* (John-Wiley & Sons, 2001).
7. Giridaran, R. (2001). "Mergers – The Emerging Reality", *IBA Bulletin,* 32-34.
8. Jarrell & Poulsen, "The Returns to Acquiring Firms in Tender Offers: Evidence from Three Decades", 12 *Financial Management* 18 (1989).
9. Jensen, "Takeovers: Their Causes and Consequences", 2 *Journal of Economic Perspectives* 21 (Winter 1988).
10. Loughran & Vijh, "Do Long-term Shareholders Benefit from Corporate A cquisitions?" 52 *Journal of Economic Perspectives.*
11. Sangita Mehta, (2001). "The Writing on the Wall", *Professional Banker,* 1.6 40-41

CHAPTER

8

STRATEGIES OF LEASE FINANCING

CHAPTER OUTLINE

- Opening Caselet
- Introduction
- Classification of Leases
- Decision to Buy, Lease vs. Hire Purchase
- Evaluation of Leasing or Buying Alternatives
- Accounting Standards of Leasing
- Problems and Solutions
- Practice Problems
- Closing Caselet
- Summary
- Keywords
- Review Questions
- References

OPENING CASELET

◈ Keeriti Financial Service (KFS) offers both lease and hire purchase to its corporate clientele. The salient features of these plans are as follows:

A. Lease Plan

Primary period 5 years.

Lease rate ₹ 28 per thousand per month.

Frequency of monthly payment in arrears.

B. Hire Purchase Plan

Hire period 3 years.

Rate of Interest 16 per cent p.a. flat.

Frequency of monthly payment in arrears.

Down payment 20 per cent.

Sigra Industrial Corporation (SIC) which is contemplating a capital expenditure of ₹ 360 lakh on modernisation and technology upgradation is evaluating the financial desirability of the two plans. The following information is available:

Useful life of plant and machinery 5 years.

Residual value after 5 years ₹ 45 lakhs.

Tax relevant rate of depreciation 25 per cent.

Marginal rate of tax 51.75 per cent.

Marginal cost of capital 16 per cent.

Marginal (pre-tax) cost of debt 20 per cent.

SIC follows the sum of the year digits method for spreading over the total charge for credit (unexpired finance charge) under the HP Plan.

◈ Find which plan is suitable to Sigra Industrial corporation to accept the service of Keeriti Financial Service.

INTRODUCTION

Leasing is effectively a sources of finance but it always relates to a specific assets. Under a lease contract, the ownership of the assets remains with the lessor whilst the use of the assets is available to the lessee in return for the payment of a fixed rental. Lease finance is very similar to debt in that the lease payment is fixed contractual obligations. Leasing will therefore, increase the level of gearing and financial risk of the company. There is need to look at the financial implications of leasing and especially at the tax implications for both lessor and lessee.

CLASSIFICATION OF LEASES

The classification of leases adopted in the accounting standard is based on the extent to which risks and rewards incidental to ownership of a leased asset lie with the lessor or the lessee. Risks include the possibilities of losses from idle capacity or technological obsolescence and of variations in return because of changing economic conditions. Rewards may be represented by the expectation of profitable operation over the asset's economic life and of gain from appreciation in value or realisation of a residual value. A lease is classified as a finance lease if it transfers substantially all the risks and rewards incidental to ownership. A lease is classified as an operating lease if it does not transfer substantially all the risks and rewards incidental to ownership.

Examples of situations that individually or in combination would normally lead to a lease being classified as a finance lease are:

(a) The lease transfers ownership of the asset to the lessee by the end of the lease term.

(b) The lessee has the option to purchase the asset at a price that is expected to be sufficiently lower than the fair value at the date the option becomes exercisable for it to be reasonably certain, at the inception of the lease, that the option will be exercised.

(c) The lease term is for the major part of the economic life of the asset even if title is not transferred.

(d) At the inception of the lease the present value of the minimum lease payments amounts to atleast substantially all of the fair value of the leased asset, and

(e) The leased assets are of such a specialised nature that only the lessee can use them without major modifications.

(f) Leases of land and of buildings are classified as operating or finance leases in the same way as leases of other assets. However, a characteristic of land is that it normally has an indefinite economic life and, if title is not expected to pass to the lessee by the end of the lease term, the lessee normally does not receive substantially all of the risks and rewards incidental to ownership in which case the lease of land will be an operating lease.

There are two types of lease *viz.*, (i) Financial Lease and (ii) Operating Lease.

1. FINANCE LEASES

A finance lease gives rise to depreciation expense for depreciable assets as well as finance expense for each reporting period. The depreciation policy for depreciable leased assets shall be consistent with that for depreciable assets that are owned, and the depreciation recognised shall be calculated in accordance with AASB 116 Property, Plant and Equipment and AASB 138 Intangible Assets. If there is no reasonable certainty that the lessee will obtain ownership by the end of the lease term, the asset shall be fully depreciated over the shorter of the lease term and its useful life.

At the commencement of the lease term, lessees shall recognise finance leases as assets and liabilities in their balance sheets at amounts equal to the fair value of the leased property or, if lower, the present value of the minimum lease payments, each determined at the inception of the lease. At the commencement of the lease term, the asset and the liability for the future lease payments are recognised in the balance sheet at the same amounts except for any initial direct costs of the lessee that are added to the amount recognised as an asset. Minimum lease payments shall be apportioned between the finance charge and the reduction of the outstanding liability. The finance charge shall be allocated to each period during the lease term so as to produce a constant periodic rate of interest on the remaining balance of the liability. In practice, in allocating the finance charge to periods during the lease term, a lessee may use some form of approximation to simplify the calculation. To determine whether a leased asset has become impaired, an entity applies AASB 136 Impairment of Assets.

Lessees shall, in addition to meeting the requirements of AASB 7 Financial Instruments: Disclosures, make the following disclosures for finance leases:

(a) For each class of asset, the net carrying amount at the reporting date.

(b) A reconciliation between the total of future minimum lease payments at the reporting date, and their present value. In addition, an entity shall disclose the total of future minimum lease payments at the reporting date, and their present value, for each of the following periods:

  (i) not later than one year.

  (ii) later than one year and not later than five years.

  (iii) later than five years.

(c) Contingent rents recognised as an expense in the period.

(d) The total of future minimum sublease payments expected to be received under non-cancellable sub-leases at the reporting date, and

(e) A general description of the lessee's material leasing arrangements including, but not limited to, the following:

(i) the basis on which contingent rent payable is determined.

(ii) the existence and terms of renewal or purchase options and escalation clauses, and

(iii) restrictions imposed by lease arrangements, such as those concerning dividends, additional debt and further leasing.

2. OPERATING LEASES

For operating leases, lease payments (excluding costs for services such as insurance and maintenance) are recognised as an expense on a straight-line basis unless another systematic basis is representative of the time pattern of the user's benefit, even if the payments are not on that basis. Lease payments under an operating lease shall be recognised as an expense on a straight-line basis over the lease term unless another systematic basis is more representative of the time pattern of the user's benefit.

Lessees shall, in addition to meeting the requirements of AASB 7, make the following disclosures for operating leases:

(a) The total of future minimum lease payments under non-cancellable operating leases for each of the following periods:

(i) not later than one year.

(ii) later than one year and not later than five years.

(iii) later than five years.

(b) The total of future minimum sublease payments expected to be received under non-cancellable subleases at the reporting date.

(c) Lease and sublease payments recognised as an expense in the period, with separate amounts for minimum lease payments, contingent rents, and sublease payments.

(d) A general description of the lessee's significant leasing arrangements including, but not limited to, the following:

(i) the basis on which contingent rent payable is determined.

(ii) the existence and terms of renewal or purchase options and escalation clauses, and

(iii) restrictions imposed by lease arrangements, such as those concerning. dividends, additional debt, and further leasing.

The major differences between these types are given in the following table:

Financial Lease vs. Operating Lease

Basis	Financial Lease	Operating Lease
Life of contract	Approximates the economic life of the assets.	Shorter than the economic life of the assets.
Maintenance	Provided by the lessee or covered separately.	Provided by the lessor and include in lease rentals.
Lease payments	Return the cost of the assets and allow a profit to the lessor.	Not sufficient to cover the cost of the asset.
Cancellation	May be cancelled only if both the lessor and the lessee agree.	May be cancelled before expiring date.

DECISION TO BUY, LEASE VS. HIRE PURCHASE

The decision to buy, hire purchase, or lease an asset will generally depend on the financing available to your business. There are different treatments for tax and accounting purposes, depending on the type of finance contract entered into, and these will need to be considered together with the VAT treatment.

1. DECISION TO BUY

Accounting Treatment: From an accounting viewpoint the actual cost of the asset is capitalised in the balance sheet and an annual charge for depreciation is shown in the accounts as an expense in the profit and loss account. This therefore has the effect of showing the asset(s) in the balance sheet at cost, reduced by the cumulative charge for depreciation. The annual depreciation charge is calculated in accordance with accounting standards, based on the useful economic life of the asset and the residual value.

VAT: Unless the asset is a car, the VAT shown on the supplier's invoice will generally be recoverable by the purchaser, if he or she is registered. Buying at the beginning of a VAT period will entail a wait of three months or more to recover the tax. VAT on cars is recoverable only in very rare circumstances.

2. DECISION TO HIRE PURCHASE

A HP agreement usually includes an option to purchase at the end of an initial period. Payment of this nominal fee transfers title of the asset and brings the legal agreement to an end.

Accounting Treatment: The asset is treated as if it had been purchased. It is, therefore, capitalised in the balance sheet and depreciation is provided on an annual basis. The obligation to pay future installments is recorded as a liability in the balance sheet. The payments are apportioned between a finance charge and a reduction of the outstanding liability. The total finance charge should be allocated to accounting periods during the HP term and is shown as an expense in the profit and loss account.

VAT: VAT charged by the finance company will be payable with the initial installment. There will be a delay of upto four months in recovering this from HM Revenue & Customs. In the case of a car, most businesses will be unable to recover any of the VAT.

EVALUATION OF LEASING OR BUYING ALTERNATIVES

Decision making problem under leasing or buying alternative involves four steps which are illustrated in the following paras:

Step 1: Find present value of cash outflows under leasing estimate using the following format:

Present Value of Cash Outflows under Leasing Alternative

Year	Lease payment	Tax shield (lease sum × tax rate)	Cash outflows after tax	PV Factor at Kd	Total PV
				Total	

Step 2: Find the amount of interest and principal amount in the loan payment using the following format:

Determination of Interest and Principal Components of Loan Installment

Year	Loan Installment	Loan at the beginning of the year	Payment		Principal outstanding at the end of the year
			Interest (3 × r)	Principal (2 - 4)	(3-5)
1	2	3	4	5	6

Annual installment = Loan/PV factor payment of installments.

Step 3: Calculate present value of cash outflows under buying alternative by applying the following table.

Present value of cash outflows under buying alternative

Year	Loan	Tax Advantage on Interest		Cash Out-flows after Taxes 2 - (3 + 4)	PV Factor	Total PV
		Interest	Depreciation			
		(I × t)	(D × t)			
1	2	3	4	5	6	7

Step 4:

Accept or Reject Criterion

- If Present Value of Cash outflow under leasing alternative greater than total present value of cash outflows under buying alternative – then buying is better.

PVCO (L) > PVCO (B) : BUY

- If Present Value of Cash outflow under buying [PVCO (B)] alternative greater than total present value of cash outflows under leasing [PVCO (L)] alternative – then leasing is better.

PVCO (B) > PVCO (L) : LEASE

ACCOUNTING STANDARDS OF LEASING

Accounting Standard (AS) 19

Leases

(This Accounting Standard includes paragraphs set in bold italic type and plain type, which have equal authority. Paragraphs in bold italic type indicate the main principles. This Accounting Standard should be read in the context of its objective and the General Instructions contained in part A of the Annexure to the Notification.)

Objective

The objective of this standard is to prescribe, for lessees and lessors, the appropriate accounting policies and disclosures in relation to finance leases and operating leases.

Scope

1. This standard should be applied in accounting for all leases other than:

   (a) Lease agreements to explore for or use natural resources, such as oil, gas, timber, metals and other mineral rights, (b) licensing agreements for items such as motion picture films, video recordings, plays, manuscripts, patents and copyrights, and (c) lease agreements to use lands.

2. This standard applies to agreements that transfer the right to use assets even though substantial services by the lessor may be called for in connection with the operation or maintenance of such assets. On the other hand, this standard does not apply to agreements that are contracts for services that do not transfer the right to use assets from one contracting party to the other.

Definitions

3. The following terms are used in this standard with the meanings specified:

   3.1 A lease is an agreement whereby the lessor conveys to the lessee in return for a payment or series of payments the right to use an asset for an agreed period of time.

   3.2 A finance lease is a lease that transfers substantially all the risks and rewards incident to ownership of an asset.

   3.3 An operating lease is a lease other than a finance lease.

   3.4 A non-cancellable lease is a lease that is cancellable only:

   (a) Upon the occurrence of some remote contingency; or

   (b) With the permission of the lessor; or

   (c) If the lessee enters into a new lease for the same or an equivalent asset with the same lessor; or

   (d) Upon payment by the lessee of an additional amount such that, at inception, continuation of the lease is reasonably certain.

   3.5 The inception of the lease is the earlier of the date of the lease agreement and the date of a commitment by the parties to the principal provisions of the lease.

   3.6 The lease term is the non-cancellable period for which the lessee has agreed to take on lease the asset together with any further periods for which the lessee has the option to continue the lease of the asset, with or without further payment, which option at the inception of the lease it is reasonably certain that the lessee will exercise.

   3.7 Minimum lease payments are the payments over the lease term that the lessee is, or can be required, to make excluding contingent rent, costs for services and taxes to be paid by and reimbursed to the lessor, together with:

(a) In the case of the lessee, any residual value guaranteed by or on behalf of the lessee; or

(b) In the case of the lessor, any residual value guaranteed to the lessor:

(i) By or on behalf of the lessee; or

(ii) By an independent third party financially capable of meeting this guarantee.

However, if the lessee has an option to purchase the asset at a price which is expected to be sufficiently lower than the fair value at the date the option becomes exercisable that, at the inception of the lease, is reasonably certain to be exercised, the minimum lease payments comprise minimum payments payable over the lease term and the payment required to exercise this purchase option.

3.8 Fair value is the amount for which an asset could be exchanged or a liability settled between knowledgeable, willing parties in an arm's length transaction.

3.9 Economic life is either:

(a) The period over which an asset is expected to be economically usable by one or more users; or

(b) The number of production or similar units expected to be obtained from the asset by one or more users.

3.10 Useful life of a leased asset is either:

(a) The period over which the leased asset is expected to be used by the lessee; or

(b) The number of production or similar units expected to be obtained from the use of the asset by the lessee.

3.11 Residual value of a leased asset is the estimated fair value of the asset at the end of the lease term.

3.12 Guaranteed residual value is:

(a) In case of the lessee, that part of the residual value which is guaranteed by the lessee or by a party on behalf of the lessee (the amount of the guarantee being the maximum amount that could, in any event, become payable); and

(b) In case of the lessor, that part of the residual value which is guaranteed by or on behalf of the lessee, or by an independent third party who is financially capable of discharging the obligations under the guarantee.

3.13 Unguaranteed residual value of a leased asset is the amount by which the residual value of the asset exceeds its guaranteed residual value.

3.14 Gross investment in the lease is the aggregate of the minimum lease payments under a finance lease from the standpoint of the lessor and any unguaranteed residual value accruing to the lessor.

3.15 Unearned finance income is the difference between:

(a) The gross investment in the lease, and

(b) The present value of:

(i) The minimum lease payments under a finance lease from the standpoint of the lessor, and

(ii) Any unguaranteed residual value accruing to the lessor, at the interest rate implicit in the lease.

3.16 Net investment in the lease is the gross investment in the lease less unearned finance income.

3.17 The interest rate implicit in the lease is the discount rate that, at the inception of the lease, causes the aggregate présent value of:

(a) The minimum lease payments under a finance lease from the standpoint of the lessor, and

(b) Any unguaranteed residual value accruing to the lessor, to be equal to the fair value of the leased asset.

3.18 The lessee's incremental borrowing rate of interest is the rate of interest the lessee would have to pay on a similar lease or, if that is not determinable, the rate that, at the inception of the lease, the lessee would incur to borrow over a similar term, and with a similar security, the funds necessary to purchase the asset.

3.19 Contingent rent is that portion of the lease payments that is not fixed in amount but is based on a factor other than just the passage of time (e.g., percentage of sales, amount of usage, price indices, market rates of interest).

4. The definition of a lease includes agreements for the hire of an asset which contain a provision giving the hirer an option to acquire title to the asset upon the fulfillment of agreed conditions. These agreements are commonly known as hire purchase agreements. Hire purchase agreements include agreements under which the property in the asset is to pass to the hirer on the payment of the last instalment and the hirer has a right to terminate the agreement at any time before the property so passes.

Classification of Leases

5. The classification of leases adopted in this standard is based on the extent to which risks and rewards incident to ownership of a leased asset lie with the lessor or the lessee. Risks include the possibilities of losses from idle capacity or technological obsolescence and of variations in return due to changing economic conditions. Rewards may be represented by the expectation of profitable operation over the economic life of the asset and of gain from appreciation in value or realisation of residual value.

6. A lease is classified as a finance lease if it transfers substantially all the risks and rewards incident to ownership. Title may or may not eventually be transferred. A lease is classified as an operating lease if it does not transfer substantially all the risks and rewards incident to ownership.

7. Since the transaction between a lessor and a lessee is based on a lease agreement common to both parties, it is appropriate to use consistent definitions. The application of these definitions to the differing circumstances of the two parties may sometimes result in the same lease being classified differently by the lessor and the lessee.

8. Whether a lease is a finance lease or an operating lease depends on the substance of the transaction rather than its form. Examples of situations which would normally lead to a lease being classified as a finance lease are:

   (a) The lease transfers ownership of the asset to the lessee by the end of the lease term.

   (b) The lessee has the option to purchase the asset at a price which is expected to be sufficiently lower than the fair value at the date the option becomes exercisable such that, at the inception of thelease, it is reasonably certain that the option will be exercised.

   (c) The lease term is for the major part of the economic life of the asset even if title is not transferred.

   (d) At the inception of the lease the present value of the minimum lease payments amounts to at least substantially all of the fair value of the leased asset, and

   (e) The leased asset is of a specialised nature such that only the lesseecan use it without major modifications being made.

9. Indicators of situations which individually or in combination could also lead to a lease being classified as a finance lease are:

   (a) If the lessee can cancel the lease, the lessor's losses associated with the cancellation are borne by the lessee.

   (b) Gains or losses from the fluctuation in the fair value of the residual fall to the lessee (for example in the form of a rent rebate equalling most of the sales proceeds at the end of the lease), and

   (c) The lessee can continue the lease for a secondary period at a rent which is substantially lower than market rent.

10. Lease classification is made at the inception of the lease. If at any time the lessee and the lessor agree to change the provisions of the lease, other than by renewing the lease, in a manner that would have resulted in a different classification of the lease under the criteria in paragraphs 5 to 9 had the changed terms been in effect at the inception of the lease, the revised agreement is

considered as a new agreement over its revised term. Changes in estimates (for example, changes in estimates of the economic life or of the residual value of the leased asset) or changes in circumstances (for example, default by the lessee), however, do not give rise to a new classification of a lease for accounting purposes.

Finance Leases

11. At the inception of a finance lease, the lessee should recognise the lease as an asset and a liability. Such recognition should be at an amount equal to the fair value of the leased asset at the inception of the lease. However, if the fair value of the leased asset exceeds the present value of the minimum lease payments from the standpoint of the lessee, the amount recorded as an asset and a liability should be the present value of the minimum lease payments from the standpoint of the lessee. In calculating the present value of the minimum lease payments the discount rate is the interest rate implicit in the lease, if this is practicable to determine; if not, the lessee's incremental borrowing rate should be used.

12. Transactions and other events are accounted for and presented in accordance with their substance and financial reality and not merely with their legal form. While the legal form of a lease agreement is that the lessee may acquire no legal title to the leased asset, in the case of finance leases the substance and financial reality are that the lessee acquires the economic benefits of the use of the leased asset for the major part of its economic life in return for entering into an obligation to pay for that right an amount approximating to the fair value of the asset and the related finance charge.

13. If such lease transactions are not reflected in the lessee's balance sheet, the economic resources and the level of obligations of an enterprise are understated thereby distorting financial ratios. It is therefore appropriate that a finance lease be recognised in the lessee's balance sheet both as an asset and as an obligation to pay future lease payments. At the inception of the lease, the asset and the liability for the future lease payments are recognised in the balance sheet at the same amounts.

14. It is not appropriate to present the liability for a leased asset as a deduction from the leased asset in the financial statements. The liability for a leased asset should be presented separately in the balance sheet as a current liability or a long-term liability as the case may be.

15. Initial direct costs are often incurred in connection with specific leasing activities, as in negotiating and securing leasing arrangements. The costs identified as directly attributable to activities performed by the lessee for a finance lease are included as part of the amount recognised as an asset under the lease.

16. Lease payments should be apportioned between the finance charge and the reduction of the outstanding liability. The finance charge should be allocated to periods during the lease term so as to produce a constant periodic rate of interest on the remaining balance of the liability for each period.

PROBLEMS AND SOLUTIONS

HIRE PURCHASE AND INSTALLMENT SALE TRANSACTIONS

Question 1

Goods with customers on 1.4.2006 (installments are not due).	3,20,000
Installments due on 1.4.2006 (customers are paying).	20,000
Goods sold on hire-purchase during the year (i.e., from 1.4.2006 to 31.3.2007).	16,00,000
Cash received from customers.	11,20,000
Goods re-possessed from customers valued at	16,000
40% Unpaid installments in respect of re-possessed goods.	40,000
Goods with customers as on 31.3.2007 (at hire-purchase price).	7,20,000

Answer

In the books of S Ltd. Hire Purchase Trading Account for the year ended on 31st March, 2007

To Hire Purchase Stock	3,20,000	By Hire Purchase Stock Reserve (W.N.1)	1,20,000
To Installments Due	20,000	By Bank A/c (cash received) Goods	11,20,000
To Goods Sold on Hire Purchase	16,00,000	By Goods Repossessed A/c	16,000
To Hire Purchase Stock	2,70,000	By Goods sold on hire Reserve (W.N.3) Purchase (loading) (W.N.2)	6,00,000
Profit and Loss A/c (balancing figure)	4,26,000	By Hire purchase stock	7,20,000
		By Installments due (W.N.4)	60,000
	26,36,000		**26,36,000**

Working Notes:

[1] Opening H.P. Stock Reserve $3,20,000 \times \frac{60}{160} = ₹\ 1,20,000$

[2] Loading on goods sold on H.P. $16,00,000 \times \frac{60}{160}$ = ₹ 6,00,000

[3] Closing H.P. Stock Reserve $7,20,000 \times \frac{60}{160}$ = ₹ 2,70,000

[4] Calculation of Installments due at the end of the year opening H.P. Stock + Opening Installments due + H.P. Sales during the year 19,40,000. (i.e., 3,20,000 + 20,000 + 16,00,000)

Less: Cash received from customers	11,20,000	
Installments unpaid for repossessed goods	40,000	
Closing balance of H.P. Stock	**7,20,000**	**18,80,000**
		60,000

Question 2

Ram & Co. acquired a motor lorry on hire-purchase basis. It has to make cash down payment of ₹ 1,00,000 at the beginning. The payments to be made subsequently are ₹ 2,63,000; ₹ 1,85,000 and ₹ 1,14,000 at the end of first year, second year and third year respectively. Interest charged is @ 14 per cent per annum. Calculate the cost price of motor lorry and interest paid in each installment.

Answer

Calculation of cost price and total interest to be paid on motor lorry

No. of Installment	Amount due at the time of Installment	Interest on Cumulative Installment	Cash Price in each Installment
III	1,14,000	$1,14,000 \times \frac{14}{114} = 14,000$	1,00,000
II	1,85,000	$2,85,000^{*} \times \frac{14}{114} = 35,000$	1,50,000
I	2,63,000	$5,13,000^{**} \times \frac{14}{114} = 63,000$	2,00,000
Cash Down Payment			1,00,000
Total		**1,12,000**	**5,50,000**

* 1,00,000 + 1,85,000 = 2,85,000.

** 2,63,000 + 1,50,000 + 1,00,000 = 5,13,000.

Question 3

Wye sells goods on Hire purchase at cost plus 50 per cent. Prepare Hire Purchase Trading Account from the information given below.

	₹
Stock with customers on hire-purchase price (opening)	1,62,000
Stock in hand at shop (opening)	3,24,000
Installments overdue (opening)	1,35,000
Purchases during the year	10,80,000
Goods repossessed (installments not due ₹ 36,000)	9,000
Stock at shop excluding repossessed goods (closing)	3,60,000
Cash received during the year	10,35,000
Installments overdue (closing)	1,62,000

The vendor spent ₹ 2,000 on goods repossessed and then sold it for ₹ 15,000.

Answer

Hire Purchase Trading Account

	₹		₹
To Opening balance		By Cash received (on instalments)	10,35,000
Hire Purchase Debtors	1,35,000	By Stock reserve (Opening) (W.N.2)	54,000
Hire Purchase Stock (Instalments overdue)	1,62,000	By Goods sold on hire purchase (loading) (W.N. 1)	5,22,000
To Goods sold on hire purchase (W.N.1)	15,66,000	By Cash received (on sale of re-) possessed goods)	15,000
To Cash	2,000	By Closing balance	
To Stock reserve (closing) (W.N.5)	2,10,000	Hire Purchase Stock (Int. Overdue) (W.N.4)	6,30,000
To Profit and loss account	3,43,000	Hire Purchase Debtors	1,62,000
	24,18,000		**24,18,000**

Working Notes:

1. Memorandum Stock at Shop Account

Particulars	₹	Particulars	₹
To Balance b/d	3,24,000	By Goods sold on hire purchase account (at cost)	10,44,000
To Purchases (at cost)	10,80,000	By Balance c/d	3,60,000
	14,04,000		**14,04,000**

Goods sold on hire purchase account (at invoice price) ₹ 15,66,000

10,44,000 × 150%

Loading ₹ 15,66,000 — ₹ 10,44,000 ₹ 5,22,000

2. Opening Stock Reserve: $\frac{1,62,000}{150} \times 50$ = **₹ 54,000**

3. Hire Purchase Debtors Account

Particulars	₹	Particulars	₹
To Balance b/d	1,35,000	By Cash received	10,35,000
To Goods sold on hire Purchase	15,66,000	By Hire purchase stock account (Bal. fig.)	5,04,000
		By Balance c/d	1,62,000
	17,01,000		**17,01,000**

4. Hire Purchase Stock Account

Particulars	₹	Particulars	₹
To Balance b/d	1,62,000	By Goods repossessed (installments not due)	36,000
To Hire Purchase Debtors A/C (W.N.3)	5,04,000	By Balance c/d (Bal. fig.)	6,30,000
	6,66,000		**6,66,000**

5. Closing Stock Reserve: $\frac{6,30,000}{150} \times 50$ = ₹ 2,10,000.

Question 4

Mr. X purchased a machine on hire-purchase system, ₹ 30,000 being paid on delivery and the balance in five instalments of ₹ 60,000 each, annually on 31st December. The cash price of the machine was ₹ 3,00,000. Compute the amount of interest for each year.

Answer

1st year	=	Amount outstanding for interest after down payment	3,00,000
2nd year	=	Amount outstanding for interest after 1st Installment	2,40,000
3rd year	=	Amount outstanding for interest after 2nd installment	1,80,000
4th year	=	Amount outstanding for interest after 3rd installment	1,20,000
5th year	=	Amount outstanding for interest after 4th installment	60,000

Total interest = Hire Purchase price — Cash Price

= 3,30,000 — 3,00,000 = 30,000.

Installment outstanding ratio = 3,00,000 : 2,40,000 : 1,80,000 : 1,20,000: 60,000

= 5 : 4 : 3 : 2 : 1

				₹
Interest for 1 year	=	$\frac{5}{15} \times 30{,}000$	=	10,000
Interest for II year	=	$\frac{4}{15} \times 30{,}000$	=	8,000
Interest for III year	=	$\frac{3}{15} \times 30{,}000$	=	6,000
Interest for IV year	=	$\frac{2}{15} \times 30{,}000$	=	4,000
Interest for V year	=	$\frac{1}{15} \times 30{,}000$	=	2,000
				30,000

Question 5

Mr. X purchased a machine on hire purchase system. He made cash payment of ₹ 30,000 and the balance was payable in 5 annual installments of ₹ 60,000 each. The cash price of the machine is ₹ 3,00,000. Assume that the purchase was made on 1st April and the annual installments are payable on 31st March of every year. Calculate the amount of interest for each year.

Answer

Hire Purchase Price = Total of all installments + Down Payment

= (5 × 60,000) + 30,000 = ₹ 3,30,000

Total interest = H.P. Price – Cash Price

= ₹ 3,30,000 – ₹ 3,00,000

= ₹ 30,000

Statement showing calculation of interest for each year:

Year			Interest ₹
I	₹ 30,000 × $\frac{5}{15}$	=	10,000
II	₹ 30,000 × $\frac{4}{15}$	=	8,000
III	₹ 30,000 × $\frac{3}{15}$	=	6,000
IV	₹ 30,000 × $\frac{2}{15}$	=	4,000
V	₹ 30,000 × $\frac{1}{15}$	=	30,000

Dr. **Cr.**

Date	Particulars	Nominal Value (₹)	Cost (₹)	Date	Particulars	Nominal Value (₹)	Cost (₹)
1.4.08	To Bank A/c (W.N.1)	5,00,000	6,15,000	31.3.09	By Bank A/c (W.N.2)	2,50,000	2,20,500
31.01.09	To Bonus Shares	2,50,000	-	31.3.09	By Balance c/d (W.N.4)	5,00,000	4,10,000
31.03.09	To Profit and Loss A/c (W.N.3)	-	15,500				
		7,50,000	**6,30,500**			**7,50,000**	**6,30,500**

Working Notes:

1. Calculation of cost of equity shares purchased on 1.4.08

$$= 5{,}000 \times ₹\ 120 + 2\%\ \text{of}\ ₹\ 6{,}00{,}000 + \frac{1}{2}\%\ \text{of}\ ₹\ 6{,}00{,}000 = ₹\ 6{,}15{,}000$$

2. Calculation of profit proceeds of equity shares sold on 31.3.09

$= 2{,}500 \times ₹\ 90 - 2\%\ \text{of}\ ₹\ 2{,}25{,}000 = ₹\ 2{,}20{,}500$

3. Calculation of profit on sale of bonus shares on 31.3.09

= Sale proceeds – Average cost

$$= 2{,}20{,}500 - 2{,}05{,}000\ \text{i.e.,} \left(6{,}15{,}000 \times \frac{2{,}50{,}000}{7{,}50{,}000}\right) = ₹\ 15{,}500$$

4. Valuation of equity shares on 31.3.09

$$\text{Cost} = 6{,}15{,}000 \times \frac{5{,}00{,}000}{7{,}50{,}000} = ₹\ 4{,}10{,}000$$

Market value = 5,000 shares × ₹ 90 = ₹ 4,50,000

Closing Balance has been valued at ₹ 4,10,000 i.e., at cost which is lower than the market value.

PRACTICE PROBLEMS

1. Meenakshi Finance Ltd., offers a hire purchase for its corporate clients on the following terms:

— Rate of interest: 12% flat

— Repayment period: 4 years

— Frequency of payment: Monthly in Arrear

— Down Payment: 25%

— Assuming investment cost to be ₹ 1,00,000 calculate:

a. The effective rate of interest per annum or the Annual Percentage Rate (APR) using:

   (i) Trial and Error Approach, and

   (ii) The Approximation Formula

b. Assuming that the payments have to be made in advance, calculate the APR using the approaches mentioned in (a) above for an investment cost of ₹ 1,00,000.

2. Sanjay Finance offers a hire purchase plan for its borrowers on the following terms.
   - Rate of interest: 14.5%
   - Repayment period: 6 years
   - Frequency of payment: Monthly in arrear
   - Down payment: 15%.

Calculate the effective rate of interest per annum or the annual percentage rate (APR) using (a) the trial and error approach and (b) the approximation formula.

CLOSING CASELET

Sridhar Financial Services offers a hire purchase plan under which the hirer is provided with hundred per cent finance on the following terms:

- Rate of interest: 15 per cent
- Repayment period: 5 years
- Frequency of payment: Quarterly

The hirer is required to invest 20% of the investment cost in the cumulative fixed deposit scheme of the company for a period of 5 years. The company offers a rate of interest of 15% p.a. compounded monthly. Calculate the APR of the scheme assuming an investment cost of ₹ 50,000.

SUMMARY

This chapter deals with strategies of leasing decision. Leasing is effectively a source of finance but it always relates to specific assets. Under a lease contract, the ownership of the assets remains with the lessor whilst the use of the assets is available to the lessee in return for the payment of a fixed rental. Lease finance is very similar to debt in that the lease payment is fixed contractual obligations. Leasing will therefore, increase the level of gearing and financial risk of the company. There is need to look at the financial implications of leasing and especially at the tax implications for both lessor and lessee. This chapter also focuses for 'Accounting Standard 19' pronounced by the Institute of Chartered Accountants of India, New Delhi.

KEYWORDS

1. **Average Rate of Return:** Also known as the Accounting Rate of Return (ARR), Return on Investment (RoI) or Return on Assets (RoA), is obtained by dividing average annual post-tax profit by the average investment.
2. **Capital Budgeting:** It is decision making process concerned with 'whether or not (i) the firm should invest funds in an attempt to make profit?' and (ii) how to choose among competing projects.

3. **Capital Rationing:** When availability of capital to a firm is limited, the firm is constrained in its choice of projects. Capital rationing is restricting capital expenditure to certain amount, even when projects with positive NPV need be rejected (which would be accepted in unlimited funds case).
4. **Certainty Equivalent:** A ratio of certain cash flow and the expected value of a risky cash flow between which the decision maker is indifferent.
5. **Financial Risk:** The added variability in earnings available to a firm's shareholders and the additional risk of insolvency caused by the use of financing sources that require a fixed return.
6. **Net Present Value:** A method of evaluation consisting of comparing the present value of all net cash flows (discounted by cost of capital as the interest rate) to the initial investment cost.
7. **Payback Period:** A method of evaluating investment proposal which determines the time a project's cash inflows will take to repay the original investment of the project. Profit Contribution – Difference between P/V income and specific programmed costs'.
8. **Risk:** Refers to a situation in which there are several possible outcomes, each outcome occurring with a probability that is known to the decisionmaker.
9. **Standard Deviation:** The degree of dispersion of possible outcomes around the expected value. It is the square root of the weighted average of the squared deviations of all possible outcomes from the expected value.
10. **Uncertainty:** Refers to situations in which there are several possible outcomes of an action whose probabilities are either not known or are not meaningful.

REVIEW QUESTIONS

1. Define 'leasing'? Explain various classification of leases with their features.
2. How do you evaluate decisions relating to leasing or buying alternatives?
3. Distinguish between financial lease and operating lease.

REFERENCES

1. Gustave Grullon, Geroge Kanatas and Piyush Kumar, "Financing Decisions and Advertising: An Empirical Study of Capital Structure and Product Market Competition", http://ssrn.com.
2. Jakhotiya G.P., *Strategic Financial Management,* Vikas Publications, New Delhi, 2007.
3. Sridhar A.N., *Strategic Financial Management,* SPD, New Delhi, 2008.

CHAPTER

9

STRATEGIES FOR FINANCIAL DISTRESS

CHAPTER OUTLINE

- Opening Caselet
- Introduction
- Causes of Financial Distress Prediction Users
- Tools to Measure
- Altman Statistical Model of Bankruptcy (or Failure or Distress)
- Turnaround Strategies
- Liquidation
- Leveraged Buy-Outs: (LBOs)
- Risk and Rewards
- Buy-back of Shares
- Joint Venture
- Disinvestment Strategies
- Valuation of PSUs
- Methodologies Adopted for Disinvestment/Privatisation
- Appendix
- Turnover Ratios/Investment Utilisation Ratios
- Profit Allocation Ratios
- Closing Caselet
- Summary
- Keywords
- Review Questions
- References

OPENING CASELET

The Use of Bankruptcy in the Resolution of Corporate Distress

As the global economic downturn continues to worsen, prospects of illiquidity and potential insolvency are becoming more likely around the world. Many countries and firms are already affected through declining demand, inability to raise financing due to the credit crunch, drops in foreign investment, and reductions in remittances. One of the important concerns for policymakers is the effectiveness of existing bankruptcy regimes. Financial crisis during the past decade (Russia, East Asia, Argentina) drew attention to the importance of effective mechanisms to resolve corporate financial distress, which facilitates the efficient reallocation of assets. The market for corporate control and the formal bankruptcy/liquidation processes of a country are two key mechanisms through which corporate assets are reallocated. Ideally, an economy would only allow the best users of economic resources to retain the right to use those assets and any sub-optimal use would result in either a take-over by a more proficient owner or an asset sale. Yet the use of formal legal bankruptcy procedures to resolve financial distress varies around the world, for example, from 0.04 per cent in India to 4.0 per cent in the United States over the 1990's. These differences can be explained by variations in legal systems, accounting standards, and regulatory frameworks, as well as differences in the development of financial and capital markets, and macroeconomic factors. These findings suggest that country and institutional characteristics affect the way that financial institutions and commercial creditors confront financial distress. Furthermore, bankruptcies are less common in countries with concentrated banking relationships, consistent with other evidence that bankruptcies are more common in firms with more complex capital structures. In practice, bankruptcy is a complicated and difficult process, and research suggests that in most countries existing bankruptcy regimes do not perform very well even in normal times. A survey of insolvency practitioners from 88 countries on debt enforcement indicates that bankruptcy procedures are time-consuming, costly and inefficient (i.e., unable to preserve the business as going concern). In only 36 per cent of countries, the business is preserved as a going concern, and an average of 48 per cent of the business value is lost in debt enforcement. In developing countries simpler procedures such as quick foreclosure and transfer of control of the firm to secured creditors work best, whereas more elaborate procedures including reorganisation (which is most likely to preserve the business as a going concern), are likely to be more successful in richer countries with greater capacity for enforcement. Furthermore, there is evidence that weaker bankruptcy regimes have a real effect on the number of firms using the formal bankruptcy system.

Discuss the significance of bankruptcy in the resolution of corporate distress.

Source: HTTP://econ.worldbank.org

INTRODUCTION

Corporate failure[1] is as much a fact of life as death or taxes, but a failing company does not have to be written-off with a requiem; it can be nursed back to life by a good turnaround strategy. Companies have been known to transform themselves into strong, profitable enterprises after a turnaround, but the strategy adopted varies from case to case. However, there are a few elements common to all such efforts. Peng S.Chan has, in an article in *Management Decision* (1993), dwelt at length on the strategies adopted by some American companies on the verge of collapse but which bounced back to good days. In India, there have been classic examples of good, profitable companies failing, a representative list being: Metal Box; Binny Limited; Standard Motor Company; Best and Crompton Engineering; Mangalore Chemicals and Fertilisers, Madras Fertilisers; Bata India; and Philips India. While the first four companies mentioned have irretrievably gone under, Bata India and Philips India have both turned around and aided, of course, by their international parent companies. Seshasayee Paper Boards is a stunning case of a wholly Indian company in great decline for a few years not only coming back to life but also achieving a considerable market share in the paper industry, which is itself in the doldrums.

A turnaround situation is usually caused by some form of financial distress – reduced sales; failing market share; posting of losses quarter after quarter; or decreasing share prices. Managements must be able to discern these trends as warning signals, quite different from normal business fluctuations. Loss in income must be considered the single most visible sign that a company is on the decline. The main reasons for company failures are:

- Inability to cope with dumping from foreign manufacturers, consequent upon the removal of tariff barriers.
- Income-generating capacity being constrained by a system of administered selling prices.
- Changes in government regulations.
- Loss of market share through poor product-quality and faulty pricing policies.
- Unrelated diversification affecting core competencies.
- Product obsolescence.

Often, company failure can be traced to poor management, and to a lesser extent, environmental factors but if the managements identify these problems early, companies have a better chance of a successful turnaround. Managements' decision making process should revolve around certain common factors in planning a turnaround. These are:

1. *Strategic Financial Management: Application of Corporate Finance*, 1st Edition Thomson ONE, Business School Edition.

- Failure of existing business plans and strategies and the failure to recognise warning signals in time. If the decline is to be checked, strategies will have to be changed, and quickly, so that there is no further loss.

An inflexible or incompatible Chief Executive Officer (CEO), who refuses to identify the problems but blames them on external factors, could be a serious handicap to any turnaround process.

One of the first steps to be initiated in the turnaround task is the replacement of the CEO, preferably with one who has had experience in retrieving a company from a troubled situation. Even when companies scout around CEOs to replace one on the verge of retirement, the choice is always a person with a proven track record. Some examples of recent appointments of CEOs are: Louis V.Gerstner Jr. at IBM; John F.Welch Jr. at General Electric; George M.C. Fisher at Eastman Kodak; and the late Roberto Goizuetta at Coca-Cola, all of whom have been performing superlatively with the companies they have joined. In fact, the incomes at Coca-Cola have increased multifold during Goizuetta's tenure.

To attract the right CEO, the compensation package will have to be commensurate with the problems he will be inheriting in the new company. As soon as a new CEO has taken-over, one of his first actions will be to find ways and means of cutting costs and reducing losses and this could be achieved by selling unproductive real estate, thereby raising cash for deployment; selling-off businesses or activities not running profitably; cutting back on workforce and abandoning projects needing large fund investment.

Re-focusing attention to the company's core competence of primary business should be the next step, as often companies find themselves in areas not intended originally but which came about due to a variety of factors. Examples of companies hiving-off unproductive activities are those of ITC hiving-off the hotels division to a separate company; Coates of India transferring its packaging-coating business to a separate company – CIBA Specialty Chemicals India Limited; and the latest restructuring by the Aditya Birla group, which is bringing all cement production under Grasim. Company failures have become increasingly identifiable with such unrelated business affecting their core competence. Many companies discover that businesses in which they had a stranglehold for several years are threatened by global competition, which is striking at the root of their existence. Caustic soda, PVC, steel and paper are some of the areas where the existing Indian companies to are finding it increasingly difficult to stay afloat with their costs of production *vis-à-vis* the international prices. While during the cost-cutting stage, CEOs need to focus their attention on a strategy of centralisation, during the refocus-and-reinvest stage, they have to adopt one of decentralisation.

The advantages of such decentralisation include the ability to provide faster response and better customer service.

The steps are the common remedial measures to effect a successful turnaround in companies and in most of the US companies mentioned, these measures produced remarkable results, as is seen from the following observations in each case.

- At Clark Equipment, sales in 1988 increased by $250 millions over 1987 sales to $1.28 billions. Losses of $60 millions in 1986 and $16.6 millions in 1987 transformed into positive net income of $46 millions. There were increases in both the earnings per share and the book value.
- At Intermedics, sales in 1987 at $193 millions were at an all-time high and it also had a turnaround in pre-tax earnings of $50 millions with the earnings per share also showing an increase.
- L.E.Meyers did not show any dramatic increase ins ales volume post-turnaround but there were other improvements such as a reduction in its long-term debt from $6 millions in 1987 to below $1 million in 1990.
- Quantum increased sales lin 1989 to $208 millions and net income to $12.9 millions.

Financial distress refering to a business failure is an unfortunate circumstance. Business failure can be considered from both an economic and a financial view point. In an economic sense, business success is associated with firms that earn an adequate return (equal to or greater than cost of capital) on their investments.

CAUSES FOR FINANCIAL DISTRESS PREDICTION USERS

1. An imbalance of skills within the top echelon. A manager tends to attract other managers of similar skills. For example, the corporate management may consist principally of individuals having a background in sales, without any one having production experience.
2. A chief executive who dominates a firm's operations without regard for the inputs of peers.
3. An inactive board of directors. The board of director's lack of interest in the financial position of the company may lead to insolvency.
4. A deficient finance function within the firm's management.
5. The absence of responsibility for the chief executive officer. Although all other managers with a company are responsible to a supervisor, the chief executive seldom must account for his actions.

Financial Distress Prediction Users

(a) Bond Raters

(b) Advisors

(c) Government Officials

(d) Researchers

(e) M&A

(f) Purchasers,

(g) Suppliers

(h) Lenders

(i) Investors

(j) Security Analysts

(k) Regulators

(l) Auditors

(m) Managers

TOOLS TO MEASURE

Traditional Ratio Analysis

The detection of company operating and financial difficulties is a subject which has been particularly amenable to analysis with financial ratios. Prior to the development of quantitative measures of company performance, agencies had been established to supply a qualitative type of information assessing the creditworthiness of particular merchants. Ratio analysis is a powerful tool of financial analysis. A ratio is defined as 'the indicated quotient of two mathematical expressions' and 'as a relationship between two or more things'. In simple language it means on number expressed in terms of another. It expresses the qualitative relationship. Ratio is used for evaluating the financial position and performance of a firm with the help of many meaningful ratios. The absolute financial figures do not add meaningful understanding of information that is already available but they show meaningful relationship between two items which helps management in drawing certain conclusions. In other words an accounting period becomes meaningful only when it is related to some relevant information.

Standard of Comparison

It involves comparison for a useful interpretation of financial statements. A single ratio in itself does not indicate favourable or unfavourable condition. It should be comparable with some standard. Standards of comparison may consist of:

- Past ratios, i.e., ratios calculated from the past financial statements of the same firm.
- Competitors ratio — ratios of some selected firms especially the most progressive and successful competitor, at the same point of time.
- Industry ratios — ratios of the industry to which the firm belongs, and
- Projected ratios, i.e., ratios developed using the projected, or pro-forma, financial statements of the same firm.

Types of Ratios:

I. LIQUIDITY RATIOS

II. ACTIVITY RATIOS

III. TURNOVER RATIOS

IV. PROFIT ABILITY RATIOS

I. LIQUIDITY RATIOS: It is extremely essential for a firm to be able to meet its obligations as they become due. Liquidity ratios measure the ability of the firm to meet its current obligations. A firm should ensure that it does not suffer from lack of liquidity will result in poor credit worthiness, loss of creditors etc., and also that it does not have excess liquidity, keeping cash idle, and idle assets earn nothing. Liquidity ratios are:

1. Current Ratios
2. Quick Ratios
3. Absolute Liquid Ratios

1. Current Ratio: Current ratio is the ratio of current assets and current liabilities. Current liabilities are liabilities which are to be repaid within a period of one year. Current ratio is a measure of the firms short-term solvency. It indicates the availability of current assets in rupees for every one rupee of current liability. It ensures the safety of funds of short-term creditors. This ratio enables the company to pay-off its liabilities with no regard to current assets, i.e., though current assets follows a declining trend.

Current ratio is calculated using the formula.

Current Ratio = Current Assets/Current Liabilities.

2. Quick Ratio: Quick ratio is the ratio of quick assets and quick liabilities. Quick assets which can be converted into cash very quickly without much loss. It shows the liquidity position of the firm, in knowing how quick it is to convert its assets to cash. Quick liabilities are liabilities which have to be necessarily be paid within one year. It stresses itself on the build up of current assets which excludes inventory and prepaid inventory and prepaid expenses.

Quick Ratio = Quick Assets/Current Liabilities

3. Absolute Liquid Ratio: It is the ratio of absolute liquid assets and current liabilities and is calculated by taking the ratio of the absolute liquid assets by the current liabilities. This ratio is calculated in order to cater to the doubt regarding the realisation of receivables into cash immediately or in time. Absolute liquid assets include cash in hand and at the bank and marketable securities or temporary investments. It is calculated using the formula:

Absolute Liquid Ratio = Absolute Liquid Assets/Current Liabilities

II. ACTIVITY RATIOS: Activity ratios measure the efficiency of effectiveness with which a firm manages its resources or assets. The ratios are also called turnover ratios because they indicate the speed with which assets are converted or turned over into sales. The funds of creditors and owners are invested in various assets to generate sales and profits. Activity ratios are employed to evaluate the efficiency with which the firm managers utilise the assets. A proper balance between sales and assets generally reflects that assets are managed well. The following turnover ratios are calculated to comment upon the liquidity or the efficiency with which the liquid resources are being used by the firm. Activity Ratios are:

1. Inventory Turnover Ratio.
2. Debtors Turnover Ratio.
3. Creditors Turnover Ratio.
4. Working Capital Turnover Ratio.
5. Fixed Assets Ratio.

III. PROFITABILITY RATIOS: These ratios measure the results of business operations or overall performances and effectiveness of the firm. These ratios are calculated to enlighten the end results of business activities which is the sole criterion of the overall efficiency of a business concern. Profits are the measure of overall efficiency of a business. The higher the profits, the more efficient is the business considered. Changes in total profits may although indicate changes in efficiency but they will not indicate the true state of efficiency of the business or profitability unless profits are related with the size of investments. Thus, overall profitability of efficiency of a business can be measured in terms of profits related to investments made in the business.

Balance Sheet – Ratios: Overall Profitability Ratios are as follows:

1. Return on Shareholders Investments of Net Worth
2. Return on Equity Capital
3. Earnings Per Share and Dividends Per Share
4. Return on Gross Capital Employed
5. Return on Net Capital Employed
6. Dividend Yield Ratio
7. Dividend Payout Ratio.

1. Net Worth: The ratio popularly known as Return on Investment (RoI) is the relationship between Net profits (after interest and taxes) and the proprietors funds. The primary objective of business is to maximise its earning, secondly, employment debt is advantageous for shareholders in two ways, as they can pay-off the creditors without sharing the control right. In future creditors may make owners equity as guarantee against its credit, when there are no chances of deriving credit. The two basic components of this ratio is shareholders funds and net profit. This ratio is of great importance to the present and prospective shareholders as well as the management of the company. It reveals how well the resources of the firm are being used. Calculated as,

RoI = Net Profit (after interest and tax)/(Share holders funds) × 100

2. **Return on Equity Capital:** This ratio depicts the relationship between profits of a company and the equity shareholders who are interested to know profits earned by the company and those profits which can be made available to pay dividends to the equity shareholder. They assume the highest rank in the company when compared to preference shareholders. The rate of dividends varies with the availability of profits in case of ordinary shareholders. Thus, ordinary shareholders are more interested in profitability of a company and the performance of a company should be judged on.

   The basis of return on equity capital of the company. It is calculated as

   Return on Equity Capital = (PAT – Pref. Dividend)/(Paid-up Equity Capital) × 100

   1. **Return on Capital Employed:** It establishes the relationship between profits and the capital employed. It is the primary ratio and is most widely used to measure the overall profitability and efficiency of business. This ratio measures the overall efficiency and indicate how well the management has used the investments made by the owners and creditors into the business. This ratio can particularly used in appraising divisional or departmental performance of big firms and in determining the selling price so as to earn a desired percentage of return on capital. Calculated as,

      Return Capital Employed = (Profit before Intrest and Tax (PBIT)/Capital Employed) × 100

   2. **Earning Per Share:** Earnings per share is the net profit after tax and preference dividend which is earned on the capital representative of one equity share. It decides the real worth of the shareholders. Business usually aims at maximising shareholders value and protecting the interest of the real owners, in profits as well as in losses. There profits must be increased with the increase in amount of risk born in by the shareholders. Their interest depends on their profits, which allow them to be with the shares. It is calculated as:

      Earnings Per Share: Profit After Tax – Preference Dividend No. of Equity Shares.

IV. **CAPITAL STRUCTURE/LEVERAGE RATIOS:** The term capital structure refers to the relationship between the various long-term forms of financing. Financing the firms assets is a very crucial problem in every business and as a general rule there should be a proper mix of debt and equity capital in financing the firms assets.

Following Ratios are to be calculated to analyze the capital structure of a firm.

1. Capital Gearing Ratio
2. Debt-Equity Ratio
3. Proprietors Ratio
4. Interest Coverage Ratio
5. Dividend Coverage Ratio
6. Fixed Assets Ratio

All the above ratios are calculated and analysed below:

1. **Capital Gearing Ratio:** It is a very important leverage ratio. It describes the relationship between equity share capital including reserves and surpluses to preference share capital and other fixed interest bearing loans. If preference share capital and other fixed interest bearing loans exceed the equity share capital including reserves, the firm is said to be geared and vice-versa. Gearing should be kept in such a way that the company is able to maintain a steady rate of dividend. Capital Gearing Ratio is calculated as below:

   Capital Gearing Ratio

   = (Preference Capital + Loan Funds)/(Equity Capital + Reserves & Surplus)

2. **Debt and Equity Ratio:** This ratio is calculated to measure the relative proportions of outsiders' funds invested in the company. This ratio is also known as external-internal equity ratio. It reflects the relative claims of creditors and shareholders against the assets of the business. Debt, usually, refers to long term liabilities. Equity includes Equity and Preference share capital and reserves. The debt to equity ratio is calculated as follows:

   Debt to Equity Ratio = (Long Term Debts/Shareholder's Funds)

3. **Proprietary Ratio:** A variant of debt to equity ratio is the proprietory ratio which shows the relationship between shareholders' funds and total assets. It is also known as equity ratio. This ratio establishes a relationship between shareholders funds and total assets of the firm. This is important for determining long-term solvency of the firm. In the total capital of the company, better is the long-term solvency position of the company. This ratio indicates the extent to which the assets of the company can be lost without affecting the interest of creditors of the company. This ratio is worked out as follows:

   Equity Ratio = (Shareholders Funds/Total Assets)

4. **Fixed Assets Ratio:** The ratio establishes the relationship between fixed assets and shareholders funds and long-term. It indicates the extent to which shareholders funds and long-term. It indicates the extent to which shareholders funds are sunk into fixed assets. It also indicates the mode of financing the fixed

assets. A financially fixed assets financed by long-term funds. It gives an idea as to what part of the capital employed has been used in purchasing the fixed assets for the concern. This is calculated as:

Fixed Assets Ratio (Net Worth) = Fixed Assets (after Dep.)/Shareholders Funds

5. **Interest Coverage Ratio:** Interest Coverage Ratio indicates the number of times, interest is covered by the profits available to pay the interest charges. It is used to test the debt-servicing capacity of the firm. The debt-equity ratio merely indicates whether there is margin of safety available to the creditors or not. But normally assets of the firm will not be sold to satisfy the claims of the creditors. The claims are usually met out of regular earnings or operating profits of the firm. These claims include interest on loans, preference dividends, repayment of their loan and redemption of preference shares from long-term creditors point of view, the financial soundness of the firm lies in its ability examined by the coverage ratio. Thus, coverage ratio may be defined as the ratio which measures the firms ability to service fixed interests bearing loan and other preference securities. The ratio is also known as Fixed Charges Cover or Times Interest Earned. Since taxes are computed after interest, this ratio is calculated by dividing earning. Before interest and tax with interest charges. It is calculated as:

   Interest Coverage Ratio = Net Profit (Before Interest and Taxes)/Fixed Interest Charges.

6. **Dividend Coverage Ratio:** It indicates the ability of a business to pay and maintain the fixed preference dividend to the preference shareholders. It is calculated as

   Dividend Coverage Ratio = PAT/Fixed Preference Dividend.

Terminology used in Ratios:

1. **Cash Reservoir or Super Quick Assets (SQA):** Cash in hand + Cash at Bank + Marketable non-trade investments.
2. **Current Assets (CA):** Inventories or Closing Stock + Quick Assets.
3. **Quick Assets (QA) or Liquid Assets (LA):** Sundry Debtors + Super Quick Assets
4. **Current Liabilities (CL):** Trade Creditors + Bills Payable + Outstanding expenses + Provisions + Bank Overdraft.
5. **Quick Liabilities (QL):** Current Liabilities – Cash Credit – Bank Overdraft — Short-term borrowings.
6. Net Working Capital (NWC) = CA – CL
7. **Cash Conversion Cycle:** Length of time for cash to complete operating cycle.
   a. Day's receivers + Day's inventory + Day's payables
8. **Receivables Conversion Period:**
   a. Cash Conversion Cycle = Operating cycle – Payments deferral period

ALTMAN STATISTICAL MODEL OF BANKRUPTCY (OR FAILURE OR DISTRESS)

Z-Score model, (Altman, 1968), has become the prototype model. Almost all of the statistical credit scoring models that are in use today are variations on a similar theme. They involve the combination of a set of quantifiable financial indicators of firm performance with, perhaps, a small number of additional variables that attempt to capture some qualitative elements of the credit process. Starting in the 1980's, some practitioners, and certainly many academicians, had been moving toward the possible elimination of ratio analysis as an analytical technique in assessing firm performance. Theorists have downgraded arbitrary rules of thumb (such as company ratio comparisons) that are widely used by practitioners. Z-Score is based on the following five variables:

- **X_1,Working Capital/Total Asset (WC/TA):** The working capital/total assets ratio is a measure of the net liquid assets of the firm relative to the total capitalization. Working capital is defined as the difference between current assets and current liabilities. Liquidity and size characteristics are explicitly considered. This ratio was the least important contributor to discrimination between the two groups. In all cases, tangible assets, not including intangibles, are used.
- **X_2, Retained Earnings/Total Assets (RE/TA):** Retained Earnings (RE) is the total amount of reinvested earnings and/or losses of a firm over its entire life. The account is also referred to as earned surplus. This is a measure of cumulative profitability over time. The age of a firm is implicitly considered in this ratio. It is likely that a bias would be created by a substantial reorganisation or stock dividend and appropriate readjustments should, in the event of this happening, be made to the accounts. In addition, the RE/TA ratio measures the leverage of a firm. Those firms with high RE relative to TA have financed their assets through retention of profits and have not utilised as much debt. This ratio highlights either the use of internally generated funds for growth (low risk capital) vs. OPM (other people's money) - higher risk capital.
- **X_3, Earnings Before Interest and Taxes/Total Assets (EBIT/TA):** This is a measure of the productivity of the firm's assets, independent of any tax or leverage factors. Since a firm's ultimate existence is based on the earning power of its assets, this ratio appears to be particularly appropriate for studies dealing with credit risk.
- **X_4, Market Value of Equity/Book Value of Total Liabilities (MVE/TL):** Equity is measured by the combined market value of all shares of stock, preferred and common, while liabilities include both current and long-term. The measure shows how much the firm's assets can decline in value (measured by market value of equity plus debt) before the liabilities exceed the assets and the firm becomes insolvent. This ratio adds a market value dimension that most other failure studies did not consider. At a later point, we will substitute the book value of net worth for

the market value in order to derive a discriminant function for privately held firms (Z) and for non-manufacturers (Z).

- **X_5, Sales/Total Assets (S/TA):** The capital-turnover ratio is a standard financial ratio illustrating the sales generating ability of the firm's assets. Net sales is used. It is a measure of management's capacity to deal with competitive conditions. This final ratio is unique because it is the least significant ratio and, on a univariate statistical significance test basis, it would not have appeared at all. However, because of its relationship to other variables in the model, the Sales/Total Assets (S/TA) ratio ranks high in its contribution to the overall discriminating ability of thc model. Still, therc is a wide variation among industries and across countries in asset turnover, and we will specify an alternative model (Z), without X_5, at a later point. Variables and their averages were measured at one financial statement prior to bankruptcy and the resulting F-statistics were observed; variables X_1 through X_4 are all significant at the 0.001 level, indicating extremely significant differences between groups. Variable X_5 does not show a significant difference between groups. On a strictly univariate level, all of the ratios indicate higher values for the nonbankrupt firms and the discriminant coefficients display positive signs, which is what one would expect. Therefore, the greater a firm's distress potential, the lower its discriminant score. Although it was clear that four of the five variables displayed significant differences between groups, the importance of MDA is its ability to separate groups using multivariate measures.

  Once the values of the discriminant co-efficients are estimated, it is possible to calculate discriminant scores for each observation in the samples, or any firm, and to assign the observations to one of the groups based on this score. The essence of the procedure is to compare the profile of an individual firm with that of the alternative groupings (distressed or non-distressed).

Z SCORE COMPONENT: DEFINITIONS

Variable	Definition	Weighing Factor
X_1	Working Capital/Total Assets	1.2
X_2	Retained Earnings/Total Assets	1.4
X_3	EBIT/Total Assets	3.3
X_4	Market Value of Equity/Book	0.6
X_5	Sales/Total Assets	0.99

Bankruptcy Score = $1.2\,X_1 + 1.4\,X_2 + 3.30\,X_3 + 0.6\,X_4 + 0.99\,X_5$.

Altman's Bankruptcy Criterion

Bankruptcy score: Less than 1.81	**Bankruptcy score Between 1.81 and 2.99**	**Bankruptcy score Greater than 2.99**
Probability of failure is high	Probability of failure is difficult to determine	Probability of failure is remote
Predict failure	— Less than 2.675 – predict failure — Greater than 2.675 – predict success	Predict success

We may conclude that a potentially failing corporation begins to invest less in current (X_1), since X_2 is a cumulative indicator of probability relative time, the findings suggest that younger companies have a greater chance of bankruptcy.

TURNAROUND STRATEGIES

The strategic turnaround choices may involve either a new way to compete in the existing business or entering an altogether new business. The strategic turnarounds around existing business focus either on increasing the market share in a given product-market frame work or by shifting the product-market relationship in a new direction by repositioning. The increase in market share can be achieved by improving product quality perception, through dealer push or even by consumer pull. However, strategic turnarounds seeking no change in the market share almost always involve a change in the product-market segment focus. 'Hoffer' has classified the turnaround strategies in two broad categories. These are strategic turnaround and operating turnarounds. A firm is said to be sick when it faces a severe cash crunch or a consistent downtrend in its operating profits. Such firms become insolvent unless appropriate internal and external actions are taken to change the financial picture of the firm. This process of recovery is called 'turnaround strategy'. Any successful turnaround strategy consists of three interrelated phases:

1. The first phase is the diagnosis of impending trouble. Many authors and research studies have indicated distinct early warning signals of corporate sickness.
2. The second phase involves analysing the causes of sickness to restore the firm on its profit track. These measures are of both short-term and long-term nature.
3. The third and final phase involves implementation of change process and its monitoring.

The operating turnaround strategies are:

a. **Cost-cutting Strategies:** Traditional costing systems do not recognise the needs of the various levels of management which require information for decision-making and, more important, do not highlight the cost of not doing a thing, that is, the cost of excess capacity. Activity-based costing is a new basis that has been found to fill this need adequately as it seeks to cost products on the basis of the resources consumed by them and not by a blanket recovery rate for overheads, irrespective of whether the products attract them or not. Quite often, the problems with managing turnarounds are the difficulty of timing and implementing the necessary changes and the inability to convince the management that something drastic needs to be done to remedy the situation. Companies should look into the need for preparing a contingency plan that will take into account uncommitted liquid cash resources; a programme for controlling cash outflows and investments; and formulating a strategic plan for the manner in which liquidation of plant, equipment or the hiving-off of unremunerative business units should be handled in the event of early warning signals showing up. Such contingency plans should be an integral part of the budgeting process and the overall long-term corporate plan.

The reduction in labour force has an immediate effect on the bottom line as the recurring cost is checked, cash is released and the profitability starts improving. Cost-cutting efforts to get the company back on the rails should be more on consideration of long-term benefits than as a knee-jerk reaction. One way to ct costs is for operations to become centralised as it helps attract good calibre professionals, eliminates duplication of staff and enables economies of scale.

b. **Combination Strategies:** A company can pursues a combination of two or more strategies simultaneously. But a combination strategy can be exceptionally risky if carried too far. No organisation can afford to pursue all the strategies that might benefit the firm. Difficult decisions must be made. Priorities must be established. Organisations like individuals have limited resources, so organisations must choose among alternative strategies. In large diversified companies, a combination strategy is commonly employed when different divisions pursue different strategies. Also, organisations struggling to survive may employ a combination of several defensive strategies.

LIQUIDATION

A legally declared bankrupt company may be liquidated. In the liquidation procedure, a referee normally is appointed to handle the administrative aspects of the bankruptcy procedure. The referee then arranges for a meeting of the creditors, and they in turn select a trustee, who liquidates the business and pay the creditor's claims according to the priority of claims. Liquidation occurs when an entire company is dissolved and its assets are sold. It is a strategy of the last resort. When there are no buyers for a business which wants to be sold, the company may be wound up and its assets may be sold to satisfy debt obligations.

Liquidation becomes the inevitable strategy under the following circumstances:

1. When an organisation has pursued both turnaround strategy and divestiture strategy, but failed.
2. When an organisation's only alternative is bankruptcy, a company can legally declare bankruptcy first and then wind up the company to raise needed funds to pay debts.
3. When the shareholders of a company can minimise their losses by selling the assets of a business.

Priority of Claims

It is the trustee's responsibility to liquidate all the firm's assets and to distribute the proceeds to the holders of provable claims. The priority of claims must be maintained by the trustee in distributing the funds from liquidation. It is important to recognise that any secured creditors have specific assets pledged as collateral and, in liquidation, receive proceeds from the sale of those assets. If these proceeds are inadequate to meet their claim, the secured creditors become unsecured, or general, creditors for the un-recovered amount, since specific collateral no longer exists. These and all other unsecured creditors, will divide up, on a pro rata basis, any funds remaining after all prior claims have been satisfied. If the proceeds from the sale of secured assets are in excess of the claims against them, the excess funds become available to meet claims of unsecured creditors.

The order of priority of claims is as follows:

1. The expenses involved in the administration of the bankruptcy.
2. Business expenses incurred after an involuntary petition has been filed but before a trustee has been appointed.
3. Wages owned for services performed prior to the bankruptcy proceedings.
4. Unpaid employee benefit plan contributions that were to be paid in the period proceedings the filling of bankruptcy or the termination of business.
5. Claims of storage.
6. Unsecured customers deposit, resulting from purchasing or leasing a good or service from the failed firm.
7. Taxes legally due and owned by the bankrupt firm to government.
8. Claims of secured creditor, who received the proceeds from the sale of collateral held, regardless of the priorities above. If the proceeds from the liquidation of the collateral are insufficient to satisfy the secured creditor's claims, the secured creditors become unsecured creditors for the unpaid amount.
9. Claims of unsecured creditors and unsatisfied portions of secured creditor's claims are all treated equally.

10. Preference shareholders, who receive an amount up to the par, or stated, value of their preference shares.
11. Equity shareholders who receive any remaining funds, which are distributed or in equal pre-share basis.

SELL-OFFS

The sell-offs are two types: (a) Divestitures and (b) Spin-offs and Spin-ups.

(a) Divestitures

A divestitures involves the sale of a division or plant or unit of one firm to another. From the seller's perspective, it is a form of contraction; from the buyer's point of view it represents expansion. This strategy is often used to raise capital for further strategic acquisition or investments. Divestiture is generally used as a part of turnaround strategy to get rid of businesses that are unprofitable, that require too much capital or that do not fit well with the firm's other activities. For example, when Cormondal Fertilizers Ltd., sold its Cement division to India cements Ltd., the size of Coramandel Fertilizers Ltd., contracted where as the size of India Cements Ltd., expanded. Hence a divestiture is the obverse of a purchase. Divestiture is an appropriate strategy to be pursued under the following circumstances:

1. When a business cannot be turned around.
2. When a business needs more resources than the company can provide.
3. When a business is responsible for a firm's overall poor performance.
4. When a business is a misfit with the rest of the organisation.
5. When a large amount of cash is required quickly.
6. When government's legal actions threaten the existence of a business.

Motives for Divestiture

- **Raising Capital:** For example CEAT sold Nylon tyre Cord plant at Gwalior to SRF for ₹ 32,50 milion.
- **Curtailment of Losses:** A prominent reason for divestiture is to cut losses. More broadly it may imply that the unit that is proposed to divest is earning a sub-normal rate of return.
- **Strategic Realignment:** The seller may divest a unit which no longer fits with its strategic plan. Often such a unit tends to be in an unrelated line and may demand a lot of managerial time.

(b) Spin-offs and Split-ups

A 'Spin-off' is a new, independent company created by detaching part of a new parent company's assets and operations. Shares in the new company are distributed.

1. Spin-offs are not taxed so long as shareholders in the parent are given at least 80 per cent of the shares in the new company.
2. If less than 80 per cent of the shares are distributed, the value of the distribution is taxed as a dividend to the investor.
3. Spin-offs widen investor's choice by allowing them to invest in just one part of the business. More important, spin-offs can improve incentives for managers. Companies sometimes refer to divisions or lines of business as 'poor profits'.
4. By spinning these businesses off, management of the parent company can concentrate on its main activity.
5. If the businesses are independent, it is easier to see the value and performance of each and reward managers accordingly. Also, spin-offs relieve investors of the worry that funds will be siphoned from one business to support unprofitable capital investment in another.

In a spin-off, a division or business unit of a company is spun-off into an independent company. After the spin-off, the parent company and the spun-off company are separate corporate entities. For example, the Information Technology Division of WIPRO Ltd was spun-off as a separate company. In a split up a company is broken up in to two or more independent companies. As a sequel, the parent company disappears as corporate entity and in its place, two or more separate companies emerge. For example, Ahmedabad Advance Mills split up into two separate companies, *viz.*, The New Ahmedabad Advance Mills and Tata Metal strips.

Rationale

Spin-offs and split-ups are regarded as devices for enhancing corporate values by raising efficiency and performance. A spin-off strengths managerial incentives and heightens in accountability. For example, the president's letter in the 1980 Annual report of Peabody's spin-offs of GEO International 'Speaking from personal experience, one of the most exciting benefits has been a rekindling of the entrepreneurial spirit and initiative with Peabody and GEO.

Equity Carve-outs

This is the Initial Public Offering (IPO) of some portion of the common stock of common stock of a wholly-owned subsidiary. These are also referred to as "split-off IPOs". An IPO of the equity of a subsidiary resembles a seasoned equity offering of the parent in that cash is received from a public sale of equity securities. But there are also differences. The IPO of the common stock of the subsidiary initiatives public trading is a new and distinct set of equity claims on the assets of the subsidiary.

Other changes often take place as well when the subsidiary equity is 'carved-out' from the consolidated entity of the parent. The management system for operating the assets is likely to be restructured in the new public entity.

LEVERAGED BUYOUTS: (LBOS)

A leveraged buyout involves a transfer of ownership consummated mainly with debt. Generally, a LBO involves an acquisition of a division or unit of a company; occasionally it entails the purchase of an entire company. A LBO entails considerable dependence on debt. Debt has a bracing effect on management, whereas equity tends to have soporific influence. Debt spurs management to perform whereas equity lulls management to relax and take things easy.

Leveraged buyouts differ from ordinary acquisitions in two immediately obvious ways. First, a large fraction of the purchase price is debt-financed. Some, often all, of this debt is junk, that is below investment-grade. Second, the LBO goes private, and its shares no longer trade on the open market. The LBO's stock is held by a partnership of investors. When this group is led by the company's management, the acquisition is called a Management Buy-out (MBO).

Main Characteristics of LBOs

1. **High Debt:** The debt is not intended to be permanent. It is designed to be paid down. The requirement to generate cash for debt service is designed to curb wasteful investment and force improvement in operating efficiency.
2. **Incentives:** Managers are given a greater stake in the business via stock options or direct ownership of shares.
3. **Private Ownership:** The LBO goes private. It is owned by a partnership of the private investors who monitor performance and can act right away if something goes awry. But private ownership is not intended to be permanent. The most successful LBO's go public again as soon as debt has been paid down sufficiently and improvements in operating performance have been demonstrated.

RISK AND REWARDS

The sponsors of a LBO are lured by the prospects of wholly (or largely) owning a company or a division thereof, with the help of substantial debt finance. They assume considerable risks in the hope of reaping handsome rewards. The success of the entire operation depends on their ability to improve the performance of the unit, contain its business risks, exercise cost controls, and liquidate disposable assets. If they fail to do so, the high fixed financial costs can jeopardise the venture.

BUY-BACK OF SHARES

Buy-back appear to serve two functions: (i) they facilitate a more efficient allocation of resources, (ii) they impart some stability to prices. Buy-backs serve useful economic functions and hence should be permitted. However, they can be abused by unscrupulous management. Hence, buy-backs need to be properly regulated to check the potential abuse of this useful device.

JOINT VENTURE

A joint venture, also referred to as a strategic alliance, represents a partnership between two or more independent companies which join hands to achieve a common purpose. Joint ventures are assuming an increasingly prominent role in the strategy of leading firms. It is usually organised as a newly created company, though the partners may choose any other form of organisation. For example, P & G, Godrej Ltd was set-up as a joint venture of Godrej soaps Ltd., & Protector & Gamble India Ltd., Joint ventures are formed for different purposes.

1. **International Joint Ventures:** In this type of joint ventures, the international partner intends to benefit from the domestic partner's local knowledge of industry conditions of a specific country. This strategy will help the international firm to hedge its risks of product development costs specific to that market. Further, some countries make it mandatory for international firms to only enter the country through a joint venture with the local partner, rather than on their own. The primary disadvantage in this type of joint venture is that the international firm might lose control of its technology to its joint venture partner. Such joint ventures will also not give the firm enough control over its joint venture, so that it could compete globally against its competitors.

2. **Diversification Joint Venture:** A firm may diversify into new products or markets through a joint venture. In such joint ventures, the specific benefits arise from transfer of technical, managerial and financial expertise from one business to another.

3. **Market Entry Joint Ventures:** In this type of joint ventures, two or more firms in different businesses enter a new business where they could capitalise on their combined capabilities. For example, India's oil majors IOCL, BPCL and ONGC formed a joint venture with GAIL India, to exploit the import channel of liquefied natural gas into the country.

Common reasons for setting-up joint ventures:

- Pooling of complementary resources
- Access to raw materials or new markets
- Diversification of risk
- Economies of scale
- Cost reduction
- Tax shelter

Examples of Joint Ventures and their Objectives

Partners	Product	Strategic Objective
AT & T/Olivetti	Computers	Foreign market
Boeings/Mitsbushi/ Fuji/Kawasaki	Small aircraft	Cut costs, Share technology
Ford/Measures	Factory overheads	Cut costs
Corning/Ciba-geigy	Lab instruments	New markets
Kodak/Cetus	Biotech diagnostics	New market, Better distribution
GM/Toyota	Autos	Cut costs
GTE/Fujit Su equipment	Communication distribution	Cut costs better

DISINVESTMENT STRATEGIES

This lesson intends to examine the models of disinvestment policy adopted by the Ministry of Disinvestment, along with suitable recent examples in this regard. It was found that these models are adopted differently according to the nature of organisation, which is proposed for disinvestment. At the same time this paper also examines the importance of strategic partner in the process of disinvestment. There are three different models *viz.*, Strategic Sale Method, selling as prospective concern, and financial restructuring before disinvestment.

The First Model Applies to Cash: Rich companies, it is also called *Strategic Sale Method* where cash receivers and other assets are de-linked from the entities that are sold. Government need not put up a majority stake for sale under this method. It is the handling over the unit that makes this method distinctive. Past examples: Balco and Videsh Sanchar Nigam Ltd (VSNL). Future assets to go on sale: State Trading Corporation (STC), Minerals and Metals Trading Corporation (MMTC), Bharat Pertroleum Corporation (BPCL) and Hindustan Petroleum Corporation (HPCL), if the specific PSU requires the money immediately for expansion or new ventures, its cash reserves will remain untouched as was done with Maruti.

Here, its foreign partner, Suzuki Motor Corporation, managed to convenience that the company require the money. In the wake of the hugely successful Maruti Udyog public issue, the Government now cleared sale of residual equity through the same route in CMC, IBP, VSNL, BALCO. This is subject to the strategic partners agreeing to this proposal. The extent of government share holding in these companies ranges from 26 per cent in CMC, IBP and VSNL to 33.95 per cent in IPCL and 49 per cent in BALCO. The IPO (Initial Public Offering) route will be taken also for the Dredging Corporation of India where 20 per cent Government equity will be sold to help the company's fleet renewal plans. The strategic partners are the Tatas in the case of CMC and VSNL, Reliance Industries for IPCL, Indian Oil Corporations for IBP and Sterlite Industries for Balco. Among the five companies, only BALCO is not yet a listed company but Mr. Shourie disclosed that there were reports that it was considering list on the London Stock Exchange.

The second model relates to PSUs where the sale of individual assets may fetch a higher price compared to the one where it is sold as an on-going concern. In such cases, properties are de-merged and sold separately. That was what was done with Hotels owned by India Tourism Development Corporation (ITDC). Recently, it was debated whether it would be more profitable to sell the individual results of the Shipping Corporation of India (SCI) rather than selling the company as a whole. The disinvestment ministry decided to pursue the latter path.

The third model adopted by the ministry is in cases like the ailing Paradip Phosphates, where prior to the sale, a financial restructuring exercise was and decoration to make to more attractive to prospective buyers. It is now being done with loss making companies like Steel Authority of India (SAIL) and Engineering Projects India (EPIL), where loans are being return off are converted into equity and non-core units hawked off. Since GoI is trying to fit future divestments into one of these three models, it is obviously confident that these can help it get better prices. On 27th May, 2003, The National Iranian Oil Company (NIOC) has decided to exit Madras Fertilizers (MFL), a joint venture between the Iranian firms and the Central Government. The NIOC holds 25.77 per cent stake in MFL, the Central Government 59.5 per cent, institutional investors around 4.54 per cent and private corporate bodies 1.54 per cent. About 8.65 per cent of the shares is held by the general public. The Government proposed to divest 33.50 per cent of its holding in the first phase to bring its stake to 26 per cent. Now that the Iranian company has agreed to exit MFL, the total offer in the first tranche of disinvestment will be 59.27 per cent. The process of disvestment of Government holding in MFL to a strategic partner has hit the speed-breaker. Any prospective suitor may not wish the presence of one more stakeholder (NIOC) sitting at MFL. The Government, too, appears to appreciate the predicament of prospective suitors.

Recently, Cabinet Committee on Disinvestment (CCD) and the Disinvestment Minister, Arun Shourie assured that the market would not be crowded as a result of option for the IPO route for the above companies. He pointed out strategic partners who had the first right of refusal would have to be persuaded to give up the option that had been provided for them in the existing shareholders and share purchase agreements.

These agreements would both have to be amended to enable the Government to go to the market. In the case the partners agree, he said the modalities for the IPOs would be worked out later in consultation with a group of ministers comprising the Disinvestment Minister, the Finance Minister and the Minister representing the administrative Ministry.

VALUATION OF PSUs

It is the prospect of gaining control by buying a chunk of Government equity that makes the buyers pay a premium over the market price. The Tatas and IOC have paid a premium over what the share market has been valuing them lately. The Tata group paid

₹ 202 per VSNL share whose last pre-privatisation quote was around ₹ 167. IOC paid a whopping 80 per cent premium to take control of IBP. It bid at ₹ 1,154 crores was almost double that of the runner-up, the Shell group (₹ 595 Crores) and more than three and a half times the reserve price (₹ 327 crores). The financial implications for the two successful bidders do end just now. Under stock market rules each of them has to make an open offer to acquire at least another 20 per cent of the equity of the company at the same price they are paying for each share brought from the government.

In conclusion, it can be observed that the different models adopted for valuation of PSU's are not agreed by many strategic partners. As in case of profit making units, the strategic partners could get more gain than in case of the loss making units. Hence, financial restructuring of loss making PSU's is the need of the hour.

METHODOLOGIES ADOPTED FOR DISINVESTMENT/ PRIVATISATION

Company	Stock sold	Total price* ₹ crores	The Methodology
Modern foods	100%	149.00	Complete sale to Hindustan Lever in two phases after minor restructuring.
BALCO	51%	826.50	Simple sale to Sterilite Industries after taking out cash reserves.
CMC	51%	152.00	The Tatas purchased stock after only they were left in the fray.
HTL	74%	55.00	Simple sale of a company that wasn't doing too well.
LAGAN JUTE MACHINERY	74%	2.53	The loss making entity was sold as an ongoing concern.
ITDC	100%	179.55	9 of its properties were demerged and sold as separate entities.
HOTEL COPORORATION	100%	242.51	3 of its properties were demerged and sold as separate entities.
IBP	33.58%	1,153.68	The stock was purchased by IOC at a fairly high premium.
VSNL	25%	3,689.00	Simple sale to the Tatas after taking out cash and delinking its real estate.
PARADEEP PHOSPHATES	74%	151.7	An incomplete financial restructuring was under taken before selling it.
JESSPO & CO	72%	18.18	Post-restructuring the loss making entity was sold as an ongoing concern.

HINDUSTAN ZINC	26%	445.00	Sterlite took it over in a simple sale transaction.
IPCL	26%	1,491.00	To stop creation of a monopoly, one of its units was sold off before hand.
MARUTI UDYOG	50%	2,424.00**	For the first time, a part of the money will flow back in to the company.
Mineral Exploration Corporation	100%	N.A.	Based on the recommendations of the Mines Ministry.

Note: * Includes cash taken out the company prior to disinvestment in the form of dividends and dividend tax.

** Minimum expected realisation to the Government in a 3-phase disinvestment.

Models of Disinvestment or Privatisation

There are several models available to the Government with respect to privatisation. M.B. Athreya has proposed four models of privatisation or disinvestment.

- **Government Majority Enterprise:** The Government sells a portion of the enterprise's equity while retaining 51 per cent or more with itself.
- **Government Controlled Enterprise:** The Government retains 26 to 49 per cent of the enterprise's equity while disinvesting the balance.
- **Joint Sector Enterprise:** The Government keeps 26 per cent of the equity, sells 25 per cent to a private sector partner, and offers the balance 49 per cent to the general investing public.
- **Private Sector Enterprise:** The entire equity is transferred to non-governmental bonds.

APPENDIX
110 WAYS TO FIND FINANCIAL PATH OF THE COMPANY

Formulae

Liquidity Ratios:

1. Absolute Cash Ratio = Cash Reservoir/Current Liabilities
2. Cash Position to Total Assets = Cash Reservoir/Total Assets
3. Interval Measure = Cash Reservoir/Average daily cash expenditure
4. Current Ratio = CA/CL

5. Super quick Ratio = SQA/QL
6. Absolute Liquidity Ratio Or Quick Ratio = QA/QL
7. Ending Inventory to NWC = Closing Stock/NWC
8. Defensive Interval Ratio = Liquid Assets/Projected Daily cash requirement
9. Projected daily cash requirement = Projected Cash operating expenditure/No. of days in a year.

Working Capital Ratios:

10. Inventory to Working Capital: Inventory/Working Capital
11. Fixed Assets to Working Capital: FA/WC
12. Debtors to Working Capital: Debtors/WC
13. Debtors to Current Assets (CA) : Drs/CA
14. CA to Net worth: CA/Net worth
15. CA to Debt: CA/Debt
16. CA to Total Assets: CA/Total Assets
17. CL to Net worth: CL/Net worth
18. CL to Debt: CL/Debt
19. CL to Total Liabilities: CL/Total Liabilities
20. WC to Net worth: WC/NW
21. WC to Debt: Debt/WC
22. WC to CL: CL/WC
23. WC to Long term Debt: LT/WC
24. WC to Total Assets: WC/TA
25. WC to Fixed Assets: WC/FA
26. Day's payables: Operating Payables/Pre-tax cash expenses per day in a year
27. Day's Receivables = Bills Receivables/Sales per day in a year
28. Day's inventory = Inventory/Cost of sales per day in a year.

TURNOVER RATIOS/INVESTMENT UTILISATION RATIOS

29. Capital Intensity or Fixed Assets Turnover: Turnover or Net Sales/Fixed Assets
30. Assets Turnover or Invested Capital Turnover: Net Sales/Total Assets
31. Sales to Owned capital: Sales/Share Capital

32. Working capital turnover: Net Sales/WC
33. Average Inventory Turnover: Net Sales/Average Inventory
34. Closing Stock Turnover: Net Sales/Closing Stock
35. Cash Turnover: Net Sales/Cash
36. Receivables Turnover: Net Sales/Bills Receivable
37. Current Assets Turnover: Net Sales/Current Assets
38. Debtors Turnover: Net Sales/Average Debtors
39. Debt Collection Period: Months or Days in a year/Debtors Turnover
    a. Debt Collection Period: Average Accounts Receivable × Months or days in a year/Credit sales for the year
    b. Accounts receivable/Average or daily credit sales
40. Creditors Turnover Ratio (creditors velocity) = Credit purchases
41. Debt Payment Period enjoyed ratio
    a. Months or days in a year/Creditors turnover
    b. Average accounts payable x months/credit purchases
    c. Average accounts payable/Average monthly or daily credit purchases
42. Days Inventory: Material consumed/average stock of raw materials
43. Days Average WIP: Cost of completed work/Average Work in progress
44. Inventory Turnover: Net Sales /Average Inventory at selling price.

Expenses Ratios

A. Direct Expenses Ratios:

45. Direct Material Expenditure Ratio: Raw material consumed/Sales × 100
46. Direct Labour Expenditure Ratio: Wages/Sales × 100
47. Direct Overhead Ratio: Production or Factory Overhead/Sales × 100.

B. Indirect Expenses Ratios:

48. Administrative Expenses/Sales × 100
49. Selling Expenses/Sales × 100
50. Distribution Expenses/Sales × 100
51. Finance charges/Sales × 100
52. Operating Ratio = Cost of goods sold + Operating Expenses/Net Sales × 100
53. Cost of goods sold ratio = Cost of goods sold/Net Sales × 100

Profitability Ratios

Return Basis:

54. GP Ratio: GP/Sales × 100
55. NP Ratio: NP/Sales × 100
56. Operating Profit Ratio = EBIT or Operating Profit/Sales × 100
57. Profit Margin = Net Profit after taxes/Net sales
58. Return on Capital Employed = Return or EBIT/Capital Employed × 100
59. Return on Gross Capital Employed = EBIT/Gross Capital Employed × 100
60. Return Total Assets = NP after taxes/total assets (or) (EAT + Interest)/(TA fictitious assets)
61. Return on Net Assets = (EAT + Interest)/(Net assets)
62. Return on Equity Share Capital = (EAT + Pref. Dividend /Equity Share Capital) × 100
63. Return on Equity Share Funds = (EAT + Pref. Dividend/Equity Share Capital + Reserves and Surplus) × 100
64. Return on Net Worth (or) Return on Proprietor' funds (or) Return on Shareholders' funds = Net Profit/Net Worth

    Hint: 1. Net worth = Equity Share Capital + Preference share capital + profits Or Net Worth = FA + CA – Outside liabilities (Long and Current)

    Hint: 2. Net Profit = Net Income After Interest and Taxes + Net non-operating income
65. Return on Investment = NP after taxes/Net total assets or EBIT/Average Capital Employed.

Note: Capital Employed refers to:

(1) Fixed Assets + Current Assets (or)

(2) Fixed Assets (or)

(3) Share Capital + Reserve + Long term loans – (Non business assets + Fictitious Assets).

Shareholder View

66. Dividend yield = (Dividend Per Share/Market Price per Share) × 100
67. Earning per share = (Earnings available to equity shareholders/No. of equity shares)
68. Primary Earnings = Net Profit – Dividend on Pref. Share Capital
69. Growth in Equity = Retention ratio × ROE or [(EPS – DPS)/EPS] × [EPS/NWPS]

70. Diluted EPS = Primary Earnings/(Equity share capital + Rights issued)
71. DPS = Total dividend on equity share capital/No. of equity shares
72. Book value per share = Ordinary shareholder's equity/No. of equity shares
73. Price-Earning Ratio = Market Price/EPS
74. Earnings Price Ratio Or Capitalisation ratio = EPS/Market price
75. Payout Ratio = DPS/EPS
76. Retained Earnings Ratio = Retained Earnings Per Share/EPS

    or Retained Earnings/Total earnings.

PROFIT ALLOCATION RATIOS

77. I.T./Net Profit
78. I.T./PBT
79. Dividend to Net Profit
80. Dividend to PBT
81. Dividend to PBIT
82. Dividend to Net profit + Depreciation
83. Dividend to Operating Profit + Depreciation
84. Retained Earning to Net Profit
85. Retained Earning to PBT

Coverage Ratio:

86. Debt-Service Coverage Ratio = Return available for debt service = Interest + Loan installment of current year
87. Interest Coverage Ratio = EBIT/Interest
88. Fixed Dividend Cover = EBIT/Pref. Dividend
89. Cover for Pref. Dividend = Earnings available for Equity Shares/Equity Dividend
90. Total Coverage ratio = [EBIT + Lease payment]/[Interest + Lease Payment + DP/(1- t)]
91. Cash Flow Coverage Ratio = EBIT + Lease payment + Depreciation]/[Interest + Lease Payment + DP/(1- t) + Installment of principal/(1- t)]
92. Fixed Coverage = EBIT + Depreciation/[Interest + Loan payment (1- tax rate)]

Leverage Ratios:

93. Degree of Operation Leverage (DOL) = % change in EBIT/% change in Sales
94. Degree of Financial Leverage (DFL) = % change in EPS/% change in EBIT
95. Degree of Combined Leverage (DCL) = DFL X DCL

Capital Structure Ratios:

96. Debt Equity Ratio = Debt/Equity

    or Long-term debt/Equity Shareholder fund

    or Total Debt/Net Worth

    or External Equity/Internal Equity

    or Total Long-term Debt/Total Long-term funds
97. Proprietary Ratio = Proprietary Fund/Total Assets

    or Owned Capital/Total Capital
98. Proprietary Fund = Fixed Assets + Current Assets

    or Equity Shares Capital + Total Liabilities

    or Equity Shares + Pref. shares + Free reserves
99. Total Liabilities to Net Worth = Total Liabilities/Net Worth
100. Total Liabilities = Secured Loans + Unsecured Loans + Current Liabilities + Provision for taxes + Advance Tax
101. Capital Gearing Ratio = (Pref. Shares + Debt + Other Loans) + (Net Worth _ Pref. Share Capital)

    or (Pref. Dividend + Debenture Dividend)/Equity Dividend
102. Interest Bearing Fund = Debentures + Pref. Share Capital + Bank OD + Short-term Loan
103. Non Interest Bearing Fund = Equity Share Capital
104. Proprietor's Net Capital Employed = Total Assets – Total outside liabilities
105. Fixed Assets Ratio = FA/Long-term funds
106. Debt Ratio = Total Debt/total Assets
107. Net Worth to Net FA = Net Worth/Net FA
108. Long-term Debt to NWC = Long-term Debt/NWC
109. Net Fixed Assets to Long-term Debt = NFA/Debt
110. Tabin's Q Ratio = It is the ratio of market value of a firm's assets (or equity and debt) to its assets' replacement cost.

    Tabin's Q = Market Value of Assets/Replacement cost of assets.

CLOSING CASELET

FINANCIAL DISTRESS IN GLOBAL TRUST BANK, INDIA (GTB)

The collapse of GTB resulted from many mistakes committed by the bank's management. GTB's problems started in 2000 and the imposition of the moratorium finally ended its independent existence. RBI's probe into GTB's accounts revealed a significant erosion of the bank's net worth and huge number of NPAs reflected its weak financials. Moreover, GTB's attempts to strengthen its capital base through investments from overseas failed due to regulatory problems, resulting in the total collapse of the bank. Since 2001, GTB's name was associated with scams and controversies, thereby casting shadows over the credibility of the bank and its management. Due to the over exposure to capital markets and huge NPAs, the bank was in a financial mess. When GTB tried to cover up its monumental NPAs through under provisioning, RBI - the Central bank and the regulatory authority for banks in India, appointed an independent team to review the finances of the bank. The review revealed various financial discrepancies kept covered by the bank. Earlier, the Reserve Bank of India (RBI) had announced that GTB's net worth had turned negative as it had incurred huge losses and accumulated a significant number of non-performing assets (NPAs). RBI stated that the numbers reported in GTB's balance sheet did not match its audited figures. Moreover, GTB failed to provide satisfactory explanations to most of RBI's queries regarding its capital market exposures and why prudent lending norms were not observed in disbursing huge amounts for investments in the stock market. RBI said the moratorium was imposed in public interest and to protect the interests of depositors. All operations of GTB were frozen and it was ordered not to give loans without RBI permission. It was allowed only to make payments for day-to-day operations or for meeting obligations entered into before the order. On July 24, 2004, the Government of India imposed a moratorium on Global Trust Bank (GTB), a leading private sector bank, on the grounds of 'wrong financial disclosures and within two days the bank was merged with Oriental Bank of Commerce (OBC), a public sector bank. With the merger becoming effective, GTB's identity came to an end and it became a part of OBC.

- Discuss the important issues in the financial distress of Global Trust Bank and the role of government in taking over it by Oriental Bank of Commerce.

Source: *http://www.icmrindia.org/casestudies/catalogue/Finance/The Rise and Fall of Global Trust Bank.htm - bot7*

SUMMARY

This chapter is intended to examine the influence of financial distress in corporate entities. Distress refers to a business failure is an unfortunate circumstance. Business failure can be considered from both an economic and a financial view point. In an economic sense, business success is associated with firms that earn an adequate return (equal to or greater than cost of capital) on their investments. 'Hoffer' has classified the turnaround strategies in two broad categories. These are strategic turnaround and operating turnarounds. A legally declared bankrupt company may be liquidated. In the liquidation procedure, a referee normally is appointed to handle the administrative aspects of the bankruptcy procedure. The referee then arranges for a meeting of the creditors, and they in turn select a trustee, who liquidates the business and pay the creditor's claims according to the priority of claims. This chapter also focuses on disinvestment procedure.

KEYWORDS

1. **Liquidation:** In the liquidation procedure, a referee normally is appointed to handle the administrative aspects of the bankruptcy procedure.
2. **Divestitures:** A divestitures involves the sale of a division or plant or unit of one firm to another.
3. **Leveraged Buy-Outs:** (LBOs): A leveraged buy-out involves a transfer of ownership consummated mainly with debt.
4. **Joint Venture:** A joint venture, also referred to as a strategic alliance, represents a partnership between two or more independent companies which join hands to achieve a common purpose.
5. **Joint Sector Enterprise:** The government keeps 26 per cent of the equity, sells 25 per cent to a private sector partner, and offers the balance 49 per cent to the general investing public.
6. **Private Sector Enterprise:** The entire equity is transferred to non-governmental bonds.

REVIEW QUESTIONS

1. What do you understand by 'Financial distress' in corporate entity?
2. Discuss various types of corporate turnaround strategies with suitable examples.
3. Define 'disinvestment' and explain the procedure of disinvestment adopted by Government of India.

REFERENCES

1. Gustave Grullon, Geroge Kanatas and Piyush Kumar, Financing Decisions and Advertising: "An Empirical Study of Capital Structure and Product Market Competition", http://ssrn.com.
2. Jakhotiya G.P., *Strategic Financial Management*, Vikas Publications, New Delhi, 2007.
3. I.M. Pandey, *Financial Management*, Vikas Publication, 2009.
4. *Strategic Financial Management: Application of Corporate Finance*, 1st Edition, Thomson, Business School Edition.
5. Sridhar A.N., *Strategic Financial Management*, SPD, New Delhi, 2008.

ജ്ജ ജ്ജ ജ്ജ

CHAPTER

10

Strategies of International Financing

CHAPTER OUTLINE

- Opening Caselet
- Introduction
- International Bonds
- Currency Options
- Types of International Bonds
- International Equity
- Interbank Clearinghouse Systems
- International Loans
- Back-to-Back Loans
- Funding from Foreign Institutional Investors
- Foreign Direct Investment
- Closing Caselet
- Summary
- Problems and Solutions
- Keywords
- Review Questions
- References

OPENING CASELET

Suppose that Sri Lanka has a choice of two possible US $ 100 million, five year Eurodollar loans. The first loan is offered at LIBOR (London Inter-bank Operating Rate) + 1 per cent with a 2.5 per cent syndication fee, where as the second loan and is priced at LIBOR + 1.5 per cent and a 0.75 per cent syndication fee. Assuming that Srilanka has 10 per cent of cost of capital, which loan is preferable?

Solution:

This problem can be solved as a capital budgeting problem. The dollar cash flows associated with these two spread-syndicate fee combinations are as follows:

1. Loan 1: 2.5 per cent fee, 1 per cent spread
2. Loan 2: 0.75 per cent fee, 1.5 per cent spread

Hence, total present value of the loan can be calculated using the following formulae:

TOTAL PRESENT VALUE = Syndication fee + Present value of spread on loan

1. STEP 1: Calculation of syndication fee : 2.5 per cent of 100 million = 2,500,000
2. STEP 2: Calculation of spread amount: 1 per cent on 100 million = 1,000,000
3. STEP 3: Find table value of spread amount: @10 per cent for 5 years = 3.791
4. STEP 4: Calculate spread amount: 1000000 × 3.791 = 3791000
5. STEP 5: Total present value = 2,500,000 + 3,760,000 = 6,291,000

INTRODUCTION

The international financing consists of the international bonds, international equity and international loans.

INTERNATIONAL BONDS

International bonds are those bonds that are initially sold outside the country of the borrower. International bonds consist of foreign bonds, Eurobonds, and global bonds. An important issue with bond financing has to do with the currency issue. The currency of issue is not necessarily the same as the country of issue, although the two may coincide. For example, if a US company sells a yen-denominated bond in Japan, the currency of issue is that of the country of issue. However, if a US company sells a dollar-denominated bond in Japan, the currency of issue is not that of the country of issue. In the former of these situations, the bond is called a foreign bond; in the latter, the bond is called a Eurobond. A global bond is hybrid in nature, because it can be sold inside as well as outside the country in whose currency it is denominated. For example, a dollar-denominated bond tradable in New York (domestic market) and Tokyo (Eurobond market) is called a global bond. Let us provide a more general description of these three international bonds: foreign bonds, Eurobonds, and global bonds.

- **Foreign Bonds:** Bonds sold in a particular national market by a foreign borrower, under-written by a syndicate of brokers from that country, and denominated in the currency of that country are called foreign bonds. Of course, foreign bonds fall under the regulatory jurisdiction of national or domestic authorities. Dollar-denominated bonds sold in New York by a Mexican firm are foreign bonds; these bonds should be registered with the US Securities and Exchange Commission (SEC). Foreign bonds are similar in many respects to the public debt sold in domestic capital markets, but their issuer is a foreigner. The first foreign bond was issued in 1958. Most large foreign-bond issues have been floated in the USA, the UK, and Switzerland. The weakening British pound in the late 1950s reduced the importance of the domestic British capital market for foreign firms. The Interest Equalization Tax (1963-74) of the USA effectively stopped New York's usefulness as a capital market for new foreign bonds. Thus, international borrowers and investors shifted their activities from the USA to Europe. This shift caused the Eurobond market to develop.

- **Euro Bonds:** Bonds underwritten by an international syndicate of brokers and sold simultaneously in many countries other than the country of the issuing entity are called Eurobonds. In other words, since the term 'foreign bonds' refers to those bonds that are issued in the external sectors of financial markets — sectors that fall outside the regulatory environment of national authorities — Euro bonds are, therefore, issued outside the country in whose currency they are denominated. The Euro bond market is almost entirely free of official regulation, but is self-regulated by the Association of International Bond Dealers. For example, dollar-denominated bonds sold outside the USA are Euro bonds; these bonds are not registered under the US Securities Act and may not be offered or sold to Americans as part of the distribution. The first Euro bond issue was launched in 1963. Euro bonds are direct claims on leading MNCs, governments, or governmental enterprises. They are sold simultaneously in many countries through multinational syndicates of underwriting brokers. The Euro bond market is similar to the Euro dollar market in one respect. Both markets are 'external', because obligations available in these markets are denominated in foreign currencies outside the country of issue.

- **Global Bonds:** These are bonds sold inside as well as outside the country in whose currency they are denominated. For example, dollar-denominated bonds sold in New York (domestic bond market) and Tokyo (Euro bond market) are called dollar global bonds. Similarly, pound-denominated bonds sold in London and Los Angeles are pound global bonds. While global bonds follow the domestic market practice of registration of bonds, they follow the Euro bond market practice regarding their distribution. Dollar global bonds combine SEC registration and US clearing arrangements with separate clearing on the Euro bond market. The World Bank issued the first such bonds in September 1989 and still remains the leading issuer of global bonds. The Bank raised $1.5 billion through a dollar global bond issue that was offered in the USA as well as in Euro bond markets. It has issued in US dollars, Euros, Japanese yen, and British pounds.

  By allowing issuers to solicit demand for a variety of markets and to offer greater liquidity to investors, global bonds have potential to reduce borrowing costs. Such cost savings might be, however, offset by the fixed costs of borrowing through the global format, such as registration and clearing arrangements. These costs for global bonds are presumably higher than for comparable Euro bond issues.

- **Currency Option Bonds:** The holders of currency option bonds are allowed to receive their interest income in the currency of their option from among two or three predetermined currencies at a predetermined exchange rate. The original bond contract contains the currencies of choice and the exchange rates. The currency option enhances the exchange guarantee for the investor. Thus, the investor will make some gain if all currencies included in the contract do not depreciate against the desired currency.

- **Currency Cocktail Bonds:** Bonds denominated in a standard 'currency basket' of several different currencies are called currency cocktail bonds. A number of these bonds have been developed to minimise or hedge foreign-exchange risk associated with single-currency bonds. The currency diversification provided by these bonds can be replicated by individual investors. Thus, currency cocktail bonds have never gained wide acceptance with Euro market borrowers.

CURRENCY OPTIONS

A currency option is no different from a stock option except that the underlying asset is foreign exchange. The basic premises remain the same: the buyer of option has the right but no obligation to enter into a contract with the seller. Therefore the buyer of a currency option has the right, to his advantage, to enter into the specified contract. In every currency transaction, one currency is bought and another sold. For example an option to buy US dollars (USD) for Indian rupees (INR) is an USD call and an INR put. Conversely, an option to sell USD for INR is an USD put and an INR call. The other basics like strike price, expiration period, American style or European style are similar to stock options. Quotation of a currency option can be done in two ways: American or direct terms, in which a currency is quoted in terms of the Indian Rupees per unit of foreign currency; and European or inverse terms, in which the Rupee is quoted in terms of units of foreign currency per rupee. The same applies to situations where the Indian Rupee is not one of the currencies.

Option Pricing

The premium quoted for a particular option at a particular time represents a consensus of the option's current value which is comprised of two elements: intrinsic value and time value. Intrinsic value is simply the difference between the spot price and the strike price. A put option will have intrinsic value only when the spot price is below the strike price. A call option will have intrinsic value only when the spot price is above the strike price. Options, which have positive intrinsic value, are said to be 'in-the-money'. When the price of a call or put option is greater than its intrinsic value, it is because of its time value. Time value is determined by five variables: the spot or underlying price, the expected volatility of the underlying currency, the exercise price, time to expiration, and the difference in the 'risk-free' rate of interest that can be earned by the two currencies. Time value falls toward zero as the expiration date approaches. An option is said to be 'out-of-the-money' if its price is comprised only of time value. A variety of complex option pricing models such as Black-Scholes and Cox-Rubinstein have been developed to determine option pricing. Another commonly used model for currency option valuation is the Garmen-Kohlhagen model.

Interest rate differentials between nations and temporary supply/demand imbalances can also have an effect on option premiums. In the final analysis, option prices (premiums) must be low enough tó induce potential buyers to buy and high enough to induce potential option writers to sell.

Types of Options

Apart from the normal call and put the following are a few basic types of currency options. In real life most of the options are combinations of these basic types.

- **Knockout Options:** These are like standard options except that they extinguish or cease to exist if the underlying market reaches a pre-determined level during the life of the option. The knockout component generally makes them cheaper than a standard Call or Put.

- **Knock-in Options:** These options are the reverse of knockout options because they don't come into existence until the underlying market reaches a certain pre-determined level, at this time a call or put option comes into life and takes on all the usual characteristics.
- **Average Rate Options:** The options have their strikes determined by an averaging process, for example at the end of every month. The profit or loss is determined by the difference between the calculated strike and the underlying market at expiry.
- **Basket Options:** A basket option has all the characteristics of a standard option, except that the strike price is based on the weighted value of the component currencies, calculated in the buyer's base currency. The buyer stipulates the maturity of the option, the foreign currency amounts which make up the basket, and the strike price, which is expressed in units of the base currency.
- **Currency Options in India:** Currency options are new comers in the Indian scenario. The Reserve Bank of India (RBI) allowed trading in rupee options from July 7th, 2003. The timing could not have been more appropriate with the government having a comfortable forex reserves position and markets mature enough to be able to exploit the opportunity. On the first day it witnessed brisk activity (trading volumes of $200-250 million with foreign as well as Indian banks like Standard Chartered, HSBC, ABN Amro, SBI, IDBI, ICICI Bank and IndusInd entering into major transactions. Big corporate houses like Reliance, HCL, Murugappa and L&T were also not far behind. Before the introduction of currency options the Indian corporates had only two alternatives: either to enter into a forward contract or leave the exposure open. The problem with forwards is that they are price fixing agreements and deny any gains of favourable movement in the market. Leaving the exposure open subjects them to the mercy of the market. Options are like insurance contracts, they protect you from the downside at the same time allowing you to reap the benefits of any upside. Allowing Rupee options would introduce greater flexibility in risk management of corporates and cost control.

TYPES OF INTERNATIONAL BONDS

Five types of international bonds are straight (fixed-rate) bonds, floating-rate notes, convertible bonds, bonds with warrants, and other bonds.

1. **Straight Bonds:** These bonds have fixed maturities and carry a fixed rate of interest. Straight bonds are repaid by amortisation or in a lump sum at the maturity date. The amortisation method refers to the retirement of a long-term debt by making a set of equal periodic payments. These periodic payments include both interest and principal. Alternatively, a borrower may retire his or her bonds by redeeming the face value of the bonds at maturity. Under this method, a fixed interest on the face value of the bonds is paid at regular intervals.

2. **Fixed-Rate Bonds:** These are technically unsecured, debenture bonds, because almost all of them are not secured by any specific property of the borrower. Because of this, debenture bondholders become general creditors in the event of default; they look to the nature of the borrower's assets, its earning power, and its general credit strength. Perhaps the greatest advantage of all types of international bonds for individual investors is that interest income on them is exempt from withholding taxes at the source. Investors must report their interest income to their national authorities, but both tax avoidance and tax evasion are extremely widespread. Official institutions hold a large portion of investment in international bonds and are not liable for tax. Another large class of investors in international bonds consists of private institutions. These private institutions legally avoid tax by being in tax-haven countries.

3. **Floating-Rate Notes:** These notes are frequently called floating-rate bonds. The rate of return on these notes is adjusted at regular intervals, usually every 6 months, to reflect changes in short-term market rates. Because one of their main objectives is to provide dollar capital for non-US banks, most roating-rate notes are issued in dollars. Like other international bonds, roating-rate notes are issued in denominations of $1,000 each. They usually carry a margin of 1/4 per cent above the LIBOR, and this margin is normally adjusted every 6 months. The link between the rate of return on roating-rate notes and LIBOR rates is intended to protect the investor against capital loss.

4. **Covertible Bonds:** Bonds of this type are convertible into parent company stock. The conversion price is usually fixed at a certain premium above the market price of the common stock on the date of the bond issue. Investors are free to convert their fixed-income securities into common stock at any time before the conversion privilege expires; the borrowing company is obliged to issue new stock for that purpose. The convertible provision is designed to increase the marketability of fixed-rate Euro bonds. Convertible bonds provide investors with a steady income and an opportunity to participate in rising stock prices. Thus, their interest rates have been 1.5 to 2 per cent below those on fixed-rate bonds. Because international investors are ratio-conscious, they prefer convertible bonds, which maintain the purchasing power of money.

5. **Bonds with Warrants:** Some international bonds are issued with warrants. A warrant is an option to buy a stated number of common shares at a stated price during a prescribed period. Warrants pay no dividends, have no voting rights, and become worthless at expiration unless the price of the common stock exceeds the exercise price. Convertible Euro bonds do not bring in additional funds. When they are converted, common stock increases, and the convertible securities are retired. When warrants are exercised, common stock and cash increase simultaneously.

6. **Other Bonds:** A major portion of other bonds consists of zero-coupon bonds, which provide all of the cash payment (interest and principal) when they mature. These bonds do not pay periodic interest, but are sold at a deep discount from their face

value. The return to the investor is the excess of the face value over the market price. Zero-coupon bonds have several advantages over conventional bonds. First, there is immedate cash inflow to the issuing company but no periodic interest to pay. Second, a big tax advantage exists for the issuing company, because any discount from the maturity value may be amortized for tax purposes by the company over the life of the bond.

INTERNATIONAL EQUITY

Besides debt instruments such as the Euro dollar and bond markets, the equity capital market is another important source of financing. Evidence indicates that the final decade of the twentieth century will go down in history as the period in which much of the world discovered the stock market as a major source of funds for their global expansion. Companies will increasingly turn to the stock market to raise money. This section focuses on how ownership in publicly owned corporations is traded throughout the world. The stock market consists of the primary market and the secondary market. The primary market is a market in which the sale of new common stock by corporations to initial investors occurs. The secondary market is a market in which the previously issued common stock is traded between investors.

New Trends in the Stock Markets

In recent years, a number of new trends have begun to emerge in the stock markets around the world:

(1) Alliance,

(2) Crosslisting, and

(3) Concentration.

1. Stock Market Alliances

There are some 150 stock exchanges in the world. Within the past 10 years, these stock exchanges have scrambled to align with each other. Markets in Paris, Amsterdam, and Brussels have agreed to form Euronext, while a group of Scandinavian markets has agreed to form Norex. Those deals prompted the London Stock Exchange and Frankfurt's Deutsche Bourse to consider a merger into a new market, but that deal fell through in September 2000. In 2001, the Lisbon Exchange decided it would join Euronext. NASDAQ has joint ventures and alliances in Japan, Hong Kong, Australia, Canada, the UK, and Germany. In September 2002, Euronext and the Tokyo Stock Exchange signed an alliance for cooperation and investor protection. In November 2002, the New Zealand Stock Exchange and the Hong Kong Stock Exchange signed an information-sharing agreement. The New York Stock Exchange has recently discussed alliances with markets in Canada, Latin America, Europe, and Asia.

There is a variety of reasons for this consolidation of stock exchanges: the growing speed and power of telecommunication links, big and small investors' keen interest in stocks from all parts of the world, and the fear of being left behind. Moreover, if national exchanges do not take the initiative, they could be bypassed by new electronic trading systems. These same forces have caused the burgeoning of online trading and have pushed national securities firms to expand their business overseas.

2. Crosslisting

With the rise of cross-border mergers during the 1990s and the early 2000s, there arises a need for companies to crosslist their stocks on different exchanges around the world. Companies are obligated to adhere to the securities regulations of all countries where their shares are listed. A decision to crosslist in the USA means that any company, domestic or foreign, must meet the accounting and disclosure requirements of the US Securities and Exchange Commission. Rules for listing requirements differ markedly from country to country, but analysts regard US requirements as the most restrictive in the world. Reconciliation of a company's financial statements to US standards can be a laborious process. Some foreign companies are reluctant to disclose hidden reserves and other pieces of company information. It might not appear too difficult for US companies to crosslist on certain foreign exchanges because their listing requirements are not that restrictive, but certain barriers still exist, such as a foreign country's specific rules and reporting costs. By crosslisting its shares on foreign exchanges, an MNC hopes to:

1. Allow foreign investors to buy their shares in their home market.
2. Increase the share price by taking advantage of the home country's rules and regulations.
3. Provide another market to support a new issuance.
4. Establish a presence in that country in the instance that it wishes to conduct business there.
5. Increase its visibility to its customers, creditors, suppliers, and the host government.
6. Compensate local management and employees in the foreign affiliates.

3. Stock Market Concentration

European stock markets have become more integrated since the European Union's decision to switch their monetary union from the European Currency Unit to the euro, which was launched in 1999. Increasing integration, as reflected in converging price dynamics across markets, results from various structural changes in European stock markets. There is already a large amount of crosslisting and trading among exchanges. Competition among exchanges for listing and order flow has long characterised European securities markets. In addition, exchanges have become subject to competition for order flow from alternative trading systems. Because there are benefits from achieving large size and attracting liquidity, another important response to competitive pressures has consisted of mergers among exchanges.

The concentration of stock market capitalisation is not an 'ED phenomenon', but reflects a worldwide trend toward a single global market for certain instruments. The three largest stock markets accounted for 60 per cent of the total market capitalisation in 1995 and 2001. Furthermore, the share of the five and 10 largest stock markets has increased from 1995 to 2001. These statistics indicate a trend toward concentration of the world stock markets.

INTERBANK CLEARINGHOUSE SYSTEMS

This section describes three key clearinghouse systems of inter bank fund transfers. These three systems transfer funds between banks through wire rather than through cheques. The Clearing House Interbank Payments System (CHIPS) is used to move dollars among New York offices of about 150 financial institutions that handle 95 per cent of all foreign-exchange trades and almost all Eurodollar transactions. The Clearing House Payments Assistance System (CHPAS) began its operation in 1983 and provides services similar to those of the CHIPS. It is used to move funds among the London offices of most financial institutions.

The Society for Worldwide Interbank Financial Telecommunications (SWIFT) is an interbank communication network that carries messages for financial transactions. It was founded in 1973, by European and North American banks. Since 1973, its membership has expanded to include many Asian and Latin American banks. The SWIFT network represents a common denominator in the international payment system and uses the latest communication technology. The network has vastly reduced the multiplicity of formats used by banks in different parts of the world. Banks can execute international payments more cheaply and efficiently than ever before, because of the common denominator in the international payment system and the speed of electronic transactions. Currently, 6,000 live network users send 10 million messages daily through the SWIFT; its usage increases at an annual average growth rate of 15 per cent. Messages transferred through this system include bank transfers, customer transfers, and special messages.

INTERNATIONAL LOANS

Large international loans to developing countries have become extremely important for European, Japanese, and US banks. For some banks, international loans have become as important as their domestic banking operations. On the other hand, recent global debt problems have raised serious questions about large loans to developing and former Eastern-bloc countries. Pricing an international loan, which amounts to the determination of the interest charged to the borrower, depends on a number of factors. It is also influenced by a combination of risk evaluation, market conditions, and shifts in the demand for and supply of loans. The following factors are important for determining the interest rate charged to the borrower.

The Spread and the Reference Rate

The interest paid on syndicated loans is usually computed by adding a spread to the London Interbank Offer Rate (LIBOR) or another reference rate such as the US prime rate or the Singapore Interbank Offer Rate (SIBOR). The following factors determine the spread:

1. The availability of liquidity or loanable funds relative to demand. Spreads are likely to be higher in a market that is characterised by a shortage of liquidity and excess demand for loanable funds.
2. The creditworthiness of the borrower, as high-quality borrowers are charged lower spreads than low-quality borrowers.
3. The maturity of the loan, with higher spreads charged on long-maturity loans.

Risk Sharing and Reduction

International banks use the following techniques to reduce and shift risks involved in international lending:

1. **Loan Selection and Structuring:** This process includes an analysis of credits to screen out inferior loans, application of loan limits, emphasis on booking higher quality credits and adherence to country, customer and currency limits.
2. **Participation in Loans:** Many banks participate in large loans, each taking a small portion of the amount.
3. **Use of Guarantees and Insurance:** Central government agencies, central banks, and commercial banks provide loan guarantees.
4. **Floating Rate Loans:** These loans provide protection for the lender bank against interest rate risk (risk is shifted to the borrower).

Syndicate Loans

A syndicated loan is a credit in which a group of banks makes funds available on common terms and conditions to a particular borrower. Perhaps one of the most important developments in the field of international lending for the past two decades (the 1980s and 1990s) has been the rapid growth of syndicated loans. In the Euromarket, syndicated loans compose almost half of bank lending to nonbank borrowers. Syndication is the device a group of banks adopt to handle large loans that one bank is unable or unwilling to supply. In other words, syndication differs from a direct commercial loan in that several banks participate at the outset. For example, Kuwait signed a $5.5 billion loan accord with 81 banks from 21 countries on December 13, 1991. This 5-year reconstruction deal was described as the largest syndicated loan ever extended to a sovereign borrower. A syndicated loan must, therefore, be structured and packaged so that it satisfies the demands of the lenders and the needs of the borrowers. This type of loan has become increasingly popular because of: (1) the increasing size of individual loans; (2) the need to spread risks in large loans; (3) the attractiveness of management fees; (4) the publicity for participating banks; and (5) the need to form profitable working relationships with other banks.

Advantages and Disadvanages

On the one hand, international loans have some advantages for banks:

1. International loans have been very profitable for many large banks, and have had a significant impact on the earnings of these international banks.
2. Many banks have improved risk-return performance because they can diversify international loans by country, by type of customer, and by currency.
3. Several safeguards have reduced the risk of international loans. They include credit insurance programs in the lenders' own countries, guarantees by parent companies on loans to affiliates, and guarantees by host governments on loans to private companies within their country.

Disadvantages

On the other hand, international loans have many disadvantages for banks:

1. Country risk analysis is extremely complex, because it depends on many variables.
2. International bankers recently did not anticipate dramatic increases in country risk.
3. Critics question the ability of debtor countries to service their external debt, because many loans are short-term variable loans.
4. If borrowing countries are unable to meet their obligations on time, banks will be forced to roll over their loans indefinitely.
5. The ultimate purpose of some loans is to finance balance-of-payments deficits. This type of loan does not improve the debtor country's ability to generate foreign-exchange earnings.

Direct Loans

MNCs may elect to provide investment funds to their foreign operations in the form of intra-company loans instead of increasing their equity contributions. However, the parent company lends money as an owner to its subsidiaries. The intra-company loan usually contains a specified repayment period for the loan principal and earns interest income that is taxed relatively lightly. These two features of intra-company loans compare favourably with an open-ended equity investment, which produces profits in the form of heavily taxed dividends. Parent loans to foreign subsidiaries are usually more popular than equity contributions for a number of reasons. First, parent loans give a parent company greater flexibility in repatriating funds from its foreign subsidiary. In nearly every part of the world, laws make it more difficult to return funds to the parent through dividend payments or equity reductions than through interest and principal payments. Moreover, a reduction in equity is often construed as, a plan to leave the country.

Second, tax considerations are another reason for favouring parent loans over equity contributions. In most cases, interest payments on internal loans are tax deductible in the host country, while dividends are not. Moreover, principal payments, unlike dividend payments, do not generally constitute taxable income. Thus, it is possible that both a parent and its subsidiaries will save taxes by using loans instead of equity contributions.

MNCs can also provide credit to their subsidiaries not only by making loans but also by delaying the collection of accounts receivable. The amount of credit available through these intracompany accounts is limited to the amount of goods exchanged. Moreover, governments frequently limit the length of the credit term. However, because intracompany accounts involve no formal documents, they are easier to use. In addition, most governments interfere less with payments on intracompany accounts than on loans.

Parent Guarantees

When foreign subsidiaries have difficulty in borrowing money, a parent may affix its own guarantees. While MNCs have traditionally been reluctant to guarantee.

Intra-company Loans

There are many different types of intra-company loans, but direct loans, credit swaps, and parallel loans are the most important. Direct loans involve straight dealings between the lending unit and the borrowing unit, but — credit swaps and parallel loans — normally involve an intermediary.

- **A Credit Swap:** Is a simultaneous spot-and-forward loan transaction between a private company and a bank of a foreign country. For example, a US company deposits a given amount of dollars in the Chicago office of a Mexican bank. In return for this deposit, the bank lends a given amount of pesos to the company's subsidiary in Mexico. The same contract provides that the bank returns the initial amount of dollars to the company at a specified date and that the subsidiary returns the original amount of pesos to the bank at a specified date. Credit swaps are, in fact, intracompany loans hedged and channeled through banks. These loans are also risk free from a bank's point of view, because the parent's deposit fully collateralises them. Credit swaps have several advantages over direct intra-company loans. First, credit swaps are free of foreign-exchange exposures because the parent recovers the amount of its deposit in the original parent currency from the bank. Second, cost savings may be available with credit swaps, because certain countries apply different tax rates to interest paid to the foreign parent and to interest paid to the local bank.
- **Parallel Loans:** Consist of two related but separate borrowings and typically involve four parties in two different countries. For example, a US parent lends an agreed amount in dollars to the American subsidiary of a Mexican parent. In return for this loan, the Mexican parent lends the same amount of money in pesos to the Mexican subsidiary of the US parent. These loan arrangements involve the same amount for both loans and the same loan maturity. Certainly, each loan is paid in

the subsidiary's currency. Parallel loans are frequently used to effectively repatriate blocked funds by circumventing exchange control restrictions. To see how the back-to-back loan can be used to repatriate blocked funds, suppose that the Mexican subsidiary of IBM is unable to repatriate its peso profits. It may lend the money to the Mexican subsidiary of AT&T; AT&T would, in turn, lend dollars to IBM in the USA. As a result, IBM would have the use of dollars in the USA while AT&T would obtain pesos in Mexico.

BACK-TO-BACK LOANS

A loan that involves an exchange of currencies between two parties, with a promise to re-exchange the currencies at a specified exchange rate on a specified future date, is referred to as a back-to-back loan and it involves two companies domiciled in two different countries. For example, AT&T agrees to borrow funds in the USA and then to lend those borrowed funds to Toyota in Japan, which, in return, borrows funds in Japan and then lends those funds to AT&T in the USA. By this simple arrangement, each firm has access to the capital markets in the foreign country without any actual cross-border flows of capital. Consequently, both companies avoid exchange rate risk in a back-to-back loan.

Drawbacks of Parallel and Back-to-Back Loans

While parallel and back-to-back loans offer definite benefits to participating companies, three problems limit their usefulness as financing tools. First, it is difficult to find counterparties with matching needs. Second, one party is still obligated to comply with such an agreement even if another party fails to do so. Third, such loans customarily show up on the books of the participating parties. Currency swaps can overcome these problems fully or partly, and this explains their rapid growth. First, a company in one country with a use for this type of financing must find another company in another country with matching needs; that is, mirror-image financing requirements.

These requirements include currencies, principals, types of interest payments, the frequency of interest payments, and the length of the loan period. Search costs for finding such a company may be considerable, if it is possible. Currency swaps largely resolve the problem of matching needs because they are arranged by specialised swap dealers and brokers who recruit prospective counterparties. Second, parallel and back-to-back loans are actually two loans with two separate agreements, which exist independently of each other. If the first company defaults on its obligations to the second company, the second company is not legally relieved of its obligations to the first company. To avoid this problem, a separate agreement, defining the right of offset, must be drafted. If this agreement is not registered, the situation and outcome described above may still arise. On the other hand, registration itself may cause problems. With currency swaps, however, the right of offset, is usually embodied in the agreement.

Third, parallel and back-to-back loans are carried on the books of the participating parties. In other words, the exchange of principals under these two instruments involves net increases in both assets and liabilities; these amounts are customarily recorded in full on the counterparties' books. With currency swaps, however, the principal amounts usually do not show up on the participants' books. Many commercial banks prefer currency swaps to parallel and back-to-back loans to keep the transactions off their books. These off-book transactions of currency swaps and other derivatives may enable banks to avoid increases in their capital requirements under applicable regulations. However, such off-book transactions may be disallowed in the near future, as accounting-standard setters in the USA and other countries require MNCs to include derivatives transactions in their financial statements.

Payment Adjustments

There are many different forms of payments by foreign subsidiaries to the parent company. These payments can be adjusted to remove blocked funds. Dividend payments are by far the most important form of fund flows from foreign subsidiaries to the parent company, accounting for approximately 50 per cent of all remittances to US companies. Money market countries recognise dividend payments as a method by which the earnings of a business firm can be distributed to the stockholders of the firm. Not all nations, however, allow dividends of local companies to be paid in hard currencies to the foreign parent companies. Countries characterised by balance of payments problems and foreign exchange shortages frequently place restrictions on the payment of dividends to foreign companies.

Two methods to adjust dividend payments in the case of these restrictions have become increasingly popular. These two methods artificially inflate the value of the local investment base, because the level of dividend payments depends on the company's capital. First, the parent company can magnify its subsidiary's registered capital by investing in used equipment, whose value has been artificially inflated. Second, the parent company may acquire a bankrupt local firm at a large discount from bookvalue and then merge it with its subsidiary on the basis of the failed firm's book value. Of course, this action would raise the subsidiary's equity base.

American Depository Receipts/Global Depository Receipts

The Indian companies were allowed to raise funds from abroad, through American/ Global Depository Receipts and External Commercial Borrowings (ECBs). The RBI allowed two way fungibility of ADRs/GDRs in 2002. The companies with the largest fraction of foreign ownership would obtain the highest P/Es and the lowest cost of capital. GDR/ ADRs are extremely illiquid (even after two-way fungibility) and there is no real argument in favour of their issuance for an Indian firm which can get capital in domestic market by FIIs or domestic investors. The only case for such a route would be justified in case of long-term bond financing as those are not very easily placed in India.

— **Ownership Restrictions:** Only FIIs can buy shares in India, while anyone can buy GDRs or ADRs. FIIs face restrictions on the fraction of a firm that can be purchased. This imposes ceilings on foreign ownership. In contrast, participation in the GDR or ADR market is unencumbered, and hence they enjoy a premium.

— **Transaction Costs:** Indian equity market imposed extremely large transactions costs (highly illiquid market). Indian firms used (ADR/GDR) as a way to bypass Indian markets. These instruments commanded a higher price owing to liquidity premium.

CLOSING CASELET

Suppose Sweden has a choice of two possible US $ 200 million, five year Eurodollar loans. The first loan is offered at LIBOR (London Inter-bank Operating Rate) + 1.5 per cent with a 1.5 per cent syndication fee, where as the second loan and is priced at LIBOR + 2.5 per cent and a 0.95 per cent syndication fee. Assuming that Sweden has 12 per cent of cost of capital, which loan is preferable?

Solution:

This problem can be solved as a capital budgeting problem. The dollar cash flows associated with these two spread-syndicate fee combinations are as follows:

3. Loan 1: 1.5 per cent fee, 1.5 per cent spread
4. Loan 2: 0.95 per cent fee, 2.5 per cent spread

Hence, total present value of the loan can be calculated using the following formulae:

TOTAL PRESENT VALUE = Syndication fee + present value of spread on loan

STEP 1: Calculation of syndication fee: 1.5 per cent of 200 million = 3,000,000

STEP 2: Calculation of spread amount: 1.5 per cent on 200 million = 3,000,000

STEP 3: Find table value of spread amount: @12 per cent for 5 years = 3.605

STEP 4: Calculate spread amount: 3000000 × 3.605 = 10815000

STEP 5: Total present value = 3,000,000 + 10815000 = 13815000.

SUMMARY

This chapter deals with international financing strategies, which is classified into international bonds, international equity and international bank loans. Loans are classified into two categories: foreign loans and Euro loans. Foreign loans are raised by borrowers who are foreign to the country where the loans are raised. International loans, however, mostly take the form of Euro loans or Euro credits, which are denominated in a currency other than the currency of the country where the loans are raised. Euro loans and foreign loans are also distinguished as follows. While Euro loans are financed wholly out of Euro currency funds, irrespective of whether the borrower is a resident or a nonresident of the country in question, foreign loans are domestic currency credits extended to non-resident borrowers.

PROBLEMS AND SOLUTIONS

1. Suppose that the current 180 day interbank Eurodollar rate is 9 per cent (all rates are stated on an annualised basis). If next period's rate is 9.5 per cent, what will a Eurocurrency loan priced at LIBOR plus 1% cost?

Answer

(a) Eurodollar loans are made on a floating rate basis, with the rate set at a fixed margin over LIBOR.

(b) Thus, if next period's annualised LIBOR is 13 per cent, then the Euro currency loan will be at 14 per cent (13% + 1%) on an annualised basis.

2. Citibank offers to syndicate a Euro dollar credit for the government of Poland with the following terms:

Principal	US$ 1,000,000,000
Maturity	7 years
Interest rate	LIBOR + 1.5 per cent, reset every six months
Syndication fee	1.75 per cent

[a] What are the net proceeds to Poland from this syndicated loan?

Answer

Poland will receive $982,500,000, which equals the $1 billion less the 1.75 per cent syndication fee.

[b] Assuming that six-month LIBOR is currently at 6.35 per cent, what is the effective annual interest cost to Poland for the first six months of this loan?

Answer

At 6-month LIBOR + 1.5 per cent, Poland will pay interest at an annual rate of 7.85 per cent (6.35% + 1.5%).

3. Suppose that Zimbabwe has a choice of two possible $100 million, five-year Eurodollar loans. The first loan is offered at LIBOR + 1 per cent with a 2.5 per cent syndication fee, whereas the second loan is priced at LIBOR + 1.5 per cent and a 0.75 per cent syndication fee. Assuming that Zimbabwe has a 9 per cent cost of capital, which loan is preferable? *Hint*: View this as a capital budgeting problem.

Answer

The dollar cash flows associated with these two spread-syndicate fee combinations are as follows:

Loan 1 (2.5% fee, 1% spread)
Loan 2 (.75% fee, 1.5% spread)

Using a 9 per cent discount rate, we can compare the present values of these two combinations:

$$\$2,500,000 + \sum^{5} \frac{\$1,000,000}{(1.09)^t} = \$6,389,651$$

Based on these comparisons, we can see that at a 9 per cent discount rate, the first loan fee-spread combination is the least expensive one.

$$\$750,000 + \sum_{t=1}^{5} \frac{\$1,500,000}{(1,09)^t} = \$6,584,477$$

4. ABC Ltd., needs to raise $1 billion and is trying to decide between a domestic dollar bond issue and a Eurobond issue. The U.S. bond can be issued at a coupon of 6.75 per cent, paid semiannually, with underwriting and other expenses totalling 0.95 per cent of the issue size. The Eurobond would cost only 0.55 per cent to issue but would bear an annual coupon of 6.88 per cent. Both issues would mature in 10 years.

   [a] Assuming all else is equal, which is the least expensive issue for ABC Ltd.,

Answer

The least expensive issue can be found by comparing the yield to maturity (YTM) for each bond, computed as the internal rate of return or IRR. For the domestic bond issue,

$$\$990,500,000 = \sum^{20} \frac{\$33,750,000}{(1+r)^t} + \frac{\$1,000,000,000}{(1+r)^{20}}$$

the YTM is the solution *r* to the following equation:

Where the $990,500,000 in bond proceeds equals the billion dollar issue less 0.95 per cent in issuance costs. The solution turns out to be $r = 3.44$ per cent. Since this is a semiannual yield, we must convert it to annualized basis. The annualised YTM is found as $(1.0344)^2 - 1$, or 7.00 per cent.

For the Eurobond issue, the YTM is the solution *k* to the following equation:

$$\$994,500,000 = \sum^{10} \frac{\$68,800,000}{(1+r)^t} + \frac{\$1,000,000,000}{(1+r)^{10}}$$

The solution to this equation turns out to be $k = 6.96$ per cent. Since this YTM is less than the annualised YTM for the U.S. bond, the Eurobond is the less expensive bond to issue.

Bond Valuation Problems

5. What is the price of the following bond?

Face value	$1,000
Maturity	10 years

Coupon rate	8%
Discount rate	9%

Solution:

$$\frac{\$80}{.09}\left[1-\frac{1}{(1.09)^{10}}\right]+\frac{\$1000}{(1.09)^{10}}=\$935.824$$

6. What is the price of the following bond?

Face value	\$1,000
Maturity	50 years
Coupon rate	10%
Discount rate	12%

Solution:

$$\frac{\$100}{12}\left[1-\frac{1}{(1.12)^{50}}\right]+\frac{\$1000}{(1.12)^{50}}=\$833.91$$

7. What is the value of the following semi-annual bond?

Face value	\$1,000
Maturity	10 years
Coupon rate	10%
Discount rate	9%

Solution:

$$\frac{\$}{\frac{.09}{2}}\left[1-\frac{1}{\left(1+\frac{.09}{2}\right)^{10(2)}}\right]+\frac{\$1000}{\left(1+\frac{.09}{2}\right)^{10(2)}}=\$1,065.04$$

8. What is the value of the following semi-annual bond?

Face value	\$1,000
Maturity	9.5 years
Coupon rate	7%
Discount rate	7%

Solution:

Since coupon rate = discount rate, this must be a par value bond, and the price is \$1,000, or

$$\frac{\$35}{\frac{.07}{2}}\left[1-\frac{1}{\left(1+\frac{.07}{2}\right)^{95(2)}}\right]+\frac{\$1,000}{\left(1+\frac{.07}{2}\right)^{95(2)}}=\$1,000$$

9. What is the value of the following semi-annual bond?

Face value	$1,000
Maturity	20 years
Coupon rate	9%
Discount rate	10%

Solution:

$$\frac{\$45}{\frac{.1}{2}}\left[1-\frac{1}{\left(1+\frac{.1}{2}\right)^{2(20)}}\right]+\frac{\$1,000}{\left(1+\frac{.1}{2}\right)^{2(20)}}=\$914.20$$

10. What is the price of the following quarterly bond?

Face value	1,000
Maturity	10 years
Coupon rate	10%
Discount rate	8%

Solution:

$$\frac{\$25}{\frac{.08}{4}}\left[1-\frac{1}{\left(1+\frac{.08}{4}\right)^{4(10)}}\right]+\frac{\$1,000}{\left(1+\frac{.08}{4}\right)^{4(10)}}=\$1136.78$$

11. What is the price of the following semi-annual bond?

Face value	$1,000
Maturity	10 years
Coupon rate	8%
Discount rate	9

Solution:

$$\frac{\$40}{\frac{.09}{2}}\left[1-\frac{1}{\left(1+\frac{.09}{2}\right)^{10(2)}}\right]+\frac{\$1000}{\left(1+\frac{.09}{2}\right)^{10(2)}}=\$934.96$$

Foreign Exchange Risk Management

(1) On 1st Jan 2010 when a forward contract matured for execution you are asked by an imposter customer to extend the validity of the forward contract for US $ 10,000 to a further period of three months.

Contracted Rate US $ 1 = —— 42.71 (1st Jan 2010)

Spot	₹ 41.69/– 41.95
Premium Feb	0.1100/0.1300
Premium Mar	0.2300/0.2500
Premium April	0.3500/0.3750

Calculate the cost for your customer in respect of the extension of the forward contract, selling rate ₹ 0.25%.

Solution:

Step 1: Can sell the contract at buying rate on (1st Jan 2010)

	₹
Spot	41.6900
Less: Margin 0.080%	0.0033
	41.6867
Hence buying rate is	₹ 41.69

Buying rate 10000 US$ @ ₹ 41.69 = 4169,00

Contract a rate 10000 US$ @ ₹ 42.71 = 4,27100

Difference in favour of bank 427100 – 416900 = 10200

Step 2: New contract to be booked at appropriate forward rate

Three moths forward rate is as under:

US $ 1 Spot selling	41.9500
Add April premium	0.3750
	42.3250
Add margin (0. 25%)	0.1058
	42.4308

Forward rate to be Quoted to the customer is us $ = ₹ 42.43.

Spot Rate with Expected Probability

(2) In Dec, 2010 The MNC ansersed the 2011 Spot rate for pound sterling at the following rates:

$ 2.30/--- with probability 0.20

$ 2.35/ --- with probability 0.15

$ 2.40 /---- with probability 0.10

$ 2.45 /---- with probablity 0.50

what is expected spot rate on 2011?

Solution:

$ [2.30 × 0.20] + [2.35 × 0.15] + [2.40 × 0.10] + [2.45 × 0.50]

$ [0.46 + 0.3525 + 0.24 + 1.225]

Spot Rate = 2.2775

Practice Problems

1. Calculate cross currency exchange values

   (a) 1$ = ₹ 42

   (b) 1£ = ₹ 66

   (c) 1$ = 100¥

   Find the value of 1£/1$

   Find the value of 1¥/1£

2. Calculate cross currency exchange values

   (a) 1¥ = 1.01£

   (b) 1€ = ₹ 77

   (c) 1 ₹ = 25 ¥

   Find the value of 1€/1¥

   Find the value of 1¥/1£

3. Use the exchange rate data in the table to answer the following questions. The first two exchange rates are the spot rates on those dates. The third exchange rate is the one year forward exchange rate as of February 2009.

	Feb 4, 2008	Feb 4 2009	Forward Feb 4 2010
US-Europe	1.08 $/Euro	1.25 $/Euro	1.24 $/Euro
US-S. Africa	8.55 Rand/$	6.95 Rand/$	7.42 Rand/$

(a) Calculate the rate of change of the euro value relative to the dollar between 2008 and 2009.

(b) Calculate the rate of change in the dollar value relative to the euro between 2008 and 2009.

(c) Calculate the rate of change in the dollar value relative to the South African rand between 2008 and 2009.

(d) Calculate the expected change in the dollar value relative to the Euro between 2009 and 2010.

(e) Calculate the expected change in the dollar value relative to the rand between 2009 and 2010.

4. In February 2010 the US dollar – Mexican peso exchange rate was 11p/$. The price of a hotel room in Mexico City was 1000 pesos. The price of a hotel room in New York City was $200.

   (a) Calculate the price of the Mexican hotel room in US dollars.

   (b) Calculate the price of the US hotel room in Mexican pesos. Suppose the exchange rate rises to 12 pesos per $.

   (c) What does the exchange rate change indicate has happened to the value of the US dollar? ... to the value of the Mexican peso?

5. The covered interest parity condition substitutes the forward exchange rate for the expected exchange rate. The condition is label covered because the forward contract assures a certain rate of return (i.e., without risk) on foreign deposits. In the table below is listed a spot exchange rate, a 90-day forward rate, and a 90-day money market interest rate in Germany and Canada. Use this info to answer the following questions.

	Germany	**Canada**
Spot ER	.5841 $/DM	.7451 $/C$
90-day For-ER	.5807 $/DM	.7446 $/C$
90-day Interest Rate	1.442%	.875%

   [a] What would the US 90-day interest rate have to be for the US to have the highest rate of return for a US investor? (Use the exact formulae to calculate the rates of return)

   [b] If spot exchange rates move until covered-interest parity holds exactly, then would you expect the Canadian dollar to appreciate or depreciate with respect to the DM on the next day of trading? Explain.

KEYWORDS

1. **Crosslisting:** A decision to crosslist in the USA means that any company, domestic or foreign, must meet the accounting and disclosure requirements of the US Securities and Exchange Commission.
2. **Privatisation** is a situation in which government-owned assets are sold to private individuals or groups.
3. **International Bonds** are those bonds that are initially sold outside the country of the borrower. International bonds consist of foreign bonds, Euro bonds, and global bonds.
4. **Foreign Bonds:** Bonds sold in a particular national market by a foreign borrower, underwritten by a syndicate of brokers from that country, and denominated in the currency of that country are called foreign bonds.
5. **Euro bonds:** Bonds underwritten by an international syndicate of brokers and sold simultaneously in many countries other than the country of the issuing entity are called Euro bonds.
6. **Global Bonds:** These are bonds sold inside as well as outside the country in whose currency they are denominated. For example, dollar-denominated bonds sold in New York (domestic bond market) and Tokyo (Euro bond market) are called dollar global bonds.
7. **Currency Option Bonds:** The holders of currency option bonds are allowed to receive their interest income in the currency of their option from among two or three predetermined currencies at a pre-determined exchange rate.

REVIEW QUESTIONS

1. Explain interbank clearing house system.
2. What do you understand by Euro bonds?
3. Classify different sources of international financing by banks.
4. Write a note on global bonds.
5. Define 'Bond' and categorise various types of bonds.
6. Explain drawbacks of parallel and back-to-back loans.

REFERENCES

1. http://pbfg.de/eng/financial2-3.htm
2. www.ozforex.com.au
3. www.indiainfoline.com
4. www.rbi.org.in

CHAPTER

11

Transfer Pricing Strategies

CHAPTER OUTLINE

- Opening Caselet
- Introduction
- Review of Literature
- Transfer Pricing Mechanism in Corporate Entities
- Purpose of Transfer Pricing
- India's Policy on Transfer Pricing
- Suggestions
- Case Study
- Appendix
- Closing Caselet
- Summary
- Keywords
- Review Questions
- References

OPENING CASELET

Satya Ltd., produces plastic chairs, which requires to be processed in two divisions *viz.*, A&B. Each chair is first produced at division 'A' will be transferred to division 'B' further processing and to get finished product. The finished product will be sold in the market at ₹ 1,200/- per chair. However, the semi-finished chairs can be purchased from the market at ₹ 450/- The division 'A' is transferred the semi-finished chairs to 'Division B' at 110 per cent of the manufactured cost. The following are the cost of material and labour for each division:

Particulars	Division A	Division B
Raw material cost per unit	₹ 250/-	NA
Direct Labour per unit	₹ 60/-	₹ 75/-
Direct overheads per unit	₹ 90/-	₹ 45/-

— If the number of units produced and sold are 1500 chairs. What is the profitability of each division?

Solution:

Calculation of divisional profitability:

Particulars	If it is transferred at 110% of manufacturing cost from division A	If it is purchased from the market at ₹ 450/-
DIVISION A:		
Raw material cost per unit	₹ 250/-	NA
No. of Units	1500	
Material cost	3,75,000	
Direct Labour per unit @ 60/- for 1500 units	90,000	₹ 75/-
Direct overheads per unit @ ₹ 90/- for 1500 units	1,35,000	₹ 45/-
Total cost of goods manufactured at division A	**6,00,000**	**NA**
Per unit cost	6,00,000/1500 = 400	NA
Profit at division A		

Goods transferred at 110% cost	440 x 1500 = 6,60,000	NA
Less: cost of goods manufactured	6,00,000	NA
Profit	60,000	NA
DIVISION B:		
Semi-finished product	6,60,000	450 x 1500 = 6,75,000
Direct Labour per unit @75/- for 1,500 units	1,12,500	1,12,500
Direct overheads per unit @ ₹ 45/- for 1,500 units	67,500	67,500
Total cost of goods manufactured at division B	8,40,000	8,55,000
Profit at division B		
Goods sold at ₹ 1,200/-	18,00,000	18,00,000
Less: cost of goods manufactured	8,40,000	8,55,000
Profit	9,60,000	9,75,000
Overall profit:		
	DIVISION A	**DIVISION B**
OPTION 1	**60,000**	**9,60,000**
OPTION 2	-	**9,75,000**

INTRODUCTION

Transfer Pricing generally, being the first tax consideration of any cross border transaction between related parties, developed countries such as USA and UK have had transfer pricing law for decades.[1] Transfer Pricing in common parlance, is manipulation of data. Hence, it is called TPM (Transfer Pricing Manipulation), which is fixing transfer price on non-market basis which generally results in saving total quantum of organisation's tax by shifting accounting profits from high tax to low tax jurisdiction.[2]

Transfer-pricing is a way of exploiting transnational and/or transcorporate accounting loop holes to minimise tax liabilities. The increasing concern of international taxation, especially in terms of a transfer-pricing mechanism, is certain to become a part of the economic life of all developing countries as major international transactions are tossed into the world of global taxation. Since the achievement and maintenance of equitable economic growth is an integral part of the development strategies of these countries, the impact of transfer pricing, both positive and negative, is a key policy issue. Developing countries need to understand, assess, assimilate and analyse critically this issue, while protecting their basic interests.

The prices of transactions between associated enterprises, which is referred to as transfer pricing, for tax purposes are in conformity with those which would be charged among independent enterprises. Ernst and Young (2003) found that 43 per cent of parent transnational companies believed their transfer pricing policies for administrative/ managerial services were vulnerable to Government audit, 30 per cent believed their pricing of technical services were also vulnerable. Ernst and Young argued that audits of services were increasing as a share of all transfer pricing audits, partly because few transnational corporate entities documented transfer pricing policies for administrative or managerial services. With no or minimal documentation, these transactions appears to be the 'weakest link' in transfer pricing armor. The rapid growth in offshoring business services should therefore exacerbate, already high tensions in this area of transfer pricing regulation.

In terms of tax planning, Tang[3] finds that all five MNEs he has selected use a variety of methods to reduce their overall tax rates, including setting up of holding companies in tax havens, taking full advantage of tax incentives such as the (soon-to-be-defunt) US Foreign Sales Corporation export incentive programme, and shifting income to low-tax and expenses to high-tax locations. In the light of recent corporate tax scandals, these practices would be a useful spring board for a class discussion of the ethical aspects of tax planning.

---

1. Waman Y. Kale, Transfer Pricing — Practical Issues and Controversies, *The Chartered Accountant,* October, 2005, pp. 570-579.
2. Mayank K. Agarwal, Transfer Pricing – A Beginner's Perspective, www.indiainfoline.com.
3. Roger Y.W. Tang, Current Trends and Corporate Cases in Transfer Pricing, Reviewed by Prof. Lorraine Eden, *Journal of International Business Studies,* March, 2003.

Transfer pricing is the pricing of products traded among affiliated units of a TNC. Because the prices are set in-house, there are opportunities for corporate entities to manipulate them and avoid or evade Government regulations such as customs duties and corporate income taxes. In order to curtail these opportunities, most Governments have adopted transfer-pricing regulations based on the Organisation for Economic Co-operation and Development (OECD) guidelines. These guidelines require corporate entities to follow the arm's length principle, i.e., firms must price each intra-company transaction as if it had occurred between two unrelated parties negotiating for the same product under the same circumstances as the related party firms. Transfer pricing is, and has been for many years, the most contentious issue in international taxation due to the difficulties involved in setting arm's length prices acceptable to both tax authorities and transnational companies (Ernst & Young, 2003; UNCTAD, 1999). Comparable transactions between unrelated parties are often not available for intra-firm transactions in goods, much less for intangibles and services. Thus, transfer pricing is an area fraught with difficulties and pitfalls for the unwary.

REVIEW OF LITERATURE

Transfer Prices have been described as: 'the net value per unit that records the transaction for the purposes of operating statements'. While many studies have addressed transfer pricing in transnational corporations, none to date have addressed transfer pricing specifically in the context of Transnational Financial Institutions (TFI). The lack of studies is not an indicator of the issue's importance, but rather a function of the difficulty of getting sensitive and confidential information from TFI executives. Yoon K. Choi (1998)[4] examines the relation between transfer pricing and production incentives using a model of a vertically integrated firm with divisions located in different tax jurisdictions. His study shows that if divisional profits are taxed at the same marginal rate, the transfer price should be set to minimise the compensation risk faced by the manager of the buying division.

Nicole Bastian Johnson (2006)[5] explains the divisional performance measurement and transfer pricing. He describes three methods of transfer pricing: (i) Royalty-based System (ii) Negotiated Transfer Pricing and (iii) Renegotiated Royalty-based Pricing. When multinational firms transfer intangible assets between decentralised divisions in different countries, transfer prices must play a vital role in both the determination of taxable income and in providing economic incentives for divisional managers. It was mentioned that, a royalty-based transfer price that can be renegotiated provides better investment incentives than either a non-negotiable royalty based transfer price or a purely negotiated transfer price. A royalty-based system provides the developer of the

4. Yoon K. Choi and Theodore R. Day (1998), 'Transfer Pricing, Incentive Compensation and Tax Avoidance in a Multi-division Firm', *Review of Quantitative Finance and Accounting,* 1998, pp. 139-164.
5. Nicole Bastian Johnson (2006), 'Divisional Performance Measurement and Transfer Pricing for Intangible Assets', Published Online, *Springer Science,* New York, 17 May, 2006.

intangible with some protection from a hold-up problem, but induces inefficiently low investment by the buyer. Negotiated transfer pricing provides efficient investment incentives for the buyer, but creates a hold-up problem.

For the seller, leading to underinvestment the third method, royalty-based transfer pricing with renegotiation, combines features of both royalty-based and negotiated transfer pricing, protecting the developer of the intangible from a hold-up problem and providing efficient investment incentives for the buyer. This method improves efficiency relative to pure royalty or negotiation-based transfer pricing and provides first best investment incentives for some types of investments.

Tim Baldenius, Stefan Reichestein and Savita A. Sahay (1999)[6] studied an incomplete contracting model to compare the effectiveness of alternative transfer pricing mechanisms. Transfer pricing serves the dual purpose of guiding intra-company transfers and providing incentives for upfront investments at the divisional level. When transfer prices are determined through negotiation, divisional managers will have insufficient investment incentives due to hold-up problems. While cost-based transfer pricing can avoid such hold-ups, it does suffer from distortions in intra-company transfers. Their analysis shows that negotiation frequently performs better than a cost-based pricing system, though we identify circumstances under which cost-based transfer pricing emerges as the superior alternative. In their study, a performance comparison of two commonly used schemes: negotiated and cost-based transfer pricing, is analysed. These two alternatives seems particularly prevalent in practice when there is no established external market for the intermediate goods in question. Transfer pricing serves two major purposes in their model: to guide intra-firm transfers of an intermediate product and to create incentives for divisional managers to make relationship specific investments. Such investments can take different forms, e.g., research and development (R&D), machinery and equipment, or personnel training. In one-period model, investments entail an upfront fixed cost and a subsequent reduction in the unit variable cost incurred by the supplying division. Alternatively, investments by the buying division may enhance net revenues obtained from internal transactions. The divisional incentive to invest will depend both on the transfer payments and the quantities that the divisions expect to trade.

Richard Sansing (1999)[7] used a model in which differences in organisation structure induce different investment choices, shows that transfer pricing methods based on the price charged by independent firms results in controlled foreign subsidiaries being allocated a greater amount of income (relative to its assets) than its domestic parent. The model implies that the current dispute between the Internal Revenue Service (IRS) and its foreign counterparts regarding the acceptability of the comparable profit method of determining transfer prices is consistent with the desire of each tax authority to maximise

6. Tim Baldenius, Stefan Reichestein and Savita A. Sahay (1999), Negotiated Versus Cost-Based Transfer Pricing, *Review Accounting Studies* 4, pp. 67-91, 1999, Kluwer Academic Publishers, Boston. (Manufactured in The Netherlands).

7. Richard Sansing (1999), Relationship-Specific Investments and the Transfer Pricing Paradox, *Review Accounting Studies* 4, pp. 119-134, 1999. Kluwer Academic Publishers, Boston. Manufactured in The Netherlands.

its own tax revenues in transfer pricing disputes involving US parent firms and foreign subsidiaries. Much international trade occurs between related parties. US parent firms exported $86 billion of merchandise to foreign affiliates in 1989, which accounted for 24 per cent of total US exports for that year. These US parent firms imported $72 billion from foreign affiliates in 1989, accounting for 15 per cent of all US imports. Trade between US affiliates of foreign parents is also large, accounting for $40 billion of US exports and $133 billion of US imports for 1989. The allocation of income between a parent corporation and its subsidiary depends on the prices at which intermediate goods are transferred between the producer (the upstream firm) and the user (downstream firm) of the intermediate goods. When the entities operate in different countries, the transfer price determines how much of the income earned by the joint efforts of the two entities is taxed in each country.

Transfer Pricing and Multinational Income Taxes

When divisions transfer product across tax jurisdictions, transfer prices play a role in the calculation of the company's income tax liability. In this situation, the company's transfer pricing policy can become a tax planning tool. The United States has agreements with most other nations that determine how multinational companies are taxed. These agreements, called **bilateral tax treaties**, establish rules for apportioning multinational corporate income among the nations in which the companies conduct business. These rules attempt to tax all multinational corporate income once and only once (excluding the double-taxation that occurs at the Federal and state levels). In other words, the tax treaties attempt to avoid the double-taxation that would occur if two nations taxed the same income. Since transfer prices represent revenue to the upstream division and an expense to the downstream division, the transfer price affects the calculation of divisional profits that represent taxable income in the nations where the divisions are based.

For example, if a US-based pharmaceutical company manufactures a drug in a factory that it operates in Ireland and transfers the drug to the US for sale, a high transfer price increases divisional income to the Irish division of the company, and hence, increases the company's tax liability in Ireland. At the same time, the high transfer price increases the cost of product to the US marketing division, lowers US income, and lowers US taxes. The company's incentives with regard to the transfer price depends on whether the marginal tax rate is higher in the US, or in Ireland. If the marginal tax rate is higher in the US, the company prefers a high transfer price, whereas if the marginal tax rate is higher in Ireland, the company prefers a low transfer price. The situation reverses if the drug is manufactured in the US and sold in Ireland. The general rule is that the company wants to shift income from the high tax jurisdiction to the low tax jurisdiction. There are limits to the extent to which companies can shift income in this manner. When a market price is available for the goods transferred, the taxing authorities will usually impose the market-based transfer price. When a market-based transfer price is not feasible, US, tax law specifies detailed and complicated rules that limit the extent to which companies can shift income out of the United States.

TRANSFER PRICING MECHANISM IN CORPORATE ENTITIES

Many multinational corporations essentially have two sets of book-keeping. One set, with artificially inflated transfer prices is what they use to prepare local tax returns, and show auditors in high-tax jurisdictions, and another set of books, in which management can see the true profit and lost statement, based on real cost of goods, are used for the executives to determine the actual performance of their various operations. Of course, no company should have to pay more tax than they are legally obligated to, and they are entitled to locate to any low-tax jurisdiction. The problem starts when they use fraudulent transfer pricing and other tricks to artificially shift their income from other countries to a tax-haven. According to OECD Guidelines, transfer prices should be the same as if the two companies involved were indeed two independents, not part of the same corporate structure.

As transnational companies move business services offshore, they must develop transfer pricing policies for pricing these intracompany transactions. Transfer-pricing regulations for services are much less developed than for goods and raw materials (Feinschreiber, 2004). Transnational companies are expected to follow the benefit-cost principle, with little explicit guidance as to acceptable methodologies compared to the detailed guidelines available for goods transactions.

Over the last decade, major barriers to trade among countries have decreased due to the galloping growth in information technology. This increase of information has seen many companies significantly expanding their cross-border trade. A result of this globalisation of world trade is that transactions can be executed effortlessly and at lowering marginal costs. Increasing technology and decreasing transaction costs have meant quicker clearing markets and hence, profit opportunities in products, services and geographic areas that may have been unattainable earlier. With such comprehensive and timely data, international businesses are now able to take decisions more effectively and quicker than ever before. From the perspective of tax authorities around the world, transfer pricing is fast gaining importance, necessitating change in legislation to protect tax revenue bases. In major industrial countries, such legislation has primarily been driven by developments in the US and other OECD member-states.

Microsoft Corporation recently shaved at least $500 million from its annual tax bill using a similar strategy to the one the drug industry has used for so many years. Microsoft has set up a subsidiary in Ireland, called Round Island One Ltd. This company pays more than $300 million in taxes to this small island country with only 4 million inhabitants, and most of this comes from licensing fees for copyrighted software, originally developed in the US. Interesting thing is, at the same time, Round Island paid a total of just under $17 million in taxes to about 20 other countries, with more than 300 million people. The result of this was that Microsoft's worldwide tax rate plunged to 26 per cent in 2004, from 33 per cent the year before. Almost half of the drop was due to foreign earnings taxed at lower rates, according to a Microsoft financial filing. And this is how Microsoft has radically reduced its corporate taxes in much of Europe and been able to shield billions of dollars from US taxation.

PURPOSE OF TRANSFER PRICING

Transfer pricing serves the following purposes:

1. When product is transferred between profit centers or investment centers within a decentralised firm, transfer prices are necessary to calculate divisional profits, which then affect divisional performance evaluation.
2. When divisional managers have the authority to decide whether to buy or sell internally or on the external market, the transfer price can determine whether managers' incentives align with the incentives of the overall company and its owners. The objective is to achieve **goal congruence**, in which divisional managers will want to transfer product when doing so maximises consolidated corporate profits, and at least one manager will refuse the transfer when transferring product is not the profit-maximising strategy for the company.
3. When multinational firms transfer product across international borders, transfer prices are relevant in the calculation of income taxes, and are sometimes relevant in connection with other international trade and regulatory issues.

The following table provides examples:

The transfer generates journal entries on the books of both divisions, but usually no money changes hands. The transfer price becomes an expense for the down-stream division and revenue for the up-stream division. Following is a representative example of journal entries to record the transfer of product:

Up-stream Division:

(1) Inter-company Accounts Receivable $9,000

Revenue from Inter-company Sale $9,000

	An external market price is available	**No external market price is available**
The downstream division will sell as is:	The West Coast Division of a super-market chain transfers oranges to the North-west Division, for retail sale.	A pharmaceutical company transfers a drug that is under patent protection, from its manufacturing division to its marketing division.
The downstream division will use the transferred product in its own production process.	An oil company transfers crude oil from the drilling division to the refinery, to be used in the production of gasoline.	The Parts Division of an appliance manufacturer transfers mechanical components to one of its assembly divisions.

(2) Cost of Goods Sold – Inter-company Sales	$8,000	
Finished Goods Inventory		$8,000

(To record the transfer of 500 cases of *Clear Mountain Spring Water*, at $18 per case, to the Florida marketing division, and to remove the 500 cases from finished goods inventory at the production cost of $16 per case.)

Downstream Division

(1) Finished Goods Inventory	$9,000	
Intercompany Accounts Payable		$9,000

(To record the receipt of 500 cases of *Clear Mountain Spring Water*, at $18 per case, from the bottling division in Nebraska)

Traditional Transaction Methods

The OECD Guidelines refer to the following methods as 'traditional transaction method':

— Comparable Uncontrolled Price method (CUP);

— Resale Price Method (RPM); and

— Cost Plus Method (CP method or C+);

These are described below and are different from the transactional profit methods:

— Profit Split Method (PSM); and

— Transactional Net Margin Method (TNMM).

The OECD Guidelines prefer the use of the traditional transaction methods, whereby the other methods should be used as methods of last resort (for example when there is no data available or available data cannot be used reliably). However, the Guidelines stress there is no *best-method rule*: a tax-payer is only required to show that the method used delivers a reasonable (at arm's length) result and is not required to disprove the use of each other method than the method used.

Transfer Pricing Options: There are three general methods for establishing transfer prices.

1. **Market-based Transfer Price:** In the presence of competitive and stable external markets for the transferred product, many firms use the external market price as the transfer price.

2. **Cost-based Transfer Price:** The transfer price is based on the production cost of the upstream division. A cost-based transfer price requires that the following criteria be specified:

   (a) Actual cost or budgeted (standard) cost.

   (b) Full cost or variable cost.

   (c) The amount of mark-up, if any, to allow the upstream division to earn a profit on the transferred product.

3. **Negotiated Transfer Price:** Senior management does not specify the transfer price. Rather, divisional managers negotiate a mutually-agreeable price.

INDIA'S POLICY ON TRANSFER PRICING

In the event of revenue context, India needs to organise our tax brains to formulate a comprehensive policy related to transfer pricing mechanism. Bearing in mind the rising volume of trade, which India is expected to have with rest of the world, the potential for dispute between regulatory frame-works, and for double taxation of income, could become a major issue for tax-payers in the coming years. India should come out with a common strategy, share experiences and models of developed nations in order to reap a much higher dividend in the coming years. In the speech given by the finance minister during the debate on the Finance Bill 2001, he made it clear that the presence of multinational enterprises in India and their ability to allocate profits in different jurisdictions by controlling prices in intra-group transactions has made the issue of transfer pricing a matter of serious concern. When banks, or other businesses, engage in cross-border activities, each of the foreign jurisdictions in which they conduct business must address the questions of when, to what extent, and how to tax the profits attributable to the activities relating to the taxing jurisdiction. Although international commerce has evolved in response to the globalisation of financial products trading, the various countries' tax provisions that govern these trading activities have not. Consequently, cross-border financial products trading between related parties pose significant challenges to the multinational enterprise. The ability to determine and apply global trading regulations continues to perplex tax regulators globally, especially in Japan, the United Kingdom, and the United States, where most of the global financial transactions are generated.

When transnational corporations trade internationally with their own subsidiaries they use a mechanism called transfer pricing. Sales between parts of the same company are meant to take place at the open market price, at an arm's length price. A whole accountancy industry has grown up around determining transfer prices and justifying them to tax authorities. In practice it can be very difficult to determine an open market price, particularly when trade in a particular sector is highly concentrated in a few companies.

SUGGESTIONS

- One recommendation to curtail transfer-pricing manipulations is to develop a standardized transfer-pricing policy and procedures to be implemented globally.
- A second suggestion is to mandate increased disclosures about the magnitude and effects of transfer-pricing on subsidiary income and tax liabilities in the financial reports of transnational corporations engaging in cross-border transactions.

- The third suggestion would be to institute an electronics-based transfer-pricing enforcement mechanism in accordance with its unique position as a global information technology superpower.
- Last, but not the least, gradual elimination of tax rate differentials that contribute to income-shifting and the inevitable misallocation of tax revenues.

CASE STUDY

BANANAS TO UK VIA THE CHANNEL ISLANDS? IT PAYS FOR TAX REASONS

Bananas are highly profitable - they are the largest single item sold by volume in British supermarkets and the third largest in value. Dole, the US-based company with a 26 per cent global market share, supplies bananas to Tesco in the UK. Chiquita, another US-based corporation with a further quarter of the global market, also supplies Tesco. Fresh Del Monte controls 16 per cent of world bananas, and supplies the vast majority of Asda's bananas and some of Morrison's. But governments at either end of the chain are seeing less and less of the money this banana trade generates. A Guardian investigation of the financial accounts of the three big banana companies has revealed that Dole, Chiquita and Fresh Del Monte had combined global sales of over $50bn (£24bn) in the last five years, and made $1.4bn of profits. They paid just $200m (or 14.3 per cent of profits) in taxes between them in that period. In some years the banana companies have paid an effective tax rate as low as 8 per cent, yet the standard rate of corporation tax in the US where they have their headquarters and file their accounts is 35 per cent.

Banana boats from the Windward Islands have never actually jostled with luxury yachts in its immaculate marinas, of course, but on paper a substantial volume of banana trade from the Caribbean has passed in the last 15 years through Channel Island-based offshore subsidiaries and joint ventures owned at various times by Fyffes and Geest. Fyffes accounts for about 8 per cent of the global banana market. Geest is no longer a banana trading company. Today three other transnational corporations dominate the rest of the banana trade. Dole, Chiquita and Fresh Del Monte account for more than two-thirds of the global market between them and source mainly from large industrial plantations in Latin America and West Africa. Fresh Del Monte is registered in the tax haven of the Cayman Islands, and has more than 30 subsidiaries based on the islands, where the rate of corporation tax is zero. It also has subsidiaries in other tax havens and low tax jurisdictions that include Gibraltar, Bermuda, the Dutch Antilles and the British Virgin Islands. Dole and Chiquita only identify their largest subsidiaries in their accounts but those listed include 11 subsidiaries of Chiquita in Bermuda at the end of 2006 and subsidiaries of Dole in Bermuda, Liberia and Puerto Rico.

This routing of commodity trade and its associated activities through tax havens is typical of a growing trend among transnational corporations to shift their transactions between different countries to minimise their tax bills.

John Christensen, a former economic adviser to the Jersey government who runs the Tax Justice Network, says the effect has been to turn the idea of free trade on its head. 'In a world of globalised companies, money can be routed offshore to ensure they don't pay tax. World trade theory depends on the idea that production will flow to the place that is most efficient, but tax competition is completely distorting it'.

In between, royalties for the use of brands, distribution networks, insurance, finance and marketing charged to the subsidiary in the final destination country can be made to accrue to subsidiaries based offshore in low tax areas. Through transfer pricing, the taxable profit on transactions at either end of the chain, in Latin America or in the EU or US say, is kept low. At Fresh Del Monte, the company had 48% of its sales in the US in 2005 but lost $35.2m in that country. Overseas it made a profit of $133.5m. It paid no US tax but was instead given a tax credit of $8.3m that year.

The big three banana companies openly admit they use low tax areas and tax avoidance schemes. Dole said in its 2007 first half results statement: 'Income tax benefit for the half year ended June 16, 2007 totalled approximately $6.6m. The company expects to generate a tax benefit on pre-tax income for the full fiscal year, given it expects to incur losses in the US for which benefit will be provided and earn pre-tax income in foreign jurisdictions taxed at a lower rate than in the US. For the periods presented, the company's effective income tax rate differs from the US federal statutory rate primarily due to earnings from operations being taxed in foreign jurisdictions at a net effective rate lower than the US rate'. Chiquita says the same. 'The company's taxable earnings are substantially from foreign operations being taxed in jurisdictions at a net effective rate lower that the US statutory rate,' its accounts state. While Fresh Del Monte concedes in its 2006 annual report that 'many of the countries in which we operate have favourable tax rates'. The big three banana producers have a long history of confrontation with the regulatory and tax authorities. When the US tax authorities investigated Dole's income tax returns for 1995-2001, they decided the company had paid $175m too little and imposed interest and penalties. In 2005 Dole received a tax assessment from Honduras, a producing country, of $137m, including claimed unpaid tax, penaltics and interest. Fresh Del Monte's 2007 accounts record that it has 'uncertain tax positions' to the tune of $12m, including interest and penalties of $3.7m primarily relating to tax audits in the European region that it expects to be completed this year. Its tax payments for 1988-2006 remain subject to examination by tax authorities throughout the world, including in producing countries such as Brazil, Costa Rica, Guatemala, and consuming countries such as the UK, the US, Italy, Japan, South Africa, and South Korea.

Blew the Whistle

Chiquita, Dole and Fresh Del Monte are being investigated by the European Commission after Chiquita blew the whistle on an alleged price-fixing cartel among them. Chiquita is paying a $25m fine in the US for illegally funding a Colombian armed terrorist organisation. The fair trade campaign group Banana Link has also tracked how supermarket banana price wars in the UK have corresponded with moves by the big three suppliers to drive down wages and conditions on plantations in Latin America. Fyffes, which supplies part of Asda, Morrison and Co-op demand, has its headquarters in Ireland, one of the lowest taxing regimes in Europe, where corporation tax is 12.5 per cent compared with the UK's 30 per cent. It lists six Jersey-based subsidiaries. Its 2001 accounts record •17m (£11.8m) of banana sales between its subsidiaries and joint ventures with Geest through a Jersey-based holding company. It said, however, that its banana purchasing, marketing and shipping are now located in Ireland, the UK, the Netherlands, and Germany and not in the Channel Islands. These particular activities ceased going through the Channel Islands in 2001, when Geest ended any banana trading. It paid less than •1m on its profit before tax of •15.7m in the first half of this year (i.e., a tax rate of just over 6%). Last year it paid no tax on its continuing operations, but its underlying tax position is difficult to assess because it broke up parts of the business in that period, hiving off its property holdings to a separate company with subsidiaries in tax havens. It said that its tax payments in the five years 2002 to 2006 were •71m on profits of •361m, i.e., 19.7 per cent. Dole declined to comment on the detailed allegations, saying that they involved confidential and proprietary information. Chiquita said it complied with all tax laws in the jurisdictions where it did business. It added that 'a significant portion of our earnings occur outside the US where they are subject to taxation at the local tax rate'. Both companies said they were working with Latin American unions to address workers' rights. Fresh Del Monte said it too operated in many countries and complied with all local tax law and international tax treaties. It added that it also complied with all local labour laws, was a strong proponent of freedom of association, and that the average wage of its agricultural employees in the countries where it operated exceeded the mandated minimum agricultural wage.

The Companies: Subsidiaries and Savings

Dole: A US-based company with approximately 26 per cent share of the global banana market. It supplies bananas to Tesco in the UK. It has subsidiaries in low tax regimes of Bermuda, Liberia and Puerto Rico. An investigation of its financial accounts over the last five years has found that it paid $20m a year less in actual tax than the standard US corporation tax rate.

Fresh Del Monte: US-based corporation owned by Jordanian-Palestinian Abu-Ghazalleh family. It controls about 16 per cent of world bananas and supplies the majority of Asda's bananas and some of Morrisons'. It has over 30 subsidiaries in the tax haven of the Cayman Islands, as well as in other low tax areas including Bermuda and the British Virgin Islands. Over the last five years its actual tax paid has been as much as $69m a year less than tax calculated at US corporation tax rates.

Chiquita: A US-based corporation with approximately a quarter of the global banana market. It supplies Tesco in the UK. It lists 11 subsidiaries in Bermuda in its 2006 accounts. An analysis of its finances over the last five years shows that actual tax paid was as much as $44m a year below US standard corporation tax rates.

be subject to adjustment in order to bring the financial results into line with the arm's length result. However, there developed a growing concern that the application of the arm's length standard under the 1968 regulations failed to deal correctly with the licensing of intangible assets, particularly valuable intangibles with high profit potential. For example, it was thought that companies could transfer potentially valuable technology to related parties at a very early stage in the development process and charge a typically modest royalty. When the technology became very valuable, the profits were then realised by the licensee located in a tax-favorable jurisdiction while the licensor was left with only a limited amount of royalty income. Reflecting Congressional concern about the possibility that such transfers were being made for inadequate compensation, the Tax Reform Act of 1986 amended section 482 so that the income from the transfer or license of intangibles had to be 'commensurate with the income' attributable to the intangible. This was an important distinction which brought with it a new set of problems, chief of which was what exactly was meant by 'commensurate with income', and how could it be measured? In the flurry of activity that followed, a Congressionally-sanctioned discussion of the topic, known simply as the 'White Paper', was issued† and the section 482 regulations were re-written. The final version of the new regulations was issued in 1994 and remains in effect today. As US tax regulations tightened and US enforcement of its regulations increased, other countries reacted. It should come as little surprise if we add, not always favorably! Countries such as Japan, for instance, saw US action to step up enforcement as simply a way to increase taxes collected in the US at the expense of foreign companies. More constructively, however, the US and other countries realized that by agreeing to certain common principles, they would be able to achieve a more uniform application of rules governing transfers of valuable intangibles.

CLOSING CASELET

Mukharjee Ltd., produces Rubber Tyres, which requires to be processed in two divisions *viz.*, A&B. Each tyres is first produced at division 'A' will be transferred to division 'B' further processing and to get finished product. The finished product will sold in the market at ₹ 1,000/- per tyre. However, the semi-finished tyres can be purchased from the market at ₹ 650/-. The division 'A' transferred the semi-finished chairs to 'Division B' at 120 per cent of the manufactured cost. The following are the cost of material and labour for each division:

Particulars	Division A	Division B
Raw material cost per unit	₹ 350/-	NA
Direct Labour per unit	₹ 50/-	₹ 75/-
Direct overheads per unit	₹ 70/-	₹ 95/-
Fixed expenses	75,000	45,000

† Treasury Department, Office of International Tax Counsel and Office of Tax Analysis, and the Internal Revenue Service, Office of Assistant Commissioner International.and Office of Associate Chief Counsel International., *A Study of Intercom any Pricing* Discussion Draft, October 18, 1988.

— If the number of units produced and sold are 1000 tires. What is the profitability of each division?

Solution:

Calculation of divisional profitability

Particulars: If it is transferred at 120 per cent of manufacturing cost from division A, if it is purchased from the market at ₹ 650/-.

Particulars	If it is transferred at 120% of manufacturing cost from division A	If it is purchased from the market at ₹ 650/-
DIVISION A:		
Raw material cost per unit	₹ 350/-	NA
No. of Units	1000	
Material cost	3,50,000	
Direct Labour per unit @ 50/- for 1000 units	50,000	₹ 75/-
Direct overheads per unit @ ₹ 70/- for 1000 units	70,000	₹ 95/-
Total cost of goods manufactured at division A	**4,70,000**	**NA**
Per unit cost	4,70,000/1000 = 470	NA
Profit at division A		
Goods transferred at 120% cost	565.20 × 1000 = 5,62,500	NA
Less of cost of goods manufactured	4,70,000	NA
Contribution	**92,500**	
Less: Fixed expenses	**75,000**	
Profit	17,500	NA
DIVISION B:		
Semi-finished product	5,62,500	650 × 1,000 = 6,50,000
Direct Labour per unit @ 75/- for 1,000 units	75,000	75,000
Direct overheads per unit @ ₹ 95/- for 1,000 units	95,000	95,000
Total cost of goods manufactured at division B	7,32,500	8,20,000
Profit at division B		
Goods sold at ₹ 1,000/-	10,00,000	10,00,000

Less: cost of goods manufactured	7,32,500	8,20,000
Contribution	2,67,500	1,75,000
Less: fixed expenses	45,000	45,000
	2,22,500	**1,30,000**
Overall profit:		
	DIVISION A	**DIVISION B**
OPTION 1	**17,500**	**2,22,500**
OPTION 2	-	**1,30,000**

SUMMARY

This chapter is intended to make an understanding of international transfer pricing strategies to avoid tax. Nowadays, almost all the multinational corporations are following the same strategy. Transfer Pricing generally being the first tax consideration of any cross border transaction between related parties, developed countries such as USA and UK have had transfer pricing law for decades. Transfer Pricing in common parlance, it is manipulation of data. Hence, it is called TPM (transfer pricing manipulation), which is fixing transfer price on non-market basis which generally results in saving total quantum of organization's tax by shifting accounting profits from high tax to low tax jurisdiction.

KEYWORDS

1. **Transfer Pricing:** Pricing of products of any cross border transaction between related parties.
2. **Bilateral Tax Treaties:** These agreements are made by United States with most other nations that determine how multinational companies are taxed.
3. **Goal Congruence:** Goal congruence, in which divisional managers will want to transfer product when doing so maximizes consolidated corporate profits.
4. **Market-based Transfer Price:** Many firms use the external market price as the transfer price.
5. **Cost-based Transfer Price:** The transfer price is based on the production cost of the upstream division.
6. **Negotiated Transfer Price:** Divisional managers negotiate a mutually-agreeable price.

REVIEW QUESTIONS

1. Explain the transfer pricing policy of any multinational corporate entity.
2. What are the various transfer pricing strategies adopted by corporate entities? Explain with suitable examples.

REFERENCES

1. Ernst & Young, 2003, Survey on Transfer Pricing, @Website
2. Feinschreiber, Robert (2004). *Transfer Pricing Methods: An Applications Guide* (Hoboken, NJ: John Wiley & Sons, Inc.).
3. Nicole Bastian Johnson (2006), 'Divisional Performance Measurement and Transfer Pricing for Intangible Assets', Published Online, *Springer Science*, New York, 17 May, 2006.
4. Roger Y.W. Tang, Current Trends and Corporate Cases in Transfer Pricing, Reviewed by Prof. Lorraine Eden, *Journal of International Business Studies*, March, 2003.
5. Richard Sansing (1999), Relationship-Specific Investments and the Transfer Pricing Paradox, *Review Accounting Studies* 4, 119-134, 1999. Kluwer Academic Publishers, Boston. Manufactured in The Netherlands.
6. Tim Baldenius, Stefan Reichestein and Savita A Sahay (1999), Negotiated Versus Cost-Based Transfer Pricing, *Review Accounting Studies* 4, 67-91, 1999, Kluwer Academic Publishers, Boston. (Manufactured in The Netherlands).
7. Yoon K. Choi and Theodore R. Day (1998), 'Transfer Pricing, Incentive Compensation and Tax Avoidance in a Multi-division Firm', *Review of Quantitative Finance and Accounting*, 1998, pp 139-164.
8. Waman Y. Kale, Transfer Pricing – Practical Issues and Controversies, *The Chartered Accountant*, October, 2005, pp. 570-579.
9. Mayank K. Agarwal, Transfer Pricing – A Beginner's Perspective, www.indiainfoline.com

ഌശ ഌശ ഌശ

Fyffes: Irish-based corporation supplies Asda, Morrisons and Co-op in UK. It lists six Jersey-based subsidiaries. Irish corporation tax is 12.5 per cent, compared with UK rates of 30 per cent. It was observed that its tax payments in the years 2002 to 2006 were •71m on profits of •361m, a rate of 19.7 per cent.

Finally, it can be stated that the transnational companies have developed ways of bundling up parts of their business such as intellectual property, brands, logos, marketing, insurance and finance expertise and owning them offshore. They can then charge for the use of these to other parts of their group onshore. In this way a banana may be sold by one subsidiary of a group in the country where it was grown to another group subsidiary offshore at little more than the cost of production in the originating country. The banana ends up being sold back onshore to a further subsidiary of the same company in the consuming country at a price that is close to the final retail price. Although tax havens have existed for decades, the flight of capital took off with the removal of exchange controls and the development of information technology in the late 1990s. Large corporations have been able to shift profits around between complex networks of subsidiaries in different countries, choosing where to incur costs, where to allocate overheads or locate assets, where to borrow money and where to make taxable profit. They tend to weight their costs towards countries with high rates of tax thereby reducing their taxable profits in those, and weight their profits instead towards those with minimal or no tax. The following appendix shows intangible transfer and tax treatment by United States.

APPENDIX

EVOLUTION OF US TAX TREATMENT OF INTANGIBLE TRANSFERS

The regulations that deal with the tax consequences of technology transfers are largely found in two labyrinth and, frankly, somewhat soporific sections of the Internal Revenue Code, known as section 367 and section 482. Section 482, which deals with related-party transactions generally, and to which one is directed by section 367 for guidance in determining the arm's length nature of a transfer of intangible property. In the mid-1980s, the US Congress became concerned that US companies were routinely avoiding taxes by transferring the ownership of valuable intangible assets to related manufacturing entities in low tax jurisdictions, e.g., Puerto Rico and Ireland. and charging inadequate royalties for the manufacturer's use of the intangibles. At that time, the regulations contained in section 482 dated to 1968. The purpose of the regulations was '. . . to place a controlled taxpayer on a tax parity with an uncontrolled taxpayer by determining, according to the standard of an uncontrolled taxpayer, the true taxable income from the property and business of a controlled taxpayer.'* The comparison of related to unrelated party transactions served as the basis for determining true taxable income. The IRS used these regulations to establish whether intercom any transfers were consistent with the arm's length standard. Transactions that failed to meet the test could

*Reg. §1.482-1_b._1. _1968.

CHAPTER

12

Mutual Funds – Performance Evaluation

CHAPTER OUTLINE

- Opening Caselet
- Introduction
- Origin of Mutual Funds
- Types of Schemes
- Classification by Treynor
- Different Mutual Fund Options
- Classification by Risk and Return
- Mutual Funds Industry Unit Holding Pattern (2001-2009)
- Performance Evaluation of Managed Funds
- Statistical Formulae
- Various Models Used for Performance Evaluation
- Practical Problems
- Closing Caselet
- Summary
- Keywords
- Review Questions
- References

OPENING CASELET

FRANKLIN INDIA TAX PLAN

Open-ended Equity Linked savings scheme with a lock-in-period of 3 years

Objective is to provide medium to long-term growth of capital along with income tax rebate.

Asset Allocation Patterns of the Scheme:

Type of Instruments	Normal Allocation (% of Net Assets)
Equity and Equity linked Instruments	Up to 100%
Debt Securities	Up to 20%(PSU Bonds/Debentures)
Money market instruments	Up to 20%

The fund manager: Anand Radhakrishnan

Inception Date: April 10, 1999

Entry load is 2.25 per cent in respect of each purchase/switch-in of units less than ₹ 5 Crore in value. If it is more than or equal to ₹ 5 crore in value, no entry load.

Exit load: Nil

Benchmark Index: S&P CNX 500

Investment Plan/Options: Growth Plan and Dividend Plan

Minimum Amount: For new and existing investor's minimum of ₹ 500 and in multiples of ₹ 500 thereafter.

Lock-in-Period: 3 years from the date of allotment of the respective units

Redemption Proceeds: Normally the investor can redeem the units on a business day if it is an open ended scheme and the redemption amount will be credited to the account of the investor within Transaction + 3 days, i.e., T + 3 days.

— Analyze the scheme advantages and disadvantages.

INTRODUCTION

Mutual funds have become a major vehicle for mobilisation of savings particularly from the small and household sectors for investment in the stock market. In view of their growing importance in the capital market, their expanding investor base and the decision to allow mutual fund to be set up in the joint and private sectors it has become necessary to evolve a comprehensive set of prudential guidelines for the all-round development and regulation of mutual funds and for ensuring investor protection.

The Association of Mutual Funds in India (AMFI)[1] has also played a supportive role in formulating guidelines and perfecting them in the interests of both investors and mutual funds. Based on the working of the Mutual Fund regulations for the last ten years, there are certain areas which require re-examination. One such area relates to the role of trustees and another to investor protection. The board of trustees of a mutual fund has onerous responsibilities. It has to form the asset management company has to manage the funds and also appoint and enter into an agreement with the custodian for the custody of assets.

A Fund Manager who is an investment specialist, who makes an in-depth understanding of the financial markets so as to manage the funds in a professional manner, will manage mutual funds. The diversified portfolio of Mutual Fund organisations will minimise the risk of investors. Investor is free to invest in open-ended mutual funds or closed-ended mutual funds, which facilitates liquidity of investment. One of the important objectives of mutual fund organisation is to provide income tax benefit to the small and medium size investors. Over a medium to long-term Mutual Funds have the potential and objective to provide a higher return as they invest in a diversified basket of selected companies. Mutual Funds objective is to offer a variety of schemes to enable investors to take advantage of opportunities not only in the equity, debt and money markets but also in specific industries and sectors.

In 1987, non-UTI, public sector mutual funds set up by public sector banks and Life Insurance Corporation of India (LIC) and General Insurance Corporation of India (GIC) were launched. SBI Mutual Fund was the first non-UTI mutual fund in India. By the end of 1988, UTI had ₹ 6,700 crore of assets under management. With the entry of private sector funds in 1993, a new era started in the Indian mutual fund industry, giving the Indian investors a wider choice of fund families. Also, 1993 was the year in which the first Mutual Fund Regulations came into being, under which all mutual funds, except UTI were to be registered and governed. The erstwhile Kothari Pioneer (now merged with Franklin Templeton) was the first private sector mutual fund registered in July 1993.

In a study conducted during 1994 in USA, it was found that, mutual funds have been labelled as the bank deposits of 1990's. Since the beginning of 1991, more than half a trillion dollars have been invested in units.[2]

In India, Mutual funds continue to be still largely a preserve of the Unit Trust of India (UTI), whose total corpus exceeds ₹ 1,00,000 crores by the year 2003. At present,

1. Information was available from the official website of the organisation — www.amfi.org
2. *Business India,* October 24-November 6, 1994.

private sector mutual funds had wrested a lion's share of the mutual fund assets from the UTI and the PSU bank-sponsored funds. By end-December 2003, the mutual fund industry was managing ₹ 1,40,000 crore of assets. UTI has faced a severe crisis due to irregularities in management, and non-disclosure policy of Unit Scheme-64 etc. The Net Asset Value was drastically declined. Most of the schemes of mutual fund in operation are deeply discounted to their Net Asset Value (NAV) by as much 40 to 50 per cent.

Many nationalised banks got into the mutual fund business in the early nineties and got off to a good start due to the stock market boom prevailing then. These banks did not really understand the mutual fund business and they just viewed it as another kind of banking activity. Few hired specialised staff and generally choose to transfer staff from the parent organisations. The performance of most of the schemes floated by these funds was not good. Some schemes had offered guaranteed returns and their parent organisations had to bail out these AMCs by paying large amounts of money as the difference between the guaranteed and actual returns. The service levels were also very bad. Most of these AMCs have not been able to retain staff, float new schemes etc., and it is doubtful whether, barring a few exceptions, they have serious plans of continuing the activity in a major way. Some have sold out to foreign owned companies, some have merged with others and there is general restructuring going on.

The foreign owned companies have deep pockets and have come in here with the expectation of a long haul. They can be credited with introducing many new practices such as new product innovation, sharp improvement in service standards and disclosure, usage of technology, broker education and support etc. In fact, they have forced the industry to upgrade itself and service levels of organisations like UTI have improved dramatically in the last few years in response to the competition provided by these.

ORIGIN OF MUTUAL FUNDS

Earlier investment companies are now called as Mutual Fund Companies. The first modern investment company, Scottish-American Investment Company, was founded in London in 1860, at the beginning of a stock market boom that lasted until 1875. By then, there were over 50 investment companies in Britain. Many of them failed in the stock market crisis of 1890, and public interest in the stock market waned until the boom of the 1920s renewed it. It was during 1920s, that investment companies first became important in the United States. They had existed since the 1890s, but by 1923, there were only 15 with total assets of no more than $15 million. However, as stock prices soared in the late 1920s, and small investors rushed to get in on the action, investment companies mushroomed. By 1929, there were some 400, with $3 billion assets. Most of these early investment companies were closed-end companies. Some offered 'families' of trusts with differing investment objectives, much like the mutual funds of today.

The stock market collapse between 1929 and 1933 was, of course, a catastrophe for the investment companies. Poor management and risky investment practices that had gone unnoticed in the boom became painfully apparent in the collapse. For example, many of the funds were highly leveraged, with as much as 40 per cent of their assets funded with debt or preferred stock. As long as the market rose, their common stock paid spectacular returns. When the market crashed, the value of the common stock was wiped out.

The 1930s, saw relatively rapid growth of open-end companies (mutual funds), partly because of the disrepute into which the close-end companies had fallen. In fund, the Mssachusetts Investors Trust, had been formed in Boston in 1924. It promised to redeem its shares at net asset value less $2 per share. Interest in mutual funds picked up again after World War II, when the stock market revived. During the period 1945-1965, mutual funds grew at an average rate of 18% a year. The number of share-holders grew from 3 million to over 50 million.

The funds in UK have already crossed the 1000 mark by the end of 1987. The top 25 funds in terms of performance come from Japan and the Far East growth sectors. Some of them have double their money within a period of just one year. In Australia also, these funds have been very successful particularly on account of 46.8 per cent rise to Australian All Shares Index. Mutual funds are growing in size and importance in countries like Hong Kong, Singapore, Phillippines, Thailand, South Korea etc. The mutual funds have been growing at an unprecedented pace throughout the world.

TYPES OF SCHEMES

Mutual fund schemes can be offered with any of a range of investment objectives, each corresponding to a certain point in the risk-return matrix. In a broad sense, schemes can be categorised based on tenor, asset class, position philosophy or geography.

The classification of MF schemes has been done on the basis of the asset allocation and investment pattern of the schemes concerned. This is different from the traditional offer document-based scheme classification. The classification on the basis of asset allocation and investment pattern holds more relevance as these two factors determine the risk level of MF schemes. MF schemes with equity exposure have been classified as Marginal Equity, Balanced, and Equity, on the basis of the extent of the equity exposure. Then they have been sub-classified as Diversified-Defensive, Diversified-Aggressive, and Sector schemes on the basis of their sectoral concentration.

Debt-based MF schemes have been categorised on the basis of their average allocation to Gilt securities. Then they have been sub-classified as Debt-Short-Term and Debt-Long-Term schemes, depending on their average portfolio maturity over the ranking period.

CLASSIFICATION BY TREYNOR

1. **Open-ended Schemes:** These are schemes that do not have a fixed maturity. The mutual fund ensures liquidity by announcing sale and re-purchase prices for the units of such a scheme on an ongoing basis. Investors who wish to exist from an open-ended scheme can offer their units to the mutual fund for redeemption,

generally called repurchase. Similarly, the mutual fund can sell new units to investors desirous of participating in the scheme, generally called sale. Every transaction results in a change in unit capital of the scheme. In open-ended funds, sale and repurchase of units happen on a continuous basis, at NAV related prices, from the fund itself. Units are bought and sold at their current NAV. Open end funds keep some portion of their assets in short term and money market securities to provide available funds for redeemptions. A large portion will be invested in highly liquid securities, which enables the fund to raise money by selling securities at prices very close to those used for valuations. The market price will be determined by NAV. In open-ended funds the NAV is calculated daily. Ex: HDFC Growth fund, Top 200, Core and Satellite etc., These schemes are open-ended whose objective is to generate long-term capital appreciation. These schemes have both entry and exit load. The minimum investment should be 5000 and in multiples of 100 thereafter.

2. **Close-ended Schemes:** These are issued to the public through an IPO. These funds have a stipulated maturity period ranging from 3 to 15 years. The fund is open for subscription only during a specified period. Investors can invest in the scheme at the time of the initial public issue and there after they can buy or sell the units of the scheme on the stock exchange where they are listed. If the investor wants to redeem the units they can do after the maturity period. For close-ended funds, investor approval is required for all cases of merger and takeover. The NAV will be calculated once in a week for close ended schemes. Ex: HDFC Mid-Cap Opportunities Fund.

It is a close-ended scheme for a period of 3 years with automatic conversion into open-ended scheme upon maturity. It was opened on 7th May, 2007 and closed on 8th June, 2007. The minimum investment should be 5000 and in multiples of 1000 thereafter. There is no entry and exit load for this fund. The scheme will be opened quarterly and the investor who wants to redeem can redeem on the specified dates, but the investor will be having an exit load of 4 per cent if he redeems in the 1st year, 3 per cent in the 2nd year and 2 per cent in the final year.

DIFFERENT MUTUAL FUND OPTIONS

- **Equity Diversified Funds:** Mutual Funds reduces the risk by investing in all the sectors. Instead of putting all your money in one sector or company it's better to invest in various good performing sectors as it reduces the risk of getting involved in a particular sector/company which may perform or may not. This is an ideal category for those who want to participate in stock market and knows the risk involved in stock market but have few rupees to invest in bluechip stocks. Though the short-term outlook is volatile in long-term, equity diversified funds have outperformed other categories and will lessen the amount of risk than stock markets. The average returns of equity diversified funds are 102 per cent.

- **Index Funds:** These are the index-based funds, which move with the likes of Sensex & Nifty. These fund charges NIL or very low entry/exit loads. As you have seen in last few months Nifty and Sensex have almost come down 17 per cent from their tops, it is a good time to invest in Index funds with the principal of investing at the lower levels. Though the short-term outlook is volatile in long-term Sensex and Nifty could do well with improving economic conditions. It has been seen that these Index funds have outperformed the indices making them more attractive.

- **Sector Fund:** Sector schemes follow particular sector. You have to be selective while investing in these funds, as you need to select particular sector, which will perform better in the future. Investing in these funds carries some amount of risk but also give you more returns. Sector funds have given average returns of 73 per cent for 1 year period. Auto, Steel, Cement have done well the year' 03 & the trend will continue in year' 04 but IT, FMCG sectors are experiencing downward trend due to $ depreciation, price war in FMCG respectively. Though short-term trend for pharma sector looks down in long-term, we look forward to lot more action in the sector, as there exists a long-term, strong fundamental story backed by immense growth potential for the Indian pharmaceutical companies.

- **Balanced Funds:** Balanced funds gives you the stability with the potential to grow with the equity help of equity investments. These funds invest in both Equity and Debt markets. The balanced funds are for those, who want to enjoy the appreciation effects of equity market but at the same time like to play safe with less volatile debt market. In this volatile market, it is good to invest in balanced funds as they carry less risk compare to equity funds. In the last 12 months, balanced funds have given descent returns with the up trend in the equity markets. Balanced funds average returns are 60 per cent for one-year period.

- **Equity Linked Tax Savings Schemes (ELSS):** These schemes are becoming more popular as traditional ways of tax saving becoming less interesting with declining interest rates. Equity Linked Savings Schemes (ELSS) is an ideal way to save on tax as well as staying invested in equity mutual funds. In last, 1 year, these funds have given above average returns to keep you more and more interested in saving tax as well as counting returns on your investment. The average returns for this category are 98 per cent.

- **Debt Funds:** Debt funds invest in the government securities, Corporate bonds, Treasury bills, etc. The conservative investors like to go for capital safety. From last 12 months in the declining interest rate scenario, debt funds remained flat. In three years debt funds have given average returns of 12 per cent. As equity market is looking volatile its better to invest part of your money in these funds.

- **Gilt Funds:** Gilt funds invest in government securities. The investors who like to avail the benefits of capital safety with government security. From last 6-12 months, gilt funds have given average returns. As equity market is looking volatile its better to invest part of your money in these funds as they provide adequate security to your investments. The average returns for one-year period are 10.41

per cent compare to the NSE G Sec. Composite Index has given 12.60 per cent returns.

- **Monthly Income Plans:** These schemes gives you monthly income, those who seek monthly income. In the current scenario where debt market is very volatile, it's better to invest in hybrid funds like MIP with suitable time horizon for capital appreciation. In last 6-12 months, MIP's have given descent returns compare to debt funds. The average returns of MIP's stands at 15.68 per cent, which looks good, compared to income funds.
- **Short-term Plans:** These schemes provides short-term saving option with more liquidity than FD's to park your investments. Those who seeking for income in short-term investments of 6-10 months with more liquidity than Bank fixed deposit. While savings accounts would give you 3.5 per cent per annum, bank FD's annually return up to 6.5 per cent, Liquid funds would typically give you more than 5 per cent and short-term plans 6 to 6.5 per cent per anum. In last 6-12 months, STP's have given decent returns.

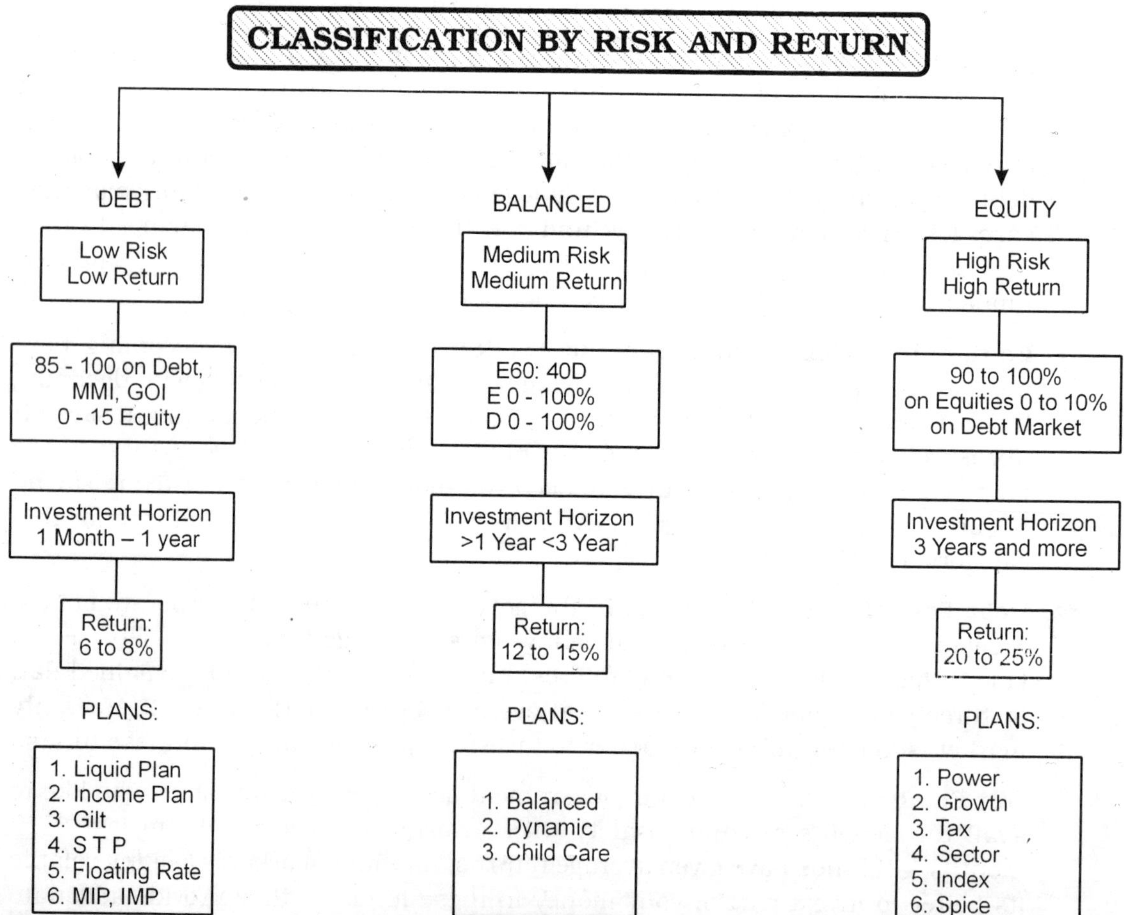

MUTUAL FUNDS INDUSTRY UNIT HOLDING PATTERN (2001-2009)

1. UNIT HOLDING PATTERN IN 2001-02

From the data collected from the mutual funds, the following has been observed

(i) As on March 31, 2002 there are a total number of 3.08 crore investors accounts (it is likely that there may be more than one folio of an investor which might have been counted more than once and actual number of investors would be less) holding units of ₹ 1,00,594 crore. Out of this total number of investors accounts, 3.02 crore are individual investors accounts, accounting for 98.04 of the total number of investors accounts and contribute ₹ 55,487 crore which is 55.16 of the total net assets.

(ii) Corporate and institutions who form only 1.46 per cent of the total number of investors accounts in the mutual funds industry, contribute a sizeable amount of ₹ 43,403 crore which is 43.15 per cent of the total net assets in the mutual funds industry.

(iii) The NRIs and OCBs constitute a very small percentage of investors accounts and contribute ₹ 306 crore (0.30 per cent) of net assets.

The details of unit holding pattern are given in the following table:

Table 1: Unit Holding Pattern of Mutual Funds Industry

As on 31st March, 2002

Categroy	Number of Investors Account	% To Total Investors Accounts	Net Assets (₹ Crore)	% To Total Net Assets
Individuals	3,02,38,065	98.04	55,487	55.16
NRIs[1]	1,54,622	0.50	1,398	1.39
FIIs	1,123	0.00	306	0.30
Corporates/ Institutions	4,50,132 /Others	1.46	43,403	43.15
TOTAL	**3,08,43,942**	**100.00**	**1,00,594**	**100.00**

FI: Financial Institutions, FII: Foreign Institutional Investors

Source: SEBI., 2002

(a) Unit Holding Pattern – Private Sector

From the analysis of data on unit holding pattern of Private Sector Mutual Funds and Public Sector Mutual Funds, the following observations are made:

1. Out of a total of 41.61 lakh investors accounts in the private sector, 40 lakhs are individual investors accounts, i.e., 96.11 per cent of the total investors accounts are in private sector mutual funds.
2. However, the private sector mutual funds manage 41,459 crores of the net assets contributes nearly 42 per cent of the total net assets.

(b) Unit Holding Pattern – Public Sector (Other than UTI)

From the analysis of data on unit holding pattern of Public Sector Mutual Funds (other than UTI), Out of a total of 2.67 lakhs investors accounts, 22.22 lakhs are individual investors accounts, i.e., 97.95 pcr cent of the total investors. Hence, the contribution made by this sector is, net asset value ₹ 7,701 cores and it is only 8 per cent of aggregate net assets.

(c) Unit Holding Pattern – Unit Trust of India

From the analysis of data on unit holding pattern of Unit Trust of India, out of a total of 24.41 lakhs investors accounts, 24.01 lakhs are individual investors accounts i.e. 98.375 per cent of the total investors. The total contribution by UTI is net asset value ₹ 51,433 cores and it is nearly 51 per cent of aggregate net assets.

Details of unit holding pattern of private sector and public sector mutual funds(other than UTI), and Unit Trust of India, are given in the following tables:

Table 2: Unit Holding Pattern of Private Sector MFs
As on 31st March, 2002

Category	Number of Investors Accounts	% To Total Investors Accounts	Net Assets (₹ Crore)	% To Total Net Assets
Individuals	40,00,117	96.11	15,024.71	36.24
NRIs	32,267	0.78	523.47	1.26
FIIs	35	0.00	288.61	0.70
Corporates/ Institutions /Others	1,29,423	3.11	25,622.19	61.80
TOTAL	**41,61,842**	**100.00**	**41,458.98**	**100.00**

Table 3: Unit Holding Pattern of Public Sector MFs (Other than UTI MF) As on 31st March, 2002

Category	Number of Investors Accounts	% To Total Investors Accounts	Net Assets (₹ Crore)	% To Total Net Assets
Individuals	22,21,362	9,795	3,116.24	40.46
NRIs	8,486	0.37	143.73	1.87
FIIs	956	0.04	0.35	0.08
Corporates/ Institutions	37,020 /Others	1.64	4,435.27	57.59
TOTAL	**22,67,824**	**100.00**	**81,939.03**	**100.00**

FI: Financial Institutions, FII: Foreign Institutional Investors

Source: SEBI, 2002.

Table 4: Unit Holding Pattern of Unit Trust of India MF As on 31st March, 2002

Category	Number of Investors Accounts	% To Total Investors Accounts	Net Assets (₹ Crore)	% To Total Net Assets
Individuals	2,40,16,586	98.37	37,345.74	72.61
NRIs	1,13,869	0.47	729.88	1.42
FIIs	132	0.00	11.06	0.02
Corporates/ Institutions	2,83,689 /Others	1.16	13,346.93	25.05
TOTAL	**2,44,14,276**	**100.00**	**51,433.61**	**100.00**

FI: Financial Institutions, FII: Foreign Institutional Investors

Source: SEBI, 2002.

2. UNIT HOLDING PATTERN IN 2008-09

From the data collected from the mutual funds, the following has been observed:-

(i) As on March 31, 2009, there are a total number of 4.76 crore investors accounts (it is likely that there may be more than one folio of an investor which might have been counted more than once and actual number of investors would be less) holding units of ₹ 4,19,321.66 crore. Out of this total number of investors accounts, 4.61 crore are individual investors accounts, accounting for 96.75 per cent of the total number of investors accounts and contribute ₹ 1,55,283.21crore which is 37.03 per cent of the total net assets.

(ii) Corporate and institutions who form only 1.21 per cent of the total number of investors accounts in the mutual funds industry, contribute a sizeable amount of ₹ 2,36,233.35 crore which is 56.34 per cent of the total net assets in the mutual funds industry.

(iii) The NRIs and FIIs constitute a very small percentage of investors accounts (2.04 per cent) and contribute ₹ 27,805.10 crore (6.63 per cent) of net assets.

The details of unit holding pattern are given in the following table:

Table 5: Unit Holding Pattern of Mutual Funds Industry

As on 31st March, 2009

Category	Number of Investors Accounts	% To Total Investors Accounts	Net Assets (₹ Crore)	% To Total Net Assets
Individuals	4,60,75,763	96.75	1,55,283.21	37.03
NRIs	9,71,430	2.04	22,821.28	5.44
FIIs	146	0.00	4,983.82	1.19
Corporates/ Institutions /Others	5,75,938	121	2,36,233.35	56.34
TOTAL	**4,76,23,277**	**100.00**	**4,19,321.66**	**100.00**

FI: Financial Institutions, FII: Foreign Institutional Investors

Source: Association of Mutual Funds in India (AMFI), 2009.

UNIT HOLDING PATTERN - PRIVATE/PUBLIC SECTOR

From the analysis of data on unit holding pattern of Private Sector Mutual Funds and Public Sector Mutual Funds, the following observations are made:

1. Out of a total of 4.76 crore investors accounts in the mutual funds industry, (it is likely that there may be more than one folio of an investor which might have been counted more than once and therefore actual number of investors may be less) 3.16 crore investors accounts, i.e., 66.27 per cent of the total investors accounts are in private sector mutual funds whereas the 1.61 crore investors accounts i.e. 33.73 per cent are with the public sector mutual funds which includes UTI Mutual Fund.

2. However, the private sector mutual funds manage 80.46 per cent of the net assets where as the public sector mutual funds own only 19.54 per cent of the assets.

   Details of unit holding pattern of private sector and public sector mutual funds are given in the following tables:

Public Sector: The Table 8 indicates the growth of Unit Trust of India Mutual Fund and Public Sector (other than UTI) during the period 2003-2009. It is observed that there is a continuous growth in assets under management by UTI MF up to the April, 2008 followed by a marginal decrease in the year 2009. It is apparent that there was a four fold increase of assets in case of UTI and 7 times increase in case of other public sector mutual funds during 2003-2009.

Table 6: Unit Holding Pattern of Private Sector MFs
As on 31st March, 2009

Category	Number of Investors Accounts	% To Total Investors Accounts	Net Assets (₹ Crore)	% To Total Net Assets
Individuals	3,03,62,538	96.21	1,21,676.51	36.06
NRIs	8,13,062	2.58	21,093.62	6.25
FIIs	128	0.00	4,888.98	1.45
Corporates/ Institutions /Others	3,83,783	1.22	1,89,723.52	56.23
TOTAL	**3,15,59,511**	**100.00**	**3,37,382.63**	**100.00**

FI: Financial Institutions, FII: Foreign Institutional Investors

Table 7: Unit Holding Pattern of Public Sector MFs
(Including UTI MF) As on 31st March, 2009

Category	Number of Investors Accounts	% To Total Investors Accounts	Net Assets (₹ Crore)	% To Total Net Assets
Individuals	15,713,225	97.82	33,606.7[illegible]	41.01
NRIs	1,58,368	0.99	1,727.66	2.11
FIIs	18	0.00	94.84	0.12
Corporates/ Institutions /Others	1,92,155	1.20	46,509.83	56.76
TOTAL	**1,60,63,766**	**100.00**	**81,939.03**	**100.00**

FI: Financial Institutions, FII: Foreign Institutional Investors

Source: Association of Mutual Funds in India (AMFI), 2009.

Private Sector: The table 9 indicates the growth of private sector mutual funds during the period 2003-2009. It is observed that there is a continuous growth up to April, 2008 and a marginal decrease in the year 2009. During 2003-08, there was nine fold growth.

Table 8: Trends in AUM of Public Sector Mutual Fund

Year	UTI ₹ Crores	Simple Index	Public Sector (other than UTI)	Simple Index
April 2003	13,532	100	7,897	100
April 2004	19,848	147	12,001	152
April 2005	20,478	151	11,924	150
April 2006	30,109	223	23,967	303
April 2007	33,517	248	29,747	376
April 2008	52,549	388	50,251	636
February, 2009	49,225	364	56,822	719
Note: Simple Index calculated based on the year April 2003.				

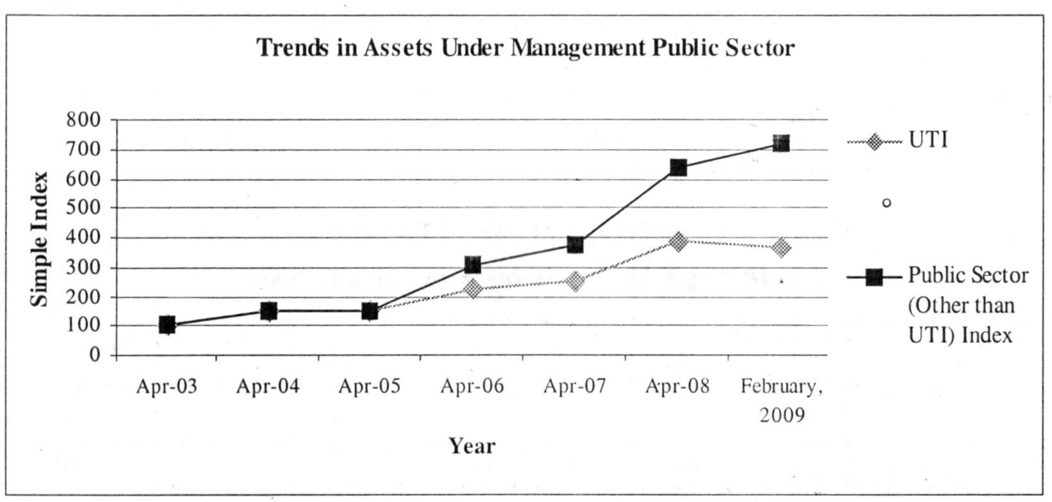

Table 9: Trends in AUM of Private Sector Mutual Funds in India

Year	Private ₹ Crores	Simple Index
April 2003	67,395	100
April 2004	1,28,211	190
April 2005	1,35,124	200.4
April 2006	2,27,420	337.4
April 2007	3,16,924	470.2
April 2008	5,15,278	764.6
February, 2009	4,51,531	669.9
Note: Simple Index calculated based on the year April 2003.		

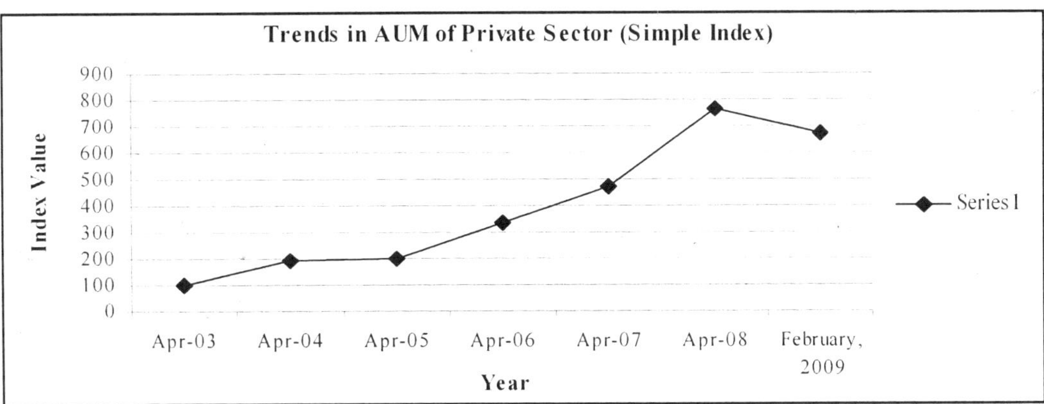

Comparative Analysis: Table 10 shows average annual growth rate in the AUM of the UTI, Public Sector (other than UTI) and the private sector mutual funds during 2003-2009. It is interesting to note that the highest percentage of overall growth is observed during the year 2005-06, followed by the year 2007-2008. Hence, we can conclude that in these two years there was positive influence of fluctuations in portfolio management. Only in the years 2004-05 and 2008-2009 there were overall negative growth rates recorded.

Table 10: Average Annual Growth Rate in AUM during April, 2003-February, 2009

Year	UTI % Growth	Public Sector (other than UTI)	Private % Growth	Overall % Growth
2003-2004	52.36	52	38.87	47.74
2004-2005	4.49	-2	-1.42	0.35
2005-2006	44.15	100	29.23	57.39
2006-2007	17.87	24.12	20.91	2.96
2007-2008	37.91	68.27	32.59	46.25
2008-2009*	-6.33	13.08	-13.67	-2.30
*Up to February, 2009				

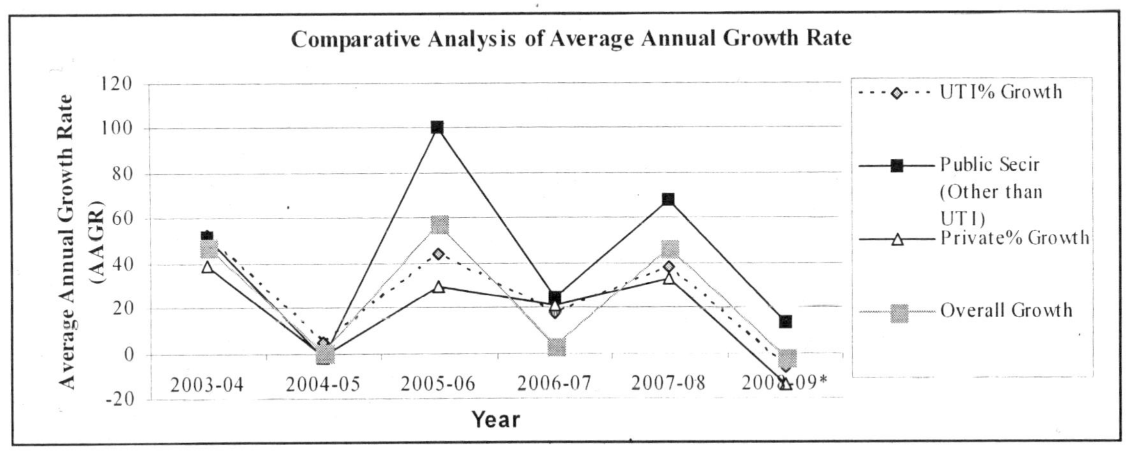

Table 11 represents the consolidated data relating to assets under management during 2003-2009. It is observed that the contribution of UTI over the period is reduced from 15 per cent in 2003, to about 8 per cent in the year 2009. At the same time, the private sector contribution increased from 76 per cent in the year 2003 to 82 per cent in the year 2009.

Table 11: Public vs. Private Sector AUM during April, 2003 – February, 2009

Year	UTI ₹	%	Public Sector (other than)	%	Private ₹ Crore	%	Overall ₹ Crore
Apr-03	13,532	(15)	7,897	(9)	67,395	(76)	88,824
Apr-04	19,848	(12)	12,001	(7)	1,28,211	(81)	1,60,060
Apr-05	20,478	(12)	11,924	(7)	1,35,124	(81)	1,67,526
Apr-06	30,109	(11)	23,967	(8)	2,27,420	(81)	2,81,496
Apr-07	33,517	(8)	29,747	(7)	3,16,924	(85)	3,80,188
Apr-08	52,549	(8)	50,251	(8)	5,15,278	(84)	6,18,078
Feb-09	49,225	(8)	56,822	(10)	4,51,531	(82)	5,57,578
Note: Figures in parentheses are percentages to row totals							

Increasing Role of Private Sector During 1994-2010

Ten years after the entry of private sector mutual funds in 1994, there was a need for re-look in to its progress. The industry has been a witness to a whole lot of unethical practices, including paying higher incentives to distributors, promising assured returns to poorly informed investors and, in some extreme cases, switching investments from scheme to scheme. The culture of numbers has created a rapacious relationship between AMCs and their distributors where one feeds off the other. At the root of the industry's crisis of confidence is its over-dependence on corporate funds for building scale. The following table focuses on the role of private sector in India's mutual fund industry, during 1994-2009.

Table 12: Increasing Role of Private Sector During 1994 to 2010

STRUCTURE	1994	2010
No. of Players	11	40
Assets Managed	₹ 62,430 Crore	₹ 6,64,599 Crore
Share of UTI & Public Sector	82.8%	23.8%
Share of Private Sector	17.2%	76.2%
Dominant Type of Funds	Close-End	Open-End
Disclosure Standards	Monthly	Daily
NAV's	Monthly	Daily
Portfolio Management	Yearly	Monthly/quarterly
Accounts	Yearly	Half -yearly

PERFORMANCE EVALUATION OF MANAGED FUNDS

Introduction

The measure of performance of financial instruments is basically dependent three important models derived independently by Sharpe, Jensen and Treynor. All three models are based on the assumption that: (1) all investors are averse to risk, and are single period expected utility of terminal wealth maximisers, (2) all investors have identical decision horizons and homogeneous expectations regarding investment opportunities, (3) all investors are able to choose among portfolios solely on the basis of expected returns and variance of returns, (4) all transactions costs and taxes are zero, and (5) all assets are infinitely divisible.

Using Benchmarks to Measure Mutual Fund Performance

Benchmark Mutual Fund, which specialises in managing exchange traded funds (ETFs), has lined up a scheme that will try to generate returns through investment in securities represented by a host of sectoral indices. The indices — the offer document sent to SEBI mentions nine of them — are owned by India Index Services and Products Ltd., the joint venture formed by NSE and CRISIL to provide a variety of indices and index-related services for the capital market. These indices cover the following sectors: Automobiles/four-wheeler, cement, electrical equipment, pharmaceutical, power, steel, telecom, services and information technology. Their names are S&P CNX Pharmaceutical Index, S&P CNX Cement and Cement Product Index, S&P CNX Power Index and the like. The ETF's investment objective is to provide returns that, before expenses, closely correspond to the total returns of the securities as represented by the index. Its performance, however, may differ due to tracking error. The plan is to use a passive or indexing approach, with no intention to beat the market. Therefore, the scheme will not try out transitory defensive positions when the market weakens or look over-valued. Here, the ETF will invest at least 90 per cent of its assets in the stocks of its underlying index, the offer document has stated.

* **Average Annual Return** is the total return for the period divided by the number of years;

* **Compound Average Return** is a time value of money computation, based on the beginning and ending value of the investment and number of years in the period. Since these two calculations result in different annual returns, it is important to use the same return measure when comparing fund performance.

To put an investment's total return into perspective, investors should compare return to the performance of an appropriate investment benchmark or index. For example, many domestic stock mutual funds are compared to the Standard and Poor's 500 stock index (S&P 500), while the Lehman Brothers Government/Corporate Bond Index is a common gauge for bond mutual funds. Many funds report total return over calendar years (January

1 through December 31). Investors should compare returns calculated over the same time period and should review a fund's performance over a variety of periods, such as one year, five years, and 10 years (or since the fund's inception), as well as year to year. The goal is to determine how successfully and consistently the fund was managed in different market environments.

1. **Beta** measures the volatility of a fund's return, relative to a given index, such as the S&P 500. The market index is assigned a beta of 1.0. Therefore, a stock fund with a beta of 1.5 has moved up and down one and one-half times more than the market as a whole. Beta does not tell investors the risk of loss, only the degree of an investment's short-term movements. And beta is a relative measure. Accordingly, a beta below 1.0 means that a fund was less volatile than the market as a whole, but the market itself may have been considerably volatile during a specific time period.

$$\beta = \frac{N(\text{"}XY) - (\text{"}X)(\text{"}Y)}{N(\text{"}X^2) - (\text{"}X)^2}.$$

2. **Alpha** takes the calculation of risk one step further. First, the return expected for a fund is determined, based on its beta. (The rationale is that risk should be proportional to reward.) Then, alpha reports how much a fund's performance differed from its expected return calculation. A positive alpha means that a fund performed better than expected for its beta, while a negative alpha means that it has underperformed. For example, a fund with an alpha of +2.3 has returned 2.3 per cent more on average than would have been expected, given its beta.

$$\alpha = \frac{\Sigma Y}{N} - \frac{\beta(\Sigma X)}{N}.$$

3. **Standard Deviation** is a measure of volatility that indicates the range of a fund's performance, relative to its average return, over the time period studied. Investors should add and subtract the standard deviation from the fund's average performance to get an idea of how much the fund's performance has varied. For example, a fund with a three-year average annual return of 10 per cent and a standard deviation of 12 means that two-thirds of the time during the three-year period, its return was between –2 per cent (10 – 12) and 22 per cent (10 + 12). A fund with a low standard deviation and a high return generally is attractive.

4. **Duration** is another way to judge volatility for fixed-income funds. Duration is calculated based on the average characteristics of the bonds in a fund's portfolio, including the maturity, the amount and frequency of bond interest payments, and the rate at which the bonds' income stream can be reinvested. The longer a fund's duration, the more dramatically its trading price will react to interest rate movements. If the average duration of a fund is not available, investors should examine the fund's average maturity. A fund with a long average maturity generally will react more to changing interest rates.

5. **Credit Quality** measures the risk of default among the bonds in a fixed income fund's portfolio. The average weighted credit quality of the bonds is often available, or the fund may state that it invests only in bonds of a minimum credit quality. Aside from risk and return, a number of other variables are relevant to a fund's performance. Many financial publications explain these variables. Two funds can be in the same general category but have distinct investment styles, which can affect their performances.

STATISTICAL FORMULAE

$$\text{Standard Deviation} = \frac{\sqrt{\text{Sum of squares of deviations from mean}}}{\text{No. of deviations}}.$$

$$\text{Coefficient of Determination} = \frac{N(\Sigma XY) - (\Sigma X)(\Sigma Y)}{\sqrt{N(\Sigma X^2) - (\Sigma X^2)}\sqrt{N(\Sigma Y^2) - (\Sigma Y^2)}}$$

A. Ratios Used to Measure Performance

1. **Sharpe Ratio:** One approach is to calculate portfolio's return in excess of the risk-free return and divide the excess return by the portfolio's standard deviation. This risk adjusted return is called, 'Sharpe Ratio'. This ratio measures reward to variability. A fund with higher Sharpe ratio in relation to another is preferable as it indicates that the fund has higher risk premium for every unit of standard deviation risk. Because Sharpe ratio adjusts return to the total portfolio risk, the implicit assumption of the Sharpe measure is that the portfolio will not be combined with any other risky portfolios.

   $$\text{Sharpe Ratio (SR)} = \frac{r_p - r_f}{\sigma_p}.$$

   Here, r_p is the rate of return of a mutual fund, r_f is the risk-free rate, r_m is the market return, s_p is the standard deviation of a mutual fund, β_p is the beta, which indicates the market risk, of a mutual fund.

2. **Treynor Ratio:** The Treynor measure adjusts excess return for systematic risk. It is computed by dividing a portfolio's excess return by its beta as shown in equation. This ratio indicates return per unit of systematic risk, it is a valid performance criterion when one wishes to evaluation a portfolio in combination with the benchmark portfolio and other actively managed portfolios.

   $$\text{Treynor Ratio (TR)} = \frac{r_p - r_f}{\beta_p}.$$

3. **Jensen Ratio:** The Jensen measure is also suitable for evaluating a portfolio's performance in combination with other portfolios because it is based on systematic

risk rather than total risk. The Jensen measure or alpha is usually very close to zero. A positive alpha means that return tends to be higher than expected given the beta statistic. Conversely, a negative alpha indicates that the fund is an underperformer. Alpha measures the value added of the portfolio given its level of systematic risk.

Jensen Ratio (JR)= $\frac{\alpha}{\beta}$.

VARIOUS MODELS USED FOR PERFORMANCE EVALUATION

Jensen Model[4]

Given the additional assumption that the capital market is in equilibrium, all three models yield the following expression for the expected one period return on any security (or portfolio) *j*:

$E(R_j) = R_F + \beta_J[E(R_m) - R_F]$

R_F = the one-period risk-free interest rate.

$\alpha_J = cov(j\, R_J, R_M)/\sigma^2 R_M$ = the measure of risk (hereafter called systematic risk) which the asset pricing model implies is crucial in determining the prices of risky assets.

$E(R_M)$ = the expected one-period return on the "Market Portfolio" which consists of an investment in each asset in the market in proportion to its fraction of the total value of all assets in the market. It implies that the expected return on any asset is equal to the risk-free rate plus a risk premium given by the product of the systematic risk of the asset and the risk premium on the market portfolio.

Fama Model[5]

In Fama's decomposition performance evaluation measure of portfolio, overall performance can be attributed to selectivity and risk. The performance due to selectivity is decomposed into net selectivity and diversification. The difference between actual return and risk-free return indicates overall performance:

$R_p - R_f$ where in,

R_p is actually return on the portfolio, which is monthly average return of fund.

R_f is monthly average return on treasury bills 91-days.

The overall performance further can be bifurcated into performance due to selectivity and risk.

Thus, $R_p - R_f = [\, R_p - R_p(\beta_{p)} + R_p(\beta_{p)} - R_f)]$

In other words, Overall performance = Selectivity + risk.

4. Michael C. Jensen, 'The Performance of Mutual Funds in the Period 1945-1964,' *Journal of Finance,* Vol. 23, 1967, pp. 389-416.
5. Fama Eugene F., 'Components of Investment Performance', *Journal of Finance,* Vol. 27, 1972, pp. 551-567.

Treynor and Mazuy Model[6]

Treynor and Mazuy developed a prudent and exclusive model to measure investment managers' market timing abilities. This formulation is obtained by adding squared extra return in the excess return version of the capital asset pricing model as given below:

$(R_{pt} - R_{ft}) = \alpha + \beta p\ (R_{mt} - R_{ft}) + yp\ (R_{mt} - R_{ft})^2 + e_{pt}$

Where,

R_{pt} is monthly return on the fund.

R_{ft} is monthly return on 91 days treasury bills.

R_{mt} is monthly return on market index.

E_{pt} is error term.

This model involves running a regression with excess investment return as dependent variable and the excess market return and squared excess market return as independent variables. The value of coefficient of squared excess return acts as a measure of market timing abilities that has been tested for significance of using t-test. Significant and positive values provide evidence in support of the investment manager's successful market timing abilities.

Statman Model:[7] Statman measured mutual funds using the following equation: eSDAR (excess Standard Deviation and Adjusted Return) = $R_f + (R_p - R_f)(Sm/Sp) - Rm$

Rf = monthly return on three-month treasury bills

Rp = monthly return on fund portfolio

Rm = monthly return on the benchmark index

Sp = standard deviation of portfolio p's return and

Sm = standard deviation of return on the bench mark index.

This model used for short-term investment analysis. The performrance is compared with it bench mark on monthly basis.

Choi Model[8]

Choi provides a theoretical foundation for an alternative portfolio performance measure that is incentive-compatible. In this model, a risk-averse portfolio manager is delegated to manage a fund, and his portfolio construction (and information-gathering) effort is not directly observable to investors. The fund manager is paid on the basis of the portfolio return that is a function of effort, managerial skill, and organisational factors. In this model, the effect of institutional factors is described by the incentive contractual form and disutility (or cost) function of managerial efforts in fund operations. It focuses on

6. Treynor, Jack L., and Mazuy, Kay K., 'Can Mutual Funds Outguess the Markets', *Harward Business Review,* 1066, Vol. 44, pp. '131-136.
7. Statman M., 'Socially Responsible Mutual Funds', *Financial Analysts Journal,* Vol. 56, 2000, pp. 30-38.
8. Yoon K. Choi, 'Relative Portfolio Performance Evaluation and Incentive Structure', Journal of Business, 2006, Vol.79, No.2, pp. 903-921.

the cost function as an organisational factor (simply, scale factor). It was assumed that the disutility function of each fund is determined by the unique nature of its operation (e.g., fund size) and is an increasing function of managerial effort at an increasing rate.

Elango Model[9]

Elango model is also compares the performance of Public Sector Funds vs. Private Sector Mutual Funds in India. In order to examine the trend in performance of NAV during the study period, growth rate in NAV was computed. The growth rate was computed based on the following formula:

Growth Rate : $Rg = (Y_t - Y_0/Y_0) \times 100$

R_g : Growth rate registered during the current year

Y_1 : Yield in current year

Y_0 : Yield in previous year.

In order to examine whether past is any indicator of future growth in the NAV, six regression analysis were carried out. NAV of base year was considered as the dependent variable and current year as in the independent variable.

Equation: $Y = A + b X$

Dependent variable: Y = NAV of 1999-2000

Independent variable: X = NAV of 2000-01.

In the same way, the second regression equation computed using NAVs of 2000-01 and 2001-02, as dependent and independent variables.

Chang, Hung and Lee Model[10]

The pricing model adopted by Jow-Ran Chang, Nao-Wei Hung and Cheng-Few Lee is based on competitive equilibrium version of intemporal asset pricing model derived in Campbell. His dynamic asset pricing model incorporates hedging risk as well as market. This model uses a loglinear approximation to the budget constraint to substitute out consumption from a standard intertemporal asset pricing model. Therefore, asset risk premia are determined by the covariances of asset returns with the market return and with news about the discounted value of all future market returns. Formally, the pricing restrictions on asset *i* imported by the conditional version of the model are:

$$E_t r_{i',t+1} - rf_{t+1} = -V_{il}/2 + \gamma V_{im} + (\gamma - 1)V_{ih}.$$

9. Elango R., Which Fund Yields More Returns? A Comparative Analysis on the NAV Performance of Select Public vs. Private/Foreign Open-ended Mutual Fund Schemes in India, *Mutual Funds*, 2003.
10. Jow-Ran Chang, Mao-Wei Hung and Cheng-Few Lee, 'An Intemporal CAPM Approach to Evaluate Mutual Fund Performance,' *Review of Quantitative Finance and Accounting*, Vol.No.20, 2003, pp. 414 433.

where:

— $E_t r_i$, $t+1$; log return on asset.

— $r f,t+1$ log return on riskless asset.

— V_{il} denotes Var $t\,(ri,t+1)$,

— γ is the agent's coefficient of relative risk aversion,

— V_{im} denotes $Cov t\,(ri,t+1, rm,t+1)$, and

— $V_{ih} = Cov t\,(ri,t+1, (Et+1 - Et),\_\infty j=1 p j\, rm,t+1+j)$, the parameter: $p = 1 - \exp(c - w)$ and $c - w$ is the mean log consumption to wealth ratio.

This states that the expected excess log return in an asset, adjusted for a Jensen's inequality effect, is a weighted average of two covariances: the covariance with the return from the market portfolio and the covariance with news about future returns on invested wealth. The intuition in this equation that assets are priced using their covariances with the return on invested wealth and future returns on invested wealth.

MM Approach[11]

Leah Modigliani and Franco Modigliani better known as M^2 in the investment literature. This measure is developed adjusting portfolio return. This adjustment is carried on the uncommitted (cash balances) part of the investment portfolio at the riskless return so as to enable all portfolio holdings to participate in the return generation process. This adjustment is needed to bring out the level playing field for portfolio risk-return and *vis-à-vis* market return. The effect of this adjustment is reported below:

M^2 = *Rp – Rm

*Rp = (Rf *(1-Sdm/Sdp)) + (Rp * Sdm/Sdp)

*Rp = Expected return

Rf = Risk-free return

Sdm = Standard deviation of market portfolio

Sdp = Standard deviation of managed portfolio.

In case the managed portfolio has twice the standard deviation of the market, then, the portfolio would be half invested in the managed portfolio and remaining half be invested at the riskless rate. Likewise, in case the managed portfolio has lower standard deviation than the market portfolio, it would be levered by borrowing money and investing the money in managed portfolio. Positive M^2 value indicate superior portfolio performance while the negative indicates actively managed portfolio manager's inability to beat the benchmark portfolio performance.

11. Modigliani, Franco and Modigliani, Leah, "Risk-Adjusted Performance", *Journal of Portfolio Management,* 1997, pp. 45-54.

Overview of Different Measures

Measures	Description	Interpretation
Standard Deviation	Standard Deviation allows us to evaluate the volatility of the fund. The standard deviation of a fund measures this risk by measuring the degree to which the fund fluctuates in relation to its mean return.	Should be near to its mean return.
Beta	Beta is a fairly commonly used measure of risk. It basically indicates the level of volatility associated with the fund as compared to the benchmark.	Beta > 1 = high risky Beta = 1 = average Beta < 1 = low risky
R-Square	R-Square measures the correlation of a fund's movement to that of an index. R-Square describes the level of association between the fund's volatility and market risk.	R-Square values range between 0 and 1, where 0 represents no correlation and 1 represents full correlation.
Alpha	Alpha is the difference between the returns one would expect from a fund, given its beta, and the return actually	Alpha, positive = returns of stock are better then market returns. Alpha, negative = return of stock are worst then market. Alpha, zero = return are same as market.
Sharpe Ratio	Sharpe Ratio = Fund return in excess of risk-fee return/Standard deviation of Fund. Sharpe ratios are ideal for comparing funds that have a mixed asset classes.	The higher the Sharpe ratio, the better a funds return relative to the amount of risk taken.
Treynor Ratio	Treynor Ratio = Fund return in excess of risk-free return/Beta of Fund. Treynor rario indicates relative measures of market risk.	The higher the Treynor ratio shows higher returns and lesser market risk of the fund.
Jensen Measure	This shows relative ratio between alpha and beta.	Jensen measure is based on systematic risk. It is also suitable for evaluating a portfolio's performance in combination with other portfolios.
M^2 Measure	It matches the risk of the market portfolio and then calculate appropriate return for that portfolio.	A high value indicates that the portfolio has outperformed and *vice versa*.
Jensen Model	$E(R_j) = R_F + \beta_J[E(R_m) - R_F]$	The expected one-period return on the 'market porfolio' which consists of an investment in each

		asset in the market in proportion to its fraction of the total value of all asset in the market.
Fama Model	Rp – Rf = [Rp – Rp($\beta_{p)}$ + Rp($\beta_{p)}$ – Rf)]	Overall performance = selectivity+ risk.
Treynor and Mazuy Model	$(R_{pt} - R_{ft}) = \alpha + \beta p\ (R_{mt} - R_{ft}) + \gamma p\ (R_{mt} - R_{ft})^2 + e_{pt}$	This model involves running a regression with excess investment return as dependent variable and the excess market return and squared excess market return as independent variables.
Statman Model	eSDAR = $R_f + (R_p - R_f)$ (Sm/Sp) – Rm	This model used for short-term investment analysis. The performance is compared with it benchmark on monthly basis.
Elango Model	Rg = $(Y_t - Y_0/Y_0) \times 100$	In order to examine whether past is any indicator of future growth in the NAV, six regression analysis were carrried out. NAV of base year was considered as the dependent variable and current year as the independent variable.

PRACTICAL PROBLEMS

1. Find NAV of the fund from the following details relating to a fund's portfolio:

Stock	Shares	Price
A	40,000	70
B	60,000	80
C	80,000	40
D	12,0000	50

The fund manager's expenses are ₹ 60,000. There are 20 lakh shares outstanding. If the fund is sold with a front end load of 5 per cent what is the sales price?

Solution:

Stock	Shares	Price	Value
A	40,000	70	28,00,000
B	60,000	80	48,00,000
C	80,000	40	32,00,000
D	1,20,000	50	6,00,00,000
Total			1,68,00,000

NAV of the Fund = (1,68,00,000 – 60,000)/20,00,000 = 8.37

Sale Price = (NAV 1+ Load %) = 8.37 (1 + 0.05) = 8.7885.

2. Calculate NAV for the following data:

S.No.	Sale Price	Repurchase Price	Entry Load	Exit Load
1	12	-	10%	-
2	-	10.5	-	8%
3	14	11.5	Nil	-
4	13.5	10.5	-	Nil

Solution:

S. No.	Sale Price	Repurchase Price	Entry Load	Exit Load	NAV = Sale Price/(1 + Load %) Or NAV = Repurchase Price/(1 – Load %)
1	12	-	10%	-	12/1.10 =10.90
2	-	10.5	-	8%	10.5/1- 0.08 =11.41
3	14	11.5	Nil	-	14 (sale price)
4	13.5	10.5	-	Nil	10.5 (repurchase price)

CLOSING CASELET

Tata Mutual Fund

Scheme	Bench Mark	Rate of return of the scheme since inception	Benchmark return since inception
Tata Equity Opportunities Fund	SENSEX	13.37%	11.95%
Tata Pure Equity Fund	SENSEX	33.83%	14.62%
Tata Select Equity Fund	SENSEX	22.26%	12.81%
Tata Life Sciences and Technology Fund	SENSEX	24.44%	16.71%
Tata Tax Saving Fund	SENSEX	27.13%	13.62%
Tata Growth Fund	SENSEX	11.02%	9.92%

All the schemes mentioned above listed by Tata Mutual Fund selected 'Sensex' as their benchmark as per their 'portfolio statement' released on 30th April, 2007. However, the rate of return for these schemes with reference to benchmark is same for one year duration (15.19 per cent), three year duration (34.87 per cent) and five year duration (32.94 per cent). It varies with respect to rate of return of the benchmark, since inception for each scheme.

SUMMARY

This lesson deals with the 'Mutual funds', which have become a major vehicle for mobilization of savings particularly from the small and household sectors for investment in the stock market. In view of their growing importance in the capital market, their expanding investor base and the decision to allow mutual fund to be set up in the joint and private sectors it has become necessary to evolve a comprehensive set of prudential guidelines for the all-round development and regulation of mutual funds and for ensuring investor protection. It also focuses types of schemes, different mutual fund options, and performance evaluation of managed funds.

Mutual fund schemes can be offered with any of a range of investment objectives, each corresponding to a certain point in the risk-return matrix. In a broad sense, schemes can be categorized based on tenor, asset class, position philosophy or geography.

KEYWORDS

1. **Balanced Fund:** A fund which invests in equities and fixed income securities so that the risk is minimised and returns are good.
2. **Closed-ended Schemes:** A scheme which is open for subscription for a short period of time and where the period of maturity is specified.
3. **Debt Fund:** Fund which invests in bonds, Govt. securities and other fixed income securities.
4. **Equity Fund:** A Fund which predominatly invests in shares and stocks.
5. **ELSS (Equity Linked Savings Scheme):** A Fund which invests mainly in equities. The investors investing in the fund get income tax exemption under 80C of Income Tax Act.
6. **Gilt Fund:** Funds which invests in Government securities and hence is totally risk-free.
7. **Growth Fund:** Funds which mainly invest in equities so that the investor gets capital appreciation of their investment. They are high risk funds.

REVIEW QUESTIONS

1. Define 'Mutual Funds' and explain various types of schemes.
2. What are the various methods of evaluating performance of mutual funds?
3. Write a brief note on historical evaluation of mutual funds.
4. What are various mutual fund options available to the investors?

REFERENCES

1. E. Gordon & K. Natarajan — *Emerging Scenario of Financial Services*, Himalaya Publishing House, Mumbai.
2. Mutual Funds in India, Marketing Strategies and Investment Practices, H. Sadhak.
3. H.R. Machiraju, *Merchant Banking: Principles and Practice*, New Age International (P) Ltd., New Delhi.
4. S. Guruswamy, *Merchant Banking and Financial Services*, Thomson South-Western.
5. M.Y. Khan, *"Financial Services'*, Tata McGraw-Hill, 3rd Edition, 2005.
6. Machiraju, *'Indian Financial System'*, Vikas Publishing House, 2nd Edition, 2002.
7. J.C. Verma, *'A Manual of Merchant Banking'*, Bharat Publishing House, New Delhi, 2001.
8. Sadhale H., *'Mutual Funds in India'*, Sage, New Delhi.

ꕤ ꕤ ꕤ

CHAPTER

13

STRATEGIES OF GLOBAL CORPORATE GOVERNANCE

CHAPTER OUTLINE

- Introduction
- Review of Literature
- Measures for Good Corporate Governance
- A to Z: A Snapshot View
- Conclusion

INTRODUCTION

Modern corporate governance may be originated from the issues of the Watergate scandal in the USA. It was found that control failures that had allowed several major corporations to make illegal political contributions and bribe Government officials. UK also saw explosive growth in earnings in the eighties ended the decade in a memorably disastrous manner. These corporate failures arose primarily out of poorly managed business practices. In India, regulation of financial sector has evolved as a product of planned development where mobilisation of savings and the corresponding investments are done through public sector at predetermined prices. For instance, Unit Trust of India and the problems it went through, three years ago, and the relief packages which had to be worked out by the Government.

In May 1991, the London Stock Exchange set up a Committee under the chairmanship of Sir Arian Cadbury to help raise the standards of corporate governance and the level of confidence in financial reporting and auditing. The Committee investigated accountability of the Board of Directors to shareholders and to the society. It submitted its report and the associated 'code of best practices' in December 1992. Being a pioneering report on corporate governance, it would perhaps be in order to make a brief reference to its recommendations which are in the nature of guidelines relating to, among other things, the Board of Directors and Reporting & Control. The issue of corporate governance was studied in depth and dealt with by the Confederation of Indian Industries (CII), Associated Chamber of Commerce and Industry (ASSOCHAM) and Securities and Exchange Board of India (SEBI).

REVIEW OF LITERATURE

There is a broader view of corporate governance, which views the subject as the methods by which suppliers of finance control managers in order to ensure that their capital cannot be expropriated and that they earn a return on their investment (Shleifer and Vishny, 1997). Macey and O'Hara (2001) argue that a broader view of corporate governance should be adopted in the case of banking institutions, arguing that because of the peculiar contractual form of banking, corporate governance mechanisms for banks should encapsulate depositors as well as shareholders. The special nature of banking requires not only a broader view of corporate governance, but also government intervention in order to restrain the behaviour of bank management. Depositors do not know the true value of a bank's loan portfolio as such information is incommunicable and very costly to reveal, implying that a bank's loan portfolio is highly fungible (Bhattacharya *et.al.*, 1998). The opaqueness of banks also makes it very costly for depositors to constrain managerial discretion through debt covenants (Capiro and Levine, 2002). Consequently, rational depositors will require some form of guarantee before they would deposit with a bank. Government-provided guarantees in the form of implicit and explicit deposit insurance might encourage economic agents to deposit their wealth with a bank, as a substantial part of the moral hazard cost is borne by the government. Nevertheless, even if the government provides deposit insurance, bank managers still have an incentive to opportunistically increase their risk taking, but now it is mainly at the government's expense. This well-known moral hazard problem can be ameliorated through the use of economic regulations such as asset restrictions, interest rate ceilings and separation of commercial banking from insurance and investment banking, and reserve requirements. Amongst the effects of these regulations is that they limit the ability of bank managers to over-issue liabilities or divert assets into high risk ventures.

The existence of deposit insurance may reduce the need for banks to raise capital from large, uninsured investors who have the incentive to exert corporate control (Capiro and Levine, 2002). Some economists argue that competition in the product or service market may act as a substitute for corporate governance mechanisms (Allen and Gale, 2000). The basic argument is that firms with inferior and expropriating management will be forced out of the market by firms possessing non-expropriating managers due to sheer competitive pressure. However, the banking industry, possibly due to its information-intensive nature, may be a lot less competitive than other business sectors (Caprio and Levine, 2002).

Government ownership of banks is a common feature in many developing economies (La Porta *et.al.*, 2002). The reasons for such ownership may include solving the severe informational problems inherent in developing financial systems, aiding the development process or supporting vested interests and distributional cartels (Arun and Turner, 2002). With a Government-owned bank, the severity of the conflict between depositors and managers very much depends upon the credibility of the government. However, given a credible Government and political stability, there will be little conflict as the government ultimately guarantees deposits. Nevertheless, in economies where there is extensive Government ownership of banks, the main corporate Governance problem is the conflict between the government/taxpayers (as owners) and the managers/bureaucrats who control the bank. The bureaucrats who control government-owned banks may have many different incentives that are not aligned with those of taxpayers. These bureaucrats may maximise a multivariate function which includes, amongst other things, consumption of prerequisites, leisure time and staff numbers. Also, bureaucrats may seek to advance their political careers, by catering to special interest groups, such as trade unions (Shleifer and Vishny, 1997). Furthermore, bureaucrats are by nature risk averse, and will therefore undertake less risk than is optimal from the taxpayers' point of view. In order to partially mitigate such opportunism, bureaucrats may be given little autonomy. In particular, banks may face regulations requiring them to allocate certain proportions of their assets to government securities and various sectors, such as agriculture and SMEs, that are deemed important from a societal viewpoint. However, in the absence of market-provided incentives, the managers of Government-owned banks may still be able to engage in opportunism at the taxpayers' expense through shirking or empire building. Perhaps this is why the Basel Committee on Banking Supervision (1999) argues that 'Government ownership of a bank has the potential to alter the strategies and objectives of the bank as well as the internal structure of governance. Consequently, the general principles of sound corporate governance are also beneficial to government-owned banks'. The inefficiencies associated with Government-owned banks, especially those emanating from a lack of adequate managerial incentives have led developing economy governments to begin divesting their ownership stakes (Arun and Turner, 2002). The divestment of Government-owned banks raises several corporate governance issues. If banks are completely privatised then there must be adequate deposit insurance schemes and supervisory arrangements, established in order to protect depositors and prevent a financial crash (Arun and Turner, 2002). On the other hand, if divestment is partial, then there may be opportunities for the government as the dominant shareholder to expropriate minority shareholders by using banks to aid fiscal problems or support certain distributional cartels.

A further issue, which complicates the corporate governance of banks in developing economies, are the activities of 'distributional cartels' (Oman, 2001). These cartels consist of corporate insiders who have very close links with or partially constitute the governing elite. The existence of such cartels will undermine the credibility of investor legal protection and may also prevent reform of the banking system. Unsurprisingly, good political governance can be considered as a prerequisite for good corporate governance (Oman, 2001). In many transition economies, it has been observed that competition is more important than change in ownership, and, could provide managers with appropriate disciplinary mechanisms (Stiglitiz, 1999). Above, it was suggested that competition might act as a substitute for corporate governance. Nevertheless, in contrast, foreign banks have made little inroads into the developing economies of Asia. Claessens *et.al.*, (2000) suggest that the entrance of foreign banks actually increases the efficiency of the developing economy banking sectors. One possible rationalisation of this finding is that foreign banks bring with them new management techniques, corporate governance mechanisms and information technologies which domestic banks have to adopt in order to effectively compete with their foreign rivals (Peek and Rosengren, 2000). A further benefit from permitting foreign bank entry is that it may result in a more stable banking system. Notably, empirical studies by Demirguc-Kunt (1998) and Levine (1999) suggest that the presence of foreign banks reduces the likelihood of banking crises and may result in banks becoming more prudentially sound.

MEASURES FOR GOOD CORPORATE GOVERNANCE

In developed economies, protection of depositors in a deregulated environment is typically provided by a system of prudential regulation, but in developing economies such protection is undermined by the lack of well-trained supervisors, inadequate disclosure requirements, the cost of raising capital and the presence of distributional cartels. In order to deal with these problems, it was suggested that developing economies need to adopt the following measures.

Firstly, liberalisation policies need to be gradual, and should be dependent upon improvements in prudential regulation. Secondly, developing economies need to expend resources enhancing the quality of their financial reporting systems. Thirdly, given that capital plays such an important role in prudential regulatory systems, it may be necessary to improve investor protection laws, increase financial disclosure and impose fiduciary duties upon directors so that firms can raise the equity capital required for regulatory purposes.

A further reason as to why this policy needs implemented is the growing recognition that the corporate governance has an important role to play in assisting supervisory institutions to perform their tasks, allowing supervisors to have a working relationship with bank management, rather than adversarial one. It was suggested that the corporate governance in developing economies is severely affected by political considerations. Firstly, given the trend towards privatisation of government-owned firms in developing economies, there is a need for the managers of such firms to be granted autonomy and be gradually introduced to the corporate governance practices of the private sector prior to divestment. Secondly, where there has only been partial divestment and governments have not relinquished any control to other shareholders, it may prove very difficult to divest further ownership stakes unless corporate governance is strengthened. Finally, given that limited entry of foreign firm may lead to increased competition, which in turn encourages domestic banks to emulate the corporate governance practices of their foreign competitors.

A TO Z: A SNAPSHOT VIEW

1. AUSTRALIA

There are approximately 1,500 public companies listed on the Australian Stock Exchange (ASX) and other public non-listed corporate entities. Australian listed companies generally have a unitary board structure with a balance of executive and non-executive directors and a separate chief executive and chairman. The ASX Corporate Governance Council acts as a central reference point for companies to understand stakeholder expectations. In order to promote and restore investor confidence, ASX convened the ASX Corporate Governance Council in August 2002. Its purpose is to develop recommendations which reflect international best practice. Australia operates under a common law system that entails courts interpreting legislation in particular factual circumstances to develop a body of precedent or common law. Judges interpret previous cases in Australia, and increasingly from overseas, in constant process of review and adaptation. The following enactments will govern the corporate governance in Australia.

- **The Corporate Law Reform Program Act, 1999:** It introduced a statutory business judgement rule, rewrote many of the revisions about director's duties, revolutionised the rules on take-overs and fund-raising, and clarified some issues about accounting standards and the rules generated by accounting standards setting bodies.

- **The Financial Service Reforms Act, 2000:** Introduced standardised regulation for all people and companies that deal in financial products or that give investment advice.
- **The Corporate Law Simplifications Act, 1995:** Amongst many other reforms, provided for a new form of company in Australia, the one person company consisting of one director and one shareholder with the aim of providing greater flexibility for small business to incorporate in Australia.

2. BHUTAN

Bhutan is the one of the most isolated and least developed nations in the world. Foreign influences and tourism are heavily regulated by the government to preserve the country's traditional culture and national identity. Though Bhutan's economy is one of the world's smallest, it has grown very rapidly with about 8 per cent in 2005 and 15 per cent in 2006. This was mainly due to the commissioning of the gigantic Tata Hydroelectricity project. A landscape that varies from hilly to ruggedly mountainous has made the building of roads, and other infrastructure difficult and expensive. This, and a lack of access to the sea, has meant that Bhutan has not been able to benefit and significant trading of its produce. The industrial sector is in a nascent stage, and though most production is cottage-industry type larger industries are being encouraged. Indo-Bhutan Friendship Treaty states that the government of the Kingdom of Bhutan and the government of the Republic of India shall cooperate closely with each other on issues relating to their national interests. The Indo-Bhutan Friendship Treaty of 2007 strengthens Bhutan's status as an independent and sovereign nation. Hence, corporate governance in Bhutan is at developing stage.

3. CANADA

Canada is originally inhabited by various Native American people, mainland Canada was explored by the English and the French. A major problem for Canada is that large segments of its economy-notably in manufacturing, petroleum and mining— are controlled by foreign, especially US interests. This deprives the nation of much of the profits of its industries and makes the economy vulnerable to development outside Canada. This situation is mitigated somewhat by the fact that Canada itself is a large foreign interest.

4. DENMARK

In Denmark, the debate on corporate governance really gathered momentum following the publication of *'The Nørby Committee's Report on Corporate Governance in Denmark – Recommendations for Corporate Governance in Denmark'* in December 2001. This meant that Denmark joined the large group of countries with a voluntary (i.e., not legally binding) code of conduct for what may be regarded as corporate governance. Prior to the publication of the Nørby Committee's report, the extensive international debate on corporate governance had caused organisations, stock exchanges, etc., in a number of countries to adopt codes of conduct. On the basis of the framework laid down in the Nørby Committee's report, including its recommendations for corporate governance that the Copenhagen Stock Exchange recommends listed companies to address in their annual reports, the Committee was also charged with:

(a) Monitoring the development of the requirements generally governing corporate governance;

(b) Collecting the companies' views and experience existing in relation to their work on the recommendations; and

(c) Assessing the need for revising the Nørby Committee's recommendations for corporate governance.

5. ENGLAND

The main corporate entities are the private limited company (private company) and the public limited company (public company). A Societas Europaea (SE) can also be registered in the UK. Most legal requirements for directors apply equally to private and public companies. Corporate governance codes and best practice apply mainly to public companies admitted to listing by the UK Listing Authority (UKLA), which is part of the Financial Services Authority (FSA) (listed companies). Corporate governance and directors' duties are regulated by: Case law, Statute, notably the Companies Act, 1985; a company's constitution, namely the memorandum and the articles of association (articles); the Listing, Prospectus and Disclosure Rules published by the UKLA. The Listing Rules apply to all companies, and their sponsors that are listed or are applying to list, on the London Stock Exchange (LSE). The Disclosure Rules apply to all companies listed on the LSE. The Prospectus Rules implement Directive 2003/71/EC on the prospectus to be published when securities are offered to the public or admitted to trading and set out when a prospectus is required. The Prospectus Rules apply to any public offer of transferable securities in the EU or for the admission of these securities to trading on an EU regulated market. In the UK this includes companies listed, or applying to list, on the LSE (but not on the Alternative Investment Market (AIM)). The Combined Code on Corporate Governance (Combined Code) applies to listed companies. Its provisions are not mandatory. However, companies should include a statement in their annual report indicating that they comply with the Combined Code and how they do this, or state that they do not comply and give reasons for this. AIM companies are also encouraged by institutional investors to adhere to the Combined Code. The Quoted Companies Alliance published a set of corporate governance guidelines for AIM companies. They are intended as a minimum standard and comprise some simple principles and recommendations for reporting corporate governance matters. Guidelines issued by bodies that represent institutional investors. These apply to listed companies and, in some respects, go further than the Combined Code. Although the guidelines are informal, institutional investors can oppose any corporate actions that contravene them. (Institutional investors, such as pension funds and insurance companies, own the vast majority of shares in UK listed companies). In the context of take-overs of public companies, the City Code on Take-overs and Mergers and rules of the Takeover Panel (Takeover Code). The Financial Services and Markets Act, 2000 (FSMA) and the FSA's Code of Market Conduct which regulates, for listed companies: the disclosure and use of confidential and price-sensitive information; and actions that could create a false market. The FSA's Disclosure Rules which regulate, for listed companies, public disclosure of confidential and price-sensitive information concerning the company. The Disclosure Rules also require transactions in shares or related securities in the issuer to be notified by directors persons discharging management responsibilities and connected persons.

6. FRANCE

The French Government has chosen to stipulate a legal 'minimum service' for corporate governance. In fact, the preparatory work for these laws (the Viénot reports in 1995 and 1999 and the Bouton report in 2002) helped to define the principles of corporate governance more precisely and completely, particularly as regards the role and structure of the Board of Directors. For example, these reports shed a great deal of new light on sensitive subjects:

(a) Issues relating to the balance of power within the Board of Directors, such as, for example, the presence of independent directors;

(b) The quality of directors and of the work of the Board: selection of directors, committees, etc.

(c) Evaluation of the Board of Directors;

(d) Communications on items not included in the balance sheet, and on the company's risks.

Two new laws have recently been passed in France with a view to strengthening the legal position on corporate governance: the NRE law (on new economic regulations) dated 15 May 2001, and the LSF, dated 1 August 2003. These laws provide the basic framework, specifically targeting transparency and ethics within companies. The regulations include the following:

- Companies whose shares are traded on a regulated market, and any of their subsidiaries, are obliged to publish details of executive pay;
- Publicity on stock options;
- The expansion of the approval procedure for related parties transactions;
- The management committee can intervene in the context of a public offering, and participate in general meetings;
- New limitations on the number of executive mandates for limited companies that can be held by one person;
- Publicity on shareholder agreements;

- The audit profession can no longer be self-regulated, and audit and consulting activities must be kept separate;
- The shares of limited companies and firms which are traded on a public market must draw up a report on the conditions governing the preparation and organisation of the work of the Board of Directors and of internal controls procedures;
- Recognition of the right for registered shareholders' associations to bring legal cases;
- In the case of a scrip issue, a portion must be set aside for employees.

7. GERMANY

The German corporate governance system is different from that of the Anglo-Saxon countries because it foresees the possibility, and even the necessity, to integrate lenders and employees in the governance of large corporations. The German corporate governance system is generally regarded as the standard example of an insider-controlled and stakeholder-oriented system. Moreover, only a few years ago, it was a consistent system in the sense of being composed of complementary elements which fit together well. The first objective of this paper is to show why and in which respect these characterisations were once appropriate. However, the past decade has seen a wave of developments in the German corporate governance system, which makes it worthwhile and indeed necessary to investigate whether German corporate governance has recently changed in a fundamental way.

The German corporate governance system is generally regarded as the standard example of what Franks and Mayer (1994) have called an insider-controlled and stakeholder-oriented system. Moreover, only a few years ago, the German corporate governance system was a consistent system in the sense of being composed of complementary elements which fit together well. The first objective of this paper is to show why and in which respect these characterisations were once appropriate. Today, however, it may no longer be appropriate to characterise German corporate governance in this way. It is worthwhile and indeed necessary to investigate whether German corporate governance has recently changed in a fundamental way. More specifically, one can ask which elements and features of German corporate governance have in fact changed, why they have changed and whether those changes which did occur constitute a structural change which have transformed the old insider-controlled system into an outsider-controlled and shareholder-oriented system, or have at least deprived the system of its former consistency.

8. HUNGARY

Hungary is small, middle income economy with a remarkable degree of integration into the world economy. The country's savings, however, are not sufficient for a catching-up growth, thus, it must fiercely compete for foreign direct investment. Under these conditions, it is obvious that she cannot risk the divergence with international trends. She has no choice but to follow international standards in all important fields including updated CG practices. Being a member of the European Union since 1 May 2004, she has to adjust to the European benchmark in the first place. Thus, new CG legal regulations and codes of conduct have been imported from the European Union extensively. Both a successfully completed transition from plan to market and the accession to the EU would have been impossible without creating a proper legal environment. Hungary's accomplishments in this field are unanimously acknowledged. There is, however, a gap between laws on the books (law extensiveness) on the one hand, and law enforcement (law effectiveness) and the real working of the economy on the other.

Hungarian civil law is German in legal origin. By the analysis of La Porta *et.al.*, (1997), this fact would suggest that the chances are not very good for investors' rights being particularly strongly protected by the laws. The sample used by La Porta *et.al.*, (1997) and La Porta *et.al.*, (1998) contained six German legal origin countries (Germany, Switzerland, Austria, Japan, South Korea, Taiwan). (The other three groups included common law-origin, French-origin, and Scandinavian-origin countries.) The general result was that outside investors' rights are best protected in common law countries, though German-origin countries perform relatively well in protecting creditors' rights. Among transition economies, Pistor (2000), identifies many other German-origin countries, such as Croatia, the Czech Republic, Estonia, Latvia, Lithuania, Poland, the Slovak Republic and Slovenia.

9. INDIA

The corporate governance of financial institutions in developing economies is important for several reasons. First, banks have an overwhelmingly dominant position in developing-economy financial systems, and are extremely important engines of economic growth (King and Levine 1993a,b; Levine 1997). Second, as financial markets are usually underdeveloped, banks in developing economies are typically the most important source of finance for the majority of firms,. Third, as well as providing a generally accepted means of payment, banks in developing countries are usually the main depository for the economy's savings. Fourth, many developing economies have recently liberalised their banking systems through privatisation/disinvestments and reducing the role of economic regulation. Consequently, managers of banks in these economies have obtained greater freedom in how they run their banks. The Reserve Bank of India (RBI) has asked all listed commercial banks to follow SEBI's committee report on corporate governance. Some of the important recommendations of the SEBI committee on corporate governance that will henceforth be applicable to listed commercial banks include, that all pecuniary relationship or transactions of the non-executive directors should be disclosed in the annual report. The committee has suggested that emphasis must be laid on the caliber of the non-executive directors, especially independent directors, since non-executive directors help bring an independent judgement to bear on the boards deliberations, especially on issues of strategy, performance, management of conflicts and standards of conduct. It has been recommended that the board of the company have an optimum combination of executive and non-executive directors with not less than 50 per cent of the board comprising the non-executive directors. The number of independent directors depends on the nature of the chairman of the board. In case, a company has a non-executive chairman, at least half of the board should be independent (mandatory recommendation).

According to the RBI circular, the audit committee of the board may look into the reasons for default in payment to depositors, debentureholders, shareholders (non-payment of dividends) and creditors, wherever there are any cases of defaults in payment. Before deregulating banking systems, much attention will need to be paid to the speedy implementation of robust corporate governance mechanisms in order to protect shareholders. The introduction of sound corporate governance principles into banking has been partially hampered by poor legal protection, weak information disclosure requirements and dominant owners. Furthermore, in many developing countries, the private banking sector is not enthusiastic to introduce corporate governance principles. For example, in India, this problem can be summarised in the corporate sector as the privileging of the interests of one group over all other interests in a company.

10. NEW ZELAND

The New Zealand corporate governance system is relatively unusual by international standards in a number of respects. First, unlike the financial systems of many countries, in New Zealand the banks form a very dominant part of the financial sector. Registered banks, of which there are currently 18, represent the lion's share of the total financial system, both in terms of total financial system assets and deposit liabilities. In terms of financial system stability, registered banks are by far the most important players in the financial system. And of the 18 registered banks, only about 5 banks could be regarded as systemically important, together holding more than 80% of total registered bank assets. The New Zealand approach is an effective way of promoting a sound financial system. It reduces the moral hazard risks associated with conventional banking supervision, and strengthens the effectiveness of market discipline on banks. New Zealand's approach to financial sector regulation seeks to create an environment conducive to robust market disciplines. This is achieved through a number of measures, including the promotion of a relatively open, contestable banking sector, a competitively neutral approach to regulation — enabling banks and non-banks to compete on largely equal terms - and the absence of deposit insurance. In addition, the Reserve Bank's approach to responding to a bank failure stresses the importance of being able to manage a bank failure in ways that avoid the need for a government-funded bail-out, and seeks to ensure that shareholders, subordinated creditors and senior creditors, including depositors, bear their fair share of losses.

11. SCOTLAND

The Scottish Parliament has legislative authority for all other areas relating to Scotland and has limited power to vary income-tax but has never exercised this power.

Scottish Parliament can defer devolved matters back to Westminister to be considered as part of United Kingdom-wise legislation by passing a legislative by passing a legislative consent motion if UK-wise legislation is considered to be more appropriate for certain issues. The programmes of legislation enacted by the Scottish Parliament have been a divergence in the provision of public services compared to the next of United Kingdom.

12. UAE

The United Arab Emirates (UAE) is a middle eastern federation of seven states which are termed as emirates, *viz.*, Abu Dhabi, Ajman, Dubai, Fujairah, Ras Al-Khaiman, Sharjah and Ummalquwain. UAE is rich in oil and it expects recent additional economic diversification to draw more financial and banking firms. The GDP per capita is curreny third in the world, while at $168 billion in 2006. The presidency and premiership of UAE is hereditary to Al Nahyan clan of Abu Dhabi and Al Makotum clan of Dubai respectively. The supreme council will be consisting of the rulers of the seven emirates. Petroleum and natural gas exports till play an important role in the economy, especially in Abu Dhabi. A massive construction boom, an expanding manufacturing base, and a thriving service sector are helping the UAE. At present, $350 billion worth of active construction projects are undertaken by UAE. Third place goes to tourism industry.

CONCLUSION

Corporate governance in banking sector is being implemented under the guidance and regulations of SEBI and RBI. Indian financial markets are a facing some problems while implementing corporate governance. Since most of corporate entities in India are protected by the government rules and regulations, the employees are also somewhat negligent towards implementation of corporate governance. However, now all public sector firms are facing severe competition from private sector. In this context, the implementation of corporate governance in a systematic and strategic manner is becoming the need of the hour.

In developed economies, protection of depositors in a deregulated environment is typically provided by a system of prudential regulation, but in developing economies such protection is undermined by the lack of well-trained supervisors, inadequate disclosure requirements, the cost of raising capital and the presence of distributional cartels. This paper gives awareness of corporate governance practices in Australia, Canada, New Zealand, Iceland, India, Scotland and UAE.

ꕥ ꕥ ꕥ

CHAPTER

14

Regulatory Mechanism for Mergers and Acquisitions

CHAPTER OUTLINE

- Scheme of Merger/Amalgamation
- Procedure for Amalgamation
- Conclusion
- Closing Caselet
- Summary

Laws Regulating Merger: Following are the laws that regulate the merger of the company:

(I) The Companies Act, 1956: Section 390 to 395 of Companies Act, 1956, deal with arrangements, amalgamations, mergers and the procedure to be followed for getting the arrangement, compramise or the scheme of amalgamation approved. Though, section 391 deals with the issue of compromise or arrangement which is different from the issue of amalgamation as deal with under section 394, as section 394 too refers to the procedure under section 391 etc., all the section are to be seen together while understanding the procedure of getting the scheme of amalgamation approved. Again, it is true that while the procedure to be followed in case of amalgamation of two companies is wider than the scheme of compromise or arrangement though there exist substantial overlapping.

The procedure to be followed, while getting the scheme of amalgamation and the important points, are as follows:

(1) Any company, creditors of the company, class of them, members or the class of members can file an application under section 391, seeking sanction of any scheme of compromise or arrangement. However, by its very nature it can be understood that the scheme of amalgamation is normally presented by the company. While filing an application either under section 391 or section 394, the applicant is supposed to disclose all material particulars in accordance with the provisions of the Act.

(2) Upon satisfying that the scheme is prima facie workable and fair, the Tribunal order for the meeting of the members, class of members, creditors or the class of creditors. Rather, passing an order calling for meeting, if the requirements of holding meetings with class of shareholders or the members, are specifically dealt with in the order calling meeting, then, there won't be any subsequent litigation. The scope of conduct of meeting with such class of members or the shareholders is wider in case of amalgamation than where a scheme of compromise or arrangement is sought for under section 391.

(3) The scheme must get approved by the majority of the stake holders, *viz.*, the members, class of members, creditors or such class of creditors. The scope of conduct of meeting with the members, class of members, creditors or such class of creditors will be restrictive some what in an application seeking compromise or arrangement.

(4) There should be due notice disclosing all material particulars and annexing the copy of the scheme as the case may be while calling the meeting.

(5) In a case where amalgamation of two companies is sought for, before approving the scheme of amalgamation, a report is to be received form the registrar of companies that the approval of scheme will not prejudice the interests of the shareholders.

(6) The Central Government is also required to file its report in an application seeking approval of compromise, arrangement or the amalgamation as the case may be under section 394A.

(7) After complying with all the requirements, if the scheme is approved, then, the certified copy of the order is to be filed with the concerned authorities.

(II) The Competition Act, 2002: Following provisions of the Competition Act, 2002, deals with mergers of the company:

(1) Section 5 of the Competition Act, 2002, deals with 'Combinations' which defines combination by reference to assets and turnover

(a) exclusively in India and

(b) in India and outside India.

For example, an Indian company with turnover of ₹ 3,000 crores cannot acquire another Indian company without prior notification and approval of the Competition Commission. On the other hand, a foreign company with turnover outside India of more than USD 1.5 billion (or in excess of ₹ 4,500 crores) may acquire a company in India with sales just short of ₹ 1,500 crores without any notification to (or approval of) the Competition Commission being required.

(2) Section 6 of the Competition Act, 2002, states that, no person or enterprise shall enter into a combination which causes or is likely to cause an appreciable adverse effect on competition within the relevant market in India and such a combination shall be void.

All types of intra-group combinations, mergers, demergers, reorganizations and other similar transactions should be specifically exempted from the notification procedure and appropriate clauses should be incorporated in sub-regulation 5(2) of the Regulations. These transactions do not have any competitive impact on the market for assessment under the Competition Act, Section 6.

(III) Foreign Exchange Management Act, 1999: The foreign exchange laws relating to issuance and allotment of shares to foreign entities are contained in The Foreign Exchange Management (Transfer or Issue of Security by a person residing out of India) Regulation, 2000, issued by RBI *vide* GSR no. 406(E) dated 3rd May, 2000. These regulations provide general guidelines on issuance of shares or securities by an Indian entity to a person residing outside India or recording in its books any transfer of security from or to such person. RBI has issued detailed guidelines on foreign investment in India vide 'Foreign Direct Investment Scheme' contained in Schedule 1 of said regulation.

(IV) SEBI Take Over Code 1994: SEBI Takeover Regulations permit consolidation of shares or voting rights beyond 15 per cent up to 55 per cent, provided the acquirer does not acquire more than 5 per cent of shares or voting rights of the target company in any financial year. [Regulation 11(1) of the SEBI Takeover Regulations] However, acquisition of shares or voting rights beyond 26 per cent would apparently attract the notification procedure under the Act. It should be clarified that notification to CCI will not be required for consolidation of shares or voting rights permitted under the SEBI Takeover Regulations. Similarly the acquirer who has already acquired control of a company (say a listed company), after adhering to all requirements of SEBI Takeover Regulations and also the Act, should be exempted from the Act for further acquisition of shares or voting rights in the same company.

(V) The Indian Income Tax Act (ITA), 1961: Merger has not been defined under the ITA but has been covered under the term 'amalgamation' as defined in section 2(1B) of the Act. To encourage restructuring, merger and demerger has been given a special treatment in the Income Tax Act since the beginning. The Finance Act, 1999, clarified many issues relating to Business Reorganisations thereby facilitating and making business restructuring tax neutral. As per Finance Minister this has been done to accelerate internal liberalisation. Certain provisions applicable to mergers/demergers are as under: Definition of Amalgamation/Merger - Section 2(1B). Amalgamation means merger of either one or more companies with another company or merger of two or more companies to form one company in such a manner that:

(1) All the properties and liabilities of the transferor company/companies become the properties and liabilities of Transferee Company.

(2) Shareholders holding not less than 75 per cent of the value of shares in the transferor company (other than shares which are held by, or by a nominee for, the transferee company or its subsidiaries) become shareholders of the transferee company.

The following provisions would be applicable to merger only if the conditions laid down in section 2(1B) relating to merger are fulfilled:

(1) Taxability in the hands of Transferee Company - Section 47(vi) & section 47

(a) The transfer of shares by the shareholders of the transferor company in lieu of shares of the transferee company on merger is not regarded as transfer and hence gains arising from the same are not chargeable to tax in the hands of the shareholders of the transferee company. [Section 47(vii)]

(b) In case of merger, cost of acquisition of shares of the transferee company, which were acquired in pursuant to merger will be the cost incurred for acquiring the shares of the transferor company. [Section 49(2)]

(VI) Mandatory Permission by the Courts: Any scheme for mergers has to be sanctioned by the courts of the country. The company act provides that the high court of the respective states where the transferor and the transferee companies have their respective registered offices have the necessary jurisdiction to direct the winding up or regulate the merger of the companies registered in or outside India.

The high courts can also supervise any arrangements or modifications in the arrangements after having sanctioned the scheme of mergers as per the section 392 of the Company Act. Thereafter the courts would issue the necessary sanctions for the scheme of mergers after dealing with the application for the merger if they are convinced that the impending merger is 'fair and reasonable'.

The courts also have a certain limit to their powers to exercise their jurisdiction which have essentially evolved from their own rulings. For example, the courts will not allow the merger to come through the intervention of the courts, if the same can be effected through some other provisions of the Companies Act; further, the courts cannot allow for the merger to proceed if there was something that the parties themselves could not agree to; also, if the merger, if allowed, would be in contravention of certain conditions laid down by the law, such a merger also cannot be permitted. The courts have no special jurisdiction with regard to the issuance of writs to entertain an appeal over a matter that is otherwise 'final, conclusive and binding' as per the section 391 of the Company act.

(VII) Stamp Duty: Stamp Act varies from State to State. As per Bombay Stamp Act, conveyance includes an order in respect of amalgamation; by which property is transferred to or vested in any other person. As per this Act, rate of stamp duty is 10 per cent.

Intellectual Property Due Diligence in Mergers and Acquisitions: The increased profile, frequency, and value of intellectual property related transactions have elevated the need for all legal and financial professionals and Intellectual Property (IP) owner to have thorough understanding of the assessment and the valuation of these assets, and their role in commercial transaction. A detailed assessment of intellectual property asset is becoming an increasingly integrated part of commercial transaction. Due diligence is the process of investigating a party's ownership, right to use, and right to stop others from using the IP rights involved in sale or merger — the nature of transaction and the rights being acquired will determine the extent and focus of the due diligence review. Due Diligence in IP for valuation would help in building strategy, where in:

(a) If Intellectual Property asset is underplayed the plans for maximisation would be discussed.

(b) If the Trademark has been maximised to the point that it has lost its cachet in the market place, reclaiming may be considered.

(c) If mark is undergoing generalisation and is becoming generic, reclaiming the mark from slipping to generic status would need to be considered.

(d) Certain events can devalue an Intellectual Property Asset, in the same way a fire can suddenly destroy a piece of real property. These sudden events in respect of IP could be adverse publicity or personal injury arising from a product. An essential part of the due diligence and valuation process accounts for the impact of product and company-related events on assets - management can use risk information revealed in the due diligence.

(e) Due diligence could highlight contingent risk, which do not always arise from Intellectual Property law itself but may be significantly affected by product liability and contract law and other non Intellectual Property realms.

Therefore Intellectual Property due diligence and valuation can be correlated with the overall legal due diligence to provide an accurate conclusion regarding the asset present and future value.

Legal Procedure for Bringing about Merger of Companies:

(1) **Examination of object clauses:** The MOA of both the companies should be examined to check the power to amalgamate is available. Further, the object clause of the merging company should permit it to carry on the business of the merged company. If such clauses do not exist, necessary approvals of the share holders, board of directors, and company law board are required.

(2) **Intimation to stock exchanges:** The stock exchanges where merging and merged companies are listed should be informed about the merger proposal. From time to time, copies of all notices, resolutions, and orders should be mailed to the concerned stock exchanges.

(3) **Approval of the draft merger proposal by the respective boards:** The draft merger proposal should be approved by the respective BOD's. The board of each company should pass a resolution authorizing its directors/executives to pursue the matter further.

(4) **Application to high courts:** Once the drafts of merger proposal is approved by the respective boards, each company should make an application to the high court of the state where its registered office is situated, so that it can convene the meetings of shareholders and creditors for passing the merger proposal.

(5) **Dispatch of notice to shareholders and creditors:** In order to convene the meetings of shareholders and creditors, a notice and an explanatory statement of the meeting, as approved by the high court, should be dispatched by each company to its shareholders and creditors so that they get 21 days advance intimation. The notice of the meetings should also be published in two newspapers.

(6) **Holding of meetings of shareholders and creditors:** A meeting of shareholders should be held by each company for passing the scheme of mergers at least 75 per cent of shareholders who vote either in person or by proxy must approve the scheme of merger. Same applies to creditors also.

(7) **Petition to high court for confirmation and passing of HC orders:** Once the mergers scheme is passed by the share holders and creditors, the companies involved in the merger should present a petition to the HC for confirming the scheme of merger. A notice about the same has to be published in 2 newspapers.

(8) **Filing the order with the Registrar:** Certified true copies of the high court order must be filed with the Registrar of Companies within the time limit specified by the court.

(9) **Transfer of assets and liabilities:** After the final orders have been passed by both the HC's, all the assets and liabilities of the merged company will have to be transferred to the merging company.

(10) Issue of shares and debentures: The merging company, after fulfilling the provisions of the law, should issue shares and debentures of the merging company. The new shares and debentures so issued will then be listed on the stock exchange.

Waiting Period in Merger: International experience shows that 80-85 per cent of mergers and acquisitions do not raise competitive concerns and are generally approved between 30-60 days. The rest tend to take longer time and, therefore, laws permit sufficient time for looking into complex cases. The International Competition Network, an association of global competition authorities, had recommended that the straight forward cases should be dealt with within six weeks and complex cases within six months.

The Indian competition law prescribes a maximum of 210 days for determination of combination, which includes mergers, amalgamations, acquisitions etc. This however should not be read as the minimum period of compulsory wait for parties who will notify the Competition Commission. In fact, the law clearly states that the compulsory wait period is either 210 days from the filing of the notice or the order of the Commission, which ever is earlier. In the event the Commission approves a proposed combination on the 30th day, it can take effect on the 31st day. The internal time limits within the overall gap of 210 days are proposed to be built in the regulations that the Commission will be drafting, so that the over whelming proportion of mergers would receive approval within a much shorter period.

The time lines prescribed under the Act and the Regulations do not take cognizance of the compliances to be observed under other statutory provisions like the SEBI (Substantial Acquisition of Shares and Takeovers) Regulations, 1997 ('SEBI Takeover Regulations'). SEBI Takeover Regulations require the acquirer to complete all procedures relating to the public offer including payment of consideration to the shareholders who have accepted the offer, within 90 days from the date of public announcement. Similarly, mergers and amalgamations get completed generally in 3-4 months' time. Failure to make payments to the shareholders in the public offer within the time stipulated in the SEBI Takeover Regulations entails payment of interest by the acquirer at a rate as may be specified by SEBI. [Regulation 22(12) of the SEBI Takeover Regulations] It would therefore be essential that the maximum turn around time for CCI should be reduced from 210 days to 90 days.

SCHEME OF MERGER/AMALGAMATION

Wherever two/more companies agree to merge with each other, they have to prepare a scheme of amalgamation. The acquiring company should prepare the scheme in consultation with its merchant banker(s)/financial consultants. The main contents of a model scheme, inter-alia, are as listed below.

- Description of the transfer and the transferee company and the business of the transferor.

- Their authorized, issued and subscribed/paid-up capital.
- Basis of scheme: Main terms of the scheme in selfcontained paragraphs on the recommendation of valuation report, covering transfer of assets/liabilities, transfer date, reduction or consolidation of capital, application to financial institutions as lead institution for permission and so on.
- Change of name, object clause and accounting year.
- Protection of employment.
- Dividend position and prospects.
- Management: Board of directors, their number and participation of transferee company's directors on the board.
- Application under section 291 and 394 of the Companies Act, 1956 to obtain Higher Court's approval.
- Expenses of amalgamation.
- Conditions of the scheme to become effective and operative, effective date of amalgamation.

The basis of merger/amalgamation in the scheme should be the reports of the valuers of assets of both the merger partner companies. The scheme should be prepared on the basis of the valuer's report, reports of chartered accountants engaged for financial analysis and fixation of exchange ratio, report of auditors and audited accounts of both the companies prepared up to the appointed date. It should be ensured that the scheme is just and equitable to the shareholders, employees of each of the amalgamating company and to the public.

Essential Features of Scheme of Amalgamation: The essential features or pre-requisites for any scheme of amalgamation are as enumerated below.

Determination of Transfer Date (Appointed Date): This involves fixing of the cut-off date from which all properties, movable as well as immovable and rights attached thereto are sought to be transferred from amalgamating company to the amalgamated company. This date is known as transfer date or the appointed date and is normally the first day of the financial year preceding the financial year for which the audited accounts are available with the company.

Determination of Effective Date: By when all the required approvals under various statutes, *viz.*, the Companies Act 1956. The Companies (Court) Rules 1959, Income Tax Act, 1961. Sick Industrial Companies (Special Provisions) Act, 1985, would be obtained and the transfer and vesting of the undertaking of amalgamating company with the amalgamated company would take effect. This date is called effective date. A scheme of amalgamation normally should also contain conditions to be satisfied for the scheme to become effective. The effective date is important for income tax purposes the Companies Act does not provide for such a date but it is a practical necessity so that a court passing an order under Section 394(2) dealing with vesting of properties in the transferee company has before it a meaningful date contained in the scheme serving the purpose and in the contemplation of the applicant companies who are free to choose any date which will be binding one. While sanctioning the scheme the court also approves this date. The effective date may be either retrospective or prospective with reference to the application to the court. The effect of the requirement is that a mere order for the transfer of the properties/ assets and liabilities to the transferee company would cause the vesting only from the date of that order. For tax considerations, the mention in the order of the date of vesting is of material consequences.

(i) The scheme should state clearly the arrangements with secured and unsecured creditors including the debentureholders.

(ii) It should also state the exchange ratio, at which the shareholders of the amalgamating company would be offered shares in the amalgamated company. The ratio has to be worked out based on the valuation of shares of the respective companies as per the accepted methods of valuation, guidelines and the audited accounts of the company.

(iii) The scheme should also provide for transfer of whole or part of the undertaking to the amalgamated company, continuation of level proceedings between the amalgamating and the amalgamated companies, absorption of employees of the amalgamating company, obtaining the consent of dissenting shareholders and so on.

Approvals for the Scheme: The scheme of merger/amalgamation is governed by the provisions of section 391-394 of the Companies Act. The legal process requires approval to the schemes as detailed below.

Approvals from Shareholders: In terms of section 391, shareholders of both the amalgamating and the amalgamated companies should hold their respective meetings under the directions of the respective high courts and consider the scheme of amalgamation. A separate meeting of both preference and equity share holders should be convened for this purpose. further, in terms of section 81(1A), the shareholders of the amalgamated company are required to pass a special resolution for issue of shares to the shareholders of the amalgamating company in terms of the scheme of amalgamation.

Approval from Creditors/Financial Institutions/Banks:

Approvals are required from the creditors, banks and financial institutions to the scheme of amalgamation in terms of their respective agreements/arrangements with each of the amalgamating and the amalgamated companies as also under section 391.

Approval from Respective High Court(s): Approvals of the respective high court(s) in terms of section 391-394, confirming the scheme of amalgamation are required. The courts issue orders for dissolving the amalgamating company without winding-up on receipt of the reports from the official liquidator and the regional director, Company Law Board, that the affairs of the amalgamating company have not been conducted in a manner prejudicial to the interests of its members or to public interests.

PROCEDURE FOR AMALGAMATION

Object Clause: The first step is to examine the objects clauses of the memorandum of association of the transferor and the transferee companies so as to ascertain whether the power of amalgamation exists or not. The objects clause of transferee company should allow for carrying on the business of the transferor company. If it is not so, it is necessary to amend the objects clause. Similarly, it should be ascertained whether the authorized capital of the transferee company would be sufficient after the merger/amalgamation. If is not so, this clause should also be amended. Suitable provisions for these could be incorporated in the scheme itself.

Meetings/Information

(i) Holding of meeting of the board of directors of both the transferor and the transferee companies (a) to decide the appointed date and the effective date, (b) to approve the scheme of amalgamation and exchange ratio and (c) to authorize directors/ officers to make applications to the appropriate high court for necessary action

(ii) Inform the stock exchanges concerned about the proposed amalgamation immediately after the board meetings.

(iii) The shareholders and other members of the companies should also be informed through press release.

(iv) The transferor the and transferee companies should inform the financial institutions, bankers/debenture- trustees at least 45 days before the board meeting so that their approval is available to the proposed amalgamation at the time of board meeting.

Application for Amalgamation: An application for amalgamation can be submitted by the company, members or even any of the creditors. A member, in this context means any person who has agreed to be a member and whose name appears on the register of members. A creditor includes all persons having pecuniary claims against the company for some amount whether present or future, definite or contingent. Even one member or one such creditor can make an application for amalgamation. Where the application is proposed to be made by the company, only a person authorized by the company in this behalf can make an application for amalgamation. It is, therefore, essential that the company should authorize the director(s) or other officer (s) to make an application to the appropriate high courts and take necessary action as may be required from time to time. The directors can, however, apply for amalgamation only when requisite power appears in the articles of association originally or by way of amendment.

Separate applications under section 291 are required to be submitted to the appropriate high courts by the amalgamating and the amalgamated companies for the purpose of the respective high courts issuing directions to convene meetings of shareholders separately for preference and equity shareholders to approve the scheme of amalgamation. It is incumbent on both the transferor and the transferee companies to obtain sanction of high courts having jurisdiction over them. However, where both the companies are under the jurisdiction of the same high court, a joint-application may be made. Such an application can be moved even when an order for winding up has been made. However, the transferee company need not obtain approval under section 391 when the transferor company is a wholly owned subsidiary of the transferor company.

Procedure for Application to the High Court: The procedure for making application to the high court has been laid down under the Companies (Court) Rules, 1959. An application under section 391 (1) for an order convening a meeting of creditors and/or members or any class of them should be by a judge's summons supported by an affidavit. A copy of the proposed compromise or arrangement should be annexed to the affidavit as an exhibit. The summons should be moved *ex parte*. Where the company is not the applicant, a copy of the summons and of the affidavit should be served on the company, or where the company is being wound-up, on its liquidator, not less than 14 days before the date fixed for the hearing of the summons. On receipt of the application by the high court, a hearing takes place in the judge's chamber, and after the hearing the judge may either dismiss the summons or order a meeting of the members or may give such directions as he may think necessary. But it is incumbent on the court to be satisfied that prima facie the scheme is genuine, *bona fide* and largely in the interest of company and its members. On being not satisfied with the scheme, the court may not even order the calling of meeting of creditors even if the consent of the creditors has been withheld or malafide or arbitrary even if the court considers the scheme reasonable and beneficial to the creditors. The court may dispense with the requirement of convening a meeting where all the members of a particular class have consented to the scheme and have entered into necessary agreement with the transferee company. Having known the proposed meeting the creditors may also move the court for rejection of the scheme and the court may entertain such an application and after reasonable scrutiny may call off the meeting.

Holding of Meeting: The next step is to hold separate meetings of the shareholders and creditors of the company to seek approval to the scheme. The resolution approving the scheme may be passed by voting in person or by proxy as per the directions of the high court. At least three-fourth in value of the members or class of members or creditors must vote in favour of the resolution approving the scheme of amalgamation. The members and the creditors are required to be classified into different classes for the purpose of convening meetings. This process has to be followed immediately on receipt of application under section 391 (1). If meetings of incorrect classification are convened and objection is taken with regard to any particular creditor of having interest competing with others, the company runs the risk of the scheme being dismissed. After classification, the court may order convening of the respective meetings of members and/or creditors.

For the purpose of convening meetings the court may give directions as it may deem fit regarding the following:

(i) Fixing the time and place of such meetings(s);

(ii) Determining the class or classes of creditors and/or members have to be held for considering the proposed compromise or arrangement;

(iii) Appointing a chairman or chairmen for the meeting(s) to be held, as the case may be;

(iv) Fixing the quorum and the procedure to be followed at the meeting(s) including voting by proxy;

(v) Determining the values of creditors and/or the members of any class, as the case may be, whose meetings have to be held;

(vi) Notice to be given of the meeting(s) and the advertisement of such notice;

(vii) The time within which the chairman of the meeting is to report to the court the results of the meeting; and such other matters as the court may deem necessary.

The notice of the meetings of members and/or creditors, should be:

(a) Sent to the members/creditors;

(b) Sent to them individually by the chairman appointed for the meeting or if the court so directs, by the company or any other person as the court may direct, by post under certificate of posting to the last known address at least 21 clear days before the date of the meeting;

(c) Accompanied by a copy of the proposed scheme of compromise or arrangement and of the statement required to be furnished under section 393 and also a form of proxy.

The approval of the registrar of the appropriate high court should be obtained in respect of notice and explanatory statements, specifying the particulars prescribed under section 393 and in accordance with the directions issued by the court. The notice of the meeting must be advertised in the prescribed form in such paper(s) as the court may direct, not less than 21 clear days before the date fixed for the meeting. In case of default, the summons should be posted before the court for such orders as it may think fit to make.

Report of Chairman to the Court: The Chairman of the meeting must within the time fixed by the court or where no time is fixed within 7 days of the date of the meeting, report the result of the meeting to the court. The report should state accurately the number of creditors or class of creditors or the numbers of members or class of members, as the case may be, who were present and who voted at the meeting either in person or by proxy, their individual values and the way the voted.

Presenting Petition Before the Court: After the proposed scheme is agreed to with or without modification in terms of section 391(2), the company must within seven days of the filing of the report by the chairman, present a petition to the court for confirmation of the compromise or arrangement. A copy of the petition should also be submitted to the regional director, company law board and others as directed by the court. The court would not sanction a scheme simply because it is recommended by the board of directors and approved by a statutory majority of the company. The court would have to see itself whether the scheme is reasonable and fair to all parties. A scheme which is proper on the face of it and in respect of which no fraud is alleged would not be rejected unless the objector shows any valid ground against it. Under section 394 (A), the court should give notice of every application made to it under section 391 or 394 to the central government/regional directors of company law board and take into consideration the representations, if any, made to it by the government before passing any order. However, the court is not bound to go by the opinion of the government/regional director as to the matters of public interest; rather it can form its independent opinion over the matte. Where the company fails to present the petition for confirmation of the proposed scheme, it is open to any creditor or contributory, with the leave of the court, to present the petition and the company would be liable for cost. Where no such petition is presented for confirmation, the report of the chairman as to the result of the meeting must be placed for consideration before the judge for such orders as may be necessary. Such a petition must be moved within 7 days of the filling of the report by the chairman. Once the scheme has been approved by the members of a company in a duly convened and held meeting, the petition filed for confirmation of the same cannot be withdrawn. The only course of action that may be followed is to appear before the court and raise the objections when the scheme comes up for consideration. In such a case, the scheme may not be sanctioned and the court may order for holding meetings of the members again. However, there is nothing to prevent a company from requisitioning a meeting to consider a proposed modification in the scheme. The court would fix a date for hearing of the petition and a notice of the hearing must be advertised in the same newspapers in which the notice of the meeting was advertised or in such other papers as the court may direct not less than 10 days before the date fixed for the hearing. The order of the court on the petition confirming the scheme should contain such directions in regard to any matter and such modifications in regard to compromise or arrangement as the judge may think fit to make for the proper working of the compromise or arrangement. The order must direct that a certified copy of the same should be filed with the registrar of companies within 14 days from the date of the order or such other time as may be fixed by the court.

The court while sanctioning the scheme should consider (i) that the provisions of the Act have been complied with; (ii) those who took part in the proceedings at the meetings are representatives of the class to which the meeting belongs and that the majority of them acted *bona fide*; and (iii) having regard to the object, background and other conditions of the scheme, the scheme on the whole is reasonable.

The high court may also direct the official liquidator for submission of reports after scrutiny of the books and papers of the amalgamating company. If the report indicates that the affairs of the company have not been conducted in a manner prejudicial to the interest of the public and the shareholders, the court may issue orders for winding up with dissolution.

Application for Direction If necessary, an application for direction of the court to provide for all or any matters indicated in section 394(1) These are:

(i) The transfer to the transferee company of the whole or any part of the undertaking, property or liabilities of any transferor company;

(ii) The allotment or appropriation by the transferee company of any shares, debentures, policies, or other like interests in that company which, under the compromise or agreement, are to be allotted or appropriated by that company to or for any person;

(iii) The continuation by or against the transferee company of any legal proceedings pending by or against any transferor company;

(iv) The dissolution, without winding-up, of any transferor company;

(v) The provision to be made for any persons who, within such time and in such manner as the court directs, dissents from the compromise or arrangement; and

(vi) Such incidental, consequential and supplemental matters as are necessary to secure that the reconstruction or amalgamation would be fully and effectively carried out.

The court would pass an order. Alternatively, by adding a suitable prayer in the main application, the court could be requested to give direction in regard to the above. In fact, such a course would provide for expeditious completion of amalgamation formalities.

Certificate: A certified copy of the order of the court dissolving the amalgamating company or giving approval to the scheme of merger, should be filed with the Registrar of Companies concerned within 30 days of the date of the court's order.

Court Order: A copy of the order of the court should be to attached to the memorandum and articles of association of the transferee company [Section 39 391(4)]. As soon as the scheme of amalgamation has become effective, the members should be intimated through the press. Government authorities, banks, creditors, customers and others should also be informed.

CONCLUSION

With the FDI policies becoming more liberalized, mergers, acquisitions and alliance talks are heating up in India and are growing with an ever increasing cadence. They are no more limited to one particular type of business. The list of past and anticipated mergers covers every size and variety of business — mergers are on the increase over the whole marketplace, providing platforms for the small companies being acquired by bigger ones. The basic reason behind mergers and acquisitions is that organizations merge and form a single entity to achieve economies of scale, widen their reach, acquire strategic skills, and gain competitive advantage. In simple terminology, mergers are considered as an important tool by companies for purpose of expanding their operation and increasing their profits, which in façade depends on the kind of companies being merged. Indian markets have witnessed burgeoning trend in mergers which may be due to business consolidation by large industrial houses, consolidation of business by multinationals operating in India, increasing competition against imports and acquisition activities. Therefore, it is ripe time for business houses and corporates to watch the Indian market and grab the opportunity.

CLOSING CASELET

GOVT MAY DILUTE 25% PIE NORM

The Government may have to dilute the recently announced rule requiring companies to maintain a minimum public shareholding of 25 per cent. That is because the new rule contradicts some of the existing regulatory guidelines like lock-in on promoters' equity and restriction on fundraising routes. There is also lack of clarity on how a pre-initial public offering (pre-IPO) placement to private equity funds will be classified. Will it fall under the promoter group or public shareholders? Also, sick companies currently under the Board for Industrial and Financial Reconstruction (BIFR), will struggle to comply with the 25 per cent rule as there won't be any takers for their shares. Present SEBI rules require the promoter of a company to continue owning at least 20 per cent of the post-issue capital for three years from the day it goes public. The rule also stipulates that the remaining equity stake of the promoter be locked-in for one year from the time of listing.

These conditions restrict the promoter of a newly-listed company from diluting his stake further. 'SEBI needs to address the lock-in on promoter's equity holding,' says Daiwa Securities' director Ambrish Singh. Sharing a similar view, Prithvi Haldea of Prime Database says the government has to relax the lock-in clause, especially for the first year, in the case of companies planning a sale offer. 'If the company is raising fresh capital then the existing lock-in on promoters' holding can continue,' Mr. Haldea says. The new rule requires companies to increase their public shareholding by 5 per cent every year till it reaches the 25 per cent level. Investment bankers say the new rule on minimum public shareholding is unfair on investors who have participated in the initial public offerings (IPOs).

This is because their stake will be reduced further in case the promoters decided to dilute their holding through issue of new shares. The Finance Ministry last week said-that those planning an IPO can sell just 10 per cent of the company, provided it has a market value of ₹ 4,000 crore. But they have to raise their public shareholding to 25 per cent gradually.

The new norm calls for amendment in the listing agreement by stock exchanges. Another problem for the promoters is that SEBI rules bar companies from selling shares to institutions through a qualified institutional placement (QIP) within a year of having raised money from the market. This means promoters will have to sell shares either in the open market or through a follow-on public offer. 'Considering that it is not in the interest of shareholders, flexibility should be given to issuers in terms of choosing instruments that are suitable for certain market conditions,' said a senior banker with a leading domestic investment bank. Mr. Haldea said that the follow-on public offer (FPO) is one of the most difficult routes for stake dilution, as seen from the response to the FPOs of NTPC and NMDC. There are at least 179 companies listed on the stock exchanges where the public float is below the new norm, according to Crisil Equities estimates. At current market prices, these companies will collectively raise ₹ 1.6 lakh crore if promoters sell their stakes. This will be nearly double the funds raised through share sales in FY10. If they attempt to achieve the 25 per cent limit through sale of new shares, they will raise ₹ 2.1 lakh crore, the report says. 'Excess supply in the market will create an overhang in stocks, putting pressure on the share price,' said an investment banker with a transnational bank, adding, 'too much supply in the primary market will depress the secondary market.'

Question: Discuss the role of SEBI in regulating mergers and acquisitions.

Source: *Economic Times*, dt. 14.06.2010

Recent Terminology on Defensive Tactics and Restructuring[1]

Divestitures:

Firms not only acquire businesses but also sell them. Divestitures are part of the market, and in recent years the number of divestitures has been half the number of the mergers (Brealey, Myers & Marcus, 2004). Weston (2001) states, that these divestitures present the sale of a section of a company to another unit. The divestiture by a seller usually produces focusing on a narrower of activities. The buying firm seeks to strengthen its strategic pro-grams. According to Ross et al. (2005), the basic idea of divestitures is to reduce the possible diversification discount connected with commingled process and to increase company focus.

Spin-offs and Equity Carve-outs:

According to Ross et al. (2005), with a spin-off the parent company distributes shares of a subsidiary to its shareholders. The consequence is that the shareholders end up with an investment in the parent as well as the subsidiary. Typically, the stock in the subsidiary is distributed *pro rata* to the parent company shareholders. No actual asset sale is involved,

1. Jennie Berggren, Carina Engström, "*Defensive Tactics in Hostile Takeovers*, JÖNKÖPING INTERNATIONAL BUSINESS SCHOOL," Jönköping University, 2007.

and the subsidiary turns out to be a completely separate company. A variant of the spin-off is called an equity curve-out (Ross *et. al.*, 2005). In an equity carve-out the company sells up to 20 percent of the stock of a segment (Weston, 2001). Ross *et. al.*, (2005) also states that occasionally a spin-off and an equity curve-out are combined.

Tracking Stock:

A tracking stock is separate classes of the common stock whose value is connected to the performance of a particular segment of the parent company's business (Weston, 2001; Ross *et. al.*, 2005). Each tracking stock is considered as common stock of the parent company for voting purposes (Weston, 2001). Tracking stock is similar to a spin-off, which gives their shareholders a pure play on a particular part of the firm (Weston, 2001; Ross *et. al.*, 2005).

The difference is, in the tracking stock relationship the committee of the parent company continues to control the activities of the tracking segment; but the spin-off becomes an independent company. Companies with tracking stocks trade separate, so dividends that are paid to shareholders of each company then can be based on their individual cash flow. One criticism of tracking stocks is that the subsidiary is still subject to control of the parent company (Weston, 2001).

Takeover Defenses:

According to Weston (2001), any company can be exposed for a potential takeover. For the target company the first step is to have a plan prepared, before an acquisition attempt is made. What will the board's response be to an unfriendly takeover and what is the different between a friendly and an unfriendly acquire? Before an attempted acquisition, what steps are appropriate to take and what steps is the company willing to take after the unwanted overture is made? According to Ross *et. al.*, (2005), target-firm management possible will take corrective action to increase stock price in order to reduce the takeover benefits. There are several of defensive tactics that can be used by target-firm managements to resist unfriendly takeover attempts.

Repurchase Standstill Agreements:

A targeted repurchase may be arranged by the managers to prevent a takeover effort. In a targeted repurchase, a firm buys back its own stock from a possible bidder, typically at a substantial premium. These premiums can be thought of as payments to possible bidders to delay or stop unfriendly takeover attempts (Ross *et. al.*, 2005). The criticism of this sort of payment often is an acceptation of a greenmail payment. According to Weston (2001), a greenmail is a performance of 'paying off' anyone who acquires a big block of the company's stocks and increases threats of acquisition. To lighten those threats, a company can simply pay that individual a premium over what he/she paid when collecting the company's stock. This sort of technique can be used in a hostile takeover situation (Weston, 2001). In addition managers of target firms may at the same time negotiate standstill agreements, which are contracts where the bidding firm agrees to limit its assets of another firm. These agreements usually lead to cancellation of takeover effort, and the message of such agreement has had a negative effect on stock price (Ross *et. al.*, 2005).

Greenmail:

As mentioned above, greenmail is a performance of 'paying off' anyone who acquires a large block of the company's stock and increases threats of acquisitions (Weston, 2001). In practice, greenmail is about buying back shares at a higher market price in order to block a hostile takeover (Hanly, 1992). Stock prices generally drop when firms pay greenmail to large shareholders who are trying to take over the firm (Grinbltt & Titman, 2002). Greenmail means that shares are repurchased by the target at a price which makes the bidder happy to agree to leave the target alone. This price does not always makes the target's shareholder happy (Brealey & Myers, 1996). However, paying greenmail may be a way to prevent the productive with less than desired effects, and it could also result in other possible acquirers stepping in to receive their greenmail as well. But on the other hand it can be a very expensive method (Weston, 2001).

Poison Pill:

According to Dolbeck (2004), poison pills can also be called shareholders rights plans, and are for example a way to make it harder for a investor to sell shares because it makes it more expensive to acquire firms shares (Dolbeck, 2004). Poison pills represent a class of securities that grant special rights to firms' holders in the event of an attempted takeover. These rights impose financial costs on possible acquirers, thereby making takeovers more costly and thus, less likely (Higgins & Nelling, 2002).

Grinblatt and Titman (2002), states that this defense is the most effective takeover defensive tactic. Poison pills are rights or securities that a firm issues to its shareholders, which are giving them the precious benefits in the event that a significant number of its shares are acquired (Grinblatt & Titman, 2002; Weston, 2001). According to Ross *et. al.*, (2005) it is generally a right to buy shares in the merged firm at a good deal price (Ross *et. al.*, 2005). Poison pills have many variants, but all share the basic characteristic that they involve a transfer from the bidder to shareholders who do not offer their shares. This makes increasing of the cost of the acquisition and decreasing the reason for target shareholders to bid at any given price (Grinblatt & Titman, 2002). Two variants are flip over and flip in plans, which may be used together. The first variant provides for a good deal purchase price of the acquirer's shares, when the second variant provides a good deal purchase price of the target company (Weston, 2001).

Flip in:

Flip in provides shareholders with the right to purchase common or preferred stock. If the tender offer for the firm is imminent, the rights allow the holder to purchase stock at a substantial discount. The holder might turn around and sell the stock at the much higher tender offer price, or might use the newly acquired stock to increase the quantity of stock needed in order for the acquirer to gain control of the firm. The rights are valid only for the original holder (Meade & Davidson, 1993).

Flip Over:

Flip over Rights Plans is according to Grinblatt and Titman (2002) the most popular poison pill defensive tactic. The target shareholders receive under this plan the right to purchase the acquiring firm's stock at a considerable discount in the event of a merger. An example can be that Alpha acquires Beta shares and then proceed with a merger. The existing Beta shareholders will then receive the rights to purchase Alpha stock at 50 percent of its value in the event the merger is completed. This would make the merger prevent expensive for Alpha, which would be unwilling to proceed with the merger unless the poison pill was annulled (Grinblatt & Titman, 2002). According to Weston (2001), a poison pill does not prevent an unwanted takeover but the board's negotiating position will be strengthened. Poison pills can in the most cases be annulling by the board of directors at an unimportant cost to allow mergers which they believe are in the shareholder's interest to be applied (Grinblatt & Titman, 2002; Weston, 2001).

White Knight and White Squire:

The target company seeks for a 'friendly' acquirer for the business, when using a white knight defense (Ross *et. al.*, 2005; Weston, 2001). Firms that rescue a target from unwanted bitters are called white knights. White knight dealings clearly are friendly (Hitt, 2001). The target firm may prefer another acquirer because it believes there is better compatibility between the two firms. Another bidder might be required because that bidder promises not to break up the target or to dismiss employees.

A white squire is similar to a white knight, but the white squire does not take control of the target firm. Instead, the target firm sells a block of stock to a white squire that is considered friendly and who will vote his/her shares with the target firm's management. There are other conditions that may be forced, such as demand the white squire to vote for management, there can also be a standstill agreement there the white squire cannot acquire more of the target firm's shares for a specified period of time, and a limit on the sale of that block of stock. The limit on the sale of that block of stock usually includes that the target company has the right of first refusal. The white squire may get a discount on the shares, a seat on the target's board, and extraordinary dividends (Weston, 2001).

Crown Jewels:

Firms often sell major assets when faced with a takeover threat (Ross *et. al.*, 2005). Instead of publicizing hidden values, the firm should eliminate those values. Rather than making the firm beautiful and the firm's market value high, the firm should make it seem as ugly, poor and worthless as possible. Crown jewels, that are the firm's most valuable assets, represent the largest reason that companies become takeover targets (Arbel & Woods, 1988, p. 36). Although, a defensive tactic for a target firm is to sell its most valuable line of business or division, which is referred to as the crown jewels. Once this business has been divested, the proceeds can be used to repurchase stock or to pay an extraordinary dividend. Once the crown jewels have been divested the hostile acquirer may withdraw its bid (Weston, 2001).

Pac-Man:

This defensive tactic is named after the popular game in which the hunted becomes the hunter. In the game, and also in real life, the objective is to eat the attacker to avoid being eaten yourself. This defense is carried out by purchase in the attacker firm, either in the open market or through a good offer. If your firm is able to acquire enough shares, you might be able to secure a position in the attackers' board of directors, and therefore gain a valuable inside position or even a vote (Arbel & Woods, 1988; Weston, Siu & Johnson, 2001).

A Pac-Man defense is an extremely aggressive and rarely used defensive tactic; in this defense the target company offers versus and launches its own acquisition attempt on the potential acquirer. An example of this is if company A begins an unfriendly takeover attempt of company B. To prevent these advances company B launch its own acquisition attempt of company A. This defensive tactic is also effective when the original acquirer is smaller than the original target company, therefore providing the original target the opportunity to finance a potential deal. This sort of defense is extremely risky. It tones down the antitrust defenses that could be offered by the original target company. The Pac-Man defensive tactic basically suggests that the target company's board and management are in favor of the acquisition, but that they disagree about which company should be in control (Weston, 2001).

Parachutes:

Parachutes are employee's agreements that are triggered when a change in control takes place (Weston, 2001). Parachutes are guarantees that incumbent management will receive certain benefits if a firm is taken over and the executive are fired or their jobs are eliminated (Hanly, 1992). According to Weston (2001), the purpose is to give the firm's managers and employees with peace of mind during acquisition discussions and the changeover. It helps the firm keep key employees who may feel threatened by a possible acquisition. The manager also gets help by the parachutes to deal with personal concerns while acting in the best interest of the stockholder. The present board and management team set up the parachutes that become effective when a possible acquirer exceeds a particular percentage of ownership in the firm. Parachutes may be establish without the agreement of stockholders and may be annulled in the case of a friendly takeover (Weston, 2001).

Parachutes can come in three different variants; the golden, the silver and a tin parachute. The first mentioned, golden parachute, is designed for the firm's most high-ranking management team, like the top 10 to 30 managers. Under this type of plan, a substantial lump sum payment is paid to a manager who is ended following an acquisition Weston, 2001). The presence of golden parachutes is prevention to hostile takeovers, because such benefits make it more expensive to purchase a firm (Arbel & Woods, 1988, p. 33).

The second mention is the silver parachute is a much wider of protection to a large number of employees and may also include middle managers. The terms of a silver parachute often cover equal to six months or one year of payment (Weston, 2001). Since the silver parachute is a large number of middle managers and employees these parachutes cost more than golden parachutes (Arbel & Woods, 1988).

The U.S. Securities and Exchange Commission, is the United States leading body which has primary respon-sibility for overseeing the rule of the securities industry. (http://encyclopedia.thefreedictionary.com/U.S.+ Securities+and+Exchange+Commission)

The last variant is a tin parachute may be put into practice, which covers an even wider circle of employees or even all employees. This program provides limited payment and may be structured as payment equal to one or two weeks of payment for every year of service (Weston, 2001). This parachutes are broad-based and are even more effective than silver or gold parachutes in preventing firms in hostile takeovers (Arbel & Woods, 1988).

Litigation:

After a hostile takeover bid has been received, the target company can challenge the acquisition through litigation. Litigation is started by the target company based on the antitrust effects of the acquisition, missing material information in SEC3 filings or other securities law insult. The target sues for a temporary order to forbid the bidder from purchasing any more shares of the target's stock until the court has an opportunity to decide on the case (Weston, 2001).

Shark Repellent:

Any tactic that makes the firm less attractive to a potential unfriendly offer is called a shark repellent (Ross *et.al.*, 2005). Firms that are making a public offering usually include a range of shark repellent, which are requirements that intended to guard against hostile takeover attempts. While planned to stop outside takeovers, shark repellent requirements can also limit the flexibility of a firm's shareholders to funding a stop to a buyer or get a control premium not shared with other stockholders. This is an example of rights plans, also called poison pills, that makes it harder for a shareholder to sells shares (Dolbeck, 2004). According to Brealey *et.al.*, (2004, p. 602), a firm often will influence shareholders to agree to shark repellent, and an example can be that any merger must be approved by a supermajority of 80 per cent of the shares rather than the normal 50 per cent.

SUMMARY

Summary of the Defensive Tactics

Name:	**Explanation:**
Anti Takeover Charter Amendments	An example is supermajority voting amendments that require two thirds, sometimes as much as 90 per cent, of the share-holders of record must agree before a change in control can be put into practice.
Repurchase Standstill Agreements	A firm buys back its own stock from a possible bidder, typically at a substantial premium. These premiums can be thought of as payments to possible bidders to delay or stop unfriendly takeover attempts.
Greenmail	Is a performance of 'paying off' anyone who acquires a large block of the company's stock and increases threats of acquisitions.
Poison pill	For example, a way to make it harder for an investor to sell shares because it makes it more expensive to acquire firm's shares. Poison pills are rights or securities that a firm issues to its shareholders, which are giving them the precious benefits in the event that a significant number of its shares are acquired.
White knight	Firms that rescue a target from unwanted bitters are called white knights. White knight dealings clearly are friendly.
White squire	A white squire is similar to a white knight, but the white squire does not take control of the target firm. Instead, the target firm sells a block of stock to a white squire.
Crown Jewels	Crown jewels, that are the firms' most valuable assets, represent the largest reason that companies become takeover targets Firms often sell major assets when faced with a takeover threat, to make the firm seem as ugly, poor and worthless as possible.
Pac-Man	The objective is to eat the attacker to avoid being eaten your-self. This defense is carried out by purchase in the attacker firm.
Parachutes	Parachutes are employee's agreements that are triggered when a change in control takes place.
Litigation	The target company can challenge the acquisition through litigation. The target sues for a temporary order to forbid the bidder from purchasing any more shares of the target's stock at the moment.
Shark repellent	Any tactic that makes the firm less attractive to a potential unfriendly offer is called a shark repellent.

ꕥ ꕥ ꕥ

APPENDIX

CHALLENGES FACED BY GLOBAL FINANCIAL MARKETS

1987-2007

Year	Challenge	Details	Country
1987	**FALL IN DJIA**	Dow Jones Industrial Average (DJIA) falls 508 points or 22.6 per cent in the steepest decline since 1929. Hence, portfolio insurance and computerised trading takes some of the blame for what ranks as the 5th largest point drop in DJIA.	**USA**
1988	**DEREGULATED MARKETS**	Deregulated S&Ls gets in over their heads, and more than 1,000 institutions fail, in many cases as the result of malfeasance and fraud. The ensuring bailout costs the US government an estimated $125 billion in direct subsidies.	**USA**
1990	**TROUBLE IN JAPANESE MARKET**	After the bank of Japan raises rates to cool its overheated economy, the Nikkei stock index plunges more than 30,000 points. It continues to struggle for more than a decade until its post-bubble low of 7,608 in 2003, down 80 per cent from its high.	**JAPAN**
1992	**UK EXITS ERM**	Britain is forced to leave European Exchange Rate Mechanism following a wave of speculative attacks on its currency.	**UK**
1995	**CAUSE FOR PROBLEM OF BARINGS BANK**	Leeson, a 28-year old trader based in Singapore, losses more than $1 billion on futures pegged to the Nifty 225 stock index in Japan and single-handedly brings down Barings Bank, the UK's oldest investment banks.	**SINGAPORE**
1997	**ASIAN FINANCIAL CRISIS**	Thailand runs out of foreign exchange reserves to support its currency and floats the baht, which	**THAILAND**

		falls 20 per cent to a record low. The prices spreads through much of Asia with the Philippines, Indonesia, South Korea and Thailand, the most effected. The IMF establishes a $40 billion programme to support these currencies.	
1998	**RUSSIAN FINANCIAL CRISIS**	The Russian economy is hit by declining oil prices in the global recession of 1998 that follows the Asian financial crisis. The Russian central bank widens the trading band for the ruble, which drops 12 per cent on the day of the announcement.The government also imposes a 90-day moratorium on foreign debt payments.	**RUSSIA**
1999	**RECESSION IN ARGENTINA**	As its exports are hurt by a devaluation of the Brazilian real, Argentina's GDP falls 4 per cent, marking the beginning of a recession that would last for three years the crisis boils over into riots in December, 2001, when the government devalued the peso and freezes bank assets.	**ARGENTIA**
2001	**FINANCIAL CRISIS IN TURKEY**	Prime Minister Bullent Ecevit clash openly with president Ahmed Necdet Sezer over reforms, triggering a crisis. Interest rates shoot upto 7,000 per cent and stock prices fall. The Turkish *lira* losses more than 40 per cent of its value as the government abandons exchange controls.	**TURKEY**

2002	**URUGUAY BANKING CRISIS**	Uruguay suffers a massive run on its banks, causing the government to freeze banking operations. Uruguay's real GDP falls by 12 per cent in 2002 as a result of its heavy dependence on neighbouring Argentina. The US treasury provides a $1.5 billion bridge loan to the Uruguayan government to tide it over to a bank-rescue fund financed by multinational organisations including the IMF.	**URUGUAY**
2007	**US SUB-PRIME MORTGAGE CRISIS**	Losses in the sub-prime market trigger a credit crunch. The risks are distributed widely through securitisation, and worries that the crisis would spread to the broader economy disrupt global financial markets for months. The Federal Reserve cuts interest rates and floods the market with liquidity.	**USA**

Source: Prepared by Gordon Plant, Global Finance, December, 2007.

ഇൽ ഇൽ ഇൽ

BIBLIOGRAPHY

- Advisory Group on Corporate Governance (AGCG) (2001), Report on Corporate Governance and International Standards, Reserve Bank of India.
- Allen, F. and Gale, D., (2000), "Corporate Governance and Competition" in Xavier Vives (Ed.) Corporate Governance: Theoretical and Empirical Perspectives, Cambridge: Cambridge University Press.
- Arun, T.G., and Turner, J.D., (2002b), "Financial Sector Reform in Developing Countries: The Indian Experience", *The World Economy*, Vol. 25, No. 3, pp. 429-445.
- Arun, T.G. and Turner, J.D., (2002c), "Financial Liberalisation in India", *Journal of International Banking Regulation* (Forthcoming).
- Arun, T.G. and Turner, J.D., (2002d), "Corporate Governance of Banking Institutions in Developing Economies: The Indian Experience", Paper Presented in the Conference on 'Finance and Development' Organised by IDPM, The University of Manchester.
- Basel Committee on Banking Supervision (BCBS) (1999), "Enhancing Corporate Governance for Banking Organisations", Bank for International Settlements, Switzerland.
- Bhattacharya, S., Boot, A.W.A., Thakor, A.V. 1998. The Economics of Bank Regulation, *Journal of Money, Credit and Banking*, Vol. 30, pp. 745-770.
- Capiro, G., Jr. and Levine, R. (2002), "Corporate Governance of Banks: Concepts and International Observations", Paper Presented in the Global Corporate Governance Forum Research Network Meeting, April 5.
- Claessens, S., Demirguc-Kunt, A. and Huizanga, H., (2000), "The Role of Foreign Banks in Domestic Banking Systems" in S. Claessens and M. Jansen, (Eds.) The Internationalisation of Financial Services: Issues and Lessons for Developing Countries, Boston, MA: Kluwer Academic Press.
- Goswami, O., (2001), "The Tide Rises, Gradually: Corporate Governance in India", OECD Development Centre Discussion Paper.
- Gilson, Stuart, Kose John and Larry Lang, (1990), "Troubled Debt Restructurings: An Empirical Study of Private Reorganisation of Firms in Default", *Journal of Financial Economics*, Vol.27, pp.315-353.
- International Monetary Fund (IMF) (2001), "India: Recent Economic Developments and Selected Issues", IMF Country Report No. 01/181.

- Hickson, C.R. and Turner, J.D., (2003), "Free Banking and the Stability of Early Joint-stock Banking", *Cambridge Journal of Economics* (Forthcoming).
- La Porta, R., Lopez-de-Silanes, F., Shleifer, A. and Vishny, R.W. (2000), "Investor Protection and Corporate Governance", *Journal of Financial Economics*, Vol.58, pp. 3-27.
- La Porta, R., Lopez-de-Silanes, F. and Shleifer, A., (1999), "Corporate Ownership Around the World", *Journal of Finance*, Vol. 54, pp. 471-517.
- Levine, R., (1999), "Foreign Bank Entry and Capital Control Liberalisation: Effects on Growth and Stability", University of Minnesota, Mimeo.
- Macey, J.R. and O'Hara, M., (2001), "The Corporate Governance of Banks", Federal Reserve Bank of New York, *Economic Policy Review.*
- Oman, C.P., (2001), "Corporate Governance and National Development", OECD Development Centre Technical Papers, Number 180.
- Peek, J. and Rosengren, E., (2000), "Implications of the Globalisation of the Banking Sector: The Latin American Experience", *New England Economic Review*, Sept./Oct., pp.45-62.
- Shleifer, A. and Vishny, R., (1997), "A Survey of Corporate Governance", *Journal of Finance*, Vol. 52, pp. 737-783.
- Stiglitz, J.E., (1994), "The Role of the State in Financial Markets", Proceedings of the World Bank Annual Conference on Development Economics 1993, pp.19-52.
- Vives, X., (2000), "Corporate Governance: Does it Matter", in Xavier Vives (Ed.) Corporate Governance: Theoretical and Empirical Perspectives, Cambridge: Cambridge University Press.

ꕤ ꕤ ꕤ